People, Penguins, and Plastic Trees

People, Penguins, and Plastic Trees

Basic Issues in Environmental Ethics

Edited by

Donald VanDeVeer and Christine Pierce

Wadsworth Publishing Company
Belmont, California
A Division of Wadsworth, Inc.

Philosophy Editor: Ken King
Editorial Associate: Debbie Fox
Production Editor: Gary Mcdonald
Managing Designer: Paula Shuhert
Print Buyer: Karen Hunt
Designer: Vargas/Williams/Design
Copy Editor: Toni Haskell
Compositor: Kachina Typesetting, Tempe, Arizona
Cover: Paula Shuhert

Printed in the United States of America
1 2 3 4 5 6 7 8 9 10—90 89 88 87 86

ISBN 0-534-06312-8

Library of Congress Cataloging-in-Publication Data
Main entry under title:

People, penguins, and plastic trees.

   Bibliography: p.
   1. Nature conservation—Moral and ethical aspects.   2. Nature conservation—Philosophy.   3. Environmental protection—Moral and ethical aspects.   4. Environmental protection—Philosophy.   I. VanDeVeer, Donald, 1939–   . II. Pierce, Christine.
QH75.P46   1986   179   85-22534
ISBN 0-534-06312-8

To Hank and Heidi.
D.V.

To my mother, Mildred Pierce.
C.P.

Contents

Preface viii
General Introduction 1

I.   The Other Animals: Mere Resources?   19

Preview 20
Animal Liberation, *Peter Singer* 24
The Case for Animal Rights, *Tom Regan* 32
Rights, Interests, Desires and Beliefs, *R. G. Frey* 40
The Limits of Trooghaft, *Desmond Stewart* 46
Interspecific Justice, *Donald VanDeVeer* 51
Trans-species Organ Transplantation 66

II.   The Broader Environment: Other Lives of Value?   67

Land and Trees: Inanimate Victims?   68

Preview 68
The Land Ethic, *Aldo Leopold* 73
Should Trees Have Standing?—Toward Legal Rights for Natural Objects,
   Christopher D. Stone 83
The Good of Trees, *Robin Attfield* 96

The Preservation of Species: Are They Special?   106

Preview 106
The Sinking Ark, *Norman Myers* 111
Why Do Species Matter?, *Lilly-Marlene Russow* 119
Cetaceans: A Litany of Cain, *Peter M. Dobra* 127

Wilderness: What Is It "Good For"?   135

Preview 135
The Wilderness Experience, *René Dubos* 137
Faking Nature, *Robert Elliot* 142

III. Constructing an Environmental Ethic: Which Foundation? 151

Preview 152

Duties Concerning Islands, *Mary Midgley* 156
Ecological Sensibility, *John Rodman* 165
The Ethics of Respect for Nature, *Paul W. Taylor* 169
Animal Liberation: A Triangular Affair, *J. Baird Callicott* 184
The Rights View, *Tom Regan* 203

IV. Economics, Ethics, and Ecology: How Much Common Ground? 207

Letting the Market Decide: Is Efficiency Overrated? 208

Preview 208

People or Penguins, *William F. Baxter* 214
The Ethical Basis of the Economic View of the Environment, *A. Myrick Freeman III* 218
At the Shrine of Our Lady of Fàtima, or Why Political Questions Are Not All Economic, *Mark Sagoff* 227

Cost-Benefit Analysis: Are We Bewitched by Numbers? 238

Preview 238

Cost-Benefit Analysis: An Ethical Critique, *Steven Kelman* 242
Cost-Benefit Analysis Defended, *Herman B. Leonard and Richard J. Zeckhauser* 249
Ways Not to Think about Plastic Trees: New Foundations for Environmental Law, *Laurence H. Tribe* 253

Selected Bibliography 263

Organizations Concerned with the Environment and/or Animals 268

Preface

Why give a damn about the planet—or its nonhuman residents? Historically, the dominant portion of our species seldom has found reason to care to any considerable extent. In the United States, the development of increased public concern about our planet and its creatures has been erratic—from George Perkins Marsh in 1864, through Giffort Pinchot and John Muir around the turn of the century, through the emergence of ecology in the 1930s and 1940s until Earth Day in 1970. However, this growing public concern has provoked (at long last) the initial stages of a serious, systematic, philosophical inquiry into fundamental questions about our environment, about ecology, and the deeply embedded ethical assumptions underlying various views about our dealings with our environment (what to do about environmental crises or whether there are any crises). In the 1970s and early 1980s a series of landmark essays emerged in Australia, the United States, Germany, Great Britain, and other nations. These discussions have generated and placed their stamp on an increasingly lively, ongoing set of debates. Consider, for example, the emergence of the "green" political parties in England and various European nations. Our goal in this volume has been to collect, in a balanced fashion, a fair representation of these innovative, influential, and often controversial writings.

A word is in order about what this volume is not. It is not a primer in ecology, ethology, economics, or environmental science. Neither is it a collection of essays by writers who think scientific considerations are unimportant. Indeed, we believe the collection is empirically rich, unlike some philosophical collections. Many environmental volumes, with titles like "our endangered planet," tend to elaborate in great detail many of the harms that have been done, or are being done, to the environment. Those same volumes often tend to castigate those who think that some pollution is desirable (all things considered), some killing of animals is justifiable, and so on. Although the essays here almost invariably exhibit some sort of positive concern about our planet, or parts of it, we have sought to focus on controversy and *the questioning of fundamental assumptions*—traditional anthropocentric assumptions but also many of the recent antianthropocentric assumptions. On both sides one can find occasional sloganeering, flag-waving, and name-calling—rhetoric without careful, explicit argument. However, the collective insights of the cross-disciplinary essays herein promise to raise environmental discussion and the search for an adequate environmental ethic to a higher level.

At various points, many of the essays focus on more or less specific *policy* issues: Should we constrain or eliminate factory farming? Ought we preserve all or certain species? Why are certain entities—the oceans or the air—"overexploited"? More typically the essays focus on foundational questions—answers to which must be presupposed in order to *begin* developing conclusions about specific (derivative) policy issues. For example, are members of our species the only entities of intrinsic value on the planet? Could or do (certain or all) animals have rights? Do plants? Ecosystems? Do we have any duties at all to future generations (of people, of others)? If so, why? If not, why not? If so, what are they? Can all that we value about nature be captured by some monetary yardstick? Human life? The beauty of the Grand Canyon? Answers to many of these questions often (not always) are simply presupposed, or barely discussed, in many standard economics texts—as well as in many environmental-science volumes. Until recent years, a similar complaint well might have been voiced about much philosophical writing. A new concern for developing a cogent and comprehensive environmental ethic, however, is in the air—as the later essays make clear. It is worth stressing that the breadth and depth of this concern emerges slowly and piecemeal as the various essays add broad, or smaller, strokes to the developing picture.

A comment is in order about selection and organization of the materials. Essays can be grouped by various criteria: chronologically, according to object of focus (trees, animals, wilderness, and so on), or by position of the author (rights theorist, utilitarian, and so on). This fact creates difficulties, of course. In some cases a given essay has important ideas with regard to a number of issues. For example, Callicott's essay in Part III well might have been placed in Part I. Instructors may choose to assign essays in a different order from that found here. However, there is a method in our editorial madness. Part I questions the anthropocentric paradigm on restricted, well-defined grounds: by exploring our treatment of animals and the assumptions underlying such treatment. Part II expands the reassessment of anthropocentric views by looking at the broader commitment of some to the value of whole ecosystems (as in Aldo Leopold's writings) and the innovative proposals of Christopher Stone (to extend legal rights to trees and rivers—not just sentient animals). Part II also questions whether we should preserve species and why—as well as exploring similar matters with regard to wildernesses. Part III provokes the reader to step further back and consider even more explicitly what is required to construct (or identify!) an adequate environmental ethic. The different strands, approaches, and tensions in environmental ethics are the focus of many of the essays in III. The outlines of something like emerging "schools of thought" are more evident there than in prior sections (holism versus individualism, rights versus utilitarianism, strong versus weak anthropocentrism, deep versus shallow ecology, and so on). *Even if* there is rational agreement about many of the fundamental issues raised in Parts I through III, recalcitrant disagreements persist. In Part IV the essays concern the strength and weakness of the market mechanism as a way of "deciding" certain environmental issues (for example, controlling pollution, regulating consumption of "resources"), the acceptability of the assumptions involved in economic theory and cost-benefit analysis and the use of such in governmental intervention to pursue public policy aims relating to environmental matters. Further puzzles are associated with assigning values to human (or other!) lives—or, if one prefers, to increases in the probability of an organism's prematurely dying. Such weighing and calculation seems unavoidable if one is to adjudicate certain conflicts of interests in arriving at this or that environmental policy. However, some think that such assignments are impossible, totally arbitrary, or morally repugnant; others that they are possible, potentially reasonable, and absolutely necessary. Of course, on the (narrowly construed) anthropocentric paradigm, only human well-being or human lives directly count in the calculus of determining social policy. The acceptability of this assumption is explored in Parts I and II. In Part IV Laurence Tribe questions whether a morally enriched cost-benefit calculus is feasible. The question is, indeed, an important one.

The above overview is a sketch of the broad path this volume cuts through the jungle of environmental ethics. As philosophers, as citizens, and earthlings, the editors are not neutral to the questions discussed; indeed we find ourselves in wild disagreement with some of the positions defended herein. (Very briefly, our own views reject both strong anthropocentrism as well as biotic egalitarian outlooks.) However, our task as editors here is not to advocate, cheerlead, or proselytize; rather it is to facilitate a systematic, reasoned joining of the issues. To this end, we have included one piece of fiction, some articles that are empirically oriented, and other essays that represent both moderate and "extreme" outlooks—when we believed their viewpoint should not go undefended and when they promise to enrich teaching or learning.

Originally, when we were more naive about the economics of publishing, our hope was for a more comprehensive volume. However, we have had to omit much that is valuable, for example, material on duties to future generations, the threats posed by (human) population growth, nuclear power, nuclear war, and so on. In many cases we have had to perform major or minor surgery on the essays in order to include them. The curious student or scholar will be advised to search out the original for the full text or for full footnote documentation.

A word about our title. In an essay that appears later in this volume, William Baxter claims that penguins are important (if at all) only because people like to watch them walk about on rocks. If capacity to promote satisfaction of human wants were the only criterion for the value of nonhuman organisms, then there may be no good reason not to accept the suggestion of one writer namely, in some contexts, to replace real with plastic trees (which survive much better on the Los Angeles freeways). The expression "people, penguins, and plastic trees" thus alludes to serious and fundamental problems of environmental ethics.

That the earth and its living creatures matter to some degree we all know. However, that is where arguments begin, not end. What on earth matters? How much? Why? What sorts of trade-offs may we make? Ought we to make? Answering these questions is both the intellectually intriguing and practically compelling task before us. We can abuse the earth, but we cannot both abuse the earth and move elsewhere. When it comes to certain forms of environmental degradation, "we all live downwind."

For their suggestions in planning this volume, we would like to thank J. Baird Callicott, Robert Hoffman, Dale Jamieson, Tom Regan, Holmes Rolston III, and Mark Sagoff, and our colleagues—who put up with our travails and "Penguins meetings." We also thank the publisher's reviewers: Thomas H. Birch, University of Montana; Allen Carlson, University of Alberta; Richard Haynes, University of Florida; John Martin,

University of Cincinnati; Edward Quest, California State University, Long Beach; and Holmes Rolston III, Colorado State University. We are also indebted to Ken King. He would have made a good drill sergeant, but as philosophy editor at Wadsworth his talents are not wasted; our effort to get things to him "yesterday" sped us forward. Also moving us forward were Ann Rives, from the outset, and Adea Allen, there at the finish line— and at the word processor.

Finally, we add that we welcome suggestions or comments from instructors or students who use *Penguins* in university classes.

Donald VanDeVeer and Christine Pierce
Department of Philosophy and Religion
North Carolina State University, Box 8103
Raleigh, North Carolina   27695-8103

People, Penguins, and Plastic Trees

General Introduction

1. The Elusive Broader View

Our lives are filled with familiar concerns: getting the car fixed; making a dental appointment; deciding on a gift for Aunt Sarah, whether to fight the traffic ticket, spray the crabgrass, or take an aerobics class. Given such understandable preoccupations, it is not easy to attend to more global issues. It is difficult to set aside temporarily one's personal aims and consider one's position as one of about four billion members of *Homo sapiens* living in one period in the history of this planet.

To smooth the path to taking a broader view, it is worth recalling that the earth is about 4.5 billion years old, that life on earth is estimated to have begun about 4 billion years ago, and the appearance of *Homo sapiens* 250,000 to 100,000 years ago.[1] Historical records date back only about 5,000 years. In terms of our understanding of matters now taken for granted, it has been only the last four centuries that we have known that the earth is not flat, about three centuries that we have known of the circulation of the blood, a little over one century that we have known of evolution, and about a quarter of a century since we began to understand nuclear fission and fusion, and the biochemical dynamics of the genetic basis of life. In the span of human history, then, it is only in a most recent "moment" that we members of *Homo sapiens* have learned how to tinker, in profound ways, with the course of life on earth—by the employment, especially, of nuclear power and genetic engineering. A few members of the four billion members of one species, itself one among thousands of species, now are capable of radically altering the fate of all species, and indeed the larger environment.

Against our concerns about the aerobics class, the leaky roof, or the crabgrass, these global matters deserve attention and critical reflection—even though we may be tempted to view ourselves as comparatively more able to influence closer-to-home events and thus let others contemplate and consciously influence our larger environment and the future of life. However, it is not as if anyone could comply with the request "Stop the world; I want to get off." What happens to our lives, our children's lives, the lives of others, and our planet depends on what we do. What we are doing and what we collectively *will do* depends in large part on what we *believe*—about the way things are, will be, or can be—and (importantly) what is good, what is right, or what it is permissible to do. Hence, if we are to think clearly about these earthly matters, we need the best scientific knowledge obtainable. We also need to be clear conceptually; that is, we need to know what we mean when we use terms such as *environment, nature, life, pollution, waste, future generations, natural resources, wilderness, cost, benefit,* and *species.* Further, we need a rationally defensible ethical theory or viewpoint. For without one we can only understand what is, was, or will be— and not have any rational basis for deciding how we ought, or ought not, treat others, or our larger environment. We need, in short, a defensible environmental ethic. Whether it is one that can be fashioned on the basis of older ethical principles, or a more radical one requiring wholesale rejection of much traditional ethical theorizing, is itself a question of current controversy—a point evident in many of the articles in this volume. What is less controversial is that given the comparatively new scientific understanding of our environment, our new capacity to radically alter the environment (including the evolution of our own species) is more pressing than it has been since human life began. Given the risks and opportunities inherent in having such capacities, the need for a coherent, comprehensive, rationally persuasive environmental ethic is imperative. The growing interest in ecologically sensitive ethics, thus, is propelled by urgent questions and problems—of both a theoretical and an eminently practical nature. As much as we might prefer simple answers, and as much as our educational institutions tend to reward students for short "correct" answers, our questions are diverse and complex. Simple answers are suspect. At the very least we must reassess traditional answers; indeed, we should go further and scrutinize critically whether we have been asking the right questions. Let us begin to sort out some fundamental issues—in order to develop a general overview of the core of environmental ethics—and perhaps to unearth matters too little noticed—or even new issues on which this volume only touches. First, some moral matters.

2. The Concept of Moral Standing: The Anthropocentric Paradigm

Reasonable people of good will agree that ordinarily it is wrong to murder or rape. However, it is not so easy to arrive at agreement about certain other questions, for example, whether one nation legitimately can intervene in the affairs of another nation to secure human rights, whether civil disobedience is justifiable given the nuclear arms race, whether "reverse discrimination" policies are morally defensible, or whether it is all right to let radically defective infants die. In cases of controversy over ethical matters—what we ought to do (or avoid doing) or what it is permissible to do—it is natural to think that we can, and ought to engage in discussion, debate, negotiation, or compromise in order to arrive at some mutually satisfactory solution to problems we confront. However, one rather obvious (on reflection) fact often gets overlooked: Those who do or can engage in such discussion, inquiry, or negotiation constitute only a small subset of those who will be affected by the views or policies agreed on or adopted as a matter of public policy. To emphasize a point, virtually all such discussants, or readers of this sentence, are characterizable as (1) adult, (2) competent, (3) literate, and (4) members of *Homo sapiens.* It typically is thought, however, that the *boundaries of legitimate moral concern* extend beyond those who satisfy conditions (1) through (4). *How far beyond* is one absolutely fundamental question of ethics and, hence, environmental ethics.

To make this central point even more vivid let us make up a label for those who are literate (L), adult (A), competent (C) members of *Homo sapiens* (H): LACHites. Although LACHites are the formulators, discussants, and adjudicators of ethical disputes or questions, they constitute only a small fraction of the population of *Homo sapiens.* It is commonly thought that LACHites possess certain rights or are owed certain duties (for example, they normally ought not to be caused pain, destroyed, raised for food, driven from their native habitat, and so on). It also is widely held that not only LACHites but all members of "our" species, that is, all humans, possess certain rights or are owed certain duties. Hence, we rightly concern ourselves with the well-being of children or incompetent adults as well. Thus, it is even clearer that the set of moral decision makers (discussants, theory formulators, and so on) is only a *subset* of the set of those thought to be owed certain duties. As some would put the matter, the class of *moral agents* (those capable of moral reflection and decision) is included in, but not identical to, the class of *moral patients* (those owed certain duties).

In order to formulate one important question central to environmental ethics it is useful to introduce here the important related concept of *moral standing*. Prior to defining the concept, it is worth explaining another concept to which it seems analogous, namely the (different) concept of *legal standing*. These are quasi-technical matters, and will call for a certain amount of attention—and patience—until their usefulness is apparent. Some people in a country (for example, illegal aliens) may have no legal standing as citizens; that is, they may enjoy none (or few) of the constitutional protections guaranteed to those who occupy the status of being a citizen. For certain purposes at least they are not owed certain legal duties, and they lack certain rights. To have the legal standing of being a citizen, then, is to be regarded as a being whose interests must be positively weighed in governmental decisions about what may be done. The state is thought to have at least a presumptive duty not to disregard or subvert the basic interests (say, in continued life, bodily integrity, or freedom of movement) of one who possesses legal standing. That these interests must be given positive weight in the decision making of others is a point usually implicit in claims that such interest bearers have rights or that we owe them certain duties.

Now let us turn to the concept of *moral standing*. Quite apart from what laws prevail at a given moment, or the shape of a particular nation's constitution (if it has one!), we commonly think that the interest or well-being of certain things (normally, certain organisms) must be positively weighed in deciding what it is permissible to do.[2] Thus, it morally is wrong to

kill LACHites for food when one is hungry. Similarly, it seems wrong to cause premature death to young (human) children to achieve the same goal. (Compare a simple taxonomy of the world: division into Edibles and Inedibles.) However, most people have few reservations about causing premature death to young nonhuman "children" (offspring) for culinary purposes. The different outlooks presupposed in these latter differential judgments may be couched in terms of moral standing. Let us stipulate, for any thing, X,[3]

> X has moral standing
> if and only if
> the continued existence of X or its
> interests in well-being have positive
> moral weight.

Explicitly or implicitly, one traditional view, often called the "anthropocentric paradigm," answers the basic *question*

> *Which things* have moral standing?

by proposing that

> All and only human beings have moral standing.

This latter view, in effect, assumes that the most defensible answer to another question

> What is the appropriate *criterion of moral standing?*

is

> Membership in *Homo sapiens.*

This proposed criterion has several virtues, one of which is reasonable clarity. However, there are hard cases: Does it include human fetal progeny, brain-dead yet breathing humans, recently dead humans, anencephalic babies? Also worrisome is what the anthropocentric criterion excludes; based on such a criterion, the well-being of nonhuman animals, nonhuman members or parts of the ecosystem, or even intelligent, "personable," alien beings does not, in itself, count. *If* by *natural resource* we mean anything not a human being (or part of one), such things are, on the view under consideration, mere resources to be used to pursue human goals.[4] This pervasive and traditional outlook has come under sharp attack in the last decade—as the following essays demonstrate.

3. Environmental Duties According to the Anthropocentric Criterion

Shortly, we shall return to questions about *(a)* the implications of the anthropocentric criterion of moral standing, and *(b)* competing criteria. First, it is useful to reflect on the relation of questions of duty to the issue of moral standing. If we could settle the issue of what is the appropriate *criterion* of moral standing, then, in principle, we could ascertain *which things* have moral standing (technically, the extension of "things with moral standing"). Suppose these difficult problems were resolved. What are the implications of recognizing that something has moral standing, that is, that its continued existence or interests in well-being have positive moral weight? A plausible answer is that, if so, then we moral agents (those who have the freedom and rational capacities to be responsible for choices) have a presumptive duty not to terminate, or undermine the interests of, those entities with moral standing. If this is right, matters are clarified somewhat. However, most of the important questions are left to be tackled, for reasons that will become clearer as we proceed.

If something *lacks* moral standing, its well-being just does not itself morally count (by definition of *moral standing*). However, if something *has* moral standing its well-being does count and is the basis of a presumptive duty *to* that thing. Presumptive duties, however, can be overridden under certain circumstances. Consider the fact that most of us think that ordinary persons have moral standing. Thus, we have a presumptive duty not to kill them—roughly a duty not to kill them in the absence of morally compelling reasons for doing so. Most people, however, think that *some* killings in self-defense, or in defense of other innocents against aggressor-persons, is morally justifiable. The contrary view, that we have an "absolute" or "categorical" duty never to kill persons

(those paradigmatic beings with moral standing!) is held by few (not even those who talk of the sanctity or infinite value of life or all human life) and is hard to defend rationally. The appeal to what most people think is not a compelling consideration. The more basic point is this: Even with regard to those paradigms of beings with moral standing (persons), there well may be important issues to be decided, regarding legitimate treatment of such beings, *even if* we take it as settled that such beings have moral standing. The moral of this story is twofold:

1. Whether we have a presumptive *duty to* some entity depends on settling the dispute over whether it has moral standing

and

2. however, even if we settle (1) there are still perplexities about just what reasons would serve to justify our going ahead and thwarting the interests of a being that has moral standing.

To stress a point, a *necessary but not sufficient* condition of formulating an adequate ethical theory (and, hence, an adequate environmental ethic) is determining the most defensible criterion of moral standing. Beyond that, there are other recalcitrant and challenging issues. The issue of moral standing, however, is more basic. Further, it is the one most neglected, because historically very few writers questioned the anthropocentric position. Like other deeply entrenched assumptions it often has functioned like a pair of lenses through which we view and conceptualize the environment—and not as itself an object in view, as something to be subjected to philosophical scrutiny.

Let us return to some reflection about the implications of the anthropocentric viewpoint—and the assumption that all and only humans have moral standing. On such a view, only the well-being or the lives of humans in themselves count. Does this mean that it is all right to burn cats for recreational purposes? Or poison one's privately owned lake? Or blow up a small planet to entertain those with astronomical curiosities? Or fertilize our gardens with the cadavers of those who died a natural death (and, perhaps, earlier voiced no objection)? Or *if* I knew I was the last person on earth, would it be all right for me to trigger (if I could) all the nuclear weapons already in place—when I was ready to say "farewell," of course? After all, according to one view the well-being of all and only humans counts! The answer to these questions (except perhaps the last one), according to the anthropocentric view, surely is: not necessarily.

To explain, or call to mind, why not, it is useful to consider the distinction between *(a)* duties *to* something and *(b)* duties *regarding* something. If you have moral standing, then I have a presumptive duty *to* you not to harm you. Suppose that nonliving things lack moral standing—as the anthropocentric paradigm implies. Then your car lacks moral standing. I cannot have duties *to* it since, we may suppose, one can have (direct) duties only to (or toward) entities with moral standing. Still, the anthropocentric view reasonably can account for why it is wrong for me to destroy your car without your consent. Were I to do so, it would damage the legitimate interests of a being with moral standing, namely, you. Hence, I have duties *regarding* your car (for example, not to destroy it) even though its well-being *in itself* does not count; that is, it lacks moral standing. In principle then, even though the anthropocentric criterion of moral standing excludes everything nonhuman (mountains, penguins, real or plastic trees, blue whales, and so on) from possessing such standing, humans have certain duties to protect or not harm the nonhuman "furniture of the earth." A key feature, of course, is that according to this view any such duties will obtain *only if* they are *derivative* from duties we have toward human beings. Some writers make this (or a similar) point in terms of *intrinsic* versus *extrinsic* value. Certain things, for example, human beings (their existence or their well-being), are thought to be valuable in themselves, or intrinsically valuable; hence, certain duties are owed to them. In contrast, other things are thought to lack intrinsic value, and if valuable at all are valuable *only if valued by* beings that are intrinsically valuable. It is worth emphasizing that according to such views duties *regarding* certain things, or value being assigned to them, are *contingent* on their being valued by, or being objects whose

existence is in the legitimate interest of, beings with moral standing. That certain animals, for example, are extrinsically valuable (so are humans) is noncontroversial. That no duties are owed *to* animals, that they utterly lack intrinsic value, is *not* noncontroversial. Similar points may be proposed with regard to mountains, oceans, redwood trees, and marshes. Such claims are among the central sources of contention in environmental ethics.

4. Competing Criteria of Moral Standing

So far we have focused on only one proposed criterion of moral standing, albeit a pervasive and influential one: membership in *Homo sapiens.* As several of the selections to follow make clear, other views have been proposed as more defensible. A list of some of the leading competing candidates would include these (or some combination):

1. personhood
2. potential personhood
3. rationality
4. linguistic capacity
5. sentience
6. being alive
7. being an integral part of an ecosystem

Some brief commentary on these proposals is of interest. The different criteria, generally, will select out different sets of beings (or entities) as possessing moral standing; some of the criteria clearly are more inclusive than others. Those who, like Schweitzer, trouble to maneuver a housefly outside rather than kill it may be committed to, or presuppose, criterion 6 as the proper criterion. Criterion 7 promises to be even more inclusive since, according to this view, even things not themselves alive (for example, a mountain) may be part of an ecosystem. Some persons, of course, are inclined toward vitalism, understood as asserting that all things are, in some sense, alive. Others would insist that at least the earth's surface and atmosphere, the biosphere, should be thought of as a dynamic, living system—even like a gigantic, somewhat diffuse, organism. In recent years, the atmospheric chemist James Lovelock in his book, *Gaia,* has argued that the earth's biosphere behaves like "a single organism, even a living creature." This view revives after a fashion the predominant ancient conception of the earth as a goddess, as alive and a fitting referent of the expression "sister" or "earth mother" used both by Plato and St. Francis. Some contemporary environmentalists think it no small matter, and indeed of the greatest consequence, that a shift occurred (about the time of Descartes and Newton, in the seventeenth and eighteenth centuries) from conceptualizing the earth as alive, and a bountiful partner, to the earth as an object, as a wound-up clock to be *tinkered* with instead of affectionately *tended* by humans. Evidently, the implications of accepting *being alive* as the criterion of moral standing will vary depending on what is viewed as being alive. In contrast, the famous late eighteenth, early nineteenth century English utilitarian, Jeremy Bentham, defended sentience as the criterion of moral standing. He remarked that:

The day *may come,* when the rest of the animal creation may acquire those rights which never could have been withholden from them but by the hand of tyranny. The French have already discovered that the blackness of the skin is no reason why a human being should be abandoned without redress to the caprice of a tormentor. It may come one day to be recognized, that the number of the legs, the villosity of the skin, or the termination of the *os sacrum,* are reasons equally insufficient for abandoning a sensitive being to the same fate. What else is it that should trace the insuperable line? Is it the faculty of reason, or, perhaps, the faculty of discourse? But a full-grown horse or dog is beyond comparison a more rational, as well as a more conversable animal, than an infant of a day, or a week, or even a month, old. But suppose the case were otherwise, what would it avail? the question is not, Can they *reason?* nor, Can they *talk?* but, Can they *suffer?*[5]

Thus, in Bentham's view the central question is whether a being can suffer or experience satisfaction—is it *sentient* (criterion 5)—and not whether it possesses the capacity to reason (criterion 3) or the capacity to use language (criterion 4). In a possibly ambiguous passage the famous seventeenth century French philosopher and mathematician René Descartes seems to have taken the view that nonhuman animals lack linguistic capacity and, for this reason, that they lack a mental-psychological life. Thus, animals are not sentient. If so, of course, they cannot be caused pain—appearances to the contrary. Hence, there could be no duty not to cause them pain. In Cartesian language they are mere *automata;* in modern language they are like programmed robots. Thus, if Descartes is right—even if sentience is the most defensible criterion of moral standing—nonhuman animals fail to have such standing. Some people may side with Descartes in his denial of sentience to (any) animals, but his view seems indefensible.

It is worth noting that the criterion of sentience not only would include certain animals (those that are sentient; contrary to Descartes, we assume many are) but also would exclude nonsentient humans. Which humans are not sentient? Possibly: the irreversibly comatose, some anencephalic (brainless or partly brainless) babies, first trimester fetuses, perhaps later fetal stages as well. In any case, the boundary around sentient creatures certainly does not coincide with the boundary around members of *Homo sapiens.* At least three reasons may be offered for accepting sentience, as opposed to membership in our species, as the most defensible criterion. (1) Drawing the line around our own species is entirely arbitrary—much like what, in effect, the racist or sexist does in favoring his (or her) own race or gender; (2) it is implausible to think that some humans, for example, the irreversibly comatose, have moral standing; (3) if suffering is an evil that *ceteris paribus* ought to be prevented, it is arbitrary to regard only human suffering as an evil. These points are somewhat controversial; to note them here is merely to hint at some of the debates that are part of the current reassessment of our dealings with animals. They are discussed in later essays.

Criterion 4, linguistic capacity, finds few defenders today. Even if it were the most defensible criterion of moral standing, two implications are of interest. First, it would imply that certain very seriously retarded humans lack moral standing. That we have no presumptive duties to such beings is a view many find repugnant. Second, a plausible case can be made that some nonhuman primates (at least) satisfy this condition—given the success in teaching Ameslan (American Sign Language) to certain gorillas and chimpanzees. Whether certain animals possess linguistic competence is a matter of current dispute, mainly because of conceptual disagreement over what counts as "possessing a language."

Criterion 3 is somewhat obscure also. What counts as being rational? If rationality is construed in a nonstringent fashion, it is likely that many animals will satisfy the condition (though not rocks or rivers). If the concept of rationality is construed stringently, although it may exclude all animals it is likely to exclude certain humans as well, for example, the severely retarded. Those who accept the sentience criterion or the anthropocentric one will find this an intolerable implication. Some philosophers who regard rationality as the proper criterion (as do some who accept sentience) do not hesitate to conclude that some members of *Homo sapiens* lack moral standing. Others, finding this implication repugnant, seek to avoid it by defending other proposals. According to one view, if something is a member of a species whose paradigm members (for example, normal adult members) are rational, then any member is classifiable as a rational creature. Thus, although no one would say of a human zygote (fertilized egg) that it can reason, one contemporary philosopher, Alan Donagan, for example, views it as a rational creature, and, hence, deserving of the respect owed to rational creatures.[6] According to this view, of course, it is clear that *actual* possession of the (allegedly) crucial trait, rationality, is not judged necessary for moral standing.

Donagan's view should be contrasted with various "potentiality principles." Suppose, for example, one were to propose that actual-rationality-or-potential-rationality (either trait or both) is the proper criterion of moral standing. On this criterion, normal persons, infants, and embryos (maybe zygotes too)[7] have moral standing. Embryos would have it, of course, because of their potential to become actually rational. On this criterion, however, an anencephalic infant is *not* potentially rational, and thus lacks moral standing. On Donagan's criterion, in contrast, it (probably) possesses moral standing. So, Donagan's extension of moral standing (though he does not employ this terminology) to "marginal members" of *Homo sapiens* diverges from potentiality principles.

It is tempting to think that, although neonates or fetuses lack rationality or certain other complex psychological characteristics, they (or most of them) directly are owed certain duties, and, hence, to presuppose that they possess moral standing. Further, it is tempting to think that such standing is possessed because of their prospect of developing into beings who uncontroversially are agreed to have standing, namely, normal persons. Some claim that although certain adult primates may exhibit "more personality" or have capacities for rational choice not possessed by neonatal humans, a reason for attributing moral standing to such humans but not to such primates is that the former have a unique potential that the latter do not. According to this line of thought it may not be thought that membership in *Homo sapiens as such* is the proper criterion of moral standing; rather, it is actual or potential personhood (or rationality according to a variant view). This criterion tends to include virtually all humans (though not the most severely retarded, anencephalic infants, or those in persistent vegetative states) but probably no animals—at least if the facts support the claim that no animals are rational or none exhibit the requisites of personhood. Such a view contrasts with the anthropocentric criterion; it also allows the possibility that nonhumans (for example, possible alien creatures; consider "E.T.") possess moral standing.

In spite of the intuitive appeal of regarding a creature's potentiality as morally significant, some deny its relevance. We note one objection here. Suppose that a *sufficient* condition for possessing moral standing is that an entity, X, possess a certain trait (P), that is, is a person. Let MS stand for "moral standing." Then the supposition is that

1. For any X, if X has P, X has MS.

Defenders of the importance of potential personhood seem to assume that

2. For any X, if X potentially has P, X has MS.

Opponents of (2) wonder why we should accept (2). Claim (2) does not follow from (1). Nor does (2) follow from the weaker claim (3):

3. For any X, if X potentially has P, X potentially has MS.

To be less formal, consider some related examples. Although an acorn potentially is an adult oak tree, and adult oak trees are large, acorns are not large. Normal adult persons, it is commonly held (at least in the Western World), have a right to decide whom to marry (or at least whom to refuse to marry); human zygotes are (generally) potential normal adults, but they, arguably, lack the right in question. Even though we may agree that a certain morally important trait (for example, having certain rights) is possessed by an entity in virtue of its having certain *actual* properties (for example, being an adult person), why think that an entity that only has the potential for these properties has the relevant trait? To press the point, infants are potentially adults. Actual adults (normally) have a right to vote. Why attribute such a right to the infant? Its potential adulthood does not seem a good reason. In short, there is a puzzle as to why *potential possession* of relevant properties is morally significant as opposed to *actual possession*. Getting clear about these matters is no easy task; here we call attention only to one source of contention. Further inquiry is in order.

Those new to recent discussions may be puzzled by the implicit contrast, in the above remarks, between humans and persons. Often we use *person* and *human* interchangeably. If the terms are synonymous it is contradictory to talk of nonhuman persons—or of humans who are not persons. Some philosophers (for example, Michael Tooley and Mary Anne Warren) suggest, however, that there is a sensible distinction worth making between (1) what is a human being (a member of the biological species, *Homo sapiens*) and (2) what is a person (when *person* is not used loosely simply to refer to humans in the biological sense). Concerning the view in question, to put matters *roughly*, it is suggested that something is a person if and only if it *(a)* is sentient, *(b)* is aware of itself as an entity existing over time (or self-aware—and not just an organism that scans its environment), and perhaps *(c)* is capable (minimally) of reasoned choice. We have sketched the seeming implications of employing personhood as the criterion of moral standing.

A standard objection to this view is that such a position expresses an arbitrary strategy of some philosophers aimed at including, or allowing them to include, only those beings that they otherwise favor in the category of entities with moral standing. If one can define *personhood* as one wishes, the definer indeed has a "do-it-yourself construction kit" for setting the boundaries of the moral community (those possessing moral standing). Several responses to this point deserve reflection. Although dominant and influential, the anthropocentric criterion (membership in *Homo sapiens*) hardly seems self-evident in the light of current criticisms; it also needs defense against the charge of arbitrariness—as would other "natural boundaries" such as race or gender. Further, one conception of personhood—as something with personality and psychological character (having beliefs about oneself, one's environment, having preferences, and capable of choice)—hardly seems a new and stipulative use of *person*. According to this at least intelligible conception of persons it seems correct to say that human fetuses and neonates are not persons.

Another perspective is worth noting here. One might think that the *most* stringent duties of all are directly owed to persons (in the psychological as opposed to the biological interpretation) and yet other entities, say the merely sentient ones, also possess moral standing. Thus, one might think that there is a sort of *moral hierarchy* of entities; for example, all and only sentient creatures have moral standing but among these with such standing, the well-being or lives of some morally count more heavily than others. Thus, although there is a presumption against destroying or causing pain to any sentient creature, in certain conflicts of interest between persons and the merely sentient it is all right (or obligatory) to sacrifice the interests of the latter. If a baboon heart can be transplanted to a human baby to save the latter's life (but the baboon will die), it is, according to this view, proper that the transplant be carried out. Even some staunch advocates of animal liberation or animal rights (for example, Peter Singer or Tom Regan) accept this judgment. *Why* it should be accepted is, however, a matter of considerable controversy. If one is to include both persons and others (say, the merely sentient) within the moral community—but views some as, in *some* sense, second-class citizens, serious perplexities arise. *Is there a nonarbitrary basis for such differentiations within the set of beings possessing moral standing?* If so, what is it? And if rationality, for example, is invoked, will that not suggest that we can, or ought to, discriminate (differentiate) among humans—according to possession (or not) of rationality (or even degrees of rationality)? Further, does such a view open the door to, or commit one to, a policy of invidious discrimination? If not, why not?

---

5. *Human Organisms*

Talk of environmental ethics, ecological ethics, the preservation of nature calls to mind concerns about protection of individual animals or rare species; preserving clean air, wilderness areas, groves of redwood trees; avoiding the destruction of the wonders of nature such as the Grand Canyon; or the sense of loss when woods and pastures are transformed into concatenations of steel, concrete, plastic, and neon. It is a bit surprising, then, when the suggestion is made that there is a link between some of the basic issues in environmental ethics and certain

perplexing issues often classified as matters of biomedical ethics such as abortion. Given our prior discussion, however, the link is more evident. If we agree that normal postnatal human beings have moral standing, whether "all things human" do is a matter of some dispute. Several sorts of entities deserve special consideration: (1) human fetuses, (2) anencephalic or (less but) radically defective infants, (3) irreversibly comatose humans, (4) newly dead human bodies. Let us use *NPH* to stand for these nonparadigmatic humans. Do any or all NPH have moral standing? If so, what sorts of duties are directly owed to NPH? Must we make equally stringent efforts to preserve or protect (or somehow "respect") such beings—as are required in our dealings with normal humans?

If the familiar contrast between "man and nature" is to be understood as one between normal neonatal humans and things that cannot be so classified, that is, everything else, then NPH are a part of "nature." As noted, according to one view what is part of nature (other than paradigm humans) can be used as a natural resource, for example, for the benefit of (paradigm) humans. Reasoning rather like this may be behind the view that we ought to put to good use, for example, aborted fetuses, the recently dead (where all respiratory and circulatory functions have irreversibly ceased), or those in a persistent vegetative state (sometimes described as brain-dead). There is a great need for organs for transplantation, a need for blood, for growth hormone, and so on. Hence, some regard the failure to "mine" NPH (or some subset) as a shameful waste—given the scarcity of resources valuable to paradigmatic humans. Disputes about these matters depend in part on ascertaining the appropriate criterion of moral standing. As we have noted, if by *natural resource* what is meant is "what it is morally permissible to use to benefit those with moral standing," one theoretical (and practical) connection of environmental ethics and biomedical ethics is clear. If we are to reassess or query *What's so important about animals?* Or rare species, jungles, wilderness, mountains, or redwoods? it is not out of place to consider What's so important about people?—Or nonparadigmatic humans—as well.

6. Traditional Ethical Theories

Natural Law Morality and Judeo-Christian Morality

Traditional morality is often associated with the view that there is a certain natural and morally defensible hierarchy of beings. There is, it is claimed, a natural order according to which inanimate objects are to serve animate ones; further, plants are here for the sake of animals, and animals for the sake of humans. It is, thus, right and proper, for the "higher" to use the "lower," as the former see fit. Throughout history this view has rarely been questioned. It is a view implicit in much (at least) of natural law theory dating back to Aristotle (384–322 B.C.) and in Thomas Aquinas's (1225–1274) theological revision of Aristotelianism. In theological versions, of course, the natural order is seen as part of the divine order—and people are around for the sake of God—and are to function within the constraints laid down by divine purposes.

In *The Politics* Aristotle says,

plants exist for the sake of animals. . . . all other animals exist for the sake of man, tame animals for the use he can make of them as well as for the food they provide; and as for wild animals, most though not all of these can be used for food and are useful in other ways; clothing and instruments can be made out of them. If then we are right in believing that nature makes nothing without some end in view, nothing to no purpose, it must be that nature has made all things specifically for the sake of man.[8]

Elsewhere in *The Politics* Aristotle compares the function of women to that of animals in an effort to explain the low position of each in the hierarchy of being:

As between male and female the former is by nature superior and ruler, the latter inferior and subject. . . . Wherever there is the same wide discrepancy between two sets of human beings as there is between mind and body or between man and beast, then the inferior of the two sets, those whose condition is such that their function is the use of their bodies and nothing better can be expected of them, those, I say, are slaves by nature.[9]

In short, those with less rationality exist to serve the needs, interests, or good of those with more. One's place in the hierarchy of being reflects Aristotle's judgment concerning one's rational abilities.

Aquinas, like Aristotle, makes it clear that to kill and otherwise use animals for human purposes is part of the natural order of things. In the *Summa Contra Gentiles*, Aquinas says,

we refute the error of those who claim that it is a sin for man to kill brute animals. For animals are ordered to man's use in the natural course of things, according to divine providence. Consequently, man uses them without any injustice, either by killing them or by employing them in any other way. For this reason, God said to Noe: "As the green herbs, I have delivered all flesh to you." (Genesis 9:3)[10]

In Aquinas's view, animals have no independent moral standing or intrinsic goodness. Aquinas thought that we ought not to be cruel to animals, not because animals have an interest in not suffering, but because if such cruelty is allowed, humans may learn callousness and inflict it on their fellow humans:

Man's affections may be either of reason or of sentiment. As regards the former, it is indifferent how one behaves towards animals, since God has given him dominion over all as it is written, 'thou has subjected all things under his feet.' It is in this sense that St. Paul says that God has no care for oxen or other animals. . . . As to affection arising from sentiment, it is operative with regard to animals. . . . And if he is often moved in this way, he is more likely to have compassion for his fellowmen. . . . Therefore, the Lord, in order to stir to compassion the Jewish people, naturally inclined to cruelty, wished to exercise them in pity even to animals by forbidding certain practices savouring of cruelty to them.[11]

According to Genesis, God has given human beings dominion over the earth: "Be fruitful and multiply, and replenish the earth, and subdue it; and have dominion over the fish of the sea, and over the fowl of the air, and over every living thing that moveth upon the earth."[12] There is, in the recent literature on animal liberation and environmental ethics, a dispute over the interpretation of the Biblical notion of dominion. Some say that (1) dominion permits humans to do whatever they want with animals, plants, rivers, and rocks. Others claim that (2) dominion means stewardship. According to this view God expects us to exercise some responsibility toward the earth. The earth belongs to God and we are commanded to take care of it and the creatures that dwell therein.

A stewardship interpretation may be committed to an acceptance of a traditional private property view. That is, humans should not ruthlessly exploit the earth because the earth is God's. If we ought to treat the earth in a responsible and virtuous way, it is not because the earth and its creatures have independent moral standing or intrinsic goodness, but because it is God's property. It is important to note that this result—the lack of independent moral standing on the part of any being except humans—seems to follow from either interpretation of dominion. This is not a surprising outcome. In the history of ethics, Aristotle and Aquinas exemplify what is called *virtue ethics*. In this tradition, for example, if one is not cruel to animals, it is because one believes that cruelty is a vice. It was too early in the history of thought for the notion of a right, that is, for the idea that there is something about the being or entity toward whom (or which) we act that must be respected, that makes it or them not simply the beneficiaries of our good character.

Natural Rights Theory

a. The Kantian Argument

It is generally accepted that persons are the sorts of being that have rights. Immanuel Kant, a German philosopher (1724–1804), provided the original argument that explains what persons are and why they have rights.

Kant explicates what a person is by distinguishing persons from things. Persons are rational, autonomous beings who are capable of formulating and pursuing different conceptions of the good. That is, persons have

ends of their own; things or objects in the world do not. For example, suppose I walk into a classroom and decide to break up all the chairs in order to use them for firewood. If I do this, it does not matter to the chairs.[13] Now, there may be many reasons why I should not destroy the chairs. The next class may be planning to sit on them. Presumably, somebody owns the chairs and does not want me to destroy them. However, I cannot give as a reason for refraining from breaking the chairs that it matters to the chairs. It can even be said that it is in the interests of chairs not to be broken (or in the interests of lawnmowers not to be left out in the rain), but this is not the same as claiming that chairs or lawnmowers have interests of their own if we mean by this that chairs or lawnmowers care about how they are treated. Persons care about how they are treated; things do not. According to Kant, things can be used to suit the purposes of persons, but persons are not to be used as if they were mere things, as if they had no ends or purposes of their own. Persons have rights because of their unconditional worth as rational beings, whereas the worth of things is relative to the ends of persons.

Conceptually, it is difficult, if not impossible, to extend rights to environmental objects such as rocks and streams on a Kantian analysis of rights. This is so for the following reason: According to this analysis, rights are designed to protect persons from being treated as things. Rocks and streams are paradigm cases of things or objects; they are incapable of formulating ends. *Thing*, in Kant, is a technical term. Something is a *thing* if it is incapable of autonomy in the Kantian sense which entails self-rule, that is, formulating and following rational principles. Hence, inanimate objects do not have rights in Kant's view. Nonetheless, we may have duties regarding inanimate objects. These duties, Kant maintained, are indirect duties toward human beings, as the following quotation shows:

Destructiveness is immoral; we ought not to destroy things which can still be put to some use. No man ought to mar the beauty of nature; for what he has no use for may still be of use to some one else. He need, of course, pay no heed to the thing itself, but he ought to consider his neighbor.[14]

Animals are also considered "things" in Kant's scheme. In his *Lectures on Ethics,* he referred to animals as "man's instruments."[15] Despite Kant's innovative work on the subject of rights, many older notions persist in his philosophy. The idea that animals, like any tool, exist for the use of human beings is one example. Likewise, we find in Kant the idea that our treatment of animals is a matter of our virtue. For example, in the *Lectures,* he says, "A master who turns out his ass or his dog because the animal can no longer earn its keep manifests a small mind."[16]

Some human beings are not autonomous, yet Kant accorded them rights. Since Kant defined persons as rational, autonomous beings and not merely as human beings, he had the philosophical ammunition, so to speak, to challenge the anthropocentric paradigm. That is, a little reflection shows that a rational being in the Kantian sense and a human being, that is, a member of the species *Homo sapiens,* are not one and the same. Some human beings are not rational: fetuses, infants, the permanently comatose; some rational beings may not be human beings. For example, some animals may be autonomous in the Kantian sense, even though Kant denied it. Moreover, as mentioned earlier, there may be extraterrestrial beings, like the movie character E.T., who are rational beings, but not members of our species. Not only did Kant treat *human being* and *rational being* as interchangeable (thereby attributing rights to all and only human beings); he also attributed all the traditional rights (liberty, property, and so on) to rational beings. Although autonomy may be necessary for possession of a right to liberty, one might ask why a being must be autonomous in order to have a right not to be tortured? The failure to take seriously the relevant criteria for the various rights is considered a serious weakness in classical rights theories by many contemporary philosophers.

b. Taking Qualifications Seriously

The new literature on animal liberation and animal rights has caused many to rethink the claim that humans have rights solely because they are human. If we no longer rely on this kind of argument, then right-holders must possess some morally relevant features that may turn out to be shared by humans, animals, and environmental objects alike. The method employed is to identify the morally relevant qualifications for the possession of specific rights in order to determine what rights, if any, a being or entity has. With respect to some rights, a plausible case can be made that certain qualifications are morally relevant. To do this, however, one needs to know the specific purpose of each right. For example, the right not to be tortured protects the basic interest certain beings have in not suffering. The right to liberty protects the interest in directing one's life as one sees fit without unjustified interference from others. If a being is capable of suffering, but not capable of autonomy or self-rule, it can have a right not to be tortured, but not a right to liberty. On this model, the right to life must protect some specific interest or desire. One plausible candidate, suggested by Michael Tooley,[17] is a desire to continue into the future, that is, to continue to live.

The desire for continued existence presupposes the capacity to have a concept of oneself as a continuing self—as an entity existing over time. Of course, each right, according to the view we have been developing, presupposes some morally relevant capacity. The right not to be tortured presupposes a capacity for suffering. The right to liberty presupposes a capacity for autonomy. Once we figure out the morally relevant capacity for any given right, only those beings or entities that have the relevant capacity have the right. Thus, only sentient beings have a right not to be tortured, only autonomous beings have a right to liberty, and only self-conscious beings a right to life. Most adult human beings can meet the self-consciousness requirement, as may some animals. However, as Tooley points out, some adult human beings do not have the requisite capacity, nor do human fetuses or newborn infants. It is worth noting that the self-consciousness requirement is a fairly sophisticated one. According to a view like Tooley's, mere consciousness or sentience may be sufficient for having a right not to be tortured, but not for having a right to life.

According to the above approach to rights, many animals fare rather well. Some animals most certainly have a right not to be tortured, and quite possibly a right to life. Environmental objects, such as rocks and plants, however, appear to fare rather badly. For example, it would be absurd to claim that rocks have a right not to be tortured if they are incapable of suffering. If environmental objects are not sentient or conscious, it is hard to see how they would qualify for any rights. Peter Singer claims that plants have no conscious experiences, and thus I do nothing seriously wrong if I pull out weeds from my garden.[18] Nonetheless, some people believe that plants have feelings, and some, like Christopher Stone, think that the entire planet is at some level conscious. So, there are matters of disagreement about who or what has certain capacities, but the important point here is that the challenge to the anthropocentric paradigm has changed the character of the rights debate into one about capacities and the moral relevance of capacities.

c. Rights and Duties

Rights can be correlative with duties. For example, correlated with my duty not to kill you is your right not to have me kill you. Some philosophers claim there can be duties toward another without that other's possessing correlative rights; others claim that a being can possess rights without others owing that being duties. Moreover, some philosophers claim that only those who can perform duties or act from a sense of duty can have rights; others claim that beings or entities (such as animals and trees) can have rights even if they cannot act from a sense of duty.

It is doubtful that animals can act from a sense of duty. Promise keeping is a paradigm of a duty or obligation. Suppose I say to my cat as I leave in the morning, "I want you to meet me here at 5:00 P.M." Can I seriously expect her to make and keep a promise? Animals kill and eat one another (and occasionally us). As unfortunate as this may be, it does not seem to make sense to say that animals have duties not to do this.

In arguments about the correlativity of rights and duties, it is often pointed out that infants and retarded persons may be incapable of duties, yet they may have rights. If this is so, an animal's inability to perform duties does not imply that it cannot have rights. If the only requirement for rights is to be capable of having certain interests, then beings that have those interests have rights whether or not they can meet additional requirements for being able to perform duties. But this is simply to say that rights and duties are two different things. Acting out of a sense of duty presupposes certain rational capacities, whereas possession of the right not to be tortured, for example, presupposes a capacity to suffer.

If animals cannot perform duties, it is even less plausible to suggest that the "environment" can be morally responsible for the disasters it causes. Rivers overflow and damage property, forest fires destroy lives, sinkholes swallow up Porsches. The interest argument, which tenably can allocate rights (or, at least some rights) to animals, cannot do the same, with comparable ease, for environmental objects. Trees and streams not only lack the rational capacity required for duties, they appear to lack interests as well at least in the Kantian sense of caring about how one is treated. If a wilderness is destroyed to make a home for Mickey Mouse, it does not matter to the wilderness.

Utilitarianism

Utilitarian theory holds that what is right is to act so as to bring about the greatest possible balance of good consequences over bad consequences for all concerned. John Stuart Mill (1806–1873), a leading exponent of classical utilitarianism, interpreted *good* as *happiness,* and *happiness* as *pleasure.* According to Mill,

"Utility" or "the greatest happiness principle" holds that actions are right in proportion as they tend to promote happiness; wrong as they tend to produce the reverse of happiness. By happiness is intended pleasure and the absence of pain; by unhappiness, pain and the privation of pleasure.[19]

a. Quantifying Goodness

Jeremy Bentham (1748–1832), as well as Mill, interpreted *utility* in a hedonistic manner. *Hedonism,* as technically understood in moral philosophy, is the view that pleasure and pleasure alone is intrinsically good. Typically, pain is viewed as an intrinsic evil. If the goal of morality is to increase the sum of pleasure in the world, its accomplishment will be facilitated if pleasures can be measured and compared with one another. Bentham devised a "pleasure measure" known as the *hedonic calculus* in order to perform this task. To help us remember how to measure the value of a pleasure or pain, Bentham wrote the following (rather bad) poem:

Intense, long, certain, speedy, fruitful, pure—
Such marks in *pleasures* and in *pains* endure.
Such pleasure seek, if *private* be thy end:
If it be *public*, wide let them *extend*.
Such *pains* avoid, whichever be thy view:
If pains *must* come, let them *extend* to few.[20]

Mill was critical of the results of Bentham's method. According to Bentham's account, only quantitative differences between pleasures matter in establishing the value of activities. Bentham claimed that pushpin is as good as poetry if the amount of pleasure in each experience is equal. In more contemporary terms, he might have said that playing video games is as good as studying Shakespearean plays if the amounts of pleasure are equal. Mill introduced the idea of considering quality as well as quantity in determining the value of pleasures. In arguing that pleasures of the mind are superior to those of the body, Mill maintained that it is better to be Socrates dissatisfied than a pig satisfied.

In contemporary economic theory, utility is interpreted as the satisfaction of individual preferences, or want-satisfaction as it is sometimes called. Some of the theoretical difficulties with classical utilitarianism are reflected in contemporary versions of utilitarianism. One such problem is the following: One often does not know what is going to make people happy. (This is why Mill worried about pushpin and poetry.) What if a junky environment makes people happy? Worse yet, what if unjust social institutions bring about the greatest happiness? This is not an implausible suggestion. After all, it may be that unjust social institutions have persisted through the centuries because some people benefit from them. If the benefits are great enough for enough people, maximiza-

tion of utility may require certain kinds of injustice.

Mark Sagoff vividly describes the possible implications of preference-based utilitarianism for environmental quality: "Schlock on every block, K-Mart lowers the price . . . crowds for every Ho Jo, Go Go, Disco, and peep show that can be built."[21] If the value of the environment depends on what our preferences are or what we want, what objection can be made to a world of pizza parlors, pinball arcades, and plastic trees if that is what people want? According to a utilitarian view, there isn't anything wrong with plastic trees. As Tom Regan puts it, "If a *reductio* is possible in assessing theories relating to our duties regarding the environment, hedonistic utilitarianism falls victim to this form of refutation."[22]

Reductio is short for *reductio ad absurdum*, a Latin phrase that means reducing to the absurd. Elementary logic textbooks classify the reductio as one way of refuting an argument. The idea is to show that your opponent's views entail claims (presumably unnoticed by him or her) that are absurd. The hope is that your opponent will be sufficiently embarrassed upon this discovery to give up his or her original views. Reductios, however, do not always work, for some people are willing to live with implications that others find absurd.

Of course, it may be that preference-based utilitarianism may sanction plastic trees because only human preferences are taken into account. It has been suggested that animals and some natural objects have wants that must be counted along with human wants. That some animals have wants is uncontroversial; that trees and streams have wants is regarded by some as, at best, a metaphorical way of speaking. Christopher Stone maintains that "natural objects can communicate their wants (needs) to us, and in ways that are not terribly ambiguous."[23] He says, for example, the lawn tells me that it wants water[24] and a smog-endangered stand of pines wants the smog stopped.[25] If animals and trees have wants, such wants must be determined by some method other than observing their consumer behavior, the standard way economists determine a certain range of wants or preferences among humans. Animals do not go to K-Mart and buy things. This problem, along with many others, is discussed in Part IV (which is devoted to an analysis of economic methodology and related ethical assumptions).

b. Utility and Moral Standing

If maximizing happiness and minimizing pain is what morality is all about, it seems reasonable to suppose that sentience is the criterion of moral standing. Peter Singer, a contemporary utilitarian, follows Bentham in claiming that "If a being suffers, there can be no moral justification for refusing to take that suffering into consideration."[26] Nor is there any justification for the claim that human interests and consideration of suffering outweigh nonhuman interests and suffering simply because they are human. The only requirement for having an interest is the capacity for suffering and enjoyment. Thus, animals have interests according to Singer's view; at the very least, they have an interest in not suffering.

In order to reach a solution to a moral problem, utilitarians weigh the interests of all relevant parties in an attempt to discover what will maximize happiness on balance. For example, cosmetics, shampoos, food colorings, and the like are tested on animals before they are introduced into the market. Singer reports that in Great Britain alone almost 100 new cosmetics and toiletries are produced every week.[27] When we weigh the interest that animals have in not suffering against the interest humans have in having more and more choice with respect to cosmetics and shampoos, it is hardly obvious that such testing maximizes utility. Utilitarian arguments do not guarantee (prior to calculating) that the interests of animals necessarily will win out over the interests of humans, or that human interests should prevail over those of animals. Although utilitarian theory insists that animal interests be taken into account, it does not necessarily support an outcome favorable to those interests. The outcome depends upon which course of action in fact contributes most to the general happiness.

c. Utility and Rights

The appeal to maximization of utility takes priority over all other considerations in the theory of utilitarianism. Mill once put the point this way: "It is proper to state that I forgo any advantage which could be derived to my argument from the idea of abstract right as a thing independent of utility. I regard utility as the ultimate appeal on all ethical questions."[28] Many utilitarians claim there are no moral rights. Bentham, for example, referred to rights as "nonsense on stilts." Mill does not rule out the possibility of rights. However, he makes it clear that if any rights exist, they are somehow to be derived from the principle of utility. According to this view, rights cannot override considerations of the general happiness.

Those who align themselves with the (competing) rights tradition are critical of the utilitarian ideal that the basic interests or rights of individuals can be sacrificed for the sake of the greatest good. As we have seen, it may be that certain kinds of injustice can be justified if doing so contributed more to the general happiness than not doing so. On the other hand, utilitarians confront rights theorists with cases that cast doubt on a tough-minded opposition to the sacrifice of individual rights. One such imaginative example, used by John D. Arras,[29] is taken from the movie *Dr. Strangelove*. The situation is this: A nuclear war can be prevented only if someone phones the President, but the person who can make the call does not have a dime. He sees a coke machine and frantically kicks it to get a dime, to make a call, to save the world. However, a clever utilitarian will point out to a rights theorist that the property rights of Coca-Cola must be infringed in order to get the money to make a call and save the world. Hence, there seem to be some cases in which the greater good takes precedence over rights. However, another interpretation is that the property rights of Coca-Cola must be infringed to *protect the rights* of others.

7. Two Fundamental Questions

To not lose sight of the moral forest because we have looked at some trees, we emphasize that two questions stand out as absolutely basic. Any proposed solution to an environmental problem must take a stand on these questions, explicitly or otherwise. First, what sorts of things have moral standing? That is, what sorts of things are such that their continued existence or welfare is valuable in themselves? To answer this question one must defend a particular criterion of moral standing. If we can settle on an answer to the first basic question, then we need to determine what are acceptable principles to invoke to help decide what are permissible (or obligatory) trade-offs in the many cases in which the lives or welfare of some things that possess moral standing conflict with the lives or welfare of other entities possessing moral standing. Some environmental proposals or positions make no effort to grapple with these perplexities. Others address one but make little or no effort to respond to the other. Reasonably addressing these two issues, however, must be viewed as a benchmark of any plausible "environmental ethic."

8. The Importance of Theory

Part of the solution to environmental disputes involves the acquisition of more empirical information, for example, discovering whether sulfur or nitrogen, or neither, plays the dominant role in the causation of "Waldsterben," the destruction of forests in various industrial nations. However, part of the solution must be found in ascertaining the most rationally defensible moral ground for evaluating this or that environmental alternative. To decide which is the most plausible view, a starting point is to be familiar with, and comparatively assess, the different ethical theories. In the Western tradition, the major ethical theories are natural law theory, natural rights theory, and utilitarianism. Furthermore, critical acquaintance with such theories is essential to deciding whether some quite nontraditional position must be formulated in order to arrive at an adequate environmental ethic. Some essays in this volume argue for, or presuppose, some traditional theory or a variation of one;

others, especially in Part III, insist that a new ethic is needed.

Whether we should heed these new voices and whether an adequate environmental ethic requires a rejection of more traditional principles are questions that demand a careful analysis of the arguments. Attempting to identify the contours of the right theory is no easy, or brief, task. Reflection on the essays that follow will take us a few steps toward clarity and toward rational convictions about how we should deal with other lives on earth and, indeed, the planet itself. If, and only if, we know what to *believe* about such matters can we know how to *act*—to shape responsibly our private lives and public policies. The price of our not thinking about these matters—of a certain intellectual neglect or recklessness—collectively will affect the fate of the earth. We do well to avoid that popular anti-intellectualism that naively doubts that "abstract ideas" have consequences. And we must shun those counsels of despair that assume that analytic or theoretic inquiry is useless because the path to practical, political change commonly is strewn with further obstacles. History repeatedly has shown the utter foolishness of both outlooks.

Notes

1. See the essays on Life (Volume 12) and *Homo sapiens* (Volume 8) in the *Encyclopaedia Brittanica* (Chicago: The University of Chicago Press, 1981).
2. Given the "high moral tone" of many exhortations to "obey the law" one should recall the legal rights and duties that sometimes have prevailed, for example, that women could not vote, that slaves must be returned to their masters—in the United States at one time, or that Jews in Nazi Germany had to wear arm bands.
3. The term *moral standing* is not used invariably in the same way in the literature. Sometimes *moral status, possesses inherent value*, and *being morally considerable* are used in an equivalent fashion, sometimes not. Readers beware!
4. Compare also the possible lack of clarity of *nature* in *man and nature*—as well as the ambiguity of *man.*

5. As cited in *Animal Rights and Human Obligations,* edited by Tom Regan and Peter Singer (Englewood Cliffs, N.J.: Prentice-Hall, 1976), p. XXX.

6. Alan Donagan, *The Theory of Morality* (Chicago: The University of Chicago Press, 1977), p. 83.

7. The *maybe* is used because a zygote may split in the first week and "become" twins. But if one twin is normal and the other is anencephalic, should we say the zygote was potentially rational or not? Or partially or . . .?

8. Aristotle. *The Politics,* translated by T. A. Sinclair (Baltimore: Penguin Books, 1962), p. 40.

9. Aristotle. *The Politics,* pp. 33, 34.

10. Thomas Aquinas. *Summa Contra Gentiles,* Book III, Part II, 112, 12, translated by Vernon J. Bourke (Notre Dame: University of Notre Dame Press, 1975), p. 119.

11. Thomas Aquinas. *Summa Theologica,* II, I, 102, 8, David Bourke and Arthur Littledale (New York: McGraw-Hill, 1969), p. 225.

12. Genesis 1:28.

13. Mary Anne Warren puts the point this way in "The Abortion Issue," in *Border Crossings,* edited by Donald VanDeVeer and Tom Regan (New York: Random House, 1986). See also Edward Johnson, "Treating the Dirt: Environmental Ethics and Moral Theory" in *Earthbound: New Introductory Essays in Environmental Ethics,* edited by Tom Regan (New York: Random House, 1984), p. 347. Johnson is not talking about rights, but he raises the following issue: "But does morality require us to pursue a creature's good, if that creature does not *care* about its good."

14. Kant. *Lectures on Ethics,* translated by Louis Infield (Indianapolis: Hackett Publishing Company, 1979), p. 241.

15. Kant. *Lectures on Ethics,* p. 240.

16. Kant. *Lectures on Ethics,* p. 241.

17. Michael Tooley. "In Defense of Abortion and Infanticide" in *The Problem of Abortion,* edited by Joel Feinberg, 2d ed. (Belmont, Calif.: Wadsworth Publishing Company, 1984).

18. Peter Singer. *Practical Ethics* (Cambridge: Cambridge University Press, 1979), p. 92.

19. J. S. Mill. *Utilitarianism* edited by George Sher (Indianapolis: Hackett Publishing Company, 1979), p. 7.

20. Oliver Johnson. *Ethics,* 4th ed. (New York: Holt Rinehart and Winston, 1978), p. 259.

21. Mark Sagoff. "Do We Need a Land Use Ethic?" *Environmental Ethics* 3, (Winter 1981), p. 299.

22. Tom Regan. "The Nature and Possibility of an Environmental Ethic," in *All That Dwell Therein: Essays on Animal Rights and Environmental Ethics* (Berkeley: University of California Press, 1982), p. 196. It is often thought that Martin Krieger's article, "What's Wrong with Plastic Trees," is a reductio of utilitarian ethics.

23. Christopher D. Stone. *Should Trees Have Standing? Toward Legal Rights for Natural Objects* (Los Altos: William Kaufmann, Inc., 1974), p. 24.

24. Christopher D. Stone. *Should Trees Have Standing?,* p. 24.

25. Christopher D. Stone. *Should Trees Have Standing?,* p. 24.

26. Peter Singer. *Practical Ethics* (Cambridge: Cambridge University Press, 1979), p. 50.

27. Peter Singer. *Animal Liberation: A New Ethics for Our Treatment of Animals* (New York: Random House, A New York Review Book, 1975), p. 52.

28. J. S. Mill. *On Liberty,* edited by Elizabeth Rapaport (Indianapolis: Hackett Publishing Company, 1978), p. 10.

29. John D. Arras. "The Right to Die on the Slippery Slope," *Social Theory and Practice,* 8 (Fall 1982), pp. 320–21.

The Other Animals: Mere Resources?

Preview

Widespread attitudes about what is permissible treatment of animals exhibit considerable ambivalence. We spend a great deal to care for our pets, to protect them and facilitate their flourishing. We mourn their deaths and even build cemeteries for them. We find it disturbing to hear of a group of children who burn a cat as a diversion. At the same time, we raise some animals in order to kill them for food; others are killed for fur coats, rugs, oil, glue, perfume (musk), or ivory piano keys. The wildebeest is killed because its tail makes a good flyswatter. The heads or entire bodies of some animals are stuffed to decorate human habitats. Other animals are incarcerated in zoos for our viewing pleasure. Some are thrust into life-and-death struggles (for example, pit bulls and cocks) to entertain some members of our species. Some of us engage in the "sport" of killing animals with no intention, or need, to eat the remains. Other instances of causing pain to, or killing, animals strike us as less suspect, such as that involved in the acquisition of scientific knowledge, for example, testing potentially toxic substances on "animal models." It is hard to see how to reconcile these conflicting attitudes.

Initially, it is worth contrasting four possible and competing views. At one extreme is the view (in our terminology) that animals lack moral standing entirely. According to this view, their well-being or lives count not at all. Thus, we can do with them *whatever* suits our purposes—so long as in doing so we wrong nothing with moral standing, that is, humans. This view, rightly or wrongly, has been attributed to the famous seventeenth century French philosopher and mathematician René Descartes. Descartes viewed animals as "automata," as beings rather like plants that move about but are incapable of suffering. According to this view,

any prohibition on causing harm (suffering, at least) simply lacked application to animals. The Cartesian view encouraged experimenters to feel no reservations about vivisecting live animals; after all the animal "cries of pain" were only like the squeakings of a clock.[1] So it was claimed. The commonsense view today no doubt is that Descartes was wrong, and his apparent denial of sentience to *all* nonhuman animals is another instance of someone's being too much in the grip of a theory—and thus driven to embrace false conclusions. If Descartes' view were correct, it is hard to see why we should be bothered by the mentioned practices, including the burning of cats for recreational purposes.

A second logically *possible* view is that some animals have moral standing and that their interests should weigh *more* heavily than the (descriptively) like interests of humans. According to this view, if two persons and, say, a dog are on a lifeboat and all will die unless one goes overboard, then, other things being equal, one of the people should go. It is not obvious that anyone has defended this view. Still, it is useful to recognize the full spectrum of possible views (to flesh it out further, one might suppose that the view also assumes that humans lack moral standing). One important related issue concerns the conflict between the expansion of the human population and the consequent destruction of animal habitats. The question of who should remain alive (have space on the lifeboat) is not without parallel in the matter of who should be allowed space on earth, that is, a "place to live."

In between the two mentioned extreme views are various positions all of which maintain that the lives or well-being of animals (or some) is not all that matters but does not count for nothing. Whether being alive, being sentient, being conscious, or being the subject of a life is the criterion of moral standing (or another morally significant category such as being the possessor of rights or that to which duties of some sort directly are owed), some animals will be included. "Commonsense" views seem locatable in this middle territory. The contemporary Australian philosopher Peter Singer in his influential book *Animal Liberation* develops a utilitarian-based critique of much of our current dealings with animals—both in the use of "factory-farming" techniques, used to raise animals for food, and in the use of animals in scientific research.[2] In that work Singer defends the principle that *the like interests* of humans and animals should be given equal weight in determining which acts or practices are morally obligatory. In his view only sentient creatures are possessors of interests. If we weigh equal interests equally, then we must conclude, Singer maintains, that a great deal of our treatment of animals is indefensible. Here we note simply that we have a distinct third sort of view: Animal interests count and count equally with that of like interests of humans.

A fourth view (or cluster of views) is that the interests of animals, or some, count but (normally) count less than similar interests of humans. The details may vary, but with this general approach animal interests, or some, are valued but are to be discounted when set against comparable interests of normal humans. This viewpoint requires some sort of "weighting principle." Since it, in effect, defends the justifiability of differential treatment (compare "discriminating") of humans and animals in a wide range of cases—discounting the interests of animals—it is a view that may be accused of a certain arbitrariness. The arbitrariness may be thought to be like that in racism and sexism, viewpoints that command extending favorable treatment to members of a certain race or gender on the ground that racial or gender differences are in themselves morally relevant. Such is the approximate accusation involved in the pejorative label *speciesist*. However, much depends on the grounds for advocating the discounting of animal interests. One who thinks that possession of rational capacities is a morally relevant consideration consistently might advocate differential treatment of those who are rational and those who are not.[3] A policy of especially favorable treatment of the rational well may discount the interests of most animals as against most humans.

One point of contention, however, is that impartial (between species) application of such a policy *may* require subordination of the interests of certain humans, such as anencephalic babies, the comatose, or the profoundly retarded. It might be argued that our duties toward certain sentient animals are no more (and no less) stringent than those owed to impaired or less than normally capacitated humans (unless species membership *as such* is a morally significant consideration). If this claim is defensible, it is compatible with two quite diverse conclusions: (1) our duties to any such beings are less stringent than many believe (hence, for example, we ought strive less officiously to preserve the lives of the mentioned humans—or some), or (2) our duties to "marginal" humans are stringent but, to be consistent, we must recognize comparably stringent duties to certain animals. One central question, in brief, is: Are there reasonable grounds for discriminating, as we traditionally have, among marginally rational beings—whether human or not?

We have noted a range of possible views. In general, their apparent implications are quite diverse, although we have not sought to trace them in detail here. In the General Introduction we mentioned a qualification worth keeping in mind. Even with the anthropocentric paradigm there is a basis for advocating care of, or protection for, entities other than humans. However, according to this view any duties to care for, or protect, what is not human can be *derived only from duties owed to humans.* Much contemporary criticism of our treatment of animals rejects such a paradigm and rests on positions described above as intermediate views. The well-being and lives of many animals, according to such views, are in themselves morally significant.

The focus of this morally based concern can be on duties to benefit animals or on refraining from harming them. The primary emphasis has been on the latter. The slippery notion of "harm" is often cashed in two ways: *(a)* causing the premature death of, and *(b)* causing pain (or deprivation) to the being in question. Various practices involve one or both, as suggested earlier: medical experimentation, hunting, destruction of certain species, extinction of species, destruction of natural habitats, and factory farming.

It may be of interest here to consider possible grounds for the advocacy of one increasingly widespread practice, namely, vegetarianism. That quite different grounds are, or may be, invoked in its favor often is insufficiently recognized. One ground is individual prudence. Given the increased risks of meat eating (for example, cancer of the intestine) or sheer expense, a vegetarian diet may be preferable. A second argument focuses on the fact that the conversion of plant protein into protein in the form of animal flesh constitutes a "protein factory in reverse" transforming roughly three to twelve units of plant protein into one unit of animal protein. Since significant famine or malnutrition prevails among much of the world's human population, more protein, in principle, could be made available to relieve human famine.[4] In short, on purely anthropocentric grounds it may be argued that we ought to be vegetarians. The moral duty, then, may not be derived from a concession of moral standing to animals. The third argument is that the duty to be a vegetarian derives from a duty not to cause avoidable pain or deprivation to sentient creatures—as occurs in factory farming. A fourth ground is that it is wrong to cause premature death to animals—at least if the only reason for so doing is to satisfy human culinary preferences. It is sometimes overlooked that according to the latter two views meat eating *as such* is not necessarily wrong. Eating an animal killed accidentally need not be wrong. The third ground mentioned would prohibit eating neither animals raised and killed painlessly and without deprivation nor animals that fail to be sentient (for example, mollusks?). Thus, advocacy of vegetarianism may appeal to prudence, to an anthropocentric moral view, or to moral principles condemning the harming of animals (causation of pain or killing). Even according to the latter view the alleged wrongness of eating meat is derivative. The claim is not that eating meat is *in itself* wrong; rather, what is condemned is what is usually done to create the opportunity. In this connection readers might wish to reflect on cannibalism, or on the case of

the airplane downed years ago in the frozen mountains of South America—a situation in which survivors ate the flesh of dead humans in order to continue to live.[5]

To place these matters in perspective it should be observed that we commonly think it sometimes is justifiable to harm humans— either by causing pain, deprivation, or premature death. In some cases (killing in self-defense, "just wars," incarceration of criminals, and capital punishment) the primary justification is often that we may do so to protect innocents against initiators of aggression. Few, probably, would argue that it always would be wrong to kill an attacking rabid dog. Although the dog is not a moral agent, self-defense against threatening psychotic humans (also not moral agents)—sometimes labeled "innocent threats"—widely is thought permissible. Such a defense of killing animals may be invoked glibly. When humans invade or destroy animal habitats and, for example, elephants "invade" areas populated by humans, there is a nontrivial question about who is the aggressor, or initiator of aggression. Another defense of imposing pain, or risk of such, on adult humans (namely, that the party at risk gave voluntary, informed consent so to be treated) is not available in the case of animals.

In short, some defenses of causing harm seem inapplicable in the case of animals. Hence, the question of moral standing, or the weightiness of animal interests, rightly seems to dominate the scene. Seldom, if ever, can we believe that animals are to blame, are initiators of threats, or consent to the harm we cause them. Another ground widely accepted as a justification for harming people is paternalistic. Roughly, it is claimed to be all right to "harm" people (typically by intervention against their will) if it is for their own good—on balance. Thus, we might incarcerate a depressed person rather than let her commit suicide, or use force on a child to prevent his running into the traffic. The dispute over paternalism is not simple,[6] but if some paternalism toward humans is all right, the question arises as to whether we logically can be said to act paternalistically toward animals (and plants or rivers?) and, if so, whether such an appeal will go much distance toward justifying much or any of our harm-causing dealings with them. Those who say that some animals are "better off" in zoos, or on factory farms (protected from nonhuman predators), or that "if it were not for us (breeders), they would not have existed at all," may be appealing to some implicit principle of permissible paternalism. The matter deserves further exploration.

Those critics of many of our current practices who defend the moral standing of (at least some) animals tend to defend either the view that (1) we have direct duties toward animals or (2) that animals (or some) have important rights. Peter Singer, from a utilitarian standpoint, claims that we owe sentient animals equal consideration of those animal interests comparable to human interests. Thus he is in the first category. The later essay by Donald VanDeVeer argues for a direct duty to give weight to animal interests, although not from a utilitarian framework and not in accord with the "equal consideration" principle. Tom Regan, in his recent book, *The Case for Animal Rights*,[7] defends the view that many animals have important rights and that, correlatively, a utilitarian approach to the question of proper treatment of animals is unacceptable—indeed that some reforms advocated by Singer find no adequate support in the theory of utilitarianism. In a later discussion, R. G. Frey argues that if rights are based on interests, animals lack rights since, for reasons he proposes, they cannot be said to have interests.

A major part of the current reassessment of the moral grounds of environmental concern focuses on the legitimacy of our attitudes and practices involving animals. If it cannot be maintained that we directly owe nontrivial duties toward certain animals (especially those exhibiting intelligence and sentience), it seems doubtful that it can be argued that the scope of our moral concern should extend to nonsentient animals, trees, wilderness areas, or rivers—except for derivative anthropocentric reasons. Even this last claim is not entirely uncontroversial. However, if we do owe direct duties to certain animals, the anthropocentric model must be rejected.[8] Further, the door will be open to defending an even more revisionist

environmental ethic. Reassessing, in a critical manner, our customary and deeply entrenched attitudes and practices is, of course, no easy task. After all, from Aristotle (fourth century B.C.) through much of the nineteenth century, many believed and acted on the assumption that certain people were "natural slaves." It is a substantive question, however, whether our traditional subordination of animals is, also, a morally indefensible prejudice.

Notes

1. For a selection from Descartes, and a valuable source of traditional and some recent views, see *Animal Rights and Human Obligations*, edited by Tom Regan and Peter Singer (Englewood Cliffs, N.J.: Prentice-Hall, Inc., 1976).
2. See Peter Singer, *Animal Liberation* (New York: Avon Books, 1975).
3. What are defensible criteria of rationality is no easy question. This point should not go unnoticed.
4. James Rachels develops this argument lucidly in his "Vegetarianism and 'The Other Weight Problem'" in *World Hunger and Moral Obligation*, edited by William Aiken and Hugh Lafollete (Englewood Cliffs, N.J.: Prentice-Hall Inc., 1977).
5. See Pier Pauls Reid, *Alive* (Philadelphia: Lippincott & Company, 1974).
6. See Donald VanDeVeer, "Paternalism and Restrictions on Liberty" in *And Justice For All*, edited by Tom Regan and Donald VanDeVeer (Totowa, N.J.: Rowman and Littlefield, 1982); *Paternalism*, edited by Rolf Sartorious (Minneapolis: University of Minnesota Press, 1983); John Kleinig, *Paternalism* (Totowa, N.J.: Rowman and Littlefield, 1983); James Childress, *Who Should Decide?* (New York: Oxford University Press, 1982); Donald VanDeVeer, *Paternalistic Intervention* (Princeton: Princeton University Press, 1986).
7. Tom Regan, *The Case for Animal Rights* (Berkeley: University of California Press, 1983).
8. At least when that model is understood narrowly (as it is here) as denying moral standing to all nonhuman creatures.

Animal Liberation[1]

Peter Singer

I

We are familiar with Black Liberation, Gay Liberation, and a variety of other movements. With Women's Liberation some thought we had come to the end of the road. Discrimination on the basis of sex, it has been said, is the last form of discrimination that is universally accepted and practiced without pretense, even in those liberal circles which have long prided themselves on their freedom from racial discrimination. But one should always be wary of talking of "the last remaining form of discrimination." If we have learned anything from the liberation movements, we should have learned how difficult it is to be aware of the ways in which we discriminate until they are forcefully pointed out to us. A liberation movement demands an expansion of our moral horizons, so that practices that were previously regarded as natural and inevitable are now seen as intolerable.

Animals, Men and Morals is a manifesto for an Animal Liberation movement. The contributers to the book may not all see the issue this way. They are a varied group. Philosophers, ranging from professors to graduate students, make up the largest contingent. There are five of them, including the three editors, and there is also an extract from the unjustly neglected German philosopher with an English name, Leonard Nelson, who died in 1927. There are essays by two novelist/critics, Brigid Brophy and Maureen Duffy, and another by Muriel the Lady Dowding, widow of Dowding of Battle of Britain fame and the founder of "Beauty without Cruelty," a movement that campaigns against the use of animals for furs and cos-

metics. The other pieces are by a psychologist, a botanist, a sociologist, and Ruth Harrison, who is probably best described as a professional campaigner for animal welfare.

Whether or not these people, as individuals, would all agree that they are launching a liberation movement for animals, the book as a whole amounts to no less. It is a demand for a complete change in our attitudes to nonhumans. It is a demand that we cease to regard the exploitation of other species as natural and inevitable, and that, instead, we see it as a continuing moral outrage. Patrick Corbett, Professor of Philosophy at Sussex University, captures the spirit of the book in his closing words:

> . . . we require now to extend the great principles of liberty, equality and fraternity over the lives of animals. Let animal slavery join human slavery in the graveyard of the past.

The reader is likely to be skeptical. "Animal Liberation" sounds more like a parody of liberation movements than a serious objective. The reader may think: We support the claims of blacks and women for equality because blacks and women really are equal to whites and males—equal in intelligence and in abilities, capacity for leadership, rationality, and so on. Humans and nonhumans obviously are not equal in these respects. Since justice demands only that we treat equals equally, unequal treatment of humans and nonhumans cannot be an injustice.

This is a tempting reply, but a dangerous one. It commits the non-racist and non-sexist to a dogmatic belief that blacks and women really are just as intelligent, able, etc., as whites and males—and no more. Quite possibly this happens to be the case. Certainly attempts to prove that racial or sexual differences in these respects have a genetic origin have not been conclusive. But do we really want to stake our demand for equality on the assumption that there are no genetic differences of this kind between

Source: *New York Review of Books* (April 1973), pp. 17–21. Reprinted by permission.

the different races or sexes? Surely the appropriate response to those who claim to have found evidence for such genetic differences is not to stick to the belief that there are no differences, whatever the evidence to the contrary; rather one should be clear that the claim to equality does not depend on IQ. Moral equality is distinct from factual equality. Otherwise it would be nonsense to talk of the equality of human beings, since humans, as individuals, obviously differ in intelligence and almost any ability one cares to name. If possessing greater intelligence does not entitle one human to exploit another, why should it entitle humans to exploit nonhumans?

Jeremy Bentham expressed the essential basis of equality in his famous formula: "Each to count for one and none for more than one." In other words, the interests of every being that has interests are to be taken into account and treated equally with the like interests of any other being. Other moral philosophers, before and after Bentham, have made the same point in different ways. Our concern for others must not depend on whether they possess certain characteristics, though just what that concern involves may, of course, vary according to such characteristics.

Bentham, incidentally, was well aware that the logic of the demand for racial equality did not stop at the equality of humans. He wrote:

The day *may* come when the rest of the animal creation may acquire those rights which never could have been withholden from them but by the hand of tyranny. The French have already discovered that the blackness of the skin is no reason why a human being should be abandoned without redress to the caprice of a tormentor. It may one day come to be recognized that the number of the legs, the villosity of the skin, or the termination of the *os sacrum,* are reasons equally insufficient for abandoning a sensitive being to the same fate. What else is it that should trace the insuperable line? Is it the faculty of reason, or perhaps the faculty of discourse? But a full-grown horse or dog is beyond comparison a more rational, as well as a more conversable animal, than an infant of a day, or a week, or even a month old. But suppose they were otherwise, what would it avail? The question is not, Can they *reason?* nor Can they *talk?* but, Can they *suffer?*[2]

Surely Bentham was right. If a being suffers, there can be no moral justification for refusing to take that suffering into consideration, and, indeed, to count it equally with the like suffering (if rough comparisons can be made) of any other being.

So the only question is: do animals other than man suffer? Most people agree unhesitatingly that animals like cats and dogs can and do suffer, and this seems also to be assumed by those laws that prohibit wanton cruelty to such animals. Personally, I have no doubt at all about this and find it hard to take seriously the doubts that a few people apparently do have. The editors and contributors of *Animals, Men and Morals* seem to feel the same way, for although the question is raised more than once, doubts are quickly dismissed each time. Nevertheless, because this is such a fundamental point, it is worth asking what grounds we have for attributing suffering to other animals.

It is best to begin by asking what grounds any individual human has for supposing that other humans feel pain. Since pain is a state of consciousness, a "mental event," it can never be directly observed. No observations, whether behavioral signs such as writhing or screaming or physiological or neurological recordings, are observations of pain itself. Pain is something one feels, and one can only infer that others are feeling it from various external indications. The fact that only philosophers are ever skeptical about whether other humans feel pain shows that we regard such inference as justifiable in the case of humans.

Is there any reason why the same inference should be unjustifiable for other animals? Nearly all the external signs which lead us to infer pain in other humans can be seen in other species, especially "higher" animals such as mammals and birds. Behavioral signs—writhing, yelping, or other forms of calling, attempts to avoid the source of pain, and many others—are present. We know, too, that these animals are biologically similar in the relevant respects, having nervous systems like ours which can be observed to function as ours do.

So the grounds for inferring that these animals can feel pain are nearly as good as the grounds for inferring other humans do. Only nearly, for there is one behavioral sign that humans have but nonhumans, with the exception of one or two specially raised chimpanzees, do not have. This, of course, is a developed language. As the quotation from Bentham indicates, this has long been regarded as an important distinction between man and other animals. Other animals may communicate with each other, but not in the way we do. Following Chomsky, many people now mark this distinction by saying that only humans communicate in a form that is governed by rules of syntax. (For the purposes of this argument, linguists allow those chimpanzees who have learned a syntactic sign language to rank as honorary humans.) Nevertheless, as Bentham pointed out, this distinction is not relevant to the question of how animals ought to be treated, unless it can be linked to the issue of whether animals suffer.

This link may be attempted in two ways. First, there is a hazy line of philosophical thought, stemming perhaps from some doctrines associated with Wittgenstein, which maintains that we cannot meaningfully attribute states of consciousness to beings without language. I have not seen this argument made explicit in print, though I have come across it in conversation. This position seems to me very implausible, and I doubt that it would be held at all if it were not thought to be a consequence of a broader view of the significance of language. It may be that the use of a public, rule-governed language is a precondition of conceptual thought. It may even be, although personally I doubt it, that we cannot meaningfully speak of a creature having an intention unless that creature can use a language. But states like pain, surely, are more primitive than either of these, and seem to have nothing to do with language.

Indeed, as Jane Goodall points out in her study of chimpanzees, when it comes to the expression of feelings and emotions, humans tend to fall back on nonlinguistic modes of communication which are often found among apes, such as a cheering pat on the back, an exuberant embrace, a clasp of hands, and so on.[3] Michael Peters makes a similar point in his contribution to *Animals, Men and Morals* when he notes that the basic signals we use to convey pain, fear, sexual arousal, and so on are not specific to our species. So there seems to be no reason at all to believe that a creature without language cannot suffer.

The second, and more easily appreciated way of linking language and the existence of pain is to say that the best evidence that we can have that another creature is in pain is when he tells us that he is. This is a distinct line of argument, for it is not being denied that a non-language-user conceivably could suffer, but only that we could know that he is suffering. Still, this line of argument seems to me to fail, and for reasons similar to those just given. "I am in pain" is not the best possible evidence that the speaker is in pain (he might be lying) and it is certainly not the only possible evidence. Behavioral signs and knowledge of the animals' biological similarity to ourselves together provide adequate evidence that animals do suffer. After all, we would not accept linguistic evidence if it contradicted the rest of the evidence. If a man was severely burned, and behaved as if he were in pain, writhing, groaning, being very careful not to let his burned skin touch anything, and so on, but later said he had not been in pain at all, we would be more likely to conclude that he was lying or suffering from amnesia than that he had not been in pain.

Even if there were stronger grounds for refusing to attribute pain to those who do not have a language, the consequences of this refusal might lead us to examine these grounds unusually critically. Human infants, as well as some adults, are unable to use language. Are we to deny that a year-old infant can suffer? If not, how can language be crucial? Of course, most parents can understand the responses of even very young infants better than they understand the responses of other animals, and sometimes infant responses can be understood in the light of later development.

This, however, is just a fact about the relative knowledge we have of our own species and other species, and most of this knowledge is simply derived from closer contact. Those who have studied the behavior of other animals soon learn to understand their responses at least as well as we understand those of an infant. (I am not just referring to Jane Goodall's and other well-known studies of apes. Consider, for example, the degree of understanding achieved by Tinbergen from watching herring gulls.)[4] Just as we can understand infant human behavior in the light of adult human behavior, so we can understand the behavior of other species in the light of our own behavior (and sometimes we can understand our own behavior better in the light of the behavior of other species).

The grounds we have for believing that other mammals and birds suffer are, then, closely analogous to the grounds we have for believing that other humans suffer. It remains to consider how far down the evolutionary scale this analogy holds. Obviously it becomes poorer when we get further away from man. To be more precise would require a detailed examination of all that we know about other forms of life. With fish, reptiles, and other vertebrates the analogy still seems strong, with molluscs like oysters it is much weaker. Insects are more difficult, and it may be that in our present state of knowledge we must be agnostic about whether they are capable of suffering.

If there is no moral justification for ignoring suffering when it occurs, and it does occur in other species, what are we to say of our attitudes toward these other species? Richard Ryder, one of the contributors to *Animals, Men and Morals*, uses the term "speciesism" to describe the belief that we are entitled to treat members of other species in a way in which it would be wrong to treat members of our own species. The term is not euphonious, but it neatly makes the anology with racism. The non-racist would do well to bear the analogy in mind when he is inclined to defend human behavior toward nonhumans. "Shouldn't we worry about improving the lot of our own species before we concern ourselves with other species?" he may ask. If we substitute "race" for "species" we shall see that the question is better not asked. "Is a vegetarian diet nutritionally adequate?" resembles the slave-owner's claim that he and the whole economy of the South would be ruined without slave labor. There is even a parallel with skeptical doubts about whether animals suffer, for some defenders of slavery professed to doubt whether blacks really suffer in the way that whites do.

I do not want to give the impression, however, that the case for Animal Liberation is based on the analogy with racism and no more. On the contrary, *Animals, Men and Morals* describes the various ways in which humans exploit nonhumans, and several contributors consider the defenses that have been offered, including the defense of meat-eating mentioned in the last paragraph. Sometimes the rebuttals are scornfully dismissive, rather than carefully designed to convince the detached critic. This may be a fault, but it is a fault that is inevitable, given the kind of book this is. The issue is not one on which one can remain detached. As the editors state in their Introduction:

Once the full force of moral assessment has been made explicit there can be no rational excuse left for killing animals, be they killed for food, science, or sheer personal indulgence. We have not assembled this book to provide the reader with yet another manual on how to make brutalities less brutal. Compromise, in the traditional sense of the term, is simple unthinking weakness when one considers the actual reasons for our crude relationships with the other animals.

The point is that on this issue there are few critics who are genuinely detached. People who eat pieces of slaughtered nonhumans every day find it hard to believe that they are doing wrong; and they also find it hard to imagine what else they could eat. So for those who do not place nonhumans beyond the pale of morality, there comes a stage when further argument seems pointless, a stage at which one can only accuse one's opponent of hypocrisy and reach for the sort of sociological account of our practices and the way we defend them that is attempted by David Wood in his contribution to this book. On the other hand, to those unconvinced by the arguments, and unable to accept that they are rationalizing their dietary preferences and their fear of being thought peculiar, such sociological explanations can only seem insultingly arrogant.

II

The logic of speciesism is most apparent in the practice of experimenting on nonhumans in order to benefit humans. This is because the issue is rarely obscured by allegations that nonhumans are so different from humans that we cannot know anything about whether they suffer. The defender of vivisection cannot use this argument because he needs to stress the similarities between man and other animals in order to justify the usefulness to the former of experiments on the latter. The researcher who makes rats choose between starvation and electric shocks to see if they develop ulcers (they do) does so because he knows that the rat has a nervous system very similar to man's, and presumably feels an electric shock in a similar way.

Richard Ryder's restrained account of experiments on animals made me angrier with my fellow men than anything else in this book. Ryder, a clinical psychologist by profession, himself experimented on animals before he came to hold the view he puts forward in his essay. Experimenting on animals is now a large industry, both academic and commercial. In 1969, more than 5 million experiments were performed in Britain, the vast majority without anesthetic (though how many of these involved pain is not known). There are no accurate US figures, since there is no federal law on the subject, and in many cases no state law either. Estimates vary from 20 million to 200 million. Ryder suggests that 80 million may be the best guess. We tend to think that this is all for vital medical research, but of course it is not. Huge numbers of animals are used in university departments from Forestry to Psychology, and even more are used for commercial purposes, to test whether cosmetics can cause skin damage, or shampoos eye damage, or to test food additives or laxatives or sleeping pills or anything else.

A standard test for foodstuffs is the "LD50." The object of this test is to find the dosage level at which 50 percent of the test animals will die. This means that nearly all of them will become very sick before finally succumbing or surviving. When the substance is a harmless one, it may be necessary to force huge doses down the animals, until in some cases sheer volume or concentration causes death.

Ryder gives a selection of experiments, taken from recent scientific journals. I will quote two, not for the sake of indulging in gory details, but in order to give an idea of what normal researchers think they may legitimately do to other species. The point is not that the individual researchers are cruel men, but that they are behaving in a way that is allowed by our speciesist attitudes. As Ryder points out, even if only 1 percent of the experiments involve severe pain, that is 50,000 experiments in Britain each year, or nearly 150 every day (and about fifteen times as many in the United States, if Ryder's guess is right). Here then are two experiments:

O. S. Ray and R. J. Barrett of Pittsburgh gave electric shocks to the feet of 1,042 mice. They then caused convulsions by giving more intense shocks through cup-shaped electrodes applied to the animals' eyes or through pressure spring clips attached to their ears. Unfortunately some of the mice who "successfully completed Day One training were found sick or dead prior to testing on Day Two." [*Journal of Comparative and Physiological Psychology*, 1969, Vol. 67, pp. 110–116]

At the National Institute for Medical Research, Mill Hill, London, W. Feldberg and S. L. Sherwood injected chemicals into the brains of cats— "with a number of widely different substances, recurrent patterns of reaction were obtained. Retching, vomiting, defaecation, increased salivation and greatly accelerated respiration leading to panting were common features." . . .

The injection into the brain of a large dose of Tubocuraine caused the cat to jump "from the table to the floor and then straight into its cage, where it started calling more and more noisily whilst moving about restlessly and jerkily . . . finally the cat fell with legs and neck flexed, jerking in rapid clonic movements, the condition being that of a major [epileptic] convulsion . . . within a few seconds the cat got up, ran for a few yards at high speed and fell in another fit. The whole process was repeated several times within the next ten minutes, during which the cat lost faeces and foamed at the mouth."

This animal finally died thirty-five minutes after the brain injection. [*Journal of Physiology*, 1954, Vol. 123, pp. 148–167]

There is nothing secret about these experiments. One has only to open any recent volume of a learned journal, such as the *Journal of Comparative and Physiological Psychology*, to find full descriptions of experiments of this sort, together with the results obtained—results that are frequently trivial and obvious. The experiments are often supported by public funds.

It is a significant indication of the level of acceptability of these practices that, although these experiments are taking place at this moment on university campuses throughout the country, there has, so far as I know, not been the slightest protest from the student movement. Students have been rightly concerned that their universities should not discriminate on grounds of race or sex, and that they should not serve the purposes of the military or big business. Speciesism continues undisturbed, and many students participate in it. There may be a few qualms at first, but since everyone regards it as normal, and it may even be a required part of a course, the student soon becomes hardened and, dismissing his earlier feelings as "mere sentiment," comes to regard animals as statistics rather than sentient beings with interests that warrant consideration.

Argument about vivisection has often missed the point because it has been put in absolutist terms: would the abolitionist be prepared to let thousands die if they could be saved by experimenting on a single animal? The way to reply to this purely hypothetical question is to pose another: Would the experimenter be prepared to experiment on a human orphan under six months old, if it were the only way to save many lives? (I say "orphan" to avoid the complication of parental feelings, although in doing so I am being overfair to the experimenter, since the nonhuman subjects of experiments are not orphans.) A negative answer to this question indicates that the experimenter's readiness to use nonhumans is simple discrimination, for adult apes, cats, mice, and other mammals are more conscious of what is happening to them, more self-directing, and, so far as we can tell, just as sensitive to pain as a human infant. There is no characteristic that human infants possess that adult mammals do not have to the same or a higher degree.

(It might be possible to hold that what makes it wrong to experiment on a human infant is that the infant will in time develop into more than the nonhuman, but one would then, to be consistent, have to oppose abortion, and perhaps contraception, too, for the fetus and the egg and sperm have the same potential as the infant. Moreover, one would still have no reason for experimenting on a nonhuman rather than a human with brain damage severe enough to make it impossible for him to rise above infant level.)

The experimenter, then, shows a bias for his own species whenever he carries out an experiment on a nonhuman for a purpose that he would not think justified him in using a human being at an equal or lower level of sentience, awareness, ability to be self-directing, etc. No one familiar with the kind of results yielded by these experiments can have the slightest doubt that if this bias were eliminated the number of experiments performed would be zero or very close to it.

III

If it is vivisection that shows the logic of speciesism most clearly, it is the use of other species for food that is at the heart of our attitudes toward them. Most of *Animals, Men and Morals* is an attack on meat-eating—an attack which is based solely on concern for nonhumans, without reference to arguments derived from considerations of ecology, macrobiotics, health, or religion.

The idea that nonhumans are utilities, means to our ends, pervades our thought. Even conservationists who are concerned about the slaughter of wild fowl but not about the vastly greater slaughter of chickens for our tables are thinking in this way—they are worried about what we would lose if there were less wildlife. Stanley Godlovitch, pursuing the Marxist idea that our thinking is formed by the activities we undertake in satisfying our needs, suggests that man's first classification of his environment was into Edibles and Inedibles. Most animals came into the first category, and there they have remained.

Man may always have killed other species for food, but he has never exploited them so ruthlessly as he does today. Farming has succumbed to business methods, the objective being to get the highest possible ratio of output (meat, eggs, milk) to input (fodder, labor costs, etc.). Ruth Harrison's essay "On Factory Farming" gives an account of some aspects of modern methods, and of the unsuccessful British campaign for effective controls, a campaign which was sparked off by her *Animal Machines* (Stuart: London, 1964).

Her article is in no way a substitute for her earlier book. This is a pity since, as she says, "Farm produce is still associated with mental pictures of animals browsing in the fields, . . . of hens having a last forage before going to roost. . . ." Yet neither in her article nor elsewhere in *Animals, Men and Morals* is this false image replaced by a clear idea of the nature and extent of factory farming. We learn of this only indirectly, when we hear of the code of reform proposed by an advisory committee set up by the British government.

Among the proposals, which the government refused to implement on the grounds that they were too idealistic, were: "*Any animal should at least have room to turn around freely.*"

Factory farm animals need liberation in the most literal sense. Veal calves are kept in stalls five feet by two feet. They are usually slaughtered when about four months old, and have been too big to turn in their stalls for at least a month. Intensive beef herds, kept in stalls only proportionately larger for much longer periods, account for a growing percentage of beef production. Sows are often similarly confined when pregnant, which, because of artificial methods of increasing fertility, can be most of the time. Animals confined in this way do not waste food by exercising, nor do they develop unpalatable muscle.

"*A dry bedded area should be provided for all stock.*" Intensively kept animals usually have to stand and sleep on slatted floors without straw, because this makes cleaning easier.

"*Palatable roughage must be readily available to all calves after one week of age.*" In order to produce the pale veal housewives are said to prefer, calves are fed on an all-liquid diet until slaughter, even though they are long past the age at which they would normally eat grass. They develop a craving for roughage, evidenced by attempts to gnaw wood from their

stalls. (For the same reason, their diet is deficient in iron.)

"*Battery cages for poultry should be large enough for a bird to be able to stretch one wing at a time.*" Under current British practice, a cage for four or five laying hens has a floor area of twenty inches by eighteen inches, scarcely larger than a double page of the *New York Review of Books*. In this space, on a sloping wire floor (sloping so the eggs roll down, wire so the dung drops through) the birds live for a year or eighteen months while artificial lighting and temperature conditions combine with drugs in their food to squeeze the maximum number of eggs out of them. Table birds are also sometimes kept in cages. More often they are reared in sheds, no less crowded. Under these conditions all the birds' natural activities are frustrated, and they develop "vices" such as pecking each other to death. To prevent this, beaks are often cut off, and the sheds kept dark.

How many of those who support factory farming by buying its produce know anything about the way it is produced? How many have heard something about it, but are reluctant to check up for fear that it will make them uncomfortable? To nonspeciesists, the typical consumer's mixture of ignorance, reluctance to find out the truth, and vague belief that nothing really bad could be allowed seems analogous to the attitudes of "decent Germans" to the death camps.

There are, of course, some defenders of factory farming. Their arguments are considered, though again rather sketchily, by John Harris. Among the most common: "Since they have never known anything else, they don't suffer." This argument will not be put by anyone who knows anything about animal behavior, since he will know that not all behavior has to be learned. Chickens attempt to stretch wings, walk around, scratch, and even dustbathe or build a nest, even though they have never lived under conditions that allowed these activities. Calves can suffer from maternal deprivation no matter at what age they were taken from their mothers. "We need these intensive methods to provide protein for a growing population." As ecologists and famine relief organizations know, we can produce far more protein per acre if we grow the right vegetable crop, soy beans for instance, than if we use the land to grow crops to be converted into protein by animals who use nearly 90 percent of the protein themselves, even when unable to exercise.

There will be many readers of this book who will agree that factory farming involves an unjustifiable degree of exploitation of sentient creatures, and yet will want to say that there is nothing wrong with rearing animals for food, provided it is done "humanely." These people are saying, in effect, that although we should not cause animals to suffer, there is nothing wrong with killing them.

There are two possible replies to this view. One is to attempt to show that this combination of attitudes is absurd. Roslind Godlovitch takes this course in her essay, which is an examination of some common attitudes to animals. She argues that from the combination of "animal suffering is to be avoided" and "there is nothing wrong with killing animals" it follows that all animal life ought to be exterminated (since all sentient creatures will suffer to some degree at some point in their lives). Euthanasia is a contentious issue only because we place some value on living. If we did not, the least amount of suffering would justify it. Accordingly, if we deny that we have a duty to exterminate all animal life, we must concede that we are placing some value on animal life.

This argument seems to me valid, although one could still reply that the value of animal life is to be derived from the pleasures that life can have for them, so that, provided their lives have a balance of pleasure over pain, we are justified in rearing them. But this would imply that we ought to produce animals and let them live as pleasantly as possible, without suffering.

At this point, one can make the second of the two possible replies to the view that rearing and killing animals for food is all right so long as it is done humanely. This second reply is that so long as we think that a nonhuman may be killed simply so that a human can satisfy his taste for meat, we are still thinking of nonhumans as means rather than as ends in themselves. The factory farm is nothing more than the application of technology to this concept. Even traditional methods involve castration, the separation of mothers and their young, the breaking up of herds, branding or ear-punching, and of course transportation to the abattoirs and the final moments of terror when the animal smells blood and senses danger. If we were to try rearing animals so that they lived and died without suffering, we should find that to do so on anything like the scale of today's meat industry would be a sheer impossibility. Meat would become the prerogative of the rich.

I have been able to discuss only some of the contributions to this book, saying nothing about, for instance, the essays on killing for furs and for sport. Nor have I considered all the detailed questions that need to be asked once we start thinking about other species in the radically different way presented by this book. What, for instance, are we to do about genuine conflicts of interest like rats biting slum children? I am not sure of the answer, but the essential point is just that we *do* see this as a conflict of interests, that we recognize that rats have interests too. Then we may begin to think about other ways of resolving the conflict— perhaps by leaving out rat baits that sterilize the rats instead of killing them.

I have not discussed such problems because they are side issues compared with the exploitation of other species for food and for experimental purposes. On these central matters, I hope that I have said enough to show that this book, despite its flaws, is a challenge to every human to recognize his attitudes to nonhumans as a form of prejudice no less objectionable than racism or sexism. It is a challenge that demands not just a change of attitudes, but a change in our way of life, for it requires us to become vegetarians.

Can a purely moral demand of this kind succeed? The odds are certainly against it. The book holds out no inducements. It does not tell us that we will become healthier, or enjoy life more, if we cease exploiting animals. Animal Liberation will require greater altruism on the part of mankind than any other liberation movement, since animals are incapable of demanding it for themselves, or of protesting against their exploitation by votes, demonstrations, or bombs. Is man capable of such genuine altruism? Who knows? If this book does have a significant effect, however, it will be a vindication of all those who have believed that man has within himself the potential for more than cruelty and selfishness.

Notes

1. This article originally appeared as a book review of *Animals, Men and Morals*, edited by Stanley and Roslind Godlovitch and John Harris.

2. *The Principles of Morals and Legislation*, Ch. XVII, Sec. 1, footnote to paragraph 4. (Italics in original.)

3. Jane van Lawick-Goodall, *In the Shadow of Man* (Houghton Mifflin, 1971), p. 225.

4. N. Tinbergen, *The Herring Gull's World* (Basic Books, 1961).

The Case for Animal Rights

Tom Regan

I regard myself as an advocate of animal rights—as a part of the animal rights movement. That movement, as I conceive it, is committed to a number of goals, including:

1. the total abolition of the use of animals in science
2. the total dissolution of commercial animal agriculture
3. and the total elimination of commercial and sport hunting and trapping.

There are, I know, people who profess to believe in animal rights who do not avow these goals. Factory farming, they say, is wrong—violates animals' rights—but traditional animal agriculture is all right. Toxicity tests of cosmetics on animals violates their rights; but not important medical research—cancer research, for example. The clubbing of baby seals is abhorrent; but not the harvesting of adult seals. I used to think I understood this reasoning. Not any more. You don't change unjust institutions by tidying them up.

What's wrong—what's fundamentally wrong—with the way animals are treated isn't the details that vary from case to case. It's the whole system. The forlornness of the veal calf is pathetic—heart wrenching; the pulsing pain of the chimp with electrodes planted deep in her brain is repulsive; the slow, torturous death of the racoon caught in the leg hold trap, agonizing. But what is fundamentally wrong isn't the pain, isn't the suffering, isn't the deprivation. These compound what's wrong. Sometimes—often—they make it much worse. But they are not the fundamental wrong.

The fundamental wrong is the system that allows us to view animals as *our resources*, here for us—to be eaten, or surgically manipulated, or put in our cross hairs for sport or money. Once we accept this view of animals—as our resources—the rest is as predictable as it is regrettable. Why worry about their loneliness, their pain, their death? Since animals exist for us, here to benefit us in one way or another, what harms them really doesn't matter—or matters only if it starts to bother us, makes us feel a trifle uneasy when we eat our veal scampi, for example. So, yes, let us get veal calves out of solitary confinement, give them more space, a little straw, a few companions. But let us keep our veal scampi.

But a little straw, more space, and a few companions don't eliminate—don't even touch—the fundamental wrong, the wrong that attaches to our viewing and treating these animals as our resources. A veal calf killed to be eaten after living in close confinement is viewed and treated in this way: but so, too, is another who is raised (as they say) "more humanely." To right the fundamental wrong of our treatment of farm animals requires more than making rearing methods "more human"—requires something quite different—requires the total dissolution of commercial animal agriculture.

Source: *In Defense of Animals*, edited by Peter Singer (Oxford: Basil Blackwell, Inc., 1985), pp. 13–26. Reprinted by permission.

How we do this—whether we do this, or as in the case of animals in science, whether and how we abolish their use—these are to a large extent political questions. People must change their beliefs before they change their habits. Enough people, especially those elected to public office, must believe in change—must want it—before we will have laws that protect the rights of animals. This process of change is very complicated, very demanding, very exhausting, calling for the efforts of many hands—in education, publicity, political organization and activity, down to the licking of envelopes and stamps. As a trained and practicing philosopher the sort of contribution I can make is limited, but, I like to think, important. The currency of philosophy is ideas—their meaning and rational foundation—not the nuts and bolts of the legislative process, say, or the mechanics of community organization. That's what I have been exploring over the past ten years or so in my essays and talks and, more recently, in my book, *The Case for Animal Rights.*[1] I believe the major conclusions I reach in that book are true because they are supported by the weight of the best arguments. I believe the idea of animal rights has reason, not just emotion, on its side.

In the space I have at my disposal here I can only sketch, in the barest outlines, some of the main features of the book. Its main themes—and we should not be surprised by this—involve asking and answering deep foundational moral questions, questions about what morality is, how it should be understood, what is the best moral theory all considered. I hope I can convey something of the shape I think this theory is. The attempt to do this will be—to use a word a friendly critic once used to describe my work—cerebral. In fact I was told by this person that my work is "too cerebral." But this is misleading. My feelings about how animals sometimes are treated are just as deep and just as strong as those of my more volatile compatriots. Philosophers do—to use the jargon of the day—have a right side to their brains. If it's the left side we contribute—or mainly should—that's because what talents we have reside there.

How to proceed? We begin by asking how the moral status of animals has been un-derstood by thinkers who deny that animals have rights. Then we test the mettle of their ideas by seeing how well they stand up under the heat of fair criticism. If we start our thinking in this way we soon find that some people believe that we have no duties directly to an-imals—that we owe nothing *to them*—that we can do nothing that *wrongs them*. Rather, we can do wrong acts that involve animals, and so we have duties regarding them, though none to them. Such views may be called indirect duty views. By way of illustration:

Suppose your neighbor kicks your dog. Then your neighbor has done something wrong. But not to your dog. The wrong that has been done is a wrong to you. After all, it is wrong to upset people, and your neighbor's kicking your dog upsets you. So you are the one who is wronged, not your dog. Or again: by kicking your dog your neighbor damages your property. And since it is wrong to damage an-other person's property, your neighbor has done something wrong—to you, of course, not to your dog. Your neighbor no more wrongs your dog than your car would be wronged if the windshield were smashed. Your neighbor's duties involving your dog are indirect duties to you. More generally, all of our duties regarding animals are indirect duties to one another—to humanity.

How could someone try to justify such a view? One could say that your dog doesn't feel anything and so isn't hurt by your neighbor's kick, doesn't care about the pain since none is felt, is as unaware of anything as your wind-shield. Someone could say this but no rational person will since, among other considerations, such a view will commit one who holds it to the position that no human being feels pain either—that human beings also don't care about what happens to them. A second possibil-ity is that though both humans and your dog are hurt when kicked, it is only human pain that matters. But, again, no rational person can be-lieve this. Pain is pain wheresoever it occurs. If your neighbor's causing you pain is wrong be-cause of the pain that is caused, we cannot rationally ignore or dismiss the moral relevance of the pain your dog feels.

Philosophers who hold indirect duty views—and many still do—have come to understand that they must avoid the two defects just noted—avoid, that is, both the view that animals don't feel anything as well as the idea that only human pain can be morally relevant. Among such thinkers the sort of view now favored is one or another form of what is called *contractarianism*.

Here, very crudely, is the root idea: morality consists of a set of rules that individuals voluntarily agree to abide by—as we do when we sign a contract (hence the name: contractarianism). Those who understand and accept the terms of the contract are covered directly—have rights created by, and recognized and protected in, the contract. And these contractors can also have protection spelled out for others who, though they lack the ability to understand morality and so cannot sign the contract themselves, are loved or cherished by those who can. Thus young children, for example, are unable to sign and lack rights. But they are protected by the contract nonetheless because of the sentimental interests of others, most notably their parents. So we have, then, duties involving these children, duties regarding them, but no duties to them. Our duties in their case are indirect duties to other human beings, usually their parents.

As for animals, since they cannot understand the contract, they obviously cannot sign; and since they cannot sign, they have no rights. Like children, however, some animals are the objects of the sentimental interest of others. You, for example, love your dog . . . or cat. So these animals—those enough people care about: companion animals, whales, baby seals, the American bald eagle—these animals, though they lack rights themselves, will be protected because of the sentimental interests of people. I have, then, according to contractarianism, no duty directly to your dog or any other animal, not even the duty not to cause them pain or suffering; my duty not to hurt them is a duty I have to those people who care about what happens to them. As for other animals, where no or little sentimental interest is present—farm animals, for example, or laboratory rats—what duties we have grow weaker and weaker, perhaps to the vanishing point. The pain and death they endure, though real, are not wrong if no one cares about them.

Contractarianism could be a hard view to refute when it comes to the moral status of animals if it was an adequate theoretical approach to the moral status of human beings. It is not adequate in this latter respect, however, which makes the question of its adequacy in the former—regarding animals—utterly moot. For consider: morality, according to the (crude) contractarian position before us, consists of rules people agree to abide by. What people? Well, enough to make a difference—enough, that is, so that collectively they have the power to enforce the rules that are drawn up in the contract. That is very well and good for the signatories—but not so good for anyone who is not asked to sign. And there is nothing in contractarianism of the sort we are discussing that guarantees or requires that everyone will have a chance to participate equitably in framing the rules of morality. The result is that this approach to ethics could sanction the most blatant forms of social, economic, moral, and political injustice, ranging from a repressive caste system to systematic racial or sexual discrimination. Might, on this theory, does make right. Let those who are the victims of injustice suffer as they will. It matters not so long as no one else—no contractor, or too few of them—cares about it. Such a theory takes one's moral breath away . . . as if, for example, there is nothing wrong with apartheid in South Africa if too few white South Africans are upset by it. A theory with so little to recommend it at the level of the ethics of our treatment of our fellow humans cannot have anything more to recommend it when it comes to the ethics of how we treat our fellow animals.

The version of contractarianism just examined is, as I have noted, a crude variety, and in fairness to those of a contractarian persuasion it must be noted that much more refined, subtle, and ingenious varieties are possible. For example, John Rawls, in his *A Theory of Justice*, sets forth a version of contractarianism that forces the contractors to ignore the accidental features of being a human being—for example, whether one is white or black, male or female, a genius or of modest intellect. Only by ignoring such features, Rawls believes, can we insure that the principles of justice contractors would agree upon are not based on bias or prejudice.

Despite the improvement a view such as Rawls's shows over the cruder forms of contractarianism, it remains deficient: it systematically denies that we have direct duties to those human beings who do not have a sense of justice—young children, for instance, and many mentally retarded humans. And yet it seems reasonably certain that, were we to torture a young child or a retarded elder, we would be doing something that wrongs them, not something that is wrong if (and only if) other humans with a sense of justice are upset. And since this is true in the case of these humans, we cannot rationally deny the same in the case of animals.

Indirect duty views, then, including the best among them, fail to command our rational assent. Whatever ethical theory we rationally should accept, therefore, it must at least recognize that we have some duties directly to animals, just as we have some duties directly to each other. The next two theories I'll sketch attempt to meet this requirement.

The first I call the cruelty-kindness view. Simply stated, this view says that we have a direct duty to be kind to animals and a direct duty not to be cruel to them. Despite the familiar, reassuring ring of these ideas, I do not believe this view offers an adequate theory. To make this clearer, consider kindness. A kind person acts from a certain kind of motive—compassion or concern, for example. And that is a virtue. But there is no guarantee that a kind act is a right act. If I am a generous racist, for example, I will be inclined to act kindly toward members of my own race, favoring their interests above others. My kindness would be real and, so far as it goes, good. But I trust it is too obvious to require comment that my kind acts may not be above moral reproach—may, in fact, be positively wrong because rooted in injustice. So kindness, not withstanding its status as a virtue to be encouraged, simply will not cancel the weight of a theory of right action.

Cruelty fares no better. People or their acts are cruel if they display either a lack of sympathy for or, worse, the presence of enjoyment in, seeing another suffer. Cruelty in all its guises *is* a bad thing—*is* a tragic human failing. But just as a person's being motivated by kindness does not guarantee that they do what is right, so the absence of cruelty does not assure that they avoid doing what is wrong. Many people who perform abortions, for example, are not cruel, sadistic people. But that fact about their character and motivation does not settle the terribly difficult question about the morality of abortion. The case is no different when we examine the ethics of our treatment of animals. So, yes, let us be for kindness and against cruelty. But let us not suppose that being for the one and against the other answers questions about moral right and wrong.

Some people think the theory we are looking for is utilitarianism. A utilitarian accepts two moral principles. The first is a principle of equality: everyone's interests count, and similar interests must be counted as having similar weight or importance. White or black, male or female, American or Iranian, human or animal: everyone's pain or frustration matter and matter equally with the like pain or frustration of anyone else. The second principle a utilitarian accepts is the principle of utility: do that act that will bring about the best balance of satisfaction over frustration for everyone affected by the outcome.

As a utilitarian, then, here is how I am to approach the task of deciding what I morally ought to do: I must ask who will be affected if I choose to do one thing rather than another, how much each individual will be affected, and where the best results are most likely to lie—which option, in other words, is most likely to bring about the best results, the best balance of satisfaction over frustration. That option, whatever it may be, is the one I ought to choose. That is where my moral duty lies.

The great appeal of utilitarianism rests with its uncompromising *egalitarianism:* everyone's interests count and count equally with the like interests of everyone else. The kind of odious discrimination some forms of contractarianism can justify—discrimination based on race or sex, for example—seems disallowed in principle by utilitarianism, as is speciesism—systematic discrimination based on species membership.

The sort of equality we find in utilitarianism, however, is not the sort an advocate of animal or human rights should have in mind. Utilitarianism has no room for the equal moral rights of different individuals because it has no room for their equal inherent value or worth. What has value for the utilitarian is the satisfaction of an individual's interests, not the individual whose interests they are. A universe in which you satisfy your desire for water, food, and warmth, is, other things being equal, better than a universe in which these desires are frustrated. And the same is true in the case of an animal with similar desires. But neither you nor the animal have any value in your own right. Only your feelings do.

Here is an analogy to help make the philosophical point clearer: a cup contains different liquids—sometimes sweet, sometimes bitter, sometimes a mix of the two. What has value are the liquids: the sweeter the better, the bitter the worse. The cup—the container—has no value. It's what goes into it, not what they go into, that has value. For the utilitarian, you and I are like the cup; we have no value as individuals and thus no equal value. What has value is what goes into us, what we serve as receptacles for; our feelings of satisfaction have positive value, our feelings of frustration have negative value.

Serious problems arise for utilitarianism when we remind ourselves that it enjoins us to bring about the best consequences. What does this mean? It doesn't mean the best consequences for me alone, or for my family or friends, or any other person taken individually. No, what we must do is, roughly, as follows: we must add up—somehow!—the separate satisfactions and frustrations of everyone likely to be affected by our choice, the satisfactions in one column, the frustrations in the other. We must total each column for each of the options before us. That is what it means to say the theory is aggregative. And then we must choose that option which is most likely to bring about the best balance of totaled satisfactions over totaled frustrations. Whatever act would lead to this outcome is the one we morally ought to perform—is where our moral duty lies. And that act quite clearly might not be the same one that would bring about the best results for me personally, or my family or friends, or a lab animal. The best aggregated consequences for everyone concerned are not necessarily the best for each individual.

That utilitarianism is an aggregative theory—that different individual's satisfactions or frus-

trations are added, or summed, or totaled—is the key objection to this theory. My Aunt Bea is old, inactive, a cranky, sour person, though not physically ill. She prefers to go on living. She is also rather rich. I could make a fortune if I could get my hands on her money, money she intends to give me in any event, after she dies, but which she refuses to give me now. In order to avoid a huge tax bite, I plan to donate a handsome sum of my profits to a local children's hospital. Many, many children will benefit from my generosity, and much joy will be brought to their parents, relatives, and friends. If I don't get the money rather soon, all these ambitions will come to naught. The once-in-a-life-time-opportunity to make a real killing will be gone. Why, then, not really kill my Aunt Bea? Oh, of course I *might* get caught. But I'm no fool and, besides, her doctor can be counted on to cooperate (he has an eye for the same investment and I happen to know a good deal about his shady past). The deed can be done . . . professionally, shall we say. There is *very* little chance of getting caught. And as for my conscience being guilt ridden, I am a resourceful sort of fellow and will take more than sufficient comfort—as I lie on the beach at Acapulco—in contemplating the joy and health I have brought to so many others.

Suppose Aunt Bea is killed and the rest of the story comes out as told. Would I have done anything wrong? Anything immoral? One would have thought that I had. But not according to utilitarianism. Since what I did brought about the best balance of totaled satisfaction over frustration for all those affected by the outcome, what I did was not wrong. Indeed, in killing Aunt Bea the physican and I did what duty required.

This same kind of argument can be repeated in all sorts of cases, illustrating, time after time, how the utilitarian's position leads to results that impartial people find morally callous. It *is* wrong to kill my Aunt Bea in the name of bringing about the best results for others. A good end does not justify an evil means. Any adequate moral theory will have to explain why this is so. Utilitarianism fails in this respect and so cannot be the theory we seek.

What to do? Where to begin anew? The place to begin, I think, is with the utilitarian's view of the value of the individual—or, rather, lack of value. In its place suppose we consider that you and I, for example, do have value as individuals—what we'll call *inherent value*. To say we have such value is to say that we are something more than, something different from, mere receptacles. Moreover, to insure that we do not pave the way for such injustices as slavery or sexual discrimination, we must believe that all who have inherent value have it equally, regardless of their sex, race, religion, birthplace, and so on. Similarly to be discarded as irrelevant are one's talents or skills, intelligence and wealth, personality or pathology, whether one is loved and admired—or despised and loathed. The genius and the retarded child, the prince and the pauper, the brain surgeon and the fruit vendor, Mother Theresa and the most unscrupulous used car salesman—all have inherent value, all possess it equally, and all have an equal right to be treated with respect, to be treated in ways that do not reduce them to the status of things, as if they exist as resources for others. My value as an individual is independent of my usefulness to you. Yours is not dependent on your usefulness to me. For either of us to treat the other in ways that fail to show respect for the other's independent value is to act immorally—is to violate the individual's rights.

Some of the rational virtues of this view—what I call the rights view—should be evident. Unlike (crude) contractarianism, for example, the rights view *in principle* denies the moral tolerability of any and all forms of racial, sexual, or social discrimination; and unlike utilitarianism, this view *in principle* denies that we can justify good results by using evil means that violate an individual's rights—denies, for example, that it could be moral to kill my Aunt Bea to harvest beneficial consequences for others. That would be to sanction the disrespectful treatment of the individual in the name of the social good, something the rights view will not—categorically will not—ever allow.

The rights view—or so I believe—is rationally the most satisfactory moral theory. It surpasses all other theories in the degree to which it illuminates and explains the foundation of our duties to one another—the domain of human morality. On this score, it has the best reasons, the best arguments, on its side. Of course, if it were possible to show that only human beings are included within its scope, then a person like myself, who believes in animal rights, would be obliged to look elsewhere than to the rights view.

But attempts to limit its scope to humans only can be shown to be rationally defective. Animals, it is true, lack many of the abilities humans possess. They can't read, do higher mathematics, build a bookcase, or make *baba ghanoush*. Neither can many human beings, however, and yet we don't say—and shouldn't say—that they (these humans) therefore have less inherent value, less of a right to be treated with respect, than do others. It is the *similarities* between those human beings who most clearly, most noncontroversially have such value—the people reading this, for example—it is our similarities, not our differences, that matter most. And the really crucial, the basic similarity is simply this; we are each of us the experiencing subject of a life, each of us a conscious creature having an individual welfare that has importance to us whatever our usefulness to others. We want and prefer things; believe and feel things; recall and expect things. And all these dimensions of our life, including our pleasure and pain, our enjoyment and suffering, our satisfaction and frustration, our continued existence or our untimely death—all make a difference to the quality of our life as lived, as experienced by us as individuals. As the same is true of those animals who concern us (those who are eaten and trapped, for example), they, too, must be viewed as the experiencing subjects of a life with inherent value of their own.

There are some who resist the idea that animals have inherent value. "Only humans have such value," they profess. How might this narrow view be defended? Shall we say that only humans have the requisite intelligence, or autonomy, or reason? But there are many, many humans who will fail to meet these standards and yet who are reasonably viewed as having value above and beyond their usefulness to others. Shall we claim that only humans belong to the right species—the species Homo sapiens? But this is blatant speciesism. Will it be said, then, that all—and only—humans have immortal souls? Then our opponents more than have their work cut out for them. I am myself not ill-disposed to there being immortal souls. Personally, I profoundly hope I have one. But I would not want to rest my position on a controversial ethical issue on the even more controversial question about who or what has an immortal soul. That is to dig one's hole deeper, not climb out. Rationally, it is better to resolve moral issues without making more controversial assumptions than are needed. The question of who has inherent value is such a question, one that is more rationally resolved without the introduction of the idea of immortal souls than by its use.

Well, perhaps some will say that animals have some inherent value, only *less* than we do. Once again, however, attempts to defend this view can be shown to lack rational justification. What could be the basis of our having more inherent value than animals? Will it be their lack of reason, or autonomy, or intellect? Only if we are willing to make the same judgement in the case of humans who are similarly deficient. But it is not true that such humans—the retarded child, for example, or the mentally deranged—have less inherent value than you or I. Neither, then, can we rationally sustain the view that animals like them in being the experiencing subjects of a life have less inherent value. *All* who have inherent value have it *equally*, whether they be human animals or not.

Inherent value, then, belongs equally to those who are the experiencing subjects of a life. Whether it belongs to others—to rocks and rivers, trees and glaciers, for example—we do not know. And may never know. But neither do we need to know, if we are to make the case for animal rights. We do not need to know how many people, for example, are eligible to vote in the next presidential election before we can know whether I am. Similarly, we do not need to know *how many* individuals have inherent value before we can know that some do. When it comes to the case for animal rights, then what we need to know is whether the animals who, in our culture are routinely eaten, hunted, and used in our laboratories, for example, are like us in being subjects of a life. And we *do* know this. We do *know* that many—literally, billions and billions—of these animals are the subjects of a life in the sense explained and so have

inherent value if we do. And since, in order to have the best theory of our duties to one another, we must recognize our equal inherent value, as individuals, reason—not sentiment, not emotion—reason compels us to recognize the equal inherent value of these animals. And, with this, their equal right to be treated with respect.

That, *very* roughly, is the shape and feel of the case for animal rights. Most of the details of the supporting argument are missing. They are to be found in the book I alluded to earlier. Here, the details go begging and I must in closing, limit myself to four final points.

The first is how the theory that underlies the case for animal rights shows that the animal rights movement is a part of, not antagonistic to, the human rights movement. The theory that rationally grounds the rights of animals also grounds the rights of humans. Thus are those involved in the animal rights movement partners in the struggle to secure respect for human rights—the rights of women, for example, or minorities and workers. The animal rights movement is cut from the same moral cloth as these.

Second, having set out the broad outlines of the rights view, I can now say why its implications for farming and science, for example, are both clear and uncompromising. In the case of using animals in science, the rights view is categorically abolitionist. Lab animals are not our tasters; we are not their kings. Because these animals are treated—routinely, systematically—as if their value is reducible to their usefulness to others, they are routinely, systematically treated with a lack of respect, and thus are their rights routinely, systematically violated. This is just as true when they are used in trivial, duplicative, unnecessary or unwise research as it is when they are used in studies that hold out real promise of human benefits. We can't justify harming or killing a human being (my Aunt Bea, for example) just for these sorts of reasons. Neither can we do so even in the case of so lowly a creature as a laboratory rat. It is not just refinement or reduction that are called for, not just larger, cleaner cages, not just more generous use of anaesthetic or the elemination of multiple surgery, not just tidying up the system. It is replacement—completely. The best we can do when it comes to using animals in science is—not to use them. That is where our duty lies, according to the rights view.

As for commercial animal agriculture, the rights view takes a similar abolitionist position. The fundamental moral wrong here is not that animals are kept in stressful close confinement, or in isolation, or that they have their pain and suffering, their needs and preferences ignored or discounted. *All* these *are* wrong, of course, but they are not the fundamental wrong. They are symptoms and effects of the deeper, systematic wrong that allows these animals to be viewed and treated as lacking independent value, as resources for us—as, indeed, a renewable resource. Giving farm animals more space, more natural environments, more companions does not right the fundamental wrong, any more than giving lab animals more anaesthesia or bigger, cleaner cages would right the fundamental wrong in their case. Nothing less than the total dissolution of commercial animal agriculture will do this, just as, for similar reasons I won't develop at length here, morality requires nothing less than the total elimination of commercial and sport hunting and trapping. The rights view's implications, then, as I have said, are clear—and are uncompromising.

My last two points are about philosophy—my profession. It is most obviously, no substitute for political action. The words I have written here and in other places by themselves don't change a thing. It is what we do with the thoughts the words express—our acts, our deeds—that change things. All that philosophy can do, and all I have attempted, is to offer a vision of what our deeds could aim at. And the why. But not the how.

Finally, I am reminded of my thoughtful critic, the one I mentioned earlier, who chastised me for being "too cerebral." Well, cerebral I have been: indirect duty views, utilitarianism, contractarianism—hardly the stuff deep passions are made of. I am also reminded, however, of the image another friend once set before me—the image of the ballerina as expressive of disciplined passion. Long hours of sweat and toil, of loneliness and practice, of doubt and fatigue; that is the discipline of her craft. But the passion is there, too; the fierce drive to excel, to speak through her body, to do it right, to pierce our minds. That is the image of philosophy I would leave with you; not "too cerebral," but *disciplined passion*. Of the discipline, enough has been seen. As for the passion:

There are times, and these are not infrequent, when tears come to my eyes when I see, or read, or hear of the wretched plight of animals in the hands of humans. Their pain, their suffering, their loneliness, their innocence, their death. Anger. Rage. Pity. Sorrow. Disgust. The whole creation groans under the weight of the evil we humans visit upon these mute, powerless creatures. It *is* our heart, not just our head, that calls for an end, that demands of us that we overcome, for them, the habits and forces behind their systematic oppression. All great movements, it is written, go through three stages: ridicule, discussion, adoption. It is the realization of this third stage—adoption—that demands both our passion and our discipline, our heart and our head. The fate of animals is in our hands. God grant we are equal to the task.

Note

1. Tom Regan, *The Case For Animal Rights* (Berkeley: University of California Press, 1983).

Rights, Interests, Desires and Beliefs

R. G. Frey

Editorial Note: Readers should note that the original numbering of sections has been retained even though certain sections have been deleted

Source: *American Philosophical Quarterly,* Vol. 16, No. 3 (July 1979), pp. 233–39. Reprinted by permission.

I

The question of whether non-human animals possess moral rights is once again being widely argued. Doubtless the rise of ethology is partly responsible for this: as we learn more about the behavior of animals, it seems inevitable that we shall be led to focus upon the similarities between them and us, with the result that the extension of moral rights from human beings to non-human animals can appear, as the result of these similarities, to have a firm basis in nature. (Of course, this way of putting the matter assumes that human beings have moral rights, and on another occasion I should perhaps wish to challenge this assumption.) But the major impetus to renewed interest in the subject of animal rights almost certainly stems from a heightened and more critical awareness, among philosophers and non-philosophers alike, of the arguments for and against eating animals and using them in scientific research. For if animals *do* have moral rights, such as a right to live and to live free from unnecessary suffering, and if our present practices systematically tread upon these rights, then the case for eating and experimenting upon animals, especially when other alternatives are for the most part readily available, is going to have to be a powerful one indeed.

It is important, however, not to misconstrue the question: the question is not about *which* rights animals may or may not be thought to possess or about *whether* their alleged rights in a particular regard are on a par with the alleged rights of humans in this same regard but rather about the more fundamental issue of whether animals—or, in any event, the "higher" animals—are a kind of being which can be the logical subject of rights. It is this issue, and a particular position with respect to it, that I want critically to address here.

II

The position I have in mind is the widely influential one which links the possession of rights to the possession of interests. In his *System of Ethics,* Leonard Nelson is among the first, if not the first, to propound the view that all and only beings which have interests can have rights,[1] a view which has attracted an increasingly wide following ever since. For example, in his paper "Rights," H. J. McCloskey embraces the view but goes on to deny that animals have interests;[2] whereas Joel Feinberg, in his seminal paper "The Rights of Animals and Unborn Generations," likewise embraces the view but goes on to affirm that animals do have interests.[3] Nelson himself is emphatic that animals as well as human beings are, as he puts it, "carriers of interests,"[4] and he concludes, accordingly, that animals possess rights, rights which both deserve and warrant our respect. For Nelson, then, it is because animals have interests that they can be the logical subject of rights, and his claim that animals *do have* interests forms the minor premiss, therefore, in an argument for the moral rights of animals:

All and only beings which (can) have interests (can) have moral rights; Animals as well as humans (can) have interests; Therefore, animals (can) have moral rights.

Both McCloskey and Feinberg accept the major premiss of this argument, which I shall dub the interest thesis, but disagree over the truth of the minor premiss; and it is apparent that the minor premiss is indeed the key to the whole matter. For given the truth of the major premiss, given, that is, that the possession of interests *is* a criterion for the possession of rights, it is nevertheless only the truth of the minor premiss that would result in the inclusion of creatures other than human beings within the class of right-holders. This premiss is doubtful, however, and the case against it a powerful one, or so I want to suggest.

This case is not that developed by McCloskey, whose position is not free of a rather obvious difficulty. He makes the issue of whether animals have interests turn upon their failure and/or inability to grasp and so behave in accordance with the prescriptive overtone which he takes talk of "*X* is in *A*'s interests" to have, when it is not obvious that expressions like "*X* is in *A*'s interests" do have a prescriptive overtone and certainly not obvious that a prescriptive overtone is part of the meaning of such expressions. I have elsewhere tried to show how a McCloskey-like position on interests might be sustained;[5] but I do not think his way of tackling the claim that animals have interests a particularly fruitful one, and I neither adopt nor rely upon it in what follows.

III

To say that "Good health is in John's interests" is not at all the same thing as to say that "John has an interest in good health." The former is intimately bound up with having a good or well-being to which good health is conducive, so that we could just as easily have said "Good health is conducive to John's good or well-being," whereas the latter—"John has an interest in good health"—is intimately bound up with wanting, with John's wanting good health. That these two notions of "interest" are logically distinct is readily apparent: good health may well be in John's interests, in the sense of being conducive to his good or well-being, even if

John does not want good health, indeed, even if he wants to continue taking hard drugs, with the result that his health is irreparably damaged; and John may have an interest in taking drugs, in the sense of wanting to take them, even if it is apparent to him that it is not conducive to his good or well-being to continue to do so. In other words, something can be *in* John's interests without John's *having* an interest in it, and John can *have* an interest in something without its being *in* his interests.

If this is right, and there are these two logically distinct senses of "interest," we can go on to ask whether animals can have interests in either of these senses; and if they do, then perhaps the minor premiss of Nelson's argument for the moral rights of animals can be sustained.

IV

Do animals, therefore, have interests in the first sense, in the sense of having a good or well-being which can be harmed or benefited? The answer, I think, is that they certainly do have interests in this sense; after all, it is plainly not good for a dog to be fed certain types of food or to be deprived of a certain amount of exercise. This answer, however, is of little use to the Nelsonian cause; for it yields the counter-intuitive result that manmade/manufactured objects and even things have interests, and, therefore, on the interest thesis, have or at least are candidates for having moral rights. For example, just as it is not good for a dog to be deprived of a certain amount of exercise, so it is not good for prehistoric cave drawings to be exposed to excessive amounts of carbon dioxide or for Rembrandt paintings to be exposed to excessive amounts of sunlight.

If, nevertheless, one is inclined to doubt that the notion of "not being good for" in the above examples shows that the object or thing in question "has a good," consider the case of tractors: anything, including tractors, can have a good, a well-being, I submit, if it is the sort of thing that can be good of its kind; and there are obviously good and bad tractors. A tractor which cannot perform certain tasks is not a good tractor, is not good of its kind; it falls short of those standards tractors must meet in order to be good ones. Thus, to say that it is in a tractor's interests to be well-oiled means only that it is conducive to the tractor's being a good one, good of its kind, if it is well-oiled. Just as John is good of his kind (i.e., human being) only if he is in health, so tractors are good of their kind only if they are well-oiled. Of course, farmers *have an interest* in their tractors being well-oiled; but this does not show that being well-oiled is not in a tractor's interest, in the sense of contributing to its being good of its kind. It *may* show that what makes good tractors good depends upon the purposes for which *we* make them; but the fact that we make them for certain purposes in no way shows that, once they are made, they cannot have a good of their own. Their good is being good of their kind, and being well-oiled is conducive to their being good of their kind and so, in this sense, in their interests. If this is right, if tractors do have interests, then on the interest thesis they have or can have moral rights, and this is a counter-intuitive result.

It is tempting to object, I suppose, that tractors cannot be harmed and benefited and, therefore, cannot have interests. My earlier examples, however, suffice to meet this objection. Prehistoric cave drawings are (not benefited but) positively harmed by excessive amounts of carbon dioxide, and Rembrandt paintings are likewise certainly harmed through exposure to excessive amounts of sunlight. It must be emphasized that it is these objects themselves that are harmed, and that their owners are harmed only in so far as and to the extent that the objects themselves undergo harm. Accordingly, on the present objection, interests are present, and the interest thesis once again gives the result that objects or things have or can have moral rights. To accommodate those, should there be any, who just might feel that objects or things can have moral rights, when these objects or things are, e.g., significant works of art, the examples can be suitably altered, so that what is harmed is, e.g., a quite ordinary rug. But if drawings, paintings and rugs can be harmed, why not tractors? Surely a tractor is harmed by prolonged exposure to rain? And surely the harm the tractor's owner

suffers comes through and is a function of the harm to the tractor itself?

In short, it cannot be in this first sense of "interest" that the case for animals and for the truth of Nelson's minor premiss is to be made; for though animals do have interests in this sense, so, too, do tractors, with awkward results.

V

Do animals, therefore, have interests in the second sense, in the sense of having wants which can be satisfied or left unsatisfied? In this sense, of course, it appears that tractors do not have interests; for though being well-oiled may be conducive to tractors being good of their kind, tractors do not *have an interest* in being well-oiled, since they cannot *want* to be well-oiled, cannot, in fact, have any wants whatever. But farmers can have wants, and they certainly have an interest in their tractors being well-oiled.

What, then, about animals? Can they have wants? By "wants," I understand a term that encompasses both needs and desires, and it is these that I shall consider.[6]

If to ask whether animals can have wants is to ask whether they can have needs, then certainly animals have wants. A dog can need water. But *this* cannot be the sense of "want" on which having interests will depend, since it does not exclude things from the class of want-holders. Just as dogs need water in order to function normally, so tractors need oil in order to function normally; and just as dogs will die unless their need for water is satisfied, so trees and grass and a wide variety of plants and shrubs will die unless their need for water is satisfied. Though we should not give the fact undue weight, someone who in ordinary discourse says "The tractor wants oiling" certainly means the tractor needs oiling, if it is not to fall away from those standards which make tractors good of their kind. Dogs, too, need water, if they are not to fall away from the standards which make them good of their kind. It is perhaps worth emphasizing, moreover, as the cases of the tractor, trees, grass, etc., show, that needs do not require the presence either of consciousness or of knowledge of the lack which makes up the need. If, in sum, we are to agree that tractors, trees, grass, etc., do not have wants, and, therefore, interests, it cannot be the case that wants are to be construed as needs.

This, then, leaves desires, and the question of whether animals can have wants as desires. I may as well say at once that I do not think animals can have desires. My reasons for thinking this turn largely upon my doubts that animals can have beliefs, and my doubts in this regard turn partially,[7] though in large part, upon the view that having beliefs is not compatible with the absence of language and linguistic ability. I realize that the claim that animals cannot have desires is a controversial one; but I think the case to be made in support of it, complex though it is, is persuasive. This case, I should stress, consists in an analysis of desire and belief and of what it is to have and to entertain beliefs, and *not* in the adoption of anything like Chomsky's account of language as something radically unlike and completely discontinuous with animal behavior.

VI

Suppose I am a collector of rare books and desire to own a Gutenberg Bible: my desire to own this volume is *to be traced* to my belief that I do not now own such a work and that my rare book collection is deficient in this regard. By "to be traced" here, what I mean is this: if someone were to ask *how* my belief that my book collection lacks a Gutenberg Bible is connected with my desire to own such a Bible, what better or more direct reply could be given than that, without this belief, I would not have this desire? For if I believed that my rare book collection *did* contain a Gutenberg Bible and so was complete in this sense, then I would not desire a Gutenberg Bible in order to make up what I now believe to be a notable deficiency in my collection. (Of course, I might desire to own more

than one such Bible, but this contingency is not what is at issue here.)

Now what is it that I believe? I believe that my collection lacks a Gutenberg Bible; that is, I believe that the sentence "My collection lacks a Gutenberg Bible" is true. In constructions of the form "I believe that . . .," what follows upon the "that" is a declarative sentence; and *what* I believe is that that sentence is true. The same is the case with constructions of the form "He believes that . . .": what follows upon the "that" is a declarative sentence, and what the "he" in question believes is that that sentence is true. The difficulty in the case of animals should be apparent: if someone were to say, e.g., "The cat believes that the door is locked," then that person is holding, as I see it, that the cat holds the declarative sentence "The door is locked" to be true; and I can see no reason whatever for crediting the cat or any other creature which lacks language, including human infants, with entertaining declarative sentences and holding certain declarative sentences to be true.

Importantly, nothing whatever in this account is affected by changing the example, in order to rid it of sophisticated concepts like "door" and "locked," which in any event may be thought beyond cats, and to put in their place more rudimentary concepts. For the essence of this account is not about the relative sophistication of this or that concept but rather about the relationship between believing something and entertaining and regarding as true certain declarative sentences. If what is believed is that a certain declarative sentence is true, then no creature which lacks language can have beliefs; and without beliefs, a creature cannot have desires. And this is the case with animals, or so I suggest; and if I am right, not even in the sense, then, of wants as desires do animals have interests, which, to recall, is the minor premiss in the Nelsonian argument for the moral rights of animals.

But is what is believed that a certain declarative sentence is true? I think there are three arguments of sorts that shore up the claim that this *is* what is believed.

First, I do not see how a creature could have the concept of belief without being able to distinguish between true and false beliefs. When I believe that my collection of rare books lacks a

Gutenberg Bible, I believe that it is true that my collection lacks a Gutenberg Bible; put another way, I believe that it is false that my collection contains a Gutenberg Bible. I can distinguish, and do distinguish, between the sentences "My collection lacks a Gutenberg Bible" and "My collection contains a Gutenberg Bible," and it is only the former I hold to be true. According to my view, what I believe in this case is that this sentence is true; and sentences are the sorts of things we regard as or hold to be true. As for the cat, and leaving aside now all questions about the relative sophistication of concepts, I do not see how it could have the belief that the door is locked unless it could distinguish this true belief from the false belief that the door is unlocked. But what is true or false are not states of affairs which correspond to or reflect or pertain to these beliefs; states of affairs are not true or false but either are or are not the case, either do or do not obtain. If, then, one is going to credit cats with beliefs, and cats must be able to distinguish true from false beliefs, and states of affairs are not true or false, then what exactly is it that cats are being credited with distinguishing as true or false? Reflection on this question, I think, forces one to credit cats with language, in order for there to be something that can be true or false in belief; and it is precisely because they lack language that we cannot make this move.

Second, if in order to have the concept of belief a creature must be possessed of the difference between true and false belief, then in order for a creature to be able to distinguish true from false beliefs that creature must—simply must, as I see it—have some awareness of, to put the matter in the most general terms, how language connects with, links up with the world; and I see no reason to credit cats with such an awareness. My belief that my collection lacks a Gutenberg Bible is true if and only if my collection lacks a Gutenberg Bible; that is, the *truth* of this belief cannot be entertained by me without it being the case that I am aware that the truth of the sentence "My collection lacks a Gutenberg Bible" is *at the very least* partially a function of how the world is. However difficult to capture, it is this relationship between language and the world a grasp of which is necessary if a creature is to grasp the difference

between true and false belief, a distinction which it must grasp, if it is to possess the concept of belief at all.

Third, I do not see how a creature could have an awareness or grasp of how language connects with, links up with the world, to leave the matter at its most general, unless that creature was itself possessed of language; and cats are not possessed of language. If it were to be suggested, for example, that the sounds that cats make amount to a language, I should deny it. This matter is far too large and complex to be tackled here; but the general line of argument I should use to support my denial can be sketched in a very few words. Can cats lie? If they cannot, then they cannot assert anything; and if they lack assertion, I do not see how they could possess a language. And I should be strict: I do not suggest that, lacking assertion, cats possess a language in some attenuated or secondary sense; rather, I suggest that, lacking assertion, they do not possess a language *at all*.

VII

It may be suggested, of course, that there might possibly be a class of desires—let us call them simple desires—which do not involve the intervention of belief, in order to have them, and which do not require that we credit animals with language. Such simple desires, for example, might be for some object or other, and we as language-users might try to capture these simple desires in the case of a dog by describing its behavior in such terms as "The dog simply desires the bone." (This position may have to be complicated, as the result of questions about whether the dog possesses the concept "bone" or even more general concepts such as "material object," "thing" and "thing in my visual field"; but these questions I shall leave aside here.) If all the dog's desires are simple desires, and this is the point, then my arguments to show that dogs lack beliefs may well be beside the point.

A subsidiary argument is required, therefore, in order to cover this possibility. Suppose, then, the dog simply desires the bone: is the dog aware that it has this simple desire or not? If it is alleged to have this desire but to be unaware that it has it, to want but to be unaware that it wants, then a problem arises. In the case of human beings, unconscious desire can be made sense of, but only because we first make sense of conscious desire; but where no desires are conscious ones, where the creature in question is alleged to have only unconscious desires, what cash value can the use of the term "desire" have in such a case? This question must be appreciated against the backdrop of what appears to ensue as a result of the present claim. On the strength of the dog's behavior, it is claimed that the dog simply desires the bone; the desire we claim for it is one which, if we concede that it has it, it is unaware that it has; and no distinction between conscious and unconscious desire is to be drawn in the dog's case. Consider, then, a rubber plant which shuns the dark and through a series of movements, seeks the light: by parity of reasoning with the dog's case, we can endow the plant with an unconscious desire for the light, and claim as we do so that it, too, is a type of creature for whom no distinction between conscious and unconscious desire is possible. In other words, without an awareness-condition of some sort, it would seem that the world can be populated with an enormous number of unconscious desires in this way, and it no longer remains clear what, if anything, the cash value of the term "desire" is in such cases. If, however, the dog is alleged to have a simple desire for the bone and to be aware that it has this desire, then the dog is aware that it simply desires the bone; it is, in other words, self-conscious. Now my objection to regarding the dog as self-conscious is not merely founded upon the view that self-consciousness presupposes the possession of language, which is too large a subject to go into here; it is also founded upon the fact that there is nothing the dog can do which can express the difference between desiring the bone and being aware of desiring the bone. Yet, the dog would have to be capable of expressing this difference in its behavior, if one is going to hold, *on the basis of that behavior*, that the dog is aware that it has a simple desire for the bone, aware that it simply desires the bone.

Even, then, if we concede for the sake of argument that there are simple desires, desires which do not involve the intervention of belief in order to have them, the suggestion that we can credit animals with these desires, without also having to credit them with language, is at best problematic. . . .

IX

I conclude, then, that the Nelsonian position on the moral rights of animals is not a sound one: the truth of the minor premiss in his argument—that animals have interests—is doubtful at best, and animals must have interests if, in accordance with the interest thesis, they are to be a logical subject of such rights. For animals either have interests in a sense which allows objects and things to have interests, and so, on the interest thesis, to have or to be candidates for having moral rights or they do not have interests at all, and so, on the interest thesis, do not have and are not candidates for having moral rights. I have reached this conclusion, moreover, without querying the correctness of the interest thesis itself, without querying, that is, whether the possession of interests *really is* a criterion for the possession of moral rights.[8]

Notes

1. Leonard Nelson, *System of Ethics*, tr. by Norbert Guterman (New Haven, 1956), Part I, Section 2, Chapter 7, pp. 136–144.
2. H. J. McCloskey, "Rights," *Philosophical Quarterly*, vol. 15 (1965), pp. 115–127.
3. Joel Feinberg, "The Rights of Animals and Unborn Generations," in W. T. Blackstone, (ed.), *Philosophy and Environmental Crisis* (Athens, Georgia, 1974), pp. 43–68.
4. Nelson, *op. cit.*, p. 138.
5. See my paper "Interests and Animal Rights," *Philosophical Quarterly*, vol. 27 (1977), pp. 254–259.

6. See also my paper "Russell and The Essence of Desire," *Philosophy,* forthcoming.

7. I express doubts of a different kind elsewhere; see note 6.

8. An earlier version of this paper was read to a discussion group in Oxford and to a conference on the philosophy of Leonard Nelson in the University of Göttingen. I am indebted to the participants in each for helpful comments and suggestions.

The Limits of Trooghaft

Desmond Stewart

The Troogs took one century to master the planet, then another three to restock it with men, its once dominant but now conquered species. Being hierarchical in temper, the Troogs segregated *homo insipiens* into four castes between which there was no traffic except that of bloodshed. The four castes derived from the Troog experience of human beings.

The planet's new masters had an intermittent sense of the absurd; Troog laughter could shake a forest. Young Troogs first captured some surviving children, then tamed them as "housemen," though to their new pets the draughty Troog structures seemed far from house-like. Pet-keeping spread. Whole zoos of children were reared on a bean diet. For housemen, Troogs preferred children with brown or yellow skins, finding them neater and cleaner than others; this preference soon settled into an arbitrary custom. Themselves hermaphrodite, the Troogs were fascinated by the spectacle of marital couplings. Once their pets reached adolescence, they were put in cages whose nesting boxes had glass walls. Troogs would gaze in by the hour. Captivity—and this was an important discovery did not inhibit the little creatures from breeding, nor, as was feared, did the sense of being watched turn the nursing females to deeds of violence. Cannibalism was rare. Breeders, by selecting partners, could soon produce strains with certain comical features, such as cone-shaped breasts or cushion-shaped rumps.

The practice of keeping pets was fought by senior Troogs; the conservative disapproved of innovations while the fastidious found it objectionable when bean-fed humans passed malodorous wind. After the innovation became too general to suppress, the Troog elders hedged the practice with laws. No pet should be kept alive if it fell sick, and since bronchitis was endemic, pets had short lives. The young Troogs recognized the wisdom behind this rule for they too disliked the sound of coughing. But in some cases they tried to save an invalid favorite from the lethal chamber, or would surrender it only after assurances that the sick were happier dead.

Adaptability had enabled the Troogs to survive their travels through time and space; it helped them to a catholic approach to the food provided by the planet, different as this was from their previous nourishment. Within two generations they had become compulsive carnivores. The realization, derived from pet-keeping, that captive men could breed, led to the establishment of batteries of capons, the second and largest human caste. Capons were naturally preferred when young, since their bones were supple; at this time they fetched, as "eat-alls," the highest price for the lowest weight. Those kept alive after childhood were lodged in small cages maintained at a steady 22 degrees [centigrade—the editors]; the cage floors were composed of rolling bars through which the filth fell into a sluice. Capons were not permitted to see the sky or smell unfiltered air. Experience proved that a warm pink glow kept them docile and conduced to weight-gain. Females were in general preferred to males and the eradication of the tongue (sold as a separate delicacy) quietened the batteries.

The third category—the ferocious hound-

47
The Limits of Trooghaft

men—were treated even by the Troogs with a certain caution; the barracks in which they were kennelled were built as far as possible from the batteries lest the black predators escape, break in and massacre hundreds. Bred for speed, obedience and ruthlessness, they were underfed. Unleashed they sped like greyhounds. Their unreliable tempers doomed the few surreptitious efforts to employ them as pets. One night they kept their quarters keening in rhythmic sound; next day, they slumped in yellow-eyed sulks, stirring only to lunge at each other or at their keepers' tentacles. None were kept alive after the age of thirty. Those injured in the chase were slaughtered on the spot and minced for the mess bowl.

Paradoxically, the swift hound-men depended for survival on the quarry they despised and hunted: the fourth human caste, the caste most hedged with laws.

The persistence, long into the first Troog period, of lone nomadic rebels, men and women who resisted from remote valleys and caves, had perplexed the planet's rulers. Then they made an advantage out of the setback. The wits and endurance of the defeated showed that the Troogs had suppressed a menace of some mettle. This was a compliment and Troogs, like the gods of fable, found praise enjoyable. They decided to preserve a caste of the uncorralled. This fourth caste, known as quarry-men or game, were protected within limits and seasons. It was forbidden, for example, to hunt pre-adolescents or pregnant females. All members of the caste enjoyed a respite during eight months of each year. Only at the five-yearly Nova Feast—the joyous commemoration of the greatest escape in Troog history—were all rules abandoned: then the demand for protein became overpowering.

Quarry-men excited more interest in their masters than the three other castes put together. On one level, gluttonous Troogs found their flesh more appetizing than that of capons. On another, academically minded Troogs studied their behavior-patterns. Moralizing Troogs extolled their courage against hopeless odds to a Troog generation inclined to be complacent about its power. The ruins which spiked the planet were testimony to the rudimentary but numerous civilizations which, over ten millennia, men had produced, from the time when they first cultivated grains and domesticated animals till their final achievement of an environment without vegetation (except under glass) and with only synthetic protein. Men, it was true, had never reached the stage where they could rely on the telepathy that served the Troogs. But this was no reason to despise them. Originally Troogs, too, had conversed through sound hitting a tympanum; they had retained a hieroglyphic system deep into their journey through time; indeed, their final abandonment of what men called writing (and the Troogs "incising") had been an indirect tribute to men: telepathic waves were harder to decipher than symbols. It moved antiquarian Troogs to see that some men still frequented the ruined repositories of written knowledge; and though men never repaired these ancient libraries, this did not argue that they had lost the constructional talents of forbears who had built skyscrapers and pyramids. It showed shrewd sense. To repair old buildings or build new ones would attract the hound-men. Safety lay in dispersal. Libraries were a place of danger for a quarry-man, known to the contemptuous hound-men as a "book-roach." The courageous passion for the little volumes in which great men had compressed their wisdom was admired by Troogs. In their death throes quarry-men often clutched these talismans.

It was through a library that, in the fifth Troog century, the first attempt was made to communicate between the species, the conquerors and the conquered.

Curiosity was a characteristic shared by both species. Quarry-men still debated what the Troogs were and where they had come from. The first generation had known them as Extra-Terrestrials, when Terra, man's planet, was still the normative center. Just as the natives of central America had welcomed the Spaniards as gods till the stake gave the notion of the godlike a satanic quality, millions of the superstitious had identified the Troogs with angels. But Doomsday was simply Troog's Day. The planet continued spinning, the sun gave out its heat and the empty oceans rolled against their shores. Living on an earth no longer theirs, quarry-men gazed at the glittering laser beams and reflected light which made the Troog-Halls and speculated about their tenants. A tradition declared that the first space vehicles had glowed with strange pictures. The Troogs, it was correctly deduced, had originally conversed by means analogous to language but had discarded speech in order to remain opaque, untappable. This encouraged some would-be rebels. They saw in precaution signs of caution and in caution proof of fallibility. A counter-attack might one day be possible, through science or magic. Some cynics pretended to find the Troogs a blessing. They quoted a long-dead writer who had believed it was better for a man to die on his feet when not too old. This was now the common human lot. Few quarry-men lived past thirty and the diseases of the past, such as cardiac failure and carcinoma, were all but unknown. But most men dreamed simply of a longer and easier existence.

The first human to be approached by a Troog was a short, stocky youth who had survived his 'teens thanks to strong legs, a good wind and the discovery of a cellar underneath one of the world's largest libraries. Because of his enthusiasm for a poet of that name, this book-roach was known to his group as "Blake." He had also studied other idealists such as the Egyptian Akhenaten and the Russian Tolstoy. These inspired him to speculate along the most hazardous paths, in the direction, for example, of the precipice-question: might not the Troogs have something akin to human consciousness, or even conscience? If so, might man perhaps address his conqueror? Against the backspace of an insentient universe one consciousness should greet another. His friends, his woman, laughed at the notion. They had seen what the Troogs had done to their species. Some men were bred to have protuberant eyes or elongated necks; others were kept in kennels on insufficient rations, and then, at the time of the Nova Feast or in the year's open season, unleashed through urban ruins or surrounding savannah to howl after their quarry—those related by blood and experience to Blake and his fellows. "I shall never trust a Troog," said his woman's brother, "even if he gives me a gold safe-conduct."

One Troog, as much an exception among his species as Blake among his, read this hopeful brain. It was still the closed season and some four months before the quinquennial Nova Feast. Quarry-men still relaxed in safety; the hounds sang or sulked; the Troogs had yet to prepare the lights and sounds for their tumultuous celebrations. Each morning Blake climbed to the Library. It was a long, rubbish-encumbered place with aisles still occupied by books, once arranged according to subject, but now higgledy-piggledy in dust and dereliction, thrown down by earthquake or scattered in the hunt. Each aisle had its attendant bust—Plato, Shakespeare, Darwin, Marx—testifying to a regretted time when men, divided by nationality, class or color, suffered only from their fellows.

In the corner watched by Shakespeare, Blake had his reading place. He had restored the shelves to some order; he had dusted the table. This May morning a Troog's fading odor made him tremble. A new object stood on his table: a large rusty typewriter of the most ancient model. In it was a sheet of paper.

Blake bent to read.

Are you ready to communicate question.

Blake typed the single word: *yes.*

He did not linger but retreated in mental confusion to the unintellectual huddle round babies and potatoes which was his cellar. He half feared that he had begun to go mad, or that some acquaintance was playing him a trick. But few of his group read and no man could duplicate the distinctive Troog smell.

The days that followed constituted a continual seance between "his" Troog and himself. Blake contributed little to the dialogue. His Troog seemed anxious for a listener but little interested in what that listener thought. Blake was an earphone, an admiring confessor. Try as he feebly did, he got no response when he tried to evoke his woman, his children.

"Trooghaft, you are right," wrote the unseen communicator, attested each time by his no longer frightening scent, "was noble once." Blake had made no such suggestion. "The quality of being a Troog was unfrictional as space and as tolerant as time. It has become—almost human."

Then next morning: "To copy the habits of lower creatures is to sink below them. What is natural to carnivores is unnatural to us. We never ate flesh before the Nova; nor on our journey. We adopted the practice from reading the minds of lower creatures, then copying them. Our corruption shows in new diseases; earlier than in the past, older Troogs decompose. It shows in our characters. We quarrel like our quarry. Our forms are not apt for ingesting so much protein. Protein is what alcohol was to humans. It maddens; it corrupts. Protein, not earth's climate, is paling our. . . ."

Here there was a day's gap before the typewriter produced, next morning, the word *complexion*. And after it, *metaphor*. Blake had learnt that the old Troog hieroglyphs were followed by determinants, symbols showing, for example, whether the concept *rule* meant tyranny or order. Complexion could only be used metaphorically of faceless and largely gaseous creatures.

To one direct question Blake obtained a direct answer: "How," he had typed, "did you first turn against the idea of eating us?"

"My first insight flashed at our last Nova Feast. Like everyone, I had been programmed to revel. Stench of flesh filled every Troog-Hall. Amid the spurt of music, the ancient greetings with which we flare still, the coruscations, I passed a meat-shop where lights pirouetted. I looked. I saw. Hanging from iron hooks—each pierced a foot-palm—were twenty she-capons, what you call women. Each neck was surrounded by a ruffle to hide the knife-cut; a tomato shut each anus. I suddenly shuddered. Nearby, on a slab of marble, smiled a row of jellied heads. Someone had dressed their sugar-hair in the manner of your Roman empresses: "Flavian Heads." A mass of piled up, tong-curled hair in front, behind a bun encoiled by a marzipan fillet. I lowered myself and saw as though for the first time great blocks of neutral-looking matter: "Paté of Burst Liver." The owner of the shop was glad to explain. They hold the woman down, then stuff nutriment through a V-shaped funnel. The merchant was pleased by my close attention. He displayed his Sucking Capons and Little Loves, as they call the reproductive organs which half of you split creatures wear outside your bodies."

"Was this," I asked in sudden repugnance, "Trooghaft?"

Encouraged by evidence of soul, Blake brought to the Troog's notice, from the miscellaneous volumes on the shelves, quotations from his favorite writers and narrative accounts of such actions as the death of Socrates, the crucifixion of Jesus and the murder of Che Guevara. Now in the mornings he found books and encyclopedias open on his table as well as typed pages. Sometimes Blake fancied that there was more than one Troog smell; so perhaps his Troog was converting others.

Each evening Blake told Janine, his partner, of his exploits. She was at first sceptical, then half-persuaded. This year she was not pregnant and therefore could be hunted. For love of her children, the dangers of the Nova season weighed on her spirits. Only her daughter was Blake's; her son had been sired by Blake's friend, a fast-runner who had sprained his ankle and fallen easy victim to the hounds two years before. As the Nova Feast approached, the majority of the quarry-men in the city began to leave for the mountains. Not that valleys and caves were secure; but the mountains were vast and the valleys remote one from another. The hound-men preferred to hunt in the cities; concentrations of people made their game easier.

Blake refused to join them. Out of loyalty Janine stayed with him.

"I shall build," the Troog had written, "a bridge between Trooghaft and Humanity. The universe calls me to revive true Trooghaft. My Troog-Hall shall become a sanctuary, not a shed of butchers."

Blake asked: "Are you powerful? Can you make other Troogs follow your example?"

The Troog answered: "I can at least do as your Akhenaten did."

Blake flushed at the mention of his hero. Then added: "But Akhenaten's experiment lasted briefly. Men relapsed. May not Troogs do likewise?" He longed for reassurance that his Troog was more than a moral dilettante.

Instead of an answer came a statement:

"We can never be equals with *homo insipiens*. But we can accept our two species as unequal productions of one universe. Men are small, but that does not mean they cannot suffer. Not one tongueless woman moves, upside-down, towards the throat-knife, without trembling. I have seen this. I felt pity, *metaphor*. Our young Troogs argue that fear gives flesh a quivering tenderness. I reject such arguments. Why should a complex, if lowly, life—birth, youth, growth to awareness—be sacrificed for one mealtime's pleasure?"

Although Blake recognized that his Troog was soliloquizing, the arguments pleased him. Convinced of their sincerity, Blake decided to trust his Troog and remain where he was, not hide or run as on previous occasions. There was a sewer leading from his refuge whose remembered stench was horrible. He would stay in the cellar. On the first day of the Nova Feast he climbed as usual to his corner of the library. But today there was no paper in the typewriter. Instead, books and encyclopedias had been pulled from the shelves and left open; they had nothing to do with poetry or the philosophers and the stench was not that of his Troog. Sudden unease seized him. Janine was alone with the children, her brother having left to join the others in the mountains. He returned to his cellar and, as his fear already predicted, found the children alone, wailing in one corner. The elder, the boy, told the doleful tale. Two hound-men had broken in and their mother had fled down the disused sewer.

Blake searched the sewer. It was empty. His one hope, as he too hid there, lay in his Troog's intervention. But neither the next day nor the day after, when he stole to the library, watching every shadow lest it turn to a hound-man, was there any message. This silence was atoned for on the third morning.

"If we still had a written language, I should publish a volume of confessions." The message was remote, almost unrelated to Blake's anguish. He read, "A few fat-fumes blow away a resolution. It was thus, the evening of the Nova Feast's beginning. Three Troog friends, *metaphor,* came to my Hall where no flesh was burning, where instead I was pondering these puny creatures to whom we cause such suffer-

ing. 'You cannot exile yourself from your group; Trooghaft is what Troogs do together.' I resisted such blandishments. The lights and sounds of the Nova were enough. I felt no craving for protein. Their laughter at this caused the laser beams to buckle and the lights to quiver. There entered four black hound-men dragging a quarry-female, filthy from the chase, her hands bound behind her. I was impassive. Housemen staggered under a great cauldron; they fetched logs. They placed the cauldron on a tripod and filled it with water; the logs were under it."

Blake shook as he read. This was the moment for his Troog to incarnate pity and save his woman.

"They now unbound and stripped the female, then set her in the water. It was cold and covered her skin with pimples.

"Again laughter, again the trembling lights and the buckling lasers.

"We, too, have been reading, brother. We have studied one of their ways of cooking. *Place the lobster*—their name for a long extinct seathing—*in warm water. Bring the water gently to the boil. The lobster will be lulled to sleep, not knowing it is to be killed. Most experts account this the humane way of treating lobster.*

"The logs under the cauldron gave a pleasant aroma as they started to splutter. The female was not lulled. She tried to clamber out: perhaps a reflex action. The hound-men placed an iron mesh over the cauldron."

Blake saw what he could not bear to see, heard the unhearable. The Troog's confession was humble.

"The scent was so persuasive. 'Try this piece,' they flashed, 'it is so tender. It will harden your scruples.' I hesitated. Outside came the noise of young Troogs whirling in the joy of satiety. A Nova Feast comes only once in five years. I dipped my hand, *metaphor*"—(even now the Troog pedantry was present)—"in the cauldron. If one must eat protein, it is better to do so in a civilized fashion. And as for the humanity, *metaphor*, of eating protein—I should write Trooghaft—if we ate no capons, who would bother to feed them? If we hunted no quarry, who would make the game-laws or keep the hound-men? At least now they live, as we do, for a season. And while they live, they are healthy. I must stop. My stomach, *metaphor,* sits heavy as a mountain."

As Blake turned in horror from the ancient typewriter, up from his line of retreat, keening

their happiest music, their white teeth flashing, loped three lithe and ruthless hound-men. All around was the squid-like odor of their master.

Interspecific Justice

Donald VanDeVeer

I have never committed an axe-murder, bludgeoned fellow-humans to death, nor eaten any of their babies. Even though I would not think of setting fire to cats (though I am not at all fond of them), I have most of my adult life paid people to axe-murder and bludgeon to death a considerable variety of creatures, some of whom were babies, so that I might eat them; they were, in fact, tasty. That this description applied to my actions or that there were moral questions about these practices is something to which I was largely oblivious until reading Peter Singer's essay 'Animal Liberation' several years ago.[1]

The effect of Singer's early essay was sometimes—and in my case—to shake one from his "dogmatic slumbers." However, before the uptake could secure itself, Singer lost some hard-won credibility near the end of his essay by stating:

What, for instance, are we to do about genuine conflicts of interest like rats biting slum children? I am not sure of the answer, but the essential point is just that we *do* see this as a conflict of interests, that we recognize that rats have interests too.[2]

To be fair, Singer does *not* say or suggest that the interests of rats ought to be weighed equally, but his willingness to consider that there might be a serious moral question here no doubt struck some readers as a *reductio* of his position. A further factor in such a reaction

may be that there is naturally a powerful *desire* to believe that one is not party to morally outrageous practices and that arguments which suggest as much "must" be fallacious. This less than reflective reaction may have occurred, I speculate, with many initial encounters with Singer's essay.

In that essay and more explicitly in Singer's book by the same title, there is a simple, tempting argument in favor of the view that humans have some duties toward animals; one possible reconstruction is this:

1. All or virtually all human beings are sentient creatures.
2. Many animals are sentient creatures.
3. Moral agents have a duty not to cause suffering to sentient creatures.
4. So, moral agents have a duty to refrain from causing suffering to (sentient) humans and (sentient) animals.
5. The interests of *all* sentient creatures (in not suffering) must be given equal consideration.
6. So, the imposition of suffering on animals (an overriding of the duty mentioned in (4)) would have to be justified by grounds of the same moral weight as those which would be necessary to justify the imposition of suffering on humans.[3]

The argument seems plausible, and some of its premises are incontrovertible. Singer's strong and specific admonitions (e.g. to become a vegetarian) in his radical critique of almost universal current practices affecting animals ap-

Source: *Inquiry,* Vol. 22, Nos. 1–2 (Summer 1979), pp. 55–70. Reprinted by permission.

peal to this argument and to further assumptions about (a) the actual effects of existing practices on animals (e.g. experimentation, raising animals for food and other products), (b) judgments about the painfulness or disability of these practices for the animals involved, and (c) the falsity of the claim that certain human satisfactions are obtainable only by harming or killing animals. The first four claims of my reconstruction of Singer's argument are reasonable. What is meant, in (5), by giving the interests of all sentient creatures "equal consideration" is less clear. Does it mean "taking into account" all such interests? Does this mean giving *equal* moral *weight* to like interests? If not, will (6) follow? Further, since killing may be performed painlessly the constraint on causing animals suffering (even if [6] is conceded) cannot yield an adequate basis for deciding on the legitimacy of killing animals if it is done painlessly. It is not my purpose to dwell on Singer's argument in any direct way, although I shall survey some principles which proffer answers to some of the above questions. Of the views to be considered, one emerges which is reasonable and in some important ways stands in agreement with *Animal Liberation*. At points, however, it delineates a competing view on the question of how we may legitimately treat animals. While I shall allude on occasion to the views of those who have taken a stand on these matters in recent literature, e.g. Peter Singer and Tom Regan, I conceive my task as a more constructive than critical one, and I shall try to sketch some of the features which I think must be incorporated in an adequate theory. Since I will focus on conflicts of interests between humans and animals and the question of a just resolution of competing morally relevant claims, one might describe what is needed as a theory of interspecific justice.[4] Questions about the treatment of animals, like questions about non-paradigm humans (e.g. Homo sapiens fetuses) are hard cases, and even if the suggestions posed here are correct, they will fall short of a fully adequate account. Indeed, it seems to me that the formulation of an adequate theoretical basis for the legitimate treatment of animals is no simple task and cannot be done simply by extending, in any straightforward way, principles widely accepted or thought to

be uncontroversial. It is not surprising that some of the recalcitrant problems confronting the formulation of an adequate theory of justice with regard to humans have parallels in attempts to formulate an adequate theory of interspecific justice.

I. Interests and Conflicts of Interests

Of those animals capable of suffering we may assume that they have at least one interest, namely, in not suffering. By this assumption I do not mean that they are interested in not suffering (though they may be) but, roughly, that it *is in their interest* not to suffer. This last claim means that it is not conducive to an animal's well-being to suffer—whether or not the animal is capable of "consciously" wanting not to suffer. Further, the claim that it is not in the interest of an animal to suffer is, I think, a strong presumptive one. While pain *per se* is undesirable, it may be in the interest of animals to suffer *on balance* for the sake of a certain beneficial result—as in the painful removal of a gangrenous leg by surgery—as it is also for human beings. While the concept of an action's being in the interest of a creature is not transparently clear, it is contingently and commonly in the interest of a being not to suffer, although there are exceptions when it is in its over-all interest to do so. Since it is possible to cause death painlessly, an animal in whose interest it is not to suffer *may* not be such that it is in its interest not to die. However, I shall simply assume that *generally* when it is in some creature's interest not to suffer it is also in its interest not to die (and, hence, not to be killed). Let us assume, then,—somewhat more strongly than our earlier (3)—that moral agents have a duty, *ceteris paribus*, not to cause suffering to those animals which can suffer and a duty, *ceteris paribus*, not to cause animals to die. On this view there are many common practices which are not in the interests of many animals, and there is a presumptive duty not to engage in certain practices, namely, any which cause suffering or death to *those* animals in whose interest it is not to suffer or not to die. The troublesome and difficult question which arises, once one is convinced that both human beings (or many) and animals (or many) have at least some morally relevant interests, concerns how to *weigh* their respective interests in general and how to adjudicate *conflicts of interest* which arise between humans and animals. What we crucially need, to advance the current reconsideration of our treatment of animals, is an identification and assessment of principles which provide a basis for comparatively weighing such interests. We may be guided here by the standard method of testing principles by checking their implications against our deepest and strongest pre-theoretical convictions about specific cases ("intuitions" in *one* sense of the term), and also by how well such principles cohere with other defensible principles, in particular, how well principles advocating interspecific discriminations (weightings of respective interests) seem to be consistent with parallel and defensible intraspecific discriminations.[5]

II. Principles of Adjudicating Conflicts of Interests

Singer characterizes views which advocate a certain preferential weighing of human interests over that of animals as "speciesist."[6] He claims:

If a being suffers there can be no moral justification for refusing to take that suffering into consideration. No matter what the nature of the being, the principle of equality requires that its suffering be counted equally with the like suffering—in so far as rough comparisons can be made—of any other being.

The racist violates the principle of equality by giving greater weight to the interests of members of his own race when there is a clash between their interests and the interests of those of another race. The sexist violates the principle of equality by favoring the interests of his own sex. Similarly the speciesist allows the interests of his own species to override the greater interests of members of other species. The pattern is identical in each case.[7]

The quoted passage does not distinguish some relevantly different principles which may be aptly classified as speciesist views and not all of which are equally tempting. I shall identify three forms of speciesism and two non-speciesist views which I shall dub Two Factor Egalitarianism and Species Egalitarianism respectively; the first three principles may be entitled "speciesist" because they all advocate a heavier weighting of human interests over that of animals or do not concede that animals have any interests at all. The fourth principle also weights human interests more heavily but only when certain contingent conditions are satisfied; for reasons mentioned later, it would be misleading to label it a speciesist view. I list the names of the principles here, and consider each in turn:

1. Radical Speciesism
2. Extreme Speciesism
3. Interest Sensitive Speciesism
4. Two Factor Egalitarianism
5. Species Egalitarianism

In turning to Radical Speciesism we consider the only one of the five principles to be identified which in fact is incompatible with the premises of the mentioned argument appealing to animal suffering.

Radical Speciesism

Radical Speciesism is the view that:

It is morally permissible, *ceteris paribus*, to treat animals in any fashion one chooses.

One ground for this claim is the view that there is no *intrinsic* feature of any animal *per se* in virtue of which there is any moral constraint on how it may be treated. I speak of "intrinsic feature" because the radical speciesist may allow that a given animal ought not to be harmed because of its relational trait, e.g. it is Smith's pet. This view is similar to the by now familiar view of Descartes's that animals were mere automata, extended things which neither think nor are sentient. With the further assumption that only thinking or sentient things are such that something may be in their interests, it follows that animals have no interests. So, it could not be the case that the interest of any animal outweighs that of any human being. There seem to be no premises which are both strong enough to entail Radical Speciesism (RS) and plausible. The Cartesian assumption is a strong one but not at all tempting. I shall not explore it. That many animals can and do suffer intensely is quite obvious. The anti-Cartesian arguments may be found elsewhere; in general, they are the arguments against extreme scepticism about Other Minds. Since many animals can suffer, the Cartesian assumption is evidently an untenable view. I include it for purposes of contrast and completeness. The reader may wish to examine the more patient discussions in Singer's book.[8]

What are the moral implications of Radical Speciesism? On RS there is no presumption at all, based on the effects *on the animal,* against putting live puppies in one's oven, and heating them in order to watch them squirm or convulse or fall over; the reader can imagine other "perverse" experiments. The important issue here is simply put. Can animals (some) suffer? If so, it is, in general, in their interest not to suffer and moral agents have a presumptive duty to avoid causing such suffering. Hence, we must judge, if we acknowledge that animals suffer, that RS is mistaken or that the *ceteris paribus* clause is rarely satisfied.

It may be noted that Singer characterizes the "speciesist" as allowing "the interests of his own species to override the greater interests of members of other species" (see earlier quotation). While such unequal weighting of interests seems to be an objectionable feature of other principles which I have dubbed speciesist, it is worth observing that the Cartesian elaboration which may be associated with Radical Speciesism (as part of the ground for the latter) is not speciesist on Singer's criterion, for RS in its Cartesian elaboration does not weigh interests *unequally;* it simply concedes no interests at all to animals.

Those forms of speciesism which allow that animals have interests and which are compatible with the statements constituting the Suffering Argument are those remaining to be considered. They may all be regarded as principles purporting to guide action in cases of *conflicts of interests.* In examining such cases it is desirable to focus, when possible, on cases where the existence of animals is no threat to humans (e.g. not on cases of animals attacking humans) and, when possible, on "normal" before extreme or bizarre situations.

Extreme Speciesism

To distinguish two further forms of speciesism we must suppose that there is a difference between the basic and peripheral interests of a being. It would be difficult to elaborate such a distinction in a precise manner or offer a full-fledged defense of it. It is clear, however, that in the absence of certain sorts of goods many creatures cannot function in ways common to their species; they do not function in a "minimally adequate" way, for example, in the absence of food, water, oxygen or the presence of prolonged, intense pain. We may say that it is in a creature's *basic* interest to have (not have) such things. In contrast there are goods such that in their absence it is true only that the creature does not thrive and which are, then, not in its basic interest (e.g. toys for my dog). This distinction is admittedly vague but it is not empty. Its application must, in part, depend on contextual matters. Given such a distinction, Extreme Speciesism is the view that:

> When there is a conflict of interests between an animal and a human being, it is morally permissible, *ceteris paribus,* so to act that a basic interest of the animal is subordinated for the sake of promoting even a peripheral interest of a human being.

Extreme Speciesism (ES) proffers a different theoretical basis for actions affecting animals from Radical Speciesism when RS is linked to Cartesian assumptions, but, as stated, RS and ES will, in practice, sanction the same policies when there is, in fact, a requisite conflict of interests. When there is not, ES allows (is compatible with) acting to promote an animal interest, e.g. the interest in not suffering. As stated, however, ES would not prohibit puppy cooking and cat torturing as long as such acts promote some peripheral (or basic) human interest. In the end, perhaps, much may depend on *how* peripheral the human interest one is considering is or further discriminations of that sort. Nevertheless, unless we wish to defend the moral permissibility of recreational puppy cooking and like acts, ES must be rejected as well as RS. On ES the kind or level of animal interest involved in a conflict of interests is, in effect, unimportant and need not be considered; this is not true of the next form of speciesism to be considered.

Interest Sensitive Speciesism

Interest Sensitive Speciesism (ISS) is the view that:

> When there is a conflict of interests between an animal and a human being, it is morally permissible, *ceteris paribus*, so to act that an interest of the animal is subordinated for the sake of promoting a *like* interest of a human being (or a more basic one) but one may not subordinate a *basic* interest of an animal for the sake of promoting a *peripheral* human interest.

On this principle what is permissible depends importantly on whether or not the conflicting interests are basic or not; it is, thus, "interest sensitive." This principle sanctions a wide range of treatment preferential to human beings. For example, in a life raft case where the raft is overloaded and about to go under and either I or my dog will die (not both) before rescue, ISS permits me to sacrifice my dog if I so choose. In cases of conflict of *like* interests it is permissible, *ceteris paribus*, to subordinate that of the animal. Anti-speciesist principles which do *not* yield this result are hard to defend. Unlike RS and ES, which also yield this result, ISS does *not* permit puppy cooking or cat torturing for the pleasure of watching them squirm. This fact immediately makes ISS a more viable contender for the appellation, "justifiable form of speciesism."

While ISS clearly permits an evident discrimination in favor of human interests while not, in effect, assigning infinite weight to the latter, it will strike many as giving *insufficient* weight to human interests. For, on ISS, if it is in a bird's interest not to be incarcerated (as in a cage) and this interest is more basic than a hedonistic interest of a human owner in keep-

ing it there, then such acts are impermissible since they would subordinate a basic animal interest in order to promote a peripheral human one. Suppose that having musk perfume, leather wearing apparel or luggage, fur rugs, ivory piano keys, or animal derived glue are not necessary to promote basic human interests. If so, then ISS would entail that killing animals for these purposes would (supposing that doing so violates a basic interest of these animals in continuing to live), *ceteris paribus*, be impermissible. Given the mentioned suppositions some would judge ISS as "too strong" even though it plausibly prohibits cat torturing to promote sadistic pleasure. I leave the question of whether ISS is "too strong" or "too weak" open here. There is a more basic objection to ISS, namely, that it omits consideration of another factor which is morally relevant in adjudicating conflicts of interests.

The objection calls attention, in part, to the enormous diversity *among* animals whose basic interest may conflict with some human interest. In this regard, the use of the expression "speciesism" tends to suggest, perhaps, that we are only dealing with two groups and, hence, encourages formulating principles which suggest the permissibility of some sort of subordination of the interests of members of one group to the interests of members of the other.[9] This perspective reflects our tendency, Jonathan Swift to the contrary, to divide the animal world into the human and non-human or, analogously, into the inedible and the edible.[10] We ought not to forget that there are estimated to be about 1.5 million species and about 10,000 new ones discovered each year.[11] Significant differences *among* non-human species may become ignored with Interest Sensitive Speciesism. If it is in the interest of both an oyster and a chimpanzee not to be killed, ISS only requires that one consider the fact that the interest is in each case a basic and not a peripheral one. However, it is most tempting to think that while both interests are basic, the interest of the chimpanzee is of greater moral weight than that of the oyster, a judgment analogous to the one about the same-level or "like" interests of my dog and myself in my life raft case. If so, then a principle purporting to be a reasonable guide to weighting the interests of members of different species must take account of something other than whether the interests in question are "like" or "unlike." Such a consideration provides a basis for another principle, one to which we may now turn.

Two Factor Egalitarianism

It is necessary, to formulate our next principle, to recognize interests that are not basic in the sense suggested earlier yet not frivolous. I shall call such interests "serious interests." A rough criterion for serious interests would be that something is in a being's serious interest if and only if, though it can survive without it, it is difficult or costly (to its well-being) to do so. Hence, it may be in the serious interest of a lonely child to have a pet or in the serious interest of an eagle to be able to fly. Serious interests are not *as* peripheral as Jones's interest in watching cockfights. It would be less messy if interests did not exhibit degrees of importance to their possessors; unfortunately, they do. This is also true of the other factor considered by the next principle, the factor of psychological capacities.

Two Factor Egalitarianism can now be formulated; it holds that

> When there is an interspecies conflict of interests between two beings, A and B, it is morally permissible, *ceteris paribus*:

1. to sacrifice the interest of A to promote a like interest of B if A lacks significant psychological capacities possessed by B,
2. to sacrifice a basic interest of A to promote a serious interest of B if A substantially lacks significant psychological capacities possessed by B,
3. to sacrifice the peripheral interest to promote the more basic interest if the beings are similar with respect to psychological capacity (regardless of who possesses the interests).[12]

On TFE the subordination of basic animal interests (say, in living or not suffering) may be subordinated if the animal is (significantly) psychologically "inferior" to the human in question. "Psychological" is intended to include the

"mental." Let us conjecture about the implications of TFE; I leave certain assumptions tacit. On TFE killing oysters or (most kinds of) fish for food for human survival would be permissible; killing them only for the human pleasure of doing so would not be. On this view *certain* forms of hunting (recreational killing) would seem to be immoral. Similarly certain rodeo activities and bull-fighting would not be justified. The killing of seals for food by an Eskimo would be justified; the killing (and radical deprivation and suffering) of veal calves by people in agriculturally affluent areas may be wrong.[13] TFE allows the sacrifice of my dog in our life raft case. Many of these implications are plausible. In general, TFE permits scientific experiments on animals where the promised utility for humans and/or animals is very considerable but not otherwise; recent criticisms suggest that a small proportion of the millions of experiments regularly performed can be so categorized.[14] It appears, then, on TFE as well as with some other speciesist principles, that fairly *simple* generalizations about the morality of hunting, killing animals for food, and experiments on animals are unreasonable. This feature of course parallels the difficulties with familiar simple generalizations about when it is permissible to kill or experiment on humans; this consideration is not unfavorable to TFE.

So far I have neglected what will strike the traditionally minded as an unfortunate and "radical" implication of TFE. On TFE if there is a conflict of interests between a human permanently and (seriously) psychologically incapacitated by illness, injury, or senility and, on the other hand, an animal with similar or superior psychological capacities (self-awareness, capacity for purposive action, diverse emotions, affection, devotion, and so on), then the more peripheral interest must be subordinated, and the peripheral interest *may* be that of the human being. If the animal is sufficiently developed psychologically, then even a serious interest of a no more capacitated human should not take precedence over the basic interests of the animal. An example where an "under-capacity" human is involved might be this. Suppose, contrary to fact, that an infant with Tay-Sachs disease could be saved from imminent death by a kidney transplant from a healthy chimpanzee at the expense of the chimpanzee's life; TFE prohibits this way of adjudicating the conflict of interests.[15] This case would be, at best, a statistically unusual one, and is mentioned in the attempt to get clearer about principles which have implications concerning other almost universal practices, e.g. raising and killing animals for certain human purposes. An important general characteristic of TFE is that not *any* interest of *any* human morally outweighs *any* interest of *any* animal, such a consideration seems a desideratum of any acceptable principle. TFE attempts to take into account both the kind of interests at stake and also psychological traits of the beings in question.

If the core of speciesism is the belief that it is permissible to give preferential treatment to humans over animals *just because* the former are human beings, then TFE is not a speciesist view. Being a member of Homo sapiens *per se* is not assumed to justify preferential treatment of humans over animals. It is a matter of fact as to whether a given human being will match or exceed a given animal in terms of psychological capacity; usually humans will. However, TFE allows that if there were, for example, beings physiologically like apes except for large brains and more complicated central nervous systems who had intellectual and emotional lives more developed than mature humans, then in a conflict of *like* interests the interests of these ape-looking persons should take precedence.[16]

We shall return (in Section IV) to further examination of TFE. First, I shall describe a final principle purporting to adjudicate interspecific conflicts of interest. Then I shall turn to the challenge posed by those who are sharply opposed to much of our preferential treatment of humans, with the larger aim of seeing whether any principle proposed here meets the challenge and provides a satisfactory basis for justifying certain preferential treatment of humans over animals.

Species Egalitarianism

In contrast to principles which permit the subordination of animal interests in *a priori* fashion (Radical Speciesism) or do so in practice even when like interests are being considered (Extreme Speciesism), is a view which is distinctly anti-speciesist, one I label Species Egalitarianism.

> When there is a conflict of interests between an animal and a human being it is morally permissible, *ceteris paribus*, to subordinate the more peripheral to the more basic interest and not otherwise; facts not relevant to how basic the interests are, are not morally relevant to resolving this conflict.

SE is a one factor (level of interests) principle in contrast to TFE. Like TFE it plausibly denies that any interest of any human outweighs any interest of any animal. In fact it suggests, in a radical way, that species identification of the possessors of the interests is irrelevant except in so far as this might bear on a non-evaluative description of the interests in question.

It is tempting to call this view "radical egalitarianism" because it allows, like Interest Sensitive Speciesism, no weight to the many impressive and (seemingly) morally relevant psychological differences among species. On this view it is not "where you are on the evolutionary scale" or what psychological capacities you have but only how fundamental your interest is which counts. This view is unacceptable. That we should, for example, equally weigh the interest in not being killed of an oyster, earthworm, or fruitfly with that of a like interest of a human being, is an implication in virtue of which we can summarily judge, I submit, that SE indeed reduces to an absurdity. While Radical and Extreme Speciesism both give undue weight to human interests over that of animals, Species Egalitarianism swings to the opposite error of giving too little. Part of the attraction of the former views may in fact derive from the blatant ignoring of relevant differences which occurs with SE and the assumption that there are no plausible alternative positions. In view of reasons discussed to this point the least counter-intuitive principle appears to be Two Factor Egalitarianism, or possibly some variant of it. Before elaborating on such a view and considering objections to it, it will be useful to consider more thoroughly the challenge posed by those who are critical of current policies toward radically differential treatment of animals and humans. After doing so we will be in a better position to determine whether TFE is acceptable as it is, whether it requires revision, or whether it should be relegated to the wasteland of tempting but, in the end, irrational proposals.

III. The Challenge of the Critics

It has been argued by Tom Regan that the radically differential treatment that we extend toward animals as opposed to human beings cannot be justified unless "we are given some morally relevant difference that characterizes all humans, but no animals"—one that would, in other words, justify the different sorts of duties and/or rights which we commonly assume we have toward the two groups, or attribute to the two groups, respectively.[17] It is tempting to believe (as Regan allows), however, that not all animals have interests, e.g. protozoa. While protozoa, I shall assume, are not *sentient*, perhaps we should allow, to the contrary, that even for protozoa something may be in their interest, e.g. conducive to their well-being. If so, possession of some (at least one) interest will not serve as a difference, possibly a morally relevant one, between all human beings on the one hand and all animals on the other. A feature that *is* possessed by humans but not, however, by all animals is sentience. This feature, since it *is* possessed by many animals, will not, however, satisfy Regan's requirement that we be given "some morally relevant difference that characterizes *all* humans, but *no* animals" (my italics). Such a feature will not, then, serve as a justification, or part of a justification, for radically differential treatment of all humans on the one hand and *all* animals on the other. The presence or absence of sentience is, however, a morally relevant trait, and it *will* serve to justify, or as part of a justification of, differential treatment of sentient creatures on the one hand and non-sentient creatures on the other, e.g. the subordination of certain animals (non-sentient ones) for the sake of the well-being of others (sentient humans and sentient non-humans).

Hence, *some* differential treatment of humans on the one hand and *some* animals on the other is, *ceteris paribus*, justifiable, I believe, without satisfying the stringent requirement that there is "some morally relevant difference that characterizes all humans, but no animals." This conclusion serves to undermine certain arguments prohibiting radically differential treatment of non-sentient animals. The conclusion is, however, a very weak one. For most differential treatment of humans and animals which is controversial involves differential treatment *within* the class of sentient creatures. The challenge posed by critics of established practices toward animals, such as Tom Regan and, possibly, Peter Singer, is more reasonably posed in the following way: to justify radically differential treatment of creatures *all of whom are sentient* it is necessary to identify a morally relevant difference between those who receive preferential treatment and those who do not. Further, any such morally relevant difference must be sufficiently significant to justify the specific differential treatment in question.[18] Of the views previously considered the only one not subject to decisive objections (considered to this point) which also proposes a basis for subordinating the interests of animals when there is a conflict of like interests between humans and sentient animals, is Two Factor Egalitarianism. It, thus, *purports* to provide the requisite morally relevant difference which would serve to justify some, at least, of the radically differential treatment of humans and animals, treatment which is not merely the kind involved in extending preferential treatment to humans over *non-sentient* animals. TFE is, then, of special interest and, in view of current disputes, not uncontroversial. Let us examine it in more detail.

IV. Two Factor Egalitarianism Explored

Two Factor Egalitarianism assumes the relevance of two matters: (1) level or importance of interests to each being in a conflict of interests, and (2) the psychological capacities of the parties whose interests conflict. It is worth considering further the rationale for assuming their relevance. First, consider the importance of the respective interests. In familiar infelicitous situations where a conflict of interests can be resolved only by sacrificing the interest of one party, a plausible principle would seem to be that there is a *presumption* in favor of maximizing utility or at least choosing an alternative which will minimize net disutility.[19] Given our initial crude distinction between basic and peripheral interests we can classify four basic types of conflicts of interests between, to oversimplify, a human and an animal:

human interest	animal interest
1. basic	basic
2. basic	peripheral
3. peripheral	basic
4. peripheral	peripheral

The following examples illustrate (roughly) the above conflicts, e.g. (1) my life versus my dog's in the life raft case, (2) giving up my career to move to a climate where my dog will be happier, (3) my obtaining a new flyswatter by killing a Wildebeest (for its tail), (4) my spending for a new wallet for myself or spending for a toy for my dog. If we suppose that the non-satisfaction of a basic interest yields a greater disutility than the non-satisfaction of a peripheral interest and if the conflict of interests in (2) and (3) is resolved by sacrificing the basic to the peripheral interest, it is tempting to suppose that there is a net loss of aggregate utility. Giving the interests of the animal no weight in calculating utilities in (2) or (3) is speciesism with a vengeance. That tack is an obvious target of current critics of many standard ways in which animals are treated and ways in which their interests are evaluated (if indeed recognized at all). For an example of the latter, to the criticism that DDT usage damages penguins, one writer states

My criteria are oriented to people, not penguins. Damage to penguins . . . is . . . simply irrelevant . . . Penguins are important because people enjoy seeing them walk about rocks . . . I have no interest in preserving penguins for their own sake . . .

it is the only tenable starting place for analysis . . . First, no other position corresponds to the way most people really think and act . . .[20]

On the principle that utility ought to be maximized in adjudicating conflicts of interests, peripheral interests ought to be subordinated to basic ones. Such a principle seems to underlie Interest Sensitive Speciesism. For reasons mentioned earlier such a view is problematic, e.g. if it is in any animal's basic interest to live then killing cockroaches for the sake of a certain convenience to humans would be prohibited. On the assumption that satisfaction (or non-satisfaction) of like interests involves promotion (or non-attainment) of like utilities and the assumption that we should maximize aggregate utility, it is not clear how to resolve conflicts of types (1) and (4). Recall the case of my dog and myself in the overloaded life raft. The conflict is between basic interests; one has to go overboard (assume drowning is then inevitable) so that the other may live. If promoting my dog's interest will promote the same utility as promoting my own, the principle of maximizing utility will fail to require what, intuitively, seems permissible, namely, that I sadly do away with my canine friend.[21]

It is reasonable to believe, however, that in the life raft example the disutilities of my dying and my dog's dying are not really equal, even though the case seems correctly describable as one where a *basic* interest of mine is in conflict with an *equally basic* interest of my dog. But would not the assignment of different utilities to *like interests* be arbitrary—a giving of greater *weight* to interests of my own species over like interests of members of other species—and, hence, in some sense, "speciesist"? The more important question, labels aside, is whether a case can be made for giving *greater weight* to my own interest in such a case as opposed to my dog's.[22] In general, is there a justification for weighting human interests more heavily than *comparable* or *like* interests of animals in cases of conflicts of interests and, thus, justifying the extension of differential treatment toward animals in certain cases where it would not be justified if extended to (most) other humans (e.g. it may be worth comparing a life raft case like the one discussed except that the conflict is between the reader and myself)?[23] Two Factor Egalitarianism assumes an affirmative answer to this question. The basis for doing so is *not* simply that human interests are, after all, *human* interests and necessarily deserving of more weight than comparable or like interests of animals. The ground is rather that the interests of beings with more complex psychological capacities deserve greater weight than those with lesser capacities—up to a point. Let us call this the Weighting Principle.[24] What may be said in defense of the Weighting Principle? I am not sure that an adequate defense can be proposed, but let us consider some possible attempts. It might be proposed that humans are typically subject to certain kinds of suffering that animals are not. For example, humans are typically capable of suffering from the dread of impending disaster (e.g. death from terminal cancer) in a way that animals are not (e.g. a turkey will not be wary of impending Thanksgiving events). This fact, however, may only show that a given type of act (e.g. death sentence) may cause unequal disutilities to an animal and a human. However, the *same amount* of suffering may be imposed on a human and an animal on a given occasion. Would there be any reason for assigning different disutilities to the two acts respectively? There may be if we take into account not just the comparative amounts of suffering on *that* occasion but consequent suffering over time, a factor affected by life span and the capacity to remember. Suppose it were true that the pain experienced by a steer upon being castrated and the pain experienced by a woman who was raped were of the "same amount."[25] The steer would not suffer from the memory of such an experience in the way that women continue to suffer from the trauma of rape, e.g. "reliving" of the experience in dreams, and so on. What such an example suggests is that in cases where a basic interest (e.g. an interest in not being subjected to serious bodily harm) is violated, the different disutilities to the animal and human may be obscured by focusing on the fact that a "basic interest" was violated in *both* cases. The long term disutilities of each individual may be radically different, and whether this is so is very much a function of the psychological capacities of the beings involved. That the *interests* of a

human and an animal are "like or comparable" seems no sure guide to the comparative amounts of harm done in such cases. Hence, in conflicts of *like* interests between humans and animals (basic–basic, or peripheral–peripheral) it may be important to focus on the less obvious and long term disutilities which may accrue in not promoting the interest; focusing on "levels of interest" may fail to take into account matters of importance.

Another and, I believe, overlooked consideration which may be used in defense of the Weighting Principle concerns the economist's notion of "opportunity cost." Generally, in employing one's capital or one's efforts in achieving one goal, the cost of doing so can be thought of as the opportunities thereby forgone, goods and satisfactions that may not be obtained but which could have been if one's capital or efforts were employed in other ways. Most of my examples have focused on cases of inflicting pain or deprivation rather than death. The notion of opportunity cost is a useful one in trying to assign some weight to the imposition of death upon a human or an animal—as well as to weighting the imposition of pain or deprivation upon an animal or a human. Suppose that a group of rabbits is used in testing possibly toxic drugs and that the test is of the LD-50 type, where it is built into the experimental design that the experiment is complete only when fifty percent of the rabbits die (thus, Lethal Dosage—fifty percent).[26] Imagine a comparable test on a group of retarded human beings. Why are we inclined to think that if either experiment (but not both) is justified it must be the one involving rabbits? It need not be, I believe, because we think the suffering of rabbits has no weight. Neither must it be because we would deny that like interests are involved in the two cases. The psychological capabilities of even retarded human beings, such as those suffering from Downs Syndrome, are, however, far greater than those of rabbits. Even with the predictable shorter than normal life span for Downs Syndrome persons, the opportunities for a satisfying life for the retarded which would be forgone in the event of death are enormously greater than those of rabbits—or even, to take a "less favorable" case—those of typical nonhuman primates. Generally, though not necessarily nor in every case, the prospects of satisfaction are qualitatively and quantitatively greater for human beings than for animals. And this fact, this morally relevant fact, is a function of the psychological complexity of the beings in question. Further, it is clear that membership in the species Homo sapiens is no *a priori* guarantee of the existence of greater psychological capacity to experience satisfaction than that which may be possessed by beings of other species. The more basic point is that, generally, the opportunity cost of dying for humans and for animals at comparable ages, barring abnormalities, is vastly greater for the former. The harm, then, of killing in the former case is much greater than in the latter. From the fact, *if it were a fact,* that nothing could be more important to a given human than preservation of his life and that nothing could be more important to a given animal than preservation of its life, it does not follow that the disvalue of the loss of life in the two cases is equal.[27] For reasons mentioned, the discounting of the value of the preservation of the lives of many animals seems reasonable. A principle such as Two Factor Egalitarianism, based in part, then, on the Weighting Principle, is not unreasonable, and need not appeal to species membership *per se* as a basis for assigning unequal weights to like interests of animals and humans respectively.

The extent of discounting the interests of a being, or more generally—weighting its interests—will, on this view, depend on the psychological complexities of the being in question. There is no reason, except to have practical presumptions, to make, *a priori,* generalizations about the capacities of all humans, all animals, all primates, or all chimpanzees. Non-trivial variations in capacity occur in any such group.

The importance of forgone satisfactions, as I have observed in passing, is a function not only of psychological capacity but of life span. The fact that the merciful letting die of quite aged humans with terminal diseases seems more acceptable than failure to extend analogous life preserving treatment to young adult humans, may reflect an implicit acceptance of the view that the opportunity cost of death is

morally relevant and, in fact, a relevant difference in the two cases just mentioned.[28] In that respect, more familiar judgments about the comparative value of preserving human lives suggest that the emphasis here on opportunity cost accords with reflective moral judgments that are made with regard to differential treatment among human beings. Similarly, the general acceptance of allowing seriously defective infants to expire may assume the plausibility of attending to psychological capacity as part of the determination of the value of promoting or sacrificing a basic interest—such as the interest in the preservation of life.

If Two Factor Egalitarianism is correct, and for the reasons mentioned, it will *sometimes* be permissible to do what Singer regards as an arbitrary prejudice, namely, for the speciesist (or any human) to "allow the interests of his own species to override the greater interests of members of other species." The unfortunate implication of Singer's claim that this is impermissible is that it prohibits killing a minimally sentient non-human creature for the sake of a "lesser human interest" in cases where the human's psychological capacities are distinctly more complex. TFE is not anthropocentric in the way that a view is if it regards species membership in Homo sapiens as relevant *per se.* The latter assumption is what Singer takes to be invidious and arbitrary about views he labels speciesist. On this point Singer is right. If Singer, or others, were to claim that TFE is also invidious and arbitrary in its "psychocentric" emphasis, reasons need to be stated other than that it takes species membership *per se* as relevant; for it does not.

V. Some Persistent Difficulties

To this point I have argued that among the widely divergent proposals considered (Radical Speciesism, etc.), Two Factor Egalitarianism best accords with both matters of fact and considered and not unreasonable pre-theoretical convictions about how we ought to resolve conflicts of interests between humans and animals. Thus, it seems the most plausible among the five positions considered. I have further suggested an answer (or part of one) to the basic challenge posed by critics of our treatment of animals (as I would pose it): to justify radically differential treatment of creatures all of whom are sentient it is necessary to identify a morally relevant difference between those who receive preferential treatment and those who do not. The difference proposed is psychological complexity in so far as that bears on the capacity of the entity to live a satisfying life; further, to the extent that the entity lacks capacities necessary for such, it is reasonable to discount its interests. The thorny question of what counts as a reasonable discounting I have not tried to settle. I have further argued that TFE avoids the counter-intuitive implications of Singer's principle of equality which requires (of *any* being) "that its suffering be counted equally with the like suffering—in so far as rough comparisons can be made—of any other being." As I understand the principle it focuses on actual suffering and not also on forgone satisfactions. Further, TFE avoids the charge of taking species membership *per se* as a morally relevant difference serving to justify interspecific differential treatment. If the argument so far is correct (perhaps even, approximately correct), TFE stands as the most reasonable approach.

Nevertheless, TFE is subject to a number of objections not yet considered, some of which are obvious and some of which are not. Most evident, the principle is vague. There is no precise way of determining which interests are basic, which serious, and which are more peripheral or how to rank interests precisely. Similarly, no adequate account has been offered of how to determine levels of psychological complexity. I will not dwell on these problems. If they are relevant (I believe they are) we must do the best we can; perhaps these difficulties are *no more* difficult than those faced in analogous problems of intraspecies conflicts of interests. These difficulties do not strike me as *decisive* ones; in any case I do not pursue them here.

TFE is, I believe, more troubling in another respect. In regarding level of psychological complexity as morally important (rather than, say, possession or lack of fur, feathers, a tail, or claws) it may require or allow that the interests of human beings need not be assigned equal weight where it is the case that there are significant empirical differences among humans in terms of psychological capacity. If an implication exists that the interests of dull, psychologically less complicated humans (the retarded? the senile? the brain damaged?) need not be counted as much as that of other humans (in the process of coming to some all-things-considered moral judgment about acts affecting them and perhaps others), it will be tempting to judge that accepting TFE would commit one to sanctioning intraspecific injustices—perhaps on the conviction that "all human beings are of equal intrinsic worth" or convictions which appear to demand that the like interests of all human beings must be assigned equal moral weight initially regardless of final specific moral judgments. The worry is, generally, that a tempting basis for making *interspecific* discrimination entails possibly counter-intuitive results with regard to *intraspecific* discriminations.

Is there any way of reasonably weighting interests based on the psychological capacities of interest holders which will not commit one who does so to policies of intraspecific (human) discrimination of an objectionable sort. A simple principle—give greater weight to the interests of a being with greater psychological capacity than one with less, proportionately—may indeed lead to objectionable discrimination. But a plausible weighting principle need not look like this. We may well regard it as an arbitrary and unjustified extension of differential treatment to offer, other things being equal, to finance the college education of one of our children with an "I.Q." of 140 but to refuse to do so for another with an "I.Q." of 120. Possession of a capacity beyond a certain degree may not count as a morally relevant difference. Beyond a certain threshold point it may. It might not be unjustified to refuse such support for a Downs Syndrome child. Suppose we adopt a bright chimpanzee and a quite retarded Downs Syndrome child. Would it be permissible to torture either? Intuitively: no. Would it be permissible to extend differential treatment to them regarding the provision of educational opportunities? Intuitively, one would think so. My more general point is that differences in psychological capacity may, up to a point, not justify differential treatment. Beyond a certain point they may, and whether they do may depend in part on the kind of differential treatment we are considering and what difference it might make to the prospective satisfactions or dissatisfactions of the beings considered. For example, virtually all human beings are capable of understanding promises and forming expectations of their being kept. Wide variations in psychological capacity exist alongside this particular capacity. These variations may provide no reason for justifying differing presumptions about the importance of promise keeping for these humans. It is not evident that any non-human is capable of understanding promises, although some certainly seem to form expectations.[29]

To clarify, a weighting principle may recognize threshold points. Possession of certain capacities (e.g. intelligence) above a certain point may preclude certain forms of differential treatment. Below a certain point it may not. These assumptions may justify certain forms of interspecific discrimination. They also may serve to justify *certain* forms of intraspecific discrimination (among humans), e.g. treating differently an anencephalic infant, a Downs Syndrome infant, and a normal infant.[30] Because of the recognition of the importance of threshold considerations it is not obvious that a weighting principle, if applied, would lead to *objectionable* forms of intraspecific discrimination. So, the genuine worry about such a consequence does not evidently disqualify TFE (or some variant on it), which presupposes a weighting principle, from consideration. If so, more needs to be said, but I shall make no attempt to say it here (at least partly because it is beyond *my* capacity).

For the reasons discussed TFE seems more adequate than other proposals about how we ought to treat animals—in spite of its deficiencies. Some of its deficiencies may be remedied by a more specific, determinate statement of a variant on TFE. Further, supplementary principles are needed to elaborate and defend distinctions among levels of interests, as well as an elaboration of which psychological capacities are relevant or which sets of such capacities are relevant (and relevant to different forms of proposed differential treatment). That such supplementary assumptions are necessary complicates what may be called, appropriately, a theory of interspecific justice. That such a theory would be complicated may be disappointing; most of us hope for and value simplicity in a theory. TFE is not itself complicated, from one standpoint. It explicitly recognizes only two considerations as morally relevant in adjudicating interspecific conflicts of interests (levels of interests and psychological complexity of the beings). As noted, however, these considerations need more complicated elaboration and defense. Given the difficulties commonly acknowledged today in formulating and defending principles of justice for human interaction, it should not be surprising that plausible principles for just interspecific interactions turn out to be not readily or easily formulated.

In testing the proposed principles I have depended considerably on what I take to be thoughtful pre-theoretic convictions about how specific conflicts ought to be or may permissibly be resolved. Some may claim that this approach is wrong-headed at the outset, but I will leave it to others to say why. More likely, some will claim that the convictions invoked are a by-product of prejudice or are uniquely mine. I do not find this obvious, and I have tried to show that distinctions among levels of interests are supposed by those who take a somewhat different view of these matters, e.g. Peter Singer. I have also indicated how some limited weighting of interests is presupposed in what appears to be reasonable albeit differential treatment of human beings. If the admittedly incomplete account presented here is approximately correct, then certain general criteria are available for assessing which sorts of subordination of animal interests are justifiable and which are not. That some subordination of animal interests is, in general, acceptable and that some is not is evident. The important and more practical task of ascertaining which is which remains. In general, the implications of the position defended here will, I think, neither sanction many common dealings with animals nor lend support to some of the sweeping condemnations of preferential treatment set out by recent critics. But a more moderate position on the proper treatment of animals must, I think, side with recent critics in judging much of the prevailing wholesale disregard of the basic interests of higher animals as unconscionable.[31]

Notes

1. Peter Singer's essay "Animal Liberation" appeared in *The New York Review of Books* (April 5, 1973), pp. 10–15.

2. Ibid., p. 15.

3. Later references will be to Singer's book, *Animal Liberation*, Avon Books, New York 1977. In that book Singer emphasizes that his primary moral assumption is "the principle of equality" which does not require identical treatment of but "equal consideration" of beings with interests (pp. 3, 6). Further, beings with interests are only those with a capacity for suffering and enjoyment (p. 8). Recognizing complexities about killing, as opposed to the imposition of pain, he claims that "the conclusions that are argued for in this book flow from the principle of minimizing suffering alone" (p. 22). Given this last emphasis and Singer's rejection of any necessity to couch his position in terms of animal rights (see Peter Singer, "The Fable of the Fox and the Unliberated Animals," *Ethics*, Vol. 88, No. 2 [January 1978], p. 122), I have chosen to reconstruct his argument as above.

4. The parallel with current theories of justice "for" human beings, theories which attempt to adjudicate conflicting interests, is evident.

5. Of course, the radical subordination of certain *human* interests (those of "natural slaves") seemed intuitively innocent and natural to Aristotle, and, as J. S. Mill noted in *The Subjection of Women*, it is a standard mark of a deeply held prejudice that it seem perfectly *natural* to the one who holds it. There is always the danger of accepting only those principles which are compatible with our prejudices.

6. For aesthetic reasons I would prefer use of "specieism," but to avoid multiplication of variants I adhere to the current use of "speciesism."

7. Singer, op. cit., pp. 8–9.

8. Ibid., pp. 9–15.

9. It is worth noting a dissimilarity between racism or sexism on the one hand and speciesism on the other, namely, that in the former cases those whose interests are subordinated are biologically "homogeneous" with their subordinators but not in the latter case.

10. See Stanley Godlovitch, "Utilities" in *Animals, Men, and Morals*, Taplinger Publishing Company, New York 1972, p. 181.

11. A. J. Cain, *Animal Species and Their Evolution*, Harper & Row, New York 1960.

12. It would be plausible to add: (4) to use a fair (e.g. random) procedure to decide whose interest should be sacrificed if the beings are psychologically similar and the interests are like. But see the (here unincorporated) consideration in Note 19.

13. See Singer, op. cit., pp. 122–8.

14. Ibid., Ch. 2.

15. The Tay-Sachs infant will die "soon" anyway, typically by the age of five or six years and will suffer in the interim. Its interest in continuing to exist may, then, be less basic than that of the healthy chimpanzee in continuing to live. The capacities of the infant may not exceed those of the chimpanzee at the time supposed.

16. See the intriguing fictionalized thought-experiment in Desmond Stewart's "The Limits of Trooghaft" in Tom Regan and Peter Singer (Eds.), *Animal Rights and Human Obligations*, Prentice Hall, Englewood Cliffs, New Jersey 1976, pp. 238–45.

17. Tom Regan, "The Moral Basis of Vegetarianism," *Canadian Journal of Philosophy*, Vol. 5, No. 2 (October 1975), pp. 181–214.

18. Without this qualification (sufficiently . . .), someone might argue that since there is a morally relevant difference between those who commit traffic violations and those who do not, it is justified to extend capital punishment to the former but not the latter.

19. I have so far deliberately ignored a complicating factor which seems relevant, namely, how a conflict of interest arises. A fuller account of things should consider this; I make no such attempt here. To elaborate, however, conflicts of interests sometimes arise only because one party *wants* what another has, and resolution of such a conflict *may not* be a matter of balancing legitimate claims. There may be a conflict of interests between my neighbor and myself since I want his new car, or between a rapist and his victim. Many of the conflicts of interests between humans and animals are generated by human desires to do

what is harmful to animals; we eat them more than they eat us.

20. William F. Baxter, *People or Penguins: The Case for Optimal Pollution*, Columbia University Press, New York 1974, p. 5.

21. Considering utilities or disutilities to others would likely weight the case in favor of my preservation—solely on grounds of maximizing aggregate utility. But we can imagine cases where this would not be so; in any case I exclude such considerations above by assumption.

22. The relation between having rights and having interests is not clear. It is doubtful that having interests is sufficient for having rights (on this see the discussions by myself and James Rachels in Tom Regan and Peter Singer's anthology, *Animal Rights and Human Obligations*, Prentice Hall, Englewood Cliffs, New Jersey 1976, pp. 205–32). More plausible is the claim that any entity having rights must also have interests. If so, at least many entities having interests also have rights. If the interests of rightholders are regarded as very important, according those interests may be thought to be sufficiently important to override the *interests* of others—or, and this seems not insignificant—the *rights* of others (who have not only interests but rights). For example, Lawrence Haworth, who defends the view that some nonhumans have rights, maintains that when the latter rights conflict with "worthy human interests . . . then it is in general reasonable to give preference to these human concerns and violate . . . the rights of nonhumans." See Lawrence Haworth, "Rights, Wrongs, and Animals," *Ethics*, Vol. 88, No. 2 (January 1978), p. 100.

So *even if* it is allowed that some animals have *rights*, the *weightings* of the respective interests in interspecific conflicts of interests are important and may affect our ultimate "on balance" judgments concerning justified violations (or justified infringements) of rights. Hence, my aims in the text are not, I think, irrelevant *even if* it is shown that animals have rights (short of being unqualifiedly "absolute").

23. Again, I simplify. Assume that neither of us owns the boat, has a special duty to sacrifice for the other, consents to die, or agrees to "draw straws."

24. The notion of psychological complexity needs further elaboration. I do have in mind complexity bearing on capacity to experience satisfaction and dissatisfaction. After all there might be a type of psychological complexity *not* conducive to a greater capacity to experience satisfaction. Suppose a micro-computer could be implanted in a turkey so that it became an excellent chess player but in other respects remained turkey-like, e.g. still did not worry about the prospect of Thanksgiving rituals.

25. I am, of course, by-passing all sorts of difficulties about the possibility of having a cardinal measure of utility and making "interbeing" comparisons of utilities.

26. On this type of test, see Peter Singer, op. cit., p. 48.

27. While the death of an animal or a human results in its forgoing *all* the potential satisfactions either could have, still the quantity of such satisfactions would typically be different for each. Hence it is reasonable to conclude that the disvalue of the death of a normal animal is less than the disvalue of the death of a normal human (at similar stages in typical life spans) even though the death of each involves a total loss of their respective potential satisfactions. The difference in disvalues is partly a function of whatever differences there are in respective psychological capacities.

28. Compare the absence of capacities in aged humans due to their waning, their absence in defective humans, and their absence in young normal animals. Absence of capacities may be a result of natural decline, injury, disease, or one's genetic lot.

29. Who would not feel some sense of betrayal when an aged dog eagerly gets in the car for a ride but does not know that it is being taken to be put to death (commonly: "to sleep")? Further, it will not surprise me if communications with non-human primates, in Ameslan, provides evidence of a capacity for understanding promises or, indeed, a sense of regret or remorse.

30. It does not seem to me that one should shrink from the view that *some* weighting of human interests and, hence, *some* differential treatment of humans is justified. There is great danger that I shall be misunderstood here—as approving in some degree the sorts of unequal consideration intrinsic to repulsive doctrines commonly labeled racist, sexist, or Nazi-like. Respect for persons requires respecting their interests but not, I think, giving equal weight to them.

31. With regard to various facets of this essay I

have benefited from discussions with my colleagues, W. R. Carter, Robert Hoffman, Harold Levin, Tom Regan, and Alan Sparer—as well as the writings of both Tom Regan and Peter Singer. Any or all are, of course, entitled to complain that I did not benefit enough.

Trans-species Organ Transplantation

LOMA LINDA, Calif. (AP)—A baboon heart was transplanted into a 15-day-old girl because the animals are plentiful and their hearts are similar to the human organ, says the doctor who performed the historic operation.

Other species of apes might make better donors, but many of them are endangered, Dr. Leonard L. Bailey said in a release issued Saturday by Loma Linda University Medical Center.

Six of Loma Linda's Animal Care Facility's home-bred baboons, ranging from 4 months to 1 year, were tested for tissue compatibility with "Baby Fae," the girl who was given a baboon heart Friday because her own heart wasn't fully developed, spokeswoman Jayne McGill said.

Bailey said the field was narrowed to two donors, then to one after a five-day blood test.

"We're not in the business of uselessly sacrificing animals," the doctor said. "But we're forced here to make a choice—we can either decide to continue to let these otherwise healthy human babies die, because they are born with only half of their heart, or we can intervene and, in so doing, sacrifice some lesser form than our own human species."

The internal structure of the baboon's heart is similar to that of a human heart.

"The baboon has only two (aortic) arch vessels, while the human heart usually has three, but for all practical purposes, the internal structure of the baboon heart is virtually the same as the human heart," Bailey said.

Some normal human hearts also have only two aortic arch vessels.

Adult male baboons weigh as much as 90 pounds, females about half that, according to the Encyclopaedia Britannica, but Bailey said the ape's heart should grow larger in a human than it would in a baboon.

"There's nothing to suggest that the heart won't respond to the internal milieu of the baby," he said. "That's certainly been true in all our experimental work and is a well-recognized phenomenon in kidney and liver" transplants.

"Of the primates, there is evidence that the chimpanzee, orangutan or gorilla may be a better donor," Bailey said. "The problem with all of those is availability. They are either endangered species or don't procreate well in captivity.

"Baboons procreate readily in captivity," he said. "They are a problem in indigenous areas, where they are known to actually kill children every year, destroy crops and swarm over the countryside."

He emphasized that the baboons were treated with respect at the Seventh-day Adventist university's facility, where they are bred to become transplant donors. Female baboons normally have only one offspring at a time, after a seven-month pregnancy.

Baboons inhabit mostly rocky, dry areas of Africa and Arabia, living in large troops with well-developed hierarchies of leaders and subordinates. They are considered highly intelligent.

They have large canine teeth that make them dangerous adversaries, large heads and hairless, doglike muzzles ending in the nostrils. Their fur is coarse.

The Loma Linda Animal Care Facility is run by Dr. Charles Hunter, a veterinarian and associate professor of surgery at Loma Linda University School of Medicine.

Source: *Raleigh News and Observer* (Oct. 28, 1984), from The Associated Press. Reprinted by permission.

The Broader Environment: Other Lives of Value?

Land and Trees: Inanimate Victims?

Preview

The animal liberation movement grew up in partial independence of the ecology movement. The former movement, as we have seen in the last section, has tended to focus on particular abuses of individual animals by human beings. A global view tends to be absent. Broader issues such as overpopulation, species protection, and even concern for wild animals and their environment have been less central. We now turn to these larger questions: land and trees, species, wilderness.

Historical Movements: Conservation and Preservation

The *conservation movement* had scientific roots. Some of its leaders, like Gifford Pinchot (1865–1914), came from fields such as forestry. Its typical emphasis was wise management of resources over the long run.

Pinchot favored commercial development of the U.S. forest reserves for present and future American citizens. In his book *The Fight For Conservation* he maintained:

The first great fact about conservation is that it stands for development. There has been a fundamental misconception that conservation means nothing but the husbanding of resources for future generations. There could be no more serious mistake. Conservation does mean provision for the future, but it means also and first of all the recognition of the right of the present generation to the fullest necessary use of all the resources with which this country is so abundantly blessed. Conservation demands the welfare of this generation first, and afterward the welfare of the generations to follow. The first principle of conservation is development, the use of the natural resources now existing on this continent for the benefit of the people who live here now.[1]

Pinchot further emphasized that forest resources should not fall into the hands of the powerful few, for example, corporations, but should be used to make homes for the plain American citizen. Pinchot, who in 1905 became head of the newly established U.S. Forest Service, once told the Society of American Foresters, "The object of our forest policy is not to preserve the forests because they are beautiful . . . or because they are refuges for the wild creatures of the wilderness . . . but . . . the making of prosperous homes."[2] As a spokesperson for the conservationist movement and a supporter of President Theodore Roosevelt's policies, he said, "If we succeed, there will exist upon this continent a sane, strong people, living through the centuries in a land subdued and controlled for the service of the people, its rightful masters, owned by the many and not by the few."[3]

Pinchot was opposed by the *preservationist movement* headed by John Muir (1838–1914), founder of the Sierra Club. Muir wanted to preserve wilderness for aesthetic and spiritual reasons:

Watch the sunbeams over the forest awakening the flowers, feeding them every one, warming, reviving the myriads of the air, setting countless wings in motion—making diamonds of dewdrops, lakes, painting the spray of falls in rainbow colors. Enjoy the great night like a day, hinting the eternal and imperishable in nature amid the transient and material.[4]

For Muir, nature provides an experience of the sacred or holy. The experience is not simply one of inspiration, but one of recognition of the divine in nature. As Muir once reported his experience of a stroll in the woods: "How beautiful and fresh and Godful the world began to appear."[5]

One famous example of the opposition between the conservationists and the preservationists is the controversy over the Hetch Hetchy Valley in California. Muir and his followers fought for the protection of the Hetch Hetchy Valley in the Yosemite National Park. The city of San Francisco wanted to dam the area, thus flooding the park, and construct a reservoir. Pinchot, whose colleagues contemptuously referred to the preservationists as "nature lovers," threw his support behind James R. Garfield, Secretary of the Interior, who approved the city's request to build a dam. Both Pinchot and Muir brought pressure to bear on President Theodore Roosevelt who, in the end, supported Pinchot.

Despite their differences, it can be argued that both traditions, conservationism and preservationism, were anthropocentric. If so, whether the Hetch Hetchy Valley is used as a water supply for human beings or as a source of peak experiences for humans, its value lies in human use.[6] Nonetheless, one can find in the writings of Muir the idea that nature has value independent of human beings.

Rocks have a kind of life not so different from ours as we imagine. Anyhow their material beauty is only a veil covering spiritual beauty—a divine incarnation—instonation.[7]

Although this independent value may not be independent of a pantheistic view of nature, it is nevertheless independent of human beings.[8] As such, Muir and his followers influenced Aldo Leopold and later advocates of "the land ethic" and the rights of trees (those who claim that nature has value in itself or for its own sake). One of the tasks of this section is to investigate the various grounds for attempting to establish the independent value of nature.

John Rodman warns that the contemporary environmental movement is in some danger of being torn between two points of view that parallel the old conservationist/preservationist division.

On the one hand are the "Enlightened Egoists" who claim to calculate that it is useful and necessary to save the California Condor or the Furbish Lousewort in order for the human species or human civilization to survive. On the other hand are the "Nature Moralists" who would insist we have a duty to save, or at least not to exterminate, condors and louseworts because they have a right to exist.[9]

It is precisely these concerns that are reflected in one contemporary distinction between *deep* and *shallow* ecology. First, a comment may be in order about unfamiliar terminology. Whenever important distinctions need to be made, technical terminology is coined for this purpose. But the creation and standardization of technical terminology is a process that takes time, and environmental ethics as we know it today is a comparatively new field. Thus, the reader should beware that the terms *shallow* and *deep* are not used uniformly. Still, it is important to get as clear an understanding as we can of terms that are often used in the contemporary literature.

Deep ecology often is contrasted with *shallow ecology*. According to Tom Regan[10] and Edward Johnson,[11] shallow ecology is the view that nature has no value apart from the needs, interests, and good of human beings. The recognition of our status as dependent members of the biosphere is a matter of prudence. As Robin Attfield notes, trees and plants "are needed by humans many times over . . . we should literally starve and suffocate without them."[12] Hence, shallow ecology is concerned with issues such as pollution, resource depletion, and overpopulation because vital human interests are at stake. Deep ecology holds that nature has value in its own right independent of the interests of humans. Thus, proper treatment of the environment is based on something other than the value of human beings.

A Divided American Mentality

Pioneers and Puritans, says Thomas Merton, viewed nature as something to be dominated, destroyed, or transformed. Over against this tradition, transcendentalists romanticized the wild and a human need for it, thus creating a wilderness myth. Although Merton claims these conflicting traditions account for an ambiguity in the American mentality vis-à-vis nature, his main concern is with the "stupendous ecological damage" that resulted from frontier ethics and puritanical notions. However much we may claim to hold the wilderness in esteem, we have destroyed much of nature. Merton thinks that the idea that nature should be conquered and exploited is influenced by the American myth of virility. "To be in the wilderness without fighting it, or at least without killing the animals in it, is regarded as a feminine trait."[13] In the end, Merton finds the answer in Aldo Leopold's "ecological conscience," crediting Leopold with

bringing into "clear focus one of the most important moral discoveries of our time."[14]

The Origins of Environmental Ethics

Aldo Leopold (1887–1948) is a major figure in the emergence of contemporary ecological/environmental ethics. His ethical views, often referred to as "the land ethic," are found in his book, *A Sand County Almanac*. In this most influential work, Leopold tells the story of Odysseus who, after returning from the wars of Troy, hanged a dozen female slaves whom he suspected of misconduct. Because Odysseus thought of slaves as property, his concept of ethical obligation did not extend to them. He felt that he could dispose of them as he wished. Leopold draws an analogy between the former status of slaves and the current status of land. Land, Leopold argues, should not be viewed as property. The land ethic extends moral concern to "soils, waters, plants, and animals, or collectively: the land."[15] Land in Leopold's view is not a commodity that belongs to us, but a community to which we belong.[16]

A study of Leopold's work raises a host of important questions. Leopold advocated a harmonious relationship with the land. The land ethic, he said, "changes the role of *Homo sapiens* from conqueror of the land-community to plain member and citizen of it. It implies respect for his fellow-members, and also respect for the community as such."[17] But what does this respect entail? Respect for land, in his view, does not mean leaving it alone, since Leopold believed that we can alter it for the better. "The swampy forests of Caesar's Gaul were utterly changed by human use—for the better. Moses' land of milk and honey was utterly changed—for the worse."[18] In Leopold's view, an harmonious, as opposed to an exploitative, relationship with nature does not imply, as Merton suggests, that humans will refrain from killing animals. One might view this aspect of Leopold's position as macho. As John Rodman characterizes Leopold's view, "it would be pretentious to talk of a land ethic until we have . . . shot a wolf (once) and looked into its eyes as it died."[19]

It is clear that Leopold intended to extend moral standing to things that are not themselves individual humans or animals. This view we shall label Leopold's maxim: "A thing is right when it tends to preserve the integrity, stability, and beauty of the biotic community. It is wrong when it tends otherwise."[20] Leopold's views take us beyond anthropocentrism and individualism. In so doing, his views are often referred to as *holistic*. Roughly speaking, holism is the view that the entire biosphere as an interconnected system has moral standing. One clear expression of holism in a principled form is Leopold's famous maxim quoted above. One of the controversial questions addressed in later selections is whether Leopold's maxim implies that concern for the biotic system should take precedence over a more traditional concern for individuals.

The Expanding Circle

Christopher Stone, a law professor at the University of Southern California, has written an important little book entitled, *Should Trees Have Standing?* Stone, like Leopold, sees the history of moral development as an extension of the scope of our moral concern. Originally, Stone said, "each man had regard only for himself and those of a very narrow circle about him."[21] As we have seen, the circle that Aristotle drew was very narrow indeed. What we have done, according to Stone, is to view many beings and entities in the world as less than persons, and indeed as objects or things in the world that exist only for the use of persons. Our law increasingly has reflected a shift from this view by "making persons of children . . . prisoners, aliens, women (especially of the married variety), the insane, Blacks, foetuses, and Indians."[22] Many authors in this volume argue against the notion that nature exists solely for the use of human beings. Some believe that such a denial points the way to expanding the

circle of right-holders to include environmental objects such as trees and streams.

Stone suggests that as we become more sensitive we add more and more previously rightless entities to the list of persons. (A similar thesis is advocated by Laurence Tribe in a later essay: "The human capacity for empathy and identification is not static; the very process of recognizing *rights* in those higher vertebrates with whom we can already empathize could well prove the way for still further extensions as we move upward along the spiral of moral evolution.")[23] Stone's remarks on sensitivity and empathy raise questions about the role of rational argument in ethics. On what basis is the law "making persons"? In Stone's view, it is only when we perceive nature as like us that we will be able to generate the love and empathy for the environment that in turn will enable us to attribute rights to it. Does such a thesis imply that rights should be attributed to all things cute and cuddly? Suppose we identify with human fetuses. Do they have rights on that account? Must E.T. be rightless if we do not empathize with him (it)? Is there anything in the universe we will not add to the list of persons assuming we can empathize with it? Should our capacities for empathy be a determining factor in ascertaining what sorts of things possess rights?

Legal Standing

Justice Douglas, in the U.S. Supreme Court case *Sierra* v. *Morton*, 1972, cited Stone's book in support of his dissenting opinion that "Contemporary public concern for protecting nature's ecological equilibrium should lead to the conferral of standing upon environmental objects to sue for their own preservation."[24] In this landmark case, the Sierra Club tried to prevent Walt Disney Enterprises, Inc. from building a ski resort in the Mineral King Valley adjacent to Sequoia National Park. The case was not decided on the relative merits of ski resorts versus natural beauty. Rather, it was decided on the issue of standing to sue.

"Whether a party has a sufficient stake in an otherwise justiciable controversy to obtain judicial resolution of that controversy is what has traditionally been referred to as the question of standing to sue."[25] The law requires that the party seeking review must have suffered an injury or been adversely affected. The Court decided in favor of Disney and against the Sierra Club. After all, it is hard to say that the Sierra Club members suffered an injury simply because others like to ski. Mineral King Valley might have received legal consideration if trees and streams had standing to sue for their own preservation and/or injury. Much of Stone's essay is a plea for a liberalized domain of legal standing. Since trees cannot initiate proceedings on their own behalf, Stone recommends a guardianship approach similar to the one we have now with respect to incompetent human beings. Incompetent humans have legal rights even if they are unable to claim them for themselves, for example, rights to essential medical treatment.

Stone's remarks about the "planetarization" of consciousness suggest that he believes that everything in the universe is at some level conscious. Claims of this sort are at least controversial; by many they are thought to be preposterous and/or false. Stone, of course, intends some connection between the consciousness of trees and the rights of trees, but he does not spell it out in any moral theory of rights.

Robin Attfield, in an essay to follow, carefully examines a number of moral notions vis-à-vis trees. Do trees have a good of their own? Do trees have interests? Do trees care about how they are treated? Are they intrinsically good? Do trees have moral rights? Attfield believes that although trees have intrinsic value and quite possibly moral rights, they do not rank very high. The rights of trees, he says, like all other rights are "overridable from time to time: and the grounds for them, the intrinsic value of trees, would be so slender by comparison with other rights as to be outweighed most of the time, so much so as to disappear into near oblivion."[26] As the moral community gets larger, so do the problems of adjudicating conflicts. The problems of conflict and ranking are central to making progress in adjudicating con-

flicts of interests in environmental disputes. Such problems are discussed at greater length in Parts III and IV.

Notes

1. Gifford Pinchot. *The Fight for Conservation* (Seattle: University of Washington Press, 1910), pp. 42–43.

2. Samuel P. Hays. *Conservation and the Gospel of Efficiency: The Progressive Conservation Movement, 1890–1920* (Cambridge: Harvard University Press, 1959), pp. 41–42.

3. Gifford Pinchot. *The Fight for Conservation*, p. 27.

4. *John Muir. To Yosemite and Beyond, Writings from the Years 1863 to 1875*, edited by Robert Engberg and Donald Wesling (Madison: University of Wisconsin Press, 1980), p. 113.

5. *John Muir. To Yosemite and Beyond*, p. 27. Ian Barbour notes that "a recent study found that the majority of Sierra Club members considered aesthetic and spiritual experience more important than recreation or resource conservation as motives for wilderness preservation. Ian G. Barbour, *Technology, Environment, and Human Values* (New York: Praeger Publishers, 1980), p. 83.

6. Samuel Hays makes a similar point when he says that the crux of the controversy was over two public uses of the area: water supply and recreation. *Conservation and the Gospel of Efficiency*, p. 193.

7. *John Muir. To Yosemite and Beyond*, p. 113.

8. John Rodman suggests this in "Four Forms of Ecological Consciousness Reconsidered," *Ethics and the Environment*, edited by Donald Scherer and Thomas Attig (Englewood Cliffs: Prentice-Hall, 1983), p. 85.

9. Remarks made by John Rodman quoted in *Footprints on the Planet, A Search for an Environmental Ethic*, by Robert Cahn (New York: Universe Books, 1978), p. 221.

10. Tom Regan. Preface to "Environmental Ethics and the Ambiguity of the Native American's Relationship with Nature," *All That Dwell Therein: Essays on Animal Rights and Environmental Ethics* (Berkeley: University of California Press, 1982), p. 207.

11. Edward Johnson. "Treating the Dirt," *Earthbound: New Introductory Essays in Environmental Ethics* (New York: Random House, 1984), p. 352.

12. Robin Attfield. "The Good of Trees," *Journal of Value Inquiry* 15(1981), p. 47.

13. Thomas Merton. "The Wild Places," *The Center Magazine* 1 (July 1968), p. 43.

14. Thomas Merton. "The Wild Places," p. 44.

15. Aldo Leopold. *A Sand County Almanac* (New York: Ballantine Books, 1970), p. 239.

16. Aldo Leopold. *A Sand County Almanac*, p. xviii.

17. Aldo Leopold. *A Sand County Almanac*, p. 240.

18. Aldo Leopold. "The Conservation Ethic," *Journal of Forestry* 31 (1933), p. 636.

19. John Rodman. "The Liberation of Nature?" *Inquiry* 20 (1977), p. 110.

20. Aldo Leopold. *A Sand County Almanac*, p. 262.

21. Christopher Stone. *Should Trees Have Standing? Toward Legal Rights for Natural Objects* (Los Altos, Calif.: William Kaufmann, Inc., 1974), p. 3.

22. Christopher Stone. *Should Trees Have Standing*, p. 4.

23. Laurence H. Tribe. "Ways Not to Think about Plastic Trees," *The Yale Law Journal* 83 (June 1974), p. 1345.

24. *Sierra v. Morton*, 70–34, April 19, 1972.

25. *Sierra v. Morton*, quoted in Stone, p. 62.

26. Robin Attfield. "The Good of Trees," pp. 52, 53.

The Land Ethic

Aldo Leopold

When god-like Odysseus returned from the wars in Troy, he hanged all on one rope a dozen slave-girls of his household whom he suspected of misbehavior during his absence.

This hanging involved no question of propriety. The girls were property. The disposal of property was then, as now, a matter of expediency, not of right and wrong.

Concepts of right and wrong were not lacking from Odysseus' Greece: witness the fidelity of his wife through the long years before at last his black-prowed galleys clove the wine-dark seas for home. The ethical structure of that day covered wives, but had not yet been extended to human chattels. During the three thousand years which have since elapsed, ethical criteria have been extended to many fields of conduct, with corresponding shrinkages in those judged by expediency only.

The Ethical Sequence

This extension of ethics, so far studied only by philosophers, is actually a process in ecological evolution. Its sequences may be described in ecological as well as in philosophical terms. An ethic, ecologically, is a limitation on freedom of action in the struggle for existence. An ethic, philosophically, is a differentiation of social from anti-social conduct. These are two definitions of one thing. The thing has its origin in the tendency of interdependent individuals or groups to evolve modes of co-operation. The ecologist calls these symbioses. Politics and economics are advanced symbioses in which the original free-for-all competition has been replaced, in part, by cooperative mechanisms with an ethical content.

The complexity of cooperative mechanisms has increased with population density, and with the efficiency of tools. It was simpler, for example, to define the anti-social uses of sticks and stones in the days of the mastodons than of bullets and billboards in the age of motors.

The first ethics dealt with the relation between individuals; the Mosaic Decalogue is an example. Later accretions dealt with the relation between the individual and society. The Golden Rule tries to integrate the individual to society; democracy to integrate social organization to the individual.

There is as yet no ethic dealing with man's relation to land and to the animals and plants which grow upon it. Land, like Odysseus' slave-girls, is still property. The land-relation is still strictly economic, entailing privileges but not obligations.

The extension of ethics to this third element in human environment is, if I read the evidence correctly, an evolutionary possibility and an ecological necessity. It is the third step in a sequence. The first two have already been taken. Individual thinkers since the days of Ezekiel and Isaiah have asserted that the despoliation of land is not only inexpedient but wrong. Society, however, has not yet affirmed their belief. I regard the present conservation movement as the embryo of such an affirmation.

An ethic may be regarded as a mode of guidance for meeting ecological situations so new or intricate, or involving such deferred reactions, that the path of social expediency is not discernible to the average individual. Animal instincts are modes of guidance for the individual in meeting such situations. Ethics are possibly a kind of community instinct in the making.

The Community Concept

All ethics so far evolved rest upon a single premise: that the individual is a member of a community of interdependent parts. His instincts prompt him to compete for his place in the community, but his ethics prompt him also to co-operate (perhaps in order that there may be a place to compete for).

The land ethic simply enlarges the boundaries of the community to include soils, waters, plants, and animals, or collectively: the land.

This sounds simple: do we not already sing our love for and obligation to the land of the free and the home of the brave? Yes, but just what and whom do we love? Certainly not the soil, which we are sending helter-skelter downriver. Certainly not the waters, which we assume have no function except to turn turbines, float barges, and carry off sewage. Certainly not the plants, of which we exterminate whole communities without batting an eye. Certainly not the animals, of which we have already extirpated many of the largest and most beautiful species. A land ethic of course cannot prevent the alteration, management, and use of these "resources," but it does affirm their right to continued existence, and, at least in spots, their continued existence in a natural state.

In short, a land ethic changes the role of *Homo sapiens* from conqueror of the land-community to plain member and citizen of it. It implies respect for his fellow-members, and also respect for the community as such.

In human history, we have learned (I hope) that the conqueror role is eventually self-defeating. Why? Because it is implicit in such a role that the conqueror knows, *ex cathedra,* just what makes the community clock tick, and just what and who is valuable, and what and who is worthless, in community life. It always turns out that he knows neither, and this is why his conquests eventually defeat themselves.

In the biotic community, a parallel situation exists. Abraham knew exactly what the land was for: it was to drip milk and honey into Abraham's mouth. At the present moment, the assurance with which we regard this assumption is inverse to the degree of our education.

The ordinary citizen today assumes that science knows what makes the community clock tick; the scientist is equally sure that he does not. He knows that the biotic mechanism is so complex that its workings may never be fully understood.

That man is, in fact, only a member of a biotic team is shown by an ecological interpretation of history. Many historical events, hitherto explained solely in terms of human enterprise, were actually biotic interactions between people and land. The characteristics of the land determined the facts quite as potently as the characteristics of the men who lived on it.

Consider, for example, the settlement of the Mississippi valley. In the years following the Revolution, three groups were contending for its control: the native Indian, the French and English traders, and the American settlers. Historians wonder what would have happened if the English at Detroit had thrown a little more weight into the Indian side of those tipsy scales which decided the outcome of the colonial migration into the cane-lands of Kentucky. It is time now to ponder the fact that the cane-lands, when subjected to the particular mixture of forces represented by the cow, plow, fire, and axe of the pioneer, became bluegrass. What if the plant succession inherent in this dark and bloody ground had, under the impact of these forces, given us some worthless sedge, shrub, or weed? Would Boone and Kenton have held out? Would there have been any overflow into Ohio, Indiana, Illinois, and Missouri? Any Louisiana Purchase? Any transcontinental union of new states? Any Civil War?

Kentucky was one sentence in the drama of history. We are commonly told what the human actors in this drama tried to do, but we are seldom told that their success, or the lack of it, hung in large degree on the reaction of particular soils to the impact of the particular forces exerted by their occupancy. In the case of Kentucky, we do not even know where the bluegrass came from—whether it is a native species, or a stowaway from Europe.

Contrast the cane-lands with what hindsight tells us about the Southwest, where the pioneers were equally brave, resourceful, and persevering. The impact of occupancy here brought no bluegrass, or other plant fitted to withstand the bumps and buffetings of hard use. This region, when grazed by livestock, reverted through a series of more and more worthless grasses, shrubs, and weeds to a condition of unstable equilibrium. Each recession of plant types bred erosion; each increment to erosion bred a further recession of plants. The result today is a progressive and mutual deterioration, not only of plants and soils, but of the animal community subsisting thereon. The early settlers did not expect this: on the ciénegas of New Mexico some even cut ditches to hasten it. So subtle has been its progress that few residents of the region are aware of it. It is

quite invisible to the tourist who finds this wrecked landscape colorful and charming (as indeed it is, but it bears scant resemblance to what it was in 1848).

This same landscape was 'developed' once before, but with quite different results. The Pueblo Indians settled the Southwest in pre-Columbian times, but they happened *not* to be equipped with range livestock. Their civilization expired, but not because their land expired.

In India, regions devoid of any sod-forming grass have been settled, apparently without wrecking the land, by the simple expedient of carrying the grass to the cow, rather than vice versa. (Was this the result of some deep wisdom, or was it just good luck? I do not know.)

In short, the plant succession steered the course of history; the pioneer simply demonstrated, for good or ill, what successions inhered in the land. Is history taught in this spirit? It will be, once the concept of land as a community really penetrates our intellectual life.

The Ecological Conscience

Conservation is a state of harmony between men and land. Despite nearly a century of propaganda, conservation still proceeds at a snail's pace; progress still consists largely of letterhead pieties and convention oratory. On the back forty we still slip two steps backward for each forward stride.

The usual answer to this dilemma is "more conservation education." No one will debate this, but is it certain that only the *volume* of education needs stepping up? Is something lacking in the *content* as well?

It is difficult to give a fair summary of its content in brief form, but, as I understand it, the content is substantially this: obey the law, vote right, join some organizations, and practice what conservation is profitable on your own land; the government will do the rest.

Is not this formula too easy to accomplish anything worth-while? It defines no right or wrong, assigns no obligation, calls for no sacrifice, implies no change in the current philosophy of values. In respect of land-use, it urges only enlightened self-interest. Just how far will such education take us? An example will perhaps yield a partial answer.

By 1930 it had become clear to all except the ecologically blind that southwestern Wisconsin's topsoil was slipping seaward. In 1933 the farmers were told that if they would adopt certain remedial practices for five years, the public would donate CCC labor to install them, plus the necessary machinery and materials. The offer was widely accepted, but the practices were widely forgotten when the five-year contract period was up. The farmers continued only those practices that yielded an immediate and visible economic gain for themselves.

This led to the idea that maybe farmers would learn more quickly if they themselves wrote the rules. Accordingly the Wisconsin Legislature in 1937 passed the Soil Conservation District Law. This said to farmers, in effect: *We, the public, will furnish you free technical service and loan you specialized machinery, if you will write your own rules for land-use. Each county may write its own rules, and these will have the force of* law. Nearly all the counties promptly organized to accept the proffered help, but after a decade of operation, *no county has yet written a single rule.* There has been visible progress in such practices as strip-cropping, pasture renovation, and soil liming, but none in fencing woodlots against grazing, and none in excluding plow and cow from steep slopes. The farmers, in short, have selected those remedial practices which were profitable anyhow, and ignored those which were profitable to the community, but not clearly profitable to themselves.

When one asks why no rules have been written, one is told that the community is not yet ready to support them; education must precede rules. But the education actually in progress makes no mention of obligations to land over and above those dictated by self-interest. The net result is that we have more education but less soil, fewer healthy woods, and as many floods as in 1937.

The puzzling aspect of such situations is that the existence of obligations over and above self-interest is taken for granted in such rural com-

munity enterprises as the betterment of roads, schools, churches, and baseball teams. Their existence is not taken for granted, nor as yet seriously discussed, in bettering the behavior of the water that falls on the land, or in the preserving of the beauty or diversity of the farm landscape. Land-use ethics are still governed wholly by economic self-interest, just as social ethics were a century ago.

To sum up: we asked the farmer to do what he conveniently could to save his soil, and he has done just that, and only that. The farmer who clears the woods off a 75 per cent slope, turns his cows into the clearing, and dumps its rainfall, rocks, and soil into the community creek, is still (if otherwise decent) a respected member of society. If he puts lime on his fields and plants his crops on contour, he is still entitled to all the privileges and emoluments of his Soil Conservation District. The District is a beautiful piece of social machinery, but it is coughing along on two cylinders because we have been too timid, and too anxious for quick success, to tell the farmer the true magnitude of his obligations. Obligations have no meaning without conscience, and the problem we face is the extension of the social conscience from people to land.

No important change in ethics was ever accomplished without an internal change in our intellectual emphasis, loyalties, affections, and convictions. The proof that conservation has not yet touched these foundations of conduct lies in the fact that philosophy and religion have not yet heard of it. In our attempt to make conservation easy, we have made it trivial.

Substitutes for a Land Ethic

When the logic of history hungers for bread and we hand out a stone, we are at pains to explain how much the stone resembles bread. I now describe some of the stones which serve in lieu of a land ethic.

One basic weakness in a conservation system based wholly on economic motives is that most members of the land community have no economic value. Wildflowers and songbirds are examples. Of the 22,000 higher plants and animals native to Wisconsin, it is doubtful whether more than 5 per cent can be sold, fed, eaten, or otherwise put to economic use. Yet these creatures are members of the biotic community, and if (as I believe) its stability depends on its integrity, they are entitled to continuance.

When one of these non-economic categories is threatened, and if we happen to love it, we invent subterfuges to give it economic importance. At the beginning of the century songbirds were supposed to be disappearing. Ornithologists jumped to the rescue with some distinctly shaky evidence to the effect that insects would eat us up if birds failed to control them. The evidence had to be economic in order to be valid.

It is painful to read these circumlocutions today. We have no land ethic yet, but we have at least drawn nearer the point of admitting that birds should continue as a matter of biotic right, regardless of the presence or absence of economic advantage to us.

A parallel situation exists in respect of predatory mammals, raptorial birds, and fish-eating birds. Time was when biologists somewhat overworked the evidence that these creatures preserve the health of game by killing weaklings, or that they control rodents for the farmer, or that they prey only on "worthless" species. Here again, the evidence had to be economic in order to be valid. It is only in recent years that we hear the more honest argument that predators are members of the community, and that no special interest has the right to exterminate them for the sake of a benefit, real or fancied, to itself. Unfortunately this enlightened view is still in the talk stage. In the field the extermination of predators goes merrily on: witness the impending erasure of the timber wolf by fiat of Congress, the Conservation Bureaus, and many state legislatures.

Some species of trees have been "read out of the party" by economics-minded foresters because they grow too slowly, or have too low a sale value to pay as timber crops: white cedar, tamarack, cypress, beech, and hemlock are examples. In Europe, where forestry is ecologically more advanced, the non-commercial tree species are recognized as members of the native forest community, to be preserved as such, within reason. Moreover some (like beech) have been found to have a valuable function in building up soil fertility. The interdependence of the forest and its constituent tree species, ground flora, and fauna is taken for granted.

Lack of economic value is sometimes a character not only of species or groups, but of entire biotic communities: marshes, bogs, dunes, and "deserts" are examples. Our formula in such cases is to relegate their conservation to government as refuges, monuments, or parks. The difficulty is that these communities are usually interspersed with more valuable private lands; the government cannot possibly own or control such scattered parcels. The net effect is that we have relegated some of them to ultimate extinction over large areas. If the private owner were ecologically minded, he would be proud to be the custodian of a reasonable proportion of such areas, which add diversity and beauty to his farm and to his community.

In some instances, the assumed lack of profit in these "waste" areas has proved to be wrong, but only after most of them had been done away with. The present scramble to reflood muskrat marshes is a case in point.

There is a clear tendency in American conservation to relegate to government all necessary jobs that private landowners fail to perform. Government ownership, operation, subsidy, or regulation is now widely prevalent in forestry, range management, soil and watershed management, park and wilderness conservation, fisheries management, and migratory bird management, with more to come. Most of this growth in governmental conservation is proper and logical, some of it is inevitable. That I imply no disapproval of it is implicit in the fact that I have spent most of my life working for it. Nevertheless the question arises: What is the ultimate magnitude of the enterprise? Will the tax base carry its eventual ramifications? At what point will governmental conservation, like the mastodon, become handicapped by its own dimensions? The answer, if there is any, seems to be in a land ethic, or some other force which assigns more obligation to the private landowner.

Industrial landowners and users, especially lumbermen and stockmen, are inclined to wail long and loudly about the extension of government ownership and regulation to land, but (with notable exceptions) they show little disposition to develop the only visible alternative: the voluntary practice of conservation on their own lands.

When the private landowner is asked to perform some unprofitable act for the good of the community, he today assents only with outstretched palm. If the act costs him cash this is fair and proper, but when it costs only forethought, open-mindedness, or time, the issue is at least debatable. The overwhelming growth of land-use subsidies in recent years must be ascribed, in large part, to the government's own agencies for conservation education: the land bureaus, the agricultural colleges, and the extension services. As far as I can detect, no ethical obligation toward land is taught in these institutions.

To sum up: a system of conservation based solely on economic self-interest is hopelessly lopsided. It tends to ignore, and thus eventually to eliminate, many elements in the land community that lack commercial value, but that are (as far as we know) essential to its healthy functioning. It assumes, falsely, I think, that the economic parts of the biotic clock will function without the uneconomic parts. It tends to relegate to government many functions eventually too large, too complex, or too widely dispersed to be performed by government.

An ethical obligation on the part of the private owner is the only visible remedy for these situations.

The Land Pyramid

An ethic to supplement and guide the economic relation to land presupposes the existence of some mental image of land as a biotic mechanism. We can be ethical only in relation to something we can see, feel, understand, love, or otherwise have faith in.

The image commonly employed in conservation education is "the balance of nature." For reasons too lengthy to detail here, this figure of speech fails to describe accurately what little we know about the land mechanism. A much truer image is the one employed in ecology: the biotic pyramid. I shall first sketch the pyramid as a symbol of land, and later develop some of its implications in terms of land-use.

Plants absorb energy from the sun. This energy flows through a circuit called the biota, which may be represented by a pyramid consisting of layers. The bottom layer is the soil. A plant layer rests on the soil, an insect layer on the plants, a bird and rodent layer on the insects, and so on up through various animal groups to the apex layer, which consists of the larger carnivores.

The species of a layer are alike not in where they came from, or in what they look like, but rather in what they eat. Each successive layer depends on those below it for food and often for other services, and each in turn furnishes food and services to those above. Proceeding upward, each successive layer decreases in numerical abundance. Thus, for every carnivore there are hundreds of his prey, thousands of their prey, millions of insects, uncountable plants. The pyramidal form of the system reflects this numerical progression from apex to base. Man shares an intermediate layer with the bears, raccoons, and squirrels which eat both meat and vegetables.

The lines of dependency for food and other services are called food chains. Thus soil-oak-deer-Indian is a chain that has now been largely converted to soil-corn-cow-farmer. Each species, including ourselves, is a link in many chains. The deer eats a hundred plants other than oak, and the cow a hundred plants other than corn. Both, then, are links in a hundred chains. The pyramid is a tangle of chains so complex as to seem disorderly, yet the stability of the system proves it to be a highly organized structure. Its functioning depends on the cooperation and competition of its diverse parts.

In the beginning, the pyramid of life was low and squat; the food chains short and simple. Evolution has added layer after layer, link after link. Man is one of thousands of accretions to the height and complexity of the pyramid. Science has given us many doubts, but it has given us at least one certainty: the trend of evolution is to elaborate and diversify the biota.

Land, then, is not merely soil; it is a fountain of energy flowing through a circuit of soils, plants, and animals. Food chains are the living channels which conduct energy upward; death and decay return it to the soil. The circuit is not closed; some energy is dissipated in decay, some is added by absorption from the air, some is stored in soils, peats, and long-lived forests; but it is a sustained circuit, like a slowly augmented revolving fund of life. There is always a net loss by downhill wash, but this is normally small and offset by the decay of rocks. It is deposited in the ocean and, in the course of geological time, raised to form new lands and new pyramids.

The velocity and character of the upward flow of energy depend on the complex structure of the plant and animal community, much as the upward flow of sap in a tree depends on its complex cellular organization. Without this complexity, normal circulation would presumably not occur. Structure means the characteristic numbers, as well as the characteristic kinds and functions, of the component species. This interdependence between the complex structure of the land and its smooth functioning as an energy unit is one of its basic attributes.

When a change occurs in one part of the circuit, many other parts must adjust themselves to it. Change does not necessarily obstruct or divert the flow of energy; evolution is a long series of self-induced changes, the net result of which has been to elaborate the flow mechanism and to lengthen the circuit. Evolutionary changes, however, are usually slow and local. Man's invention of tools has enabled him to make changes of unprecedented violence, rapidity, and scope.

One change is in the composition of floras and faunas. The larger predators are lopped off the apex of the pyramid; food chains, for the first time in history, become shorter rather than longer. Domesticated species from other lands are substituted for wild ones, and wild ones are moved to new habitats. In this worldwide pooling of faunas and floras, some species get out of bounds as pests and diseases, others are extinguished. Such effects are seldom intended or foreseen; they represent unpredicted and often untraceable readjustments in the structure. Agricultural science is largely a race between the emergence of new pests and the emergence of new techniques for their control.

Another change touches the flow of energy through plants and animals and its return to the soil. Fertility is the ability of soil to receive, store, and release energy. Agriculture, by overdrafts on the soil, or by too radical a substitution of domestic for native species in the superstructure, may derange the channels of flow or deplete storage. Soils depleted of their storage, or of the organic matter which anchors it, wash away faster than they form. This is erosion.

Waters, like soil, are part of the energy circuit. Industry, by polluting waters or obstructing them with dams, may exclude the plants and animals necessary to keep energy in circulation.

Transportation brings about another basic change: the plants or animals grown in one region are now consumed and returned to the soil in another. Transportation taps the energy stored in rocks, and in the air, and uses it elsewhere; thus we fertilize the garden with nitrogen gleaned by the guano birds from the fishes of seas on the other side of the Equator. Thus the formerly localized and self-contained circuits are pooled on a world-wide scale.

The process of altering the pyramid for human occupation releases stored energy, and this often gives rise, during the pioneering period, to a deceptive exuberance of plant and animal life, both wild and tame. These releases of biotic capital tend to becloud or postpone the penalties of violence.

This thumbnail sketch of land as an energy circuit conveys three basic ideas:

1. That land is not merely soil.
2. That the native plants and animals kept the energy circuit open; others may or may not.
3. That man-made changes are of a different order than evolutionary changes, and have effects more comprehensive than is intended or foreseen.

These ideas, collectively, raise two basic issues: Can the land adjust itself to the new order? Can the desired alterations be accomplished with less violence?

Biotas seem to differ in their capacity to sustain violent conversion. Western Europe, for example, carries a far different pyramid than Caesar found there. Some large animals are lost; swampy forests have become meadows or plowland; many new plants and animals are introduced, some of which escape as pests; the remaining natives are greatly changed in distribution and abundance. Yet the soil is still there and, with the help of imported nutrients, still fertile; the waters flow normally; the new structure seems to function and to persist. There is no visible stoppage or derangement of the circuit.

Western Europe, then, has a resistant biota. Its inner processes are tough, elastic, resistant to strain. No matter how violent the alterations, the pyramid, so far, has developed some new *modus vivendi* which preserves its habitability for man, and for most of the other natives.

Japan seems to present another instance of radical conversion without disorganization.

Most other civilized regions, and some as yet barely touched by civilization, display various stages of disorganization, varying from initial symptoms to advanced wastage. In Asia Minor and North Africa diagnosis is confused by climatic changes, which may have been either the cause or the effect of advanced wastage. In the United States the degree of disorganization varies locally; it is worst in the Southwest, the Ozarks, and parts of the South, and least in New England and the Northwest. Better land uses may still arrest it in the less advanced regions. In parts of Mexico, South America, South Africa, and Australia a violent and accelerating wastage is in progress, but I cannot assess the prospects.

This almost world-wide display of disorganization in the land seems to be similar to disease in an animal, except that it never culminates in complete disorganization or death. The land recovers, but at some reduced level of complexity, and with a reduced carrying capacity for people, plants, and animals. Many biotas currently regarded as 'lands of opportunity' are in fact already subsisting on exploitative agriculture, i.e. they have already exceeded their sus-

tained carrying capacity. Most of South America is overpopulated in this sense.

In arid regions we attempt to offset the process of wastage by reclamation, but it is only too evident that the prospective longevity of reclamation projects is often short. In our own West, the best of them may not last a century.

The combined evidence of history and ecology seems to support one general deduction: the less violent the man-made changes, the greater the probability of successful readjustment in the pyramid. Violence, in turn, varies with human population density; a dense population requires a more violent conversion. In this respect, North America has a better chance for permanence than Europe, if she can contrive to limit her density.

This deduction runs counter to our current philosophy, which assumes that because a small increase in density enriched human life, that an indefinite increase will enrich it indefinitely. Ecology knows of no density relationship that holds for indefinitely wide limits. All gains from density are subject to a law of diminishing returns.

Whatever may be the equation for men and land, it is improbable that we as yet know all its terms. Recent discoveries in mineral and vitamin nutrition reveal unsuspected dependencies in the up-circuit: incredibly minute quantities of certain substances determine the value of soils to plants, of plants to animals. What of the down-circuit? What of the vanishing species, the preservation of which we now regard as an esthetic luxury? They helped build the soil; in what unsuspected ways may they be essential to its maintenance? Professor Weaver proposes that we use prairie flowers to reflocculate the wasting soils of the dust bowl; who knows for what purpose cranes and condors, otters and grizzlies may some day be used?

Land Health and the A-B Cleavage

A land ethic, then, reflects the existence of an ecological conscience, and this in turn reflects a conviction of individual responsibility for the health of the land. Health is the capacity of the land for self-renewal. Conservation is our effort to understand and preserve this capacity.

Conservationists are notorious for their dissensions. Superficially these seem to add up to mere confusion, but a more careful scrutiny reveals a single plane of cleavage common to many specialized fields. In each field one group (A) regards the land as soil, and its function as commodity-production; another group (B) regards the land as a biota, and its function as something broader. How much broader is admittedly in a state of doubt and confusion.

In my own field, forestry, group A is quite content to grow trees like cabbages, with cellulose as the basic forest commodity. It feels no inhibition against violence; its ideology is agronomic. Group B, on the other hand, sees forestry as fundamentally different from agronomy because it employs natural species, and manages a natural environment rather than creating an artificial one. Group B prefers natural reproduction on principle. It worries on biotic as well as economic grounds about the loss of species like chestnut, and the threatened loss of the white pines. It worries about a whole series of secondary forest functions: wildlife, recreation, watersheds, wilderness areas. To my mind, Group B feels the stirrings of an ecological conscience.

In the wildlife field, a parallel cleavage exists. For Group A the basic commodities are sport and meat; the yardsticks of production are ciphers of take in pheasants and trout. Artificial propagation is acceptable as a permanent as well as a temporary recourse—if its unit costs permit. Group B, on the other hand, worries about a whole series of biotic side-issues. What is the cost in predators of producing a game crop? Should we have further recourse to exotics? How can management restore the shrinking species, like prairie grouse, already hopeless as shootable game? How can management restore the threatened rarities, like trumpeter swan and whooping crane? Can management principles be extended to wildflowers? Here again it is clear to me that we have the same A-B cleavage as in forestry.

In the larger field of agriculture I am less

competent to speak, but there seem to be somewhat parallel cleavages. Scientific agriculture was actively developing before ecology was born, hence a slower penetration of ecological concepts might be expected. Moreover the farmer, by the very nature of his techniques, must modify the biota more radically than the forester or the wildlife manager. Nevertheless, there are many discontents in agriculture which seem to add up to a new vision of 'biotic farming.'

Perhaps the most important of these is the new evidence that poundage or tonnage is no measure of the food-value of farm crops; the products of fertile soil may be qualitatively as well as quantitatively superior. We can bolster poundage from depleted soils by pouring on imported fertility, but we are not necessarily bolstering food-value. The possible ultimate ramifications of this idea are so immense that I must leave their exposition to abler pens.

The discontent that labels itself 'organic farming,' while bearing some of the earmarks of a cult, is nevertheless biotic in its direction, particularly in its insistence on the importance of soil flora and fauna.

The ecological fundamentals of agriculture are just as poorly known to the public as in other fields of land-use. For example, few educated people realize that the marvelous advances in technique made during recent decades are improvements in the pump, rather than the well. Acre for acre, they have barely sufficed to offset the sinking level of fertility.

In all of these cleavages, we see repeated the same basic paradoxes: man the conqueror *versus* man the biotic citizen; science the sharpener of his sword *versus* science the searchlight on his universe; land the slave and servant *versus* land the collective organism. Robinson's injunction to Tristram may well be applied, at this juncture, to *Homo sapiens* as a species in geological time:

Whether you will or not
You are a King, Tristram, for you are one
Of the time-tested few that leave the world,
When they are gone, not the same place it was.
Mark what you leave.

The Outlook

It is inconceivable to me that an ethical relation to land can exist without love, respect, and admiration for land, and a high regard for its value. By value, I of course mean something far broader than mere economic value; I mean value in the philosophical sense.

Perhaps the most serious obstacle impeding the evolution of a land ethic is the fact that our educational and economic system is headed away from, rather than toward, an intense consciousness of land. Your true modern is separated from the land by many middlemen, and by innumerable physical gadgets. He has no vital relation to it; to him it is the space between cities on which crops grow. Turn him loose for a day on the land, and if the spot does not happen to be a golf links or a "scenic" area, he is bored stiff. If crops could be raised by hydroponics instead of farming, it would suit him very well. Synthetic substitutes for wood, leather, wool, and other natural land products suit him better than the originals. In short, land is something he has "outgrown."

Almost equally serious as an obstacle to a land ethic is the attitude of the farmer for whom the land is still an adversary, or a taskmaster that keeps him in slavery. Theoretically, the mechanization of farming ought to cut the farmer's chains, but whether it really does is debatable.

One of the requisites for an ecological comprehension of land is an understanding of ecology, and this is by no means co-extensive with "education"; in fact, much higher education seems deliberately to avoid ecological concepts. An understanding of ecology does not necessarily originate in courses bearing ecological labels; it is quite as likely to be labeled geography, botany, agronomy, history, or economics. This is as it should be, but whatever the label, ecological training is scarce.

The case for a land ethic would appear hopeless but for the minority which is in obvious revolt against these "modern" trends.

The "key-log" which must be moved to release the evolutionary process for an ethic is simply this: quit thinking about decent land-use as solely an economic problem. Examine each question in terms of what is ethically and esthetically right, as well as what is economically expedient. A thing is right when it tends to preserve the integrity, stability, and beauty of the biotic community. It is wrong when it tends otherwise.

It of course goes without saying that economic feasibility limits the tether of what can or cannot be done for land. It always has and it always will. The fallacy the economic determinists have tied around our collective neck, and which we now need to cast off, is the belief that economics determines *all* land-use. This is simply not true. An innumerable host of actions and attitudes, comprising perhaps the bulk of all land relations, is determined by the land-users' tastes and predilections, rather than by his purse. The bulk of all land relations hinges on investments of time, forethought, skill, and faith rather than on investments of cash. As a land-user thinketh, so is he.

I have purposely presented the land ethic as a product of social evolution because nothing so important as an ethic is ever "written." Only the most superficial student of history supposes that Moses "wrote" the Decalogue; it evolved in the minds of a thinking community, and Moses wrote a tentative summary of it for a "seminar." I say tentative because evolution never stops.

The evolution of a land ethic is an intellectual as well as emotional process. Conservation is paved with good intentions which prove to be futile, or even dangerous, because they are devoid of critical understanding either of the land, or of economic land-use. I think it is a truism that as the ethical frontier advances from the individual to the community, its intellectual content increases.

The mechanism of operation is the same for any ethic: social approbation for right actions: social disapproval for wrong actions.

By and large, our present problem is one of attitudes and implements. We are remodeling the Alhambra with a steam-shovel, and we are proud of our yardage. We shall hardly relinquish the shovel, which after all has many good points, but we are in need of gentler and more objective criteria for its successful use.

Should Trees Have Standing?—Toward Legal Rights for Natural Objects

Christopher D. Stone

Introduction: The Unthinkable

In *Descent of Man,* Darwin observes that the history of man's moral development has been a continual extension in the objects of his "social instincts and sympathies." Originally each man had regard only for himself and those of a very narrow circle about him; later, he came to regard more and more "not only the welfare, but the happiness of all his fellow-men"; then "his sympathies became more tender and widely diffused, extending to men of all races, to the imbecile, maimed, and other useless members of society, and finally to the lower animals. . . ."[1]

The history of the law suggests a parallel development. Perhaps there never was a pure Hobbesian state of nature, in which no "rights" existed except in the vacant sense of each man's "right to self-defense." But it is not unlikely that so far as the earliest "families" (including extended kinship groups and clans) were concerned, everyone outside the family was suspect, alien, rightless.[2] And even within the family, persons we presently regard as the natural holders of at least some rights had none. Take, for example, children. We know something of the early rights-status of children from the widespread practice of infanticide—especially of the deformed and female.[3] (Senicide,[4] as among the North American Indians, was the corresponding rightlessness of the aged.)[5] Maine tells us that as late as the

Patria Potestas of the Romans, the father had *jus vitae necisque*—the power of life and death—over his children. A fortiori, Maine writes, he had power of "uncontrolled corporal chastisement; he can modify their personal condition at pleasure; he can give a wife to his son; he can give his daughter in marriage; he can divorce his children of either sex; he can transfer them to another family by adoption; and he can sell them." The child was less than a person: an object, a thing.[6]

The legal rights of children have long since been recognized in principle, and are still expanding in practice. Witness, just within recent time, *In re Gault*,[7] guaranteeing basic constitutional protections to juvenile defendants, and the Voting Rights Act of 1970.[8] We have been making persons of children although they were not, in law, always so. And we have done the same, albeit imperfectly some would say, with prisoners,[9] aliens, women (especially of the married variety), the insane,[10] Blacks, foetuses,[11] and Indians.

Nor is it only matter in human form that has come to be recognized as the possessor of rights. The world of the lawyer is peopled with inanimate right-holders: trusts, corporations, joint ventures, municipalities, Subchapter R partnerships,[12] and nation-states, to mention just a few. Ships, still referred to by courts in the feminine gender, have long had an independent jural life, often with striking consequences.[13] We have become so accustomed to the idea of a corporation having "its" own rights, and being a "person" and "citizen" for so many statutory and constitutional purposes, that we forget how jarring the notion was to early jurists. "That invisible, intangible and artificial being, that mere legal entity" Chief Justice Marshall wrote of the corporation in *Bank of the United States v. Deveaux*[14]—could a suit be brought in *its* name? Ten years later, in

Source: *Should Trees Have Standing? Toward Legal Rights for Natural Objects*, by Christopher D. Stone (Los Altos: William Kaufmann, Inc., 1974), pp. 3–18, 24, 27–33, 45–46, 48–54. Reprinted by permission.

the *Dartmouth College* case,[15] he was still refusing to let pass unnoticed the wonder of an entity "existing only in contemplation of law."[16] Yet, long before Marshall worried over the personifying of the modern corporation, the best medieval legal scholars had spent hundreds of years struggling with the notion of the legal nature of those great public "corporate bodies," the Church and the State. How could they exist in law, as entities transcending the living Pope and King? It was clear how a king could bind *himself*—on his honor—by a treaty. But when the king died, what was it that was burdened with the obligations of, and claimed the rights under, the treaty *his* tangible hand had signed? The medieval mind saw (what we have lost our capacity to see)[17] how *unthinkable* it was, and worked out the most elaborate conceits and fallacies to serve as anthropomorphic flesh for the Universal Church and the Universal Empire.[18]

It is this note of the *unthinkable* that I want to dwell upon for a moment. Throughout legal history, each successive extension of rights to some new entity has been, theretofore, a bit unthinkable. We are inclined to suppose the rightlessness of rightless "things" to be a decree of Nature, not a legal convention acting in support of some status quo. It is thus that we defer considering the choices involved in all their moral, social, and economic dimensions. And so the United States Supreme Court could straight-facedly tell us in *Dred Scott* that Blacks had been denied the rights of citizenship "as a subordinate and inferior class of beings, who had been subjugated by the dominant race. . . ."[19] In the nineteenth century, the highest court in California explained that Chinese had not the right to testify against white men in criminal matters because they were "a race of people whom nature has marked as inferior, and who are incapable of progress or intellectual development beyond a certain point . . . between whom and ourselves nature has placed an impassable difference."[20] The popular conception of the Jew in the 13th Century contributed to a law which treated them as "men *ferae naturae*, protected by a quasi-forest law. Like the roe and the deer, they form an order apart."[21] Recall, too, that it was not so long ago that the foetus was "like the roe and the deer." In an early suit attempting to es-

tablish a wrongful death action on behalf of a negligently killed foetus (now widely accepted practice), Holmes, then on the Massachusetts Supreme Court, seems to have thought it simply inconceivable "that a man might owe a civil duty and incur a conditional prospective liability in tort to one not yet in being."[22] The first woman in Wisconsin who thought she might have a right to practice law was told that she did not, in the following terms:

The law of nature destines and qualifies the female sex for the bearing and nurture of the children of our race and for the custody of the homes of the world. . . . [A]ll life-long callings of women, inconsistent with these radical and sacred duties of their sex, as is the profession of the law, are departures from the order of nature; and when voluntary, treason against it. . . . The peculiar qualities of womanhood, its gentle graces, its quick sensibility, its tender susceptibility, its purity, its delicacy, its emotional impulses, its subordination of hard reason to sympathetic feeling, are surely not qualifications for forensic strife. Nature has tempered woman as little for the juridical conflicts of the court room, as for the physical conflicts of the battle field. . . .[23]

The fact is, that each time there is a movement to confer rights onto some new "entity," the proposal is bound to sound odd or frightening or laughable. This is partly because until the rightless thing receives its rights, we cannot see it as anything but a *thing* for the use of "us"—those who are holding rights at the time.[24] In this vein, what is striking about the Wisconsin case above is that the court, for all its talk about women, so clearly was never able to see women as they are (and might become). All it could see was the popular "idealized" version of *an object it needed*. Such is the way the slave South looked upon the Black.[25] There is something of a seamless web involved: there will be resistance to giving the thing "rights" until it can be seen and valued for itself; yet, it is hard to see it and value it for itself until we can bring ourselves to give it "rights"—which is almost inevitably going to sound inconceivable to a large group of people.

The reason for this little discourse on the unthinkable, the reader must know by now, if only from the title of the paper. I am quite seriously proposing that we give legal rights to forests, oceans, rivers and other so-called "natural objects" in the environment—indeed, to the natural environment as a whole.

As strange as such a notion may sound, it is neither fanciful nor devoid of operational content. In fact, I do not think it would be a misdescription of recent developments in the law to say that we are already on the verge of assigning some such rights, although we have not faced up to what we are doing in those particular terms.[26] We should do so now, and begin to explore the implications such a notion would hold.

Toward Rights for the Environment

Now, to say that the natural environment should have rights is not to say anything as silly as that no one should be allowed to cut down a tree. We say human beings have rights, but—at least as of the time of this writing—they can be executed. Corporations have rights, but they cannot plead the fifth amendment; *In re Gault* gave 15-year-olds certain rights in juvenile proceedings, but it did not give them the right to vote. Thus, to say that the environment should have rights is not to say that it should have every right we can imagine, or even the same body of rights as human beings have. Nor is it to say that everything in the environment should have the same rights as every other thing in the environment.

What the granting of rights does involve has two sides to it. The first involves what might be called the legal-operational aspects; the second, the psychic and socio-psychic aspects. I shall deal with these aspects in turn.

The Legal-Operational Aspects

What It Means to Be a Holder of Legal Rights

There is, so far as I know, no generally accepted standard for how one ought to use the term "legal rights." Let me indicate how I shall be using it in this piece.

First and most obviously, if the term is to have any content at all, an entity cannot be said to hold a legal right unless and until *some public authoritative body* is prepared to give *some amount of review* to actions that are colorably inconsistent with that "right." For example, if a student can be expelled from a university and cannot get any public official, even a judge or administrative agent at the lowest level, either (i) to require the university to justify its actions (if only to the extent of filling out an affidavit alleging that the expulsion "was not wholly arbitrary and capricious") or (ii) to compel the university to accord the student some procedural safeguards (a hearing, right to counsel, right to have notice of charges), then the minimum requirements for saying that the student has a legal right to his education do not exist.[27]

But for a thing to be *a holder of legal rights,* something more is needed than that some authoritative body will review the actions and processes of those who threaten it. As I shall use the term, "holder of legal rights," each of three additional criteria must be satisfied. All three, one will observe, go towards making a thing *count* jurally—to have a legally recognized worth and dignity in its own right, and not merely to serve as a means to benefit "us" (whoever the contemporary group of rights-holders may be). They are, first, that the thing can institute legal actions *at its behest;* second, that in determining the granting of legal relief, the court must take *injury to it* into account; and, third, that relief must run to the *benefit of it.* . . .

The Rightlessness of Natural Objects at Common Law

Consider, for example, the common law's posture toward the pollution of a stream. True, courts have always been able, in some circumstances, to issue orders that will stop the pollution. . . . But the stream itself is fundamentally rightless, with implications that deserve careful reconsideration.

The first sense in which the stream is not a rights-holder has to do with standing. The stream itself has none. So far as the common law is concerned, there is in general no way to challenge the polluter's actions save at the behest of a lower riparian—another human being—able to show an invasion of *his* rights. This conception of the riparian as the holder of the right to bring suit has more than theoretical interest. The lower riparians may simply not care about the pollution. They themselves may be polluting, and not wish to stir up legal waters. They may be economically dependent on their polluting neighbor. And, of course, when they discount the value of winning by the costs of bringing suit and the chances of success, the action may not seem worth undertaking. Consider, for example, that while the polluter might be injuring 100 downstream riparians $10,000 a year *in the aggregate*, each riparian separately might be suffering injury only to the extent of $100—possibly not enough for any one of them to want to press suit by himself, or even to go to the trouble and cost of securing co-plaintiffs to make it worth everyone's while. This hesitance will be especially likely when the potential plaintiffs consider the burdens the law puts in their way:[28] proving, *e.g.*, specific damages, the "unreasonableness" of defendant's use of the water, the fact that practicable means of abatement exist, and overcoming difficulties raised by issues such as joint causality, right to pollute by prescription, and so forth. Even in states which, like California, sought to overcome these difficulties by empowering the attorney-general to sue for abatement of pollution in limited instances, the power has been sparingly invoked and, when invoked, narrowly construed by the courts.[29]

The second sense in which the common law denies "rights" to natural objects has to do with the way in which the merits are decided in those cases in which someone is competent and willing to establish standing. At its more primitive levels, the system protected the "rights" of the property owning human with minimal weighing of any values: *Cujus est solum, ejus est usque ad coelum et ad infernos.*[30] Today we have come more and more to make balances—but only such as will adjust the economic best interests of identifiable humans. For example, continuing with the case of streams, there are commentators who speak of a "general rule" that "a riparian owner is legally entitled to have the stream flow by his land with its quality unimpaired" and observe that "an upper owner

has, prima facie, no right to pollute the water."[31] Such a doctrine, if strictly invoked, would protect the stream absolutely whenever a suit was brought; but obviously, to look around us, the law does not work that way. Almost everywhere there are doctrinal qualifications on riparian "rights" to an unpolluted stream.[32] Although these rules vary from jurisdiction to jurisdiction, and upon whether one is suing for an equitable injunction or for damages, what they all have in common is some sort of balancing. Whether under language of "reasonable use," "reasonable methods of use," "balance of convenience" or "the public interest doctrine," what the courts are balancing, with varying degrees of directness, are the economic hardships on the upper riparian (or dependent community) of abating the pollution vis-à-vis the economic hardships of continued pollution on the lower riparians. What does not weigh in the balance is the damage to the stream, its fish and turtles and "lower" life. So long as the natural environment itself is rightless, these are not matters for judicial cognizance. Thus, we find the highest court of Pennsylvania refusing to stop a coal company from discharging polluted mine water into a tributary of the Lackawana River because a plaintiff's "grievance is for a mere personal inconvenience; and . . . mere private personal inconveniences . . . must yield to the necessities of a great public industry, which although in the hands of a private corporation, subserves a great public interest."[33] The stream itself is lost sight of in "a quantitative compromise between *two* conflicting interests."[34]

The third way in which the common law makes natural objects rightless has to do with who is regarded as the beneficiary of a favorable judgment. Here, too, it makes a considerable difference that it is not the natural object that counts in its own right. To illustrate this point, let me begin by observing that it makes perfectly good sense to speak of, and ascertain, the legal damage to a natural object, if only in the sense of "making it whole" with respect to the most obvious factors. The costs of making a forest whole, for example, would include the costs of reseeding, repairing watersheds, restocking wildlife—the sorts of costs the Forest Service undergoes after a fire. Making a polluted stream whole would include the costs of restocking with fish, water-fowl, and other animal and vegetable life, dredging, washing out impurities, establishing natural and/or artificial aerating agents, and so forth. Now, what is important to note is that, under our present system, even if a plaintiff riparian wins a water pollution suit for damages, no money goes to the benefit of the stream itself to repair *its* damages. This omission has the further effect that, at most, the law confronts a polluter with what it takes to make the plaintiff riparians whole; this may be far less than the damages to the stream, but not so much as to force the polluter to desist. For example, it is easy to imagine a polluter whose activities damage a stream to the extent of $10,000 annually, although the aggregate damage to all the riparian plaintiffs who come into the suit is only $3000. If $3000 is less than the cost to the polluter of shutting down, or making the requisite technological changes, he might prefer to pay off the damages (*i.e.*, the legally cognizable damages) and continue to pollute the stream. Similarly, even if the jurisdiction issues an injunction at the plaintiffs' behest (rather than to order payment of damages), there is nothing to stop the plaintiffs from "selling out" the stream, *i.e.,* agreeing to dissolve or not enforce the injunction at some price (in the example above, somewhere between plaintiffs' damages—$3000—and defendant's next best economic alternative). Indeed, I take it this is exactly what Learned Hand had in mind in an opinion in which, after issuing an antipollution injunction, he suggests that the defendant "make its peace with the plaintiff as best it can."[35] What is meant is a peace between *them,* and not amongst them and the river.

I ought to make clear at this point that the common law as it affects streams and rivers, which I have been using as an example so far, is not exactly the same as the law affecting other environmental objects. Indeed, one would be hard pressed to say that there was a "typical" environmental object, so far as its treatment at the hands of the law is concerned. There are some differences in the law applicable to all the various resources that are held in common: rivers, lakes, oceans, dunes, air, streams (surface and subterranean), beaches, and so forth.

And there is an even greater difference as between these traditional communal resources on the one hand, and natural objects on traditionally private land, *e.g.,* the pond on the farmer's field, or the stand of trees on the suburbanite's lawn.

On the other hand, although there be these differences which would make it fatuous to generalize about a law of the natural environment, most of these differences simply underscore the points made in the instance of rivers and streams. None of the natural objects, whether held in common or situated on private land, has any of the three criteria of a rightsholder. They have no standing in their own right; their unique damages do not count in determining outcome; and they are not the beneficiaries of awards. In such fashion, these objects have traditionally been regarded by the common law, and even by all but the most recent legislation, as objects for man to conquer and master and use—in such a way as the law once looked upon "man's" relationships to African Negroes. Even where special measures have been taken to conserve them, as by seasons on game and limits on timber cutting, the dominant motive has been to conserve them *for us*—for the greatest good of the greatest number of human beings. Conservationists, so far as I am aware, are generally reluctant to maintain otherwise.[36] As the name implies, they want to conserve and guarantee *our* consumption and *our* enjoyment of these other living things. In their own right, natural objects have counted for little, in law as in popular movements.

As I mentioned at the outset, however, the rightlessness of the natural environment can and should change; it already shows some signs of doing so.

Toward Having Standing in Its Own Right

It is not inevitable, nor is it wise, that natural objects should have no rights to seek redress in their own behalf. It is no answer to say that streams and forests cannot have standing because streams and forest cannot speak. Corporations cannot speak either; nor can states, estates, infants, incompetents, municipalities or universities. Lawyers speak for them, as they customarily do for the ordinary citizen with legal problems. One ought, I think, to handle the legal problems of natural objects as one does the problems of legal incompetents— human beings who have become vegetable. If a human being shows signs of becoming senile and has affairs that he is de jure incompetent to manage, those concerned with his well being make such a showing to the court, and someone is designated by the court with the authority to manage the incompetent's affairs. The guardian (or "conservator" or "committee"—the terminology varies) then represents the incompetent in his legal affairs. Courts make similar appointments when a corporation has become "incompetent"—they appoint a trustee in bankruptcy or reorganization to oversee its affairs and speak for it in court when that becomes necessary.

On a parity of reasoning, we should have a system in which, when a friend of a natural object perceives it to be endangered, he can apply to a court for the creation of a guardianship. Perhaps we already have the machinery to do so. California law, for example, defines an incompetent as "any person, whether insane or not, who by reason of old age, disease, weakness of mind, or other cause, is unable, unassisted, properly to manage and take care of himself or his property, and by reason thereof is likely to be deceived or imposed upon by artful or designing persons."[37] Of course, to urge a court that an endangered river is "a person" under this provision will call for lawyers as bold and imaginative as those who convinced the Supreme Court that a railroad corporation was a "person" under the fourteenth amendment, a constitutional provision theretofore generally thought of as designed to secure the rights of freedmen.[38] . . .

The guardianship approach, however, is apt to raise . . . [the following objection]: a committee or guardian could not judge the needs of the river or forest in its charge; indeed, the very concept of "needs," it might be said, could be used here only in the most metaphorical way. . . .

. . . Natural objects can communicate their wants (needs) to us, and in ways that are not terribly ambiguous. I am sure I can judge with more certainty and meaningfulness whether

and when my lawn wants (needs) water, than the Attorney General can judge whether and when the United States wants (needs) to take an appeal from an adverse judgment by a lower court. The lawn tells me that it wants water by a certain dryness of the blades and soil— immediately obvious to the touch—the appearance of bald spots, yellowing, and a lack of springiness after being walked on; how does "the United States" communicate to the Attorney General? For similar reasons, the guardian-attorney for a smog-endangered stand of pines could venture with more confidence that his client wants the smog stopped, than the directors of a corporation can assert that "the corporation" wants dividends declared. We make decisions on behalf of, and in the purported interests of, others every day; these "others" are often creatures whose wants are far less verifiable, and even far more metaphysical in conception, than the wants of rivers, trees, and land. . . .

The argument for "personifying" the environment, from the point of damage calculations, can best be demonstrated from the welfare economics position. Every well-working legal-economic system should be so structured as to confront each of us with the full costs that our activities are imposing on society. Ideally, a paper-mill, in deciding what to produce—and where, and by what methods—ought to be forced to take into account not only the lumber, acid and labor that its production "takes" from other uses in the society, but also what costs alternative production plans will impose on society through pollution. The legal system, through the law of contracts and the criminal law, for example, makes the mill confront the costs of the first group of demands. When, for example, the company's purchasing agent orders 1000 drums of acid from the Z Company, the Z Company can bind the mill to pay for them, and thereby reimburse the society for what the mill is removing from alternative uses.

Unfortunately, so far as the pollution costs are concerned, the allocative ideal begins to break down, because the traditional legal institutions have a more difficult time "catching" and confronting us with the full social costs of our activities. In the lakeside mill example, major riparian interests might bring an action, forcing a court to weigh *their* aggregate losses against the costs to the mill of installing the anti-pollution device. But many other interests—and I am speaking for the moment of recognized homocentric interests—are too fragmented and perhaps "too remote" causally to warrant securing representation and pressing for recovery: the people who own summer homes and motels, the man who sells fishing tackle and bait, the man who rents rowboats. There is no reason not to allow the lake to prove damages to them as the prima facie measure of damages to it. *By doing so, we in effect make the natural object, through its guardian, a jural entity competent to gather up these fragmented and otherwise unrepresented damage claims, and press them before the court even where, for legal or practical reasons, they are not going to be pressed by traditional class action plaintiffs.* Indeed, one way—the homocentric way—to view what I am proposing so far, is to view the guardian of the natural object as the guardian of unborn generations, as well as of the otherwise unrepresented, but distantly injured, contemporary humans.[39] By making the lake itself the focus of these damages, and "incorporating" it so to speak, the legal system can effectively take proof upon, and confront the mill with, a larger and more representative measure of the damages its pollution causes.

So far, I do not suppose that my economist friends (unremittent human chauvinists, every one of them!) will have any large quarrel in principle with the concept. Many will view it as a *trompe l'oeil* that comes down, at best, to effectuate the goals of the paragon class action, or the paragon water pollution control district. Where we are apt to part company is here—I propose going beyond gathering up the loose ends of what most people would presently recognize as economically valid damages. The guardian would urge before the court injuries not presently cognizable—the death of eagles and inedible crabs, the suffering of sea lions, the loss from the face of the earth of species of commerically valueless birds, the disappearance of a wilderness area. One might, of course, speak of the damages involved as "damages" to us humans, and indeed, the widespread growth of environmental groups shows that human beings do feel these losses. But they

are not, at present, economically measurable losses: how can they have a monetary value for the guardian to prove in court?

The answer for me is simple. Wherever it carves out "property" rights, the legal system is engaged in the process of *creating* monetary worth. One's literary works would have minimal monetary value if anyone could copy them at will. Their economic value to the author is a product of the law of copyright; the person who copies a copyrighted book has to bear a cost to the copyright-holder because the law says he must. Similarly, it is through the law of torts that we have made a "right" of—and guaranteed an economically meaningful value to—privacy. (The value we place on gold—a yellow inanimate dirt—is not simply a function of supply and demand—wilderness areas are scarce and pretty too—, but results from the actions of the legal systems of the world, which have institutionalized that value; they have even done a remarkable job of stabilizing the price). I am proposing we do the same with eagles and wilderness areas as we do with copyrighted works, patented inventions, and privacy: *make* the violation of rights in them to be a cost by declaring the "pirating" of them to be the invasion of a property interest.[40] If we do so, the net social costs the polluter would be confronted with would include not only the extended homocentric costs of his pollution (explained above) but also costs to the environment *per se*.

How, though, would these costs be calculated? When we protect an invention, we can at least speak of a fair market value for it, by reference to which damages can be computed. But the lost environmental "values" of which we are now speaking are by definition over and above those that the market is prepared to bid for: they are priceless.

One possible measure of damages, suggested earlier, would be the cost of making the environment whole, just as, when a man is injured in an automobile accident, we impose upon the responsible party the injured man's medical expenses. Comparable expenses to a polluted river would be the costs of dredging, restocking with fish, and so forth. It is on the basis of such costs as these, I assume, that we get the figure of $1 billion as the cost of saving Lake

Erie.[41] As an ideal, I think this is a good guide applicable in many environmental situations. It is by no means free from difficulties, however.

One problem with computing damages on the basis of making the environment whole is that, if understood most literally, it is tantamount to asking for a "freeze" on environmental quality, even at the costs (and there will be costs) of preserving "useless" objects. Such a "freeze" is not inconceivable to me as a general goal, especially considering that, even by the most immediately discernible homocentric interests, in so many areas we ought to be cleaning up and not merely preserving the environmental status quo. In fact, there is presently strong sentiment in the Congress for a total elimination of all river pollutants by 1985,[42] notwithstanding that such a decision would impose quite large direct and indirect costs on us all. Here one is inclined to recall the instructions of Judge Hays, in remanding Consolidated Edison's Storm King application to the Federal Power Commission in *Scenic Hudson:*

The Commission's renewed proceedings must include as a basic concern the preservation of natural beauty and of natural historic shrines, keeping in mind that, in our affluent society, the cost of a project is only one of several factors to be considered.[43]

Nevertheless, whatever the merits of such a goal in principle, there are many cases in which the social price tag of putting it into effect are going to seem too high to accept. Consider, for example, an oceanside nuclear generator that could produce low cost electricity for a million homes at a savings of $1 a year per home, spare us the air pollution that comes of burning fossil fuels, but which through a slight heating effect threatened to kill off a rare species of temperature-sensitive sea urchins; suppose further that technological improvements adequate to reduce the temperature to present environmental quality would expend the entire one million dollars in anticipated fuel savings. Are we prepared to tax ourselves $1,000,000 a year on behalf of the sea urchins? In comparable problems under the present law of damages, we

work out practicable compromises by abandoning restoration costs and calling upon fair market value. For example, if an automobile is so severely damaged that the cost of bringing the car to its original state by repair is greater than the fair market value, we would allow the responsible tortfeasor to pay the fair market value only. Or if a human being suffers the loss of an arm (as we might conceive of the ocean having irreparably lost the sea urchins), we can fall back on the capitalization of reduced earning power (and pain and suffering) to measure the damages. But what is the fair market value of sea urchins? How can we capitalize their loss to the ocean, independent of any commercial value they may have to someone else?

One answer is that the problem can sometimes be sidestepped quite satisfactorily. In the sea urchin example, one compromise solution would be to impose on the nuclear generator the costs of making the ocean whole somewhere else, in some other way, *e.g.,* reestablishing a sea urchin colony elsewhere, or making a somehow comparable contribution.[44] In the debate over the laying of the trans-Alaskan pipeline, the builders are apparently prepared to meet conservationists' objections half-way by re-establishing wildlife away from the pipeline, so far as is feasible.[45]

But even if damage calculations have to be made, one ought to recognize that the measurement of damages is rarely a simple report of economic facts about "the market," whether we are valuing the loss of a foot, a foetus, or a work of fine art. Decisions of this sort are always hard, but not impossible. We have increasingly taken (human) pain and suffering into account in reckoning damages, not because we think we can ascertain them as objective "facts" about the universe, but because, even in view of all the room for disagreement, we come up with a better society by making rude estimates of them than by ignoring them.[46] We can make such estimates in regard to environmental losses fully aware that what we are really doing is making implicit normative judgments (as with pain and suffering)—laying down rules as to what the society is going to "value" rather than reporting market evaluations. In making such normative estimates decision-makers would not go wrong if they estimated on the "high side," putting the burden of trimming the figure down on the immediate human interests present. All burdens of proof should reflect common experience; our experience in environmental matters has been a continual discovery that our acts have caused more long-range damage than we were able to appreciate at the outset.

To what extent the decision-maker should factor in costs such as the pain and suffering of animals and other sentient natural objects, I cannot say; although I am prepared to do so in principle.[47] Given the conjectural nature of the "estimates" in all events, and the roughness of the "balance of conveniences" procedure where that is involved, the practice would be of more interest from the socio-psychic point of view, discussed below, than from the legal-operational. . . .

The Psychic and Socio-psychic Aspects

. . . The strongest case can be made from the perspective of human advantage for conferring rights on the environment. Scientists have been warning of the crises the earth and all humans on it face if we do not change our ways—radically—and these crises make the lost "recreational use" of rivers seem absolutely trivial. The earth's very atmosphere is threatened with frightening possibilities: absorption of sunlight, upon which the entire life cycle depends, may be diminished; the oceans may warm (increasing the "greenhouse effect" of the atmosphere), melting the polar ice caps, and destroying our great coastal cities; the portion of the atmosphere that shields us from dangerous radiation may be destroyed. Testifying before Congress, sea explorer Jacques Cousteau predicted that the oceans (to which we dreamily look to feed our booming populations) are headed toward their own death: "The cycle of life is intricately tied up with the cycle of water . . . the water system has to remain alive if we are to remain alive on

earth."[48] We are depleting our energy and our food sources at a rate that takes little account of the needs even of humans now living.

These problems will not be solved easily; they very likely can be solved, if at all, only through a willingness to suspend the rate of increase in the standard of living (by present values) of the earth's "advanced" nations, and by stabilizing the total human population. For some of us this will involve forfeiting material comforts; for others it will involve abandoning the hope someday to obtain comforts long envied. For all of us it will involve giving up the right to have as many offspring as we might wish. Such a program is not impossible of realization, however. Many of our so-called "material comforts" are not only in excess of, but are probably in opposition to, basic biological needs. Further, the "costs" to the advanced nations is not as large as would appear from Gross National Product figures. G.N.P. reflects social gain (of a sort) without discounting for the social *cost* of that gain, *e.g.*, the losses through depletion of resources, pollution, and so forth. As has well been shown, as societies become more and more "advanced," their real marginal gains become less and less for each additional dollar of G.N.P.[49] Thus, to give up "human progress" would not be as costly as might appear on first blush.

Nonetheless, such far-reaching social changes are going to involve us in a serious reconsideration of our consciousness towards the environment. . . .

A radical new conception of man's relationship to the rest of nature would not only be a step towards solving the material planetary problems; there are strong reasons for such a changed consciousness from the point of making us far better humans. If we only stop for a moment and look at the underlying human qualities that our present attitudes toward property and nature draw upon and reinforce, we have to be struck by how stultifying of our own personal growth and satisfaction they can become when they take rein of us. Hegel, in "justifying" private property, unwittingly reflects the tone and quality of some of the needs that are played upon:

A person has as his substantive end the right of putting his will into any and every thing and thereby making it his, because it has no such end in itself and derives its destiny and soul from his will. This is the absolute right of appropriation which man has over all "things."[50]

What is it within us that gives us this need not just to satisfy basic biological wants, but to extend our wills over things, to object-ify them, to make them ours, to manipulate them, to keep them at a psychic distance? Can it all be explained on "rational" bases? Should we not be suspect of such needs within us, cautious as to why we wish to gratify them? When I first read that passage of Hegel, I immediately thought not only of the emotional contrast with Spinoza, but of the passage in Carson McCullers' *A Tree, A Rock, A Cloud*, in which an old derelict has collared a twelve year old boy in a streetcar cafe. The old man asks whether the boy knows "how love should be begun?"

The old man leaned closer and whispered:

"A tree. A rock. A cloud."
. . .

"The weather was like this in Portland," he said. "At the time my science was begun. I meditated and I started very cautious. I would pick up something from the street and take it home with me. I bought a goldfish and I concentrated on the goldfish and I loved it. I graduated from one thing to another. Day by day I was getting this technique. . . .
. . .

. . . "For six years now I have gone around by myself and built up my science. And now I am a master. Son. I can love anything. No longer do I have to think about it even. I see a street full of people and a beautiful light comes in me. I watch a bird in the sky. Or I meet a traveler on the road. Everything, Son. And anybody. All stranger and all loved! Do you realize what a science like mine can mean?"[51]

To be able to get away from the view that Nature is a collection of useful senseless objects is, as McCullers' "madman" suggests, deeply involved in the development of our abilities to love—or, if that is putting it too strongly, to be able to reach a heightened awareness of our own, and others' capacities in their mutual in-terplay. To do so, we have to give up some psychic investment in our sense of separateness and specialness in the universe. And this, in turn, is hard giving indeed, because it involves us in a flight backwards, into earlier stages of civilization and childhood in which we had to trust (and perhaps fear) our environment, for we had not then the power to master it. Yet, in doing so, we—as persons—gradually free ourselves of needs for supportive illusions. Is not this one of the triumphs for "us" of our giving legal rights to (or acknowledging the legal rights of) the Blacks and women? . . .

. . . A few years ago the pollution of streams was thought of only as a problem of smelly, unsightly, unpotable water *i.e.,* to us. Now we are beginning to discover that pollution is a process that destroys wondrously subtle balances of life within the water, and as between the water and its banks. This heightened awareness enlarges our sense of the dangers to us. But it also enlarges our empathy. We are not only developing the scientific capacity, but we are cultivating the personal capacities *within us* to recognize more and more the ways in which nature—like the woman, the Black, the Indian and the Alien—is like us (and we will also become more able realistically to define, confront, live with and admire the ways in which we are all different).

The time may be on hand when these sentiments, and the early stirrings of the law, can be coalesced into a radical new theory or myth—felt as well as intellectualized—of man's relationships to the rest of nature. I do not mean "myth" in a demeaning sense of the term, but in the sense in which, at different times in history, our social "facts" and relationships have been comprehended and integrated by reference to the "myths" that we are co-signers of a social contract, that the Pope is God's agent, and that all men are created equal. Pantheism, Shinto and Tao all have myths to offer. But they are all, each in its own fashion, quaint, primitive and archaic. What is needed is a myth that can fit our growing body of knowledge of geophysics, biology and the cosmos. In this vein, I do not think it too remote that we may come to regard the Earth, as some have suggested, as one organism, of which Mankind is a functional part—the mind, perhaps: different from the rest of nature, but different as a man's brain is from his lungs. . . .

. . . As I see it, the Earth is only one organized "field" of activities—and so is the *human person*—but these activities take place at various levels, in different "spheres" of being and realms of consciousness. The lithosphere is not the biosphere, and the latter not the . . . ionosphere. The Earth is not *only* a material mass. Consciousness is not only "human"; it exists at animal and vegetable levels, and most likely must be latent, or operating in some form, in the molecule and the atom; and all these diverse and in a sense hierarchical modes of activity and consciousness should be seen integrated in and perhaps transcended by an all-encompassing and "eonic" planetary Consciousness.

. . . .

Mankind's function within the Earth-organism is to extract from the activities of all other operative systems within this organism the type of consciousness which we call "reflective" or "self"-consciousness—or, we may also say to *mentalize* and give meaning, value, and "name" to all that takes place anywhere within the Earth-field. . . .[52]

As radical as such a consciousness may sound today, all the dominant changes we see about us point in its direction. Consider just the impact of space travel, of world-wide mass media, of increasing scientific discoveries about the interrelatedness of all life processes. Is it any wonder that the term "spaceship earth" has so captured the popular imagination? The problems we have to confront are increasingly the world-wide crises of a global organism: not pollution of a stream, but pollution of the atmosphere and of the ocean. Increasingly, the death that occupies each human's imagination is not his own, but that of the entire life cycle of the planet earth, to which each of us is as but a cell to a body.

To shift from such a lofty fancy as the planetarization of consciousness to the operation of our municipal legal system is to come down to earth hard. Before the forces that are at work, our highest court is but a frail and feeble—a distinctly human—institution. Yet, the Court may be at its best not in its work of handing down decrees, but at the very task that is called for: of summoning up from the human

spirit the kindest and most generous and worthy ideas that abound there, giving them shape and reality and legitimacy. Witness the School Desegregation Cases which, more importantly than to integrate the schools (assuming they did), awakened us to moral needs which, when made visible, could not be denied. And so here, too, in the case of the environment, the Supreme Court may find itself in a position to award "rights" in a way that will contribute to a change in popular consciousness. It would be a modest move, to be sure, but one in furtherance of a large goal: the future of the planet as we know it.

How far we are from such a state of affairs, where the law treats "environmental objects" as holders of legal rights, I cannot say. But there is certainly intriguing language in one of Justice Black's last dissents, regarding the Texas Highway Department's plan to run a six-lane expressway through a San Antonio Park.[53] Complaining of the Court's refusal to stay the plan, Black observed that "after today's decision, the people of San Antonio and the birds and animals that make their home in the park will share their quiet retreat with an ugly, smelly stream of traffic. . . . Trees, shrubs, and flowers will be mowed down."[54] Elsewhere he speaks of the "burial of public parks," of segments of a highway which "devour parkland," and of the park's heartland.[55] Was he, at the end of his great career, on the verge of saying—just saying—that "nature has 'rights' on its own account"? Would it be so hard to do?

Notes

1. C. Darwin, Descent of Man 119, 120–21 (2d ed. 1874). *See also* R. Waelder, Progress and Revolution 39 *et seq.* (1967).
2. *See* Darwin, *supra* note 1, at 113–14. . . .
3. *See* Darwin, *supra* note 1, at 113. *See also* E. Westermarck, 1 The Origin and Development of the Moral Ideas 406–12 (1912). . . .
4. There does not appear to be a word "gericide" or "geronticide" to designate the killing of the aged. "Senicide" is as close as the Oxford English Dictionary comes, although, as it indicates, the

word is rare. 9 Oxford English Dictionary 454 (1933).

5. *See* Darwin, *supra* note 1, at 386–93. Westermarck, *supra* note 3, at 387–89, observes that where the killing of the aged and infirm is practiced, it is often supported by humanitarian justification; this, however, is a far cry from saying that the killing is *requested* by the victim as his right.

6. H. Maine, Ancient Law 153 (Pollock ed. 1930).

7. 387 U.S. 1 (1967).

8. 42 U.S.C. §§ 1973 *et seq.* (1970).

9. *See* Landman v. Royster, 40 U.S.L.W. 2256 (E.D. Va., Oct. 30, 1971). . . .

10. *But see* T. Szasz, Law, Liberty and Psychiatry (1963).

11. *See* note 22. The trend toward liberalized abortion can be seen either as a legislative tendency back in the direction of rightlessness for the foetus—or toward increasing rights of women. This inconsistency is not unique in the law of course; it is simply support for Hohfeld's scheme that the "jural opposite" of someone's right is someone else's "no-right." W. Hohfeld, Fundamental Legal Conceptions (1923). . . .

12. Int. Rev. Code of 1954, § 1361 (repealed by Pub. L. No. 89-389, effective Jan. 1, 1969).

13. For example, *see* United States v. Cargo of the Brig Malek Adhel, 43 U.S. (2 How.) 210 (1844). There, a ship had been seized and used by pirates. All this was done without the knowledge or consent of the owners of the ship. After the ship had been captured, the United States condemned and sold the "offending vessel." The owners objected. In denying release to the owners, Justice Story cited Chief Justice Marshall from an earlier case: "This is not a proceeding against the owner; it is a proceeding against the vessel for an offense committed by the vessel; which is not the less an offense . . . because it was committed without the authority and against the will of the owner." 43 U.S. at 234, quoting from United States v. Schooner Little Charles, 26 F. Cas. 979 (No. 15,612) (C.C.D. Va. 1818).

14. 9 U.S. (5 Cranch) 61, 86 (1809).

15. Trustees of Darmouth College v. Woodward, 17 U.S. (4 Wheat.) 518 (1819).

16. *Id.* at 636.

17. Consider, for example, that the claim of the United States to the naval station at Guantanamo Bay, at $2000-a-year rental, is based upon a treaty signed in 1903 by José Montes for the President of Cuba and a minister representing Theodore Roosevelt; it was subsequently ratified by two-thirds of a Senate no member of which is living today. Lease [from Cuba] of Certain Areas for Naval or Coaling Stations, July 2, 1903, T.S. No. 426; C. Bevans, 6 Treaties and Other International Agreements of the United States 1776–1949, at 1120 (U.S. Dep't of State Pub. 8549, 1971).

18. O. Gierke, Political Theories of the Middle Age (Maitland transl. 1927), especially at 22–30. . . .

19. Dred Scott v. Sandford, 60 U.S. (19 How.) 396, 404–05 (1856). . . .

20. People v. Hall, 4 Cal. 399, 405 (1854). . . .

21. Schechter, *The Rightlessness of Mediaeval English Jewry*, 45 Jewish Q. Rev. 121, 135 (1954) quoting from M. Bateson, *Medieval England* 139 (1904). . . .

22. Dietrich v. Inhabitants of Northampton, 138 Mass. 14, 16 (1884).

23. *In re* Goddell, 39 Wisc. 232, 245 (1875). The court continued with the following "clincher":

> And when counsel was arguing for this lady that the word, person, in sec. 32, ch. 119 [respecting those qualified to practice law], necessarily includes females, her presence made it impossible to suggest to him as *reductio ad absurdum* of his position, that the same construction of the same word . . . would subject woman to prosecution for the paternity of a bastard, and . . . prosecution for rape.

Id. at 246.

The relationship between our attitudes toward woman, on the one hand, and, on the other, the more central concern of this article—land—is captured in an unguarded aside of our colleague, Curt Berger: ". . . after all, land, like woman, was meant to be possessed. . . ." Land Ownership and Use 139 (1968).

24. Thus it was that the Founding Fathers could speak of the inalienable rights of all men, and yet maintain a society that was, by modern standards, without the most basic rights for Blacks, Indians, children and women. There was no hypocrisy; emotionally, no one *felt* that these other things were men.

25. The second thought streaming from . . . the older South [is] the sincere and passionate belief that somewhere between men and cattle, God created a *tertium quid*, and called it a Negro—a clownish, simple creature, at times even lovable within its limitations, but straitly foreordained to walk

within the Veil. W. E. B. DuBois, The Souls of Black Folk 89 (1924).

26. The statement in text is not quite true; *cf.* Murphy, *Has Nature Any Right to Life?*, 22 Hast. L. J. 467 (1971). An Irish court, passing upon the validity of a testamentary trust to the benefit of someone's dogs, observed in dictum that " 'lives' means lives of human beings, not of animals or trees in California." Kelly v. Dillon, 1932 Ir. R. 255, 261. (The intended gift over on the death of the last surviving dog was held void for remoteness, the court refusing "to enter into the question of a dog's expectation of life," although prepared to observe that "in point of fact neighbor's [sic] dogs and cats are unpleasantly long-lived. . . ." *Id.* at 260–61).

27. *See* Dixon v. Alabama State Bd. of Educ., 294 F.2d 150 (5th Cir.), *cert. denied*, 368 U.S. 930 (1961).

28. The law in a suit for injunctive relief is commonly easier on the plaintiff than in a suit for damages. *See* J. Gould, Law of Waters § 206 (1883).

29. However, in 1970 California amended its Water Quality Act to make it easier for the Attorney General to obtain relief, *e.g.,* one must no longer allege irreparable injury in a suit for an injunction. Cal. Water Code § 13350(b) (West 1971).

30. To whomsoever the soil belongs, he owns also to the sky and to the depths. *See* W. Blackstone, 2 Commentaries *18.

31. *See* Note, *Statutory Treatment of Industrial Stream Pollution*, 24 Geo. Wash. L. Rev. 302, 306 (1955); H. Farnham, 2 Law of Waters and Water Rights § 461 (1904); Gould, *supra* note 32, at § 204.

32. For example, courts have upheld a right to pollute by prescription, Mississippi Mills Co. v. Smith, 69 Miss. 299, 11 So. 26 (1882), and by easement, Luama v. Bunker Hill & Sullivan Mining & Concentrating Co., 41 F.2d 358 (9th Cir. 1930).

33. Pennsylvania Coal Co. v. Sanderson, 113 Pa. 126, 149, 6 A. 453, 459 (1886).

34. Hand, J. in Smith v. Staso Milling Co., 18 F.2d 736, 738 (2d Cir. 1927) (emphasis added). *See also* Harrisonville v. Dickey Clay Co., 289 U.S. 334 (1933) (Brandeis, J.).

35. Smith v. Staso, 18 F.2d 736, 738 (2d Cir. 1927).

36. By contrast, for example, with humane societies.

37. Cal. Prob. Code § 1460 (West Supp. 1971). . . .

38. Santa Clara County v. Southern Pac. R.R., 118 U.S. 394 (1886). . . .

39. *Cf.* Golding, *Ethical Issues in Biological Engineering*, 15 U.C.L.A. L. Rev. 443, 451–63 (1968).

40. Of course, in the instance of copyright and patent protection, the creation of the "property right" can be more directly justified on homocentric grounds.

41. *See* Schrag, *Life on a Dying Lake*, in The Politics of Neglect 167, at 173 (R. Meek & J. Straayer eds. 1971).

42. On November 2, 1971, the Senate, by a vote of 86–0, passed and sent to the House the proposed Federal Water Pollution Control Act Amendments of 1971, 117 Cong. Rec. S17464 (daily ed. Nov. 2, 1971). Sections 101(a) and (a)(1) of the bill declare it to be "national policy that, consistent with the provisions of this Act—(1) the discharge of pollutants into the navigable waters be eliminated by 1985." S.2770, 92d Cong., 1st Sess., 117 Cong. Rec. S17464 (daily ed. Nov. 2, 1971).

43. 354 F.2d 608, 624 (2d Cir. 1965).

44. Again, there is a problem involving what we conceive to be the injured entity.

45. N.Y. Times, Jan. 14, 1971, § 1, col. 2, and at 74, col. 7.

46. Courts have not been reluctant to award damages for the destruction of heirlooms, literary manuscripts or other property having no ascertainable market value. In Willard v. Valley Gas Fuel Co., 171 Cal. 9, 151 Pac. 286 (1915), it was held that the measure of damages for the negligent destruction of a rare old book written by one of plaintiff's ancestors was the amount which would compensate the owner for all detriment including sentimental loss proximately caused by such destruction. . . .

47. It is not easy to dismiss the idea of "lower" life having consciousness and feeling pain, especially since it is so difficult to know what these terms mean even as applied to humans. *See* Austin, *Other Minds*, in *Logic and Language* 342 (S. Flew ed. 1965); Schopenhauer, *On the Will in Nature*, in Two Essays by Arthur Schopenhauer 193, 281–304 (1889). Some experiments on plant sensitivity—of varying degrees of extravagance in their claims—include Lawrence, *Plants Have Feelings, Too . . .*, Organic Gardening & Farming 64 (April 1971); Woodlief, Royster & Huang, *Effect of Random Noise on Plant Growth*, 46 J. Acoustical Soc. Am. 481 (1969); Backster, *Evidence of a Primary*

Perception in Plant Life, 10 Int'l J. Parapsychology 250 (1968).

48. Cousteau, *The Oceans: No Time to Lose,* L.A. Times, Oct. 24, 1971, § (opinion), at 1, col. 4.

49. *See* J. Harte & R. Socolow, Patient Earth (1971).

50. G. Hegel, Hegel's Philosophy of Right 41 (T. Knox transl. 1945).

51. C. McCullers, The Ballad of the Sad Cafe and Other Stories 150–51 (1958).

52. D. Rudhyar, Directives for New Life 21–23 (1971).

53. 136. San Antonio Conservation Soc'y v. Texas Highway Dep't, *cert. denied,* 400 U.S. 968 (1970) (Black, J. dissenting to denial of certiorari).

54. *Id.* at 969.

55. *Id.* at 971.

The Good of Trees

Robin Attfield

My title can be taken in at least two ways: as "the good of trees" as opposed to "the harm of trees" and as "the good of trees" in the sense of "the value of trees." It might also be taken in the sense of "the use of trees," particularly by those who hold that to speak strictly trees have no good of their own, and are good only for satisfying human interests; this view, however, I consider and reject in the course of Section I. . . . But even if trees have needs and a good of their own, they may still have no value of their own and may still be due no consideration in their own right: in Section II, I examine various proposed moral grounds for preserving trees without finding in them any basis for valuing trees beyond human and animal welfare. The resulting paradox, that trees have interests but no value of their own, is explored in Section III, in which I supply an argument and a thought-experiment to show that trees can after all be of intrinsic value, even though we seldom need to take account of it in practice.

This essay is not in any way intended to derogate from arguments in support of belief in the rights of animals. Rather I hope it may contribute to the philosophy of intrinsic value and to the philosophy of ecology, and also throw light on the conceptual links between the notions of "purpose" and "interest," between "capacities" and "flourishing," between "di-versity" and "good" and between "interests," "value" and "rights." My beliefs about the feelings of trees are unalarmingly traditional: indeed trees are discussed not for the sake of some Arboreal Liberation Campaign, but because they constitute an intriguing test case of several theories in meta-ethics and normative ethics and because our attitudes to them are of considerable intrinsic interest.

I. Harm and the Needs of Trees

There is a view held widely among philosophers that, if we speak strictly, the needs of trees and other plants depend wholly on the interests of humans, that plants can only be harmed when actual or possible human desires are frustrated, and that their harm consists precisely in this frustration. This view has been held not only by contemporary writers such as . . . Joel Feinberg;[1] there are some traces of it in the writings of Aquinas,[2] who represents as instruments creatures which, unlike rational agents, do not control their actions, instruments intended solely for the use of agents possessed of intellect: and a similar belief seems to have been held by the ancient Stoics.[3] I shall try to show this view to be a confused one, about which we need to get straight not only for the sake of trees but also so as to become clearer

Source: *The Journal of Value Inquiry* 15 (1981), pp. 35–54. Reprinted by permission.

about harm and needs in general. (Some followers of Aquinas and of Kant hold a similar and in my opinion confused view about animals, but this view is contested by Feinberg, who argues in the same paper that some animals have interests and can have rights. While I agree with these conclusions of Feinberg, my own argument about the good of trees can be carried over so as to supplement his account of the interests of animals: for if the good of trees is partially or wholly independent of human interests, there can be little doubt that the same holds good of animals *a fortiori*.) . . .

Feinberg . . . doubts whether trees *do* have a good of their own, or that they have needs beyond our purposes and the norms which as a result we supply for them. What impresses him is that no-one (outside Samuel Butler's *Erewhon*) speaks of plants as having rights. He grants that "plants, after all, are not 'mere things'; they are vital objects with inherited propensities determining their natural growth. Moreover we do say that certain conditions are "good" or "bad" for plants, thereby suggesting that plants, unlike rocks, are capable of having a 'good.' " But this talk is misleading: paint can be believed bad for the walls of a house in the absence of a belief that the walls have "a good or welfare of their own."

Feinberg's basic point is that trees do not have wants or goals, and hence cannot know satisfaction or frustration, pleasure or pain. As they cannot suffer, we cannot be cruel to them: and as they lack desire and cognition, they have no interests, and hence cannot be preserved for their own sakes. Rather when redwood groves are preserved it is for the sake of humans including generations unborn.

I grant Feinberg his premise, that plants lack beliefs and desires, and also, in a strict sense of the term "cruel," that we cannot be cruel to plants. . . . What I do not see, however, is that "desires or wants are the materials interests are made of" and hence that "mindless creatures have no interests of their own." In an earlier passage,[4] Feinberg holds that the explanation why mere things, such as the Taj Mahal or a beautiful natural wilderness, have no good of their own "consists in the fact that mere things have no conative life: no conscious wishes, desires and hopes; or urges and impulses; or unconscious drives, aims and goals; or latent tendencies, direction of growth and natural fulfillments *(sic)*. Interests must be compounded somehow out of conations; hence mere things have no interests." And, if so, they have no value in their own right.

Now I have some doubt over classifying latent tendencies as conations: Feinberg's remarks about conations seem out of keeping with what they are intended to summarize. But of the two positions which might be attributed to him here, the fuller statement is preferable: latent tendencies, direction of growth and natural fulfilment do jointly seem, as Feinberg himself apparently suggests, sufficient conditions of having interests. This is not to endow machines or cities (if regarded as material objects) with interests, as they lack *natural* fulfilment even when built according to a plan; nor are these conditions satisfied by things lacking inherited capacities, such as forests, swamps or even species (as opposed to their members), though the case of species will be considered again later. It does, however, imply, contrary to Feinberg's subsequent conclusions, that all individual animals and plants have interests. For all have latent tendencies at some time or other, all have a direction of growth, and all can flourish after their natural kind. There is no need to hold that trees have unconscious goals to reach the conclusion that trees have interests: indeed where nothing counts as a conscious goal it is hard to see how anything counts as an unconscious one either. The growth and thriving of trees does not need to be regarded as a kind of wanting, nor trees as possible objects of sympathy, for us to recognize that they too have a good of their own.

Feinberg, however, rejects this construction of our ordinary beliefs about plants. He grants that we talk of their needs, but holds that things only have needs of their own, as distinct from needs for the fulfilment of the goals of some extrinsic agent, when they have a good or interests of their own. Our talk of the needs of trees, however, he holds to resemble that of the needs of cars for oil and petrol: without sunshine and water they "cannot grow and survive; but unless the growth and survival of trees are matters of human concern, affecting human interests, practical or aesthetic, the needs of trees alone will not be the basis of any claim of what is 'due' them in their own right. Plants may need things in order to discharge their functions, but their functions are assigned by human interests, not their own."

Feinberg's readers no doubt experience relief to hear that trees make no claims and have no rights: but this sentiment is really beside the point. Certainly Feinberg has by this stage advanced a theory relating interests and rights: but if both plants have no rights and the theory suggests a close connection between having rights and having interests, then that could as easily be a reason for rejecting or modifying the theory as for concluding that plants have no interests. At all events what is at stake is interests, not rights, and the real argument here has nothing to do with rights but amounts to the claim that as trees have needs only where human interests require the growth or survival that the needs are necessary for, they have no needs, and hence no good, of their own.

This argument might seem . . . difficult to controvert, . . . since any need of a tree which I represent as having no benefit for humans is likely to be regarded as an object of at least my interest: and, even if the play on the meaning of 'interest' is remarked, it will be held that objects of my investigative curiosity are also objects of my interests as a source of aesthetic enjoyment. Nevertheless the question which must be faced is whether trees would have needs if there *were* no humans, and indeed whether they had needs before humans first made their appearance. Once this question is put, the answer is obvious. Indeed Feinberg seems quite mistaken to hold that trees have no needs of their own. Trees had needs before people existed, and cannot be supposed to have lost them.

Feinberg does, however, present a reply to the view that talk of the thriving, flourishing, withering and languishing of trees shows them to have a good or interests of their own. His reply is of an etymological kind. . . . The original meaning of "flourish" was "blossom," but it was then extended to "grow luxuriantly, increase and enlarge" and to "thrive." Then it was further extended to persons: about this sense Feinberg says that "When a person flourishes, something happens to his interests analogous to what happens to a plant when it flowers, grows and spreads." (Is not more involved in a person flourishing than the progress of their

"interests"?) Finally flourishing is represented as a conscious act of disposition in the claim that "To flourish is to glory in the advancement of one's interests, in short, to be happy," an account which seems not only to degrade happiness, but also to require attitudes not required by flourishing itself.

This etymological account prepares the way for the remark "Nothing is gained by twisting the botanical metaphor back from humans to plants." Feinberg does not expect the senses of "flourish" in the two cases to be telescoped, but he does fear that the re-application of the metaphor to its source will make people believe that plants have interests "in the teeth of our actual beliefs." In Feinberg's eyes, of course, the sense of flourishing tied to interests is also tied to consciousness: and he regards this sense as merely metaphorical, as if there were no common element in the flourishing of people, animals and trees, such as the fulfilment or development of natural propensities. I do not, of course, claim that "flourishing" is used univocally of different natural kinds: but as there does seem to be a common element, I do not see the justification for holding that it is not in the *interest* of plants to flourish. Truistically they are unaware of their interests: but even creatures with cognition are often unaware of theirs, whether they are flourishing or not.

Nevertheless Feinberg tries to defend his claims by contending that "Some of our talk about flourishing plants reveals quite clearly that the interests that thrive when plants flourish are human, not 'plant interests.'" Sometimes, admittedly, there is a coincidence between our interests and a plant's natural propensities; but there are exceptions, as when we frustrate the natural propensities of a plant by removing dead flowers before the seeds have formed to encourage new flowers, and still talk of its "flourishing"; and what we then mean "is that our interest in the plant, not its own, is thriving." Now plants bred to have large, colourful or exotic flowers do, when they flower, satisfy our interests, even though flowering is only a part of their flourishing as even a cultivated plant. It is probably the overlap between their nature and our purposes which allows us to call this condition "flourishing": such talk does not however show that whether or not plants flourish turns on our interests rather than theirs. If it were our purpose to hang plastic lanterns on them, we could not claim that their bedecked condition was *ipso facto* one of flourishing: flourishing states have to be states in keeping with a plant's nature (which may, of course, be a cultivated nature).

The real exception, however, to the coincidence of plants' propensities and human interests is not the one which Feinberg believes he finds. What I have in mind is the common and garden experience of unwanted flourishing. Not only do weeds flourish contrary to our interests: so do runaway hedges, trees the roots of which block drains and the shade of which annoys the neighbors, and luxuriant undergrowth which blocks our paths and by-ways: to say nothing of the stings and scratches of plants whose propensities include protection against predators. Often we have good reason to cut back such growth: yet, even as we curse it, we cannot usually deny that the plants are flourishing after their kind—and that in no ironical or animistic sense of "flourishing." But on Feinberg's theory we cannot cut back plants which in any proper sense flourish contrary to our interests, because they are conceptually impossible. Not so easily is paradise regained.

Underlying my [criticism] of . . . Feinberg there is, of course, the Aristotelian principle that the good life for a living organism turns on the fulfilment of its nature. This principle has recently been defended and applied to animals by Stephen Clark,[5] who concludes that it harms creatures to "deprive them, whether they were man or beast, of the proper fulfilment of their genetically programmed potentialities.". . .

The same principle can be restated as follows. Let the "essential" capacities of an *x* be capacities in the absence of which from most members of a species that species would not *be* the species of *x*'s, and let "*x*" range over terms for living organisms. Then the flourishing of an *x* entails the development in it of the essential capacities of *x*'s. I have elsewhere attempted to defend the application of this principle to humans:[6] but, as Clark says of Aristotle's similar argument, the objections which might be invoked against it over humans "do not begin to touch its application in the case of beasts." To this I should add, "Or to plants,"

besides, of course, endorsing his view that the objections to its application to humans are mistaken. But this agreement of Clark and myself about humans is not here at stake, except insofar as the general principle is. This principle is also a principle governing the nature of good and harm, and suggests the kind of theory of harm. . . . It also implies that trees can be harmed in their own right, and have a "sake" for which acts can be performed, and interests and needs of their own.

What it does not imply, however, is that trees are of value in their own right, have rights, or ought to be shown consideration. To issues like these I now turn, by considering the grounds for preserving trees. Whether the fact that trees have a good of their own is a reason for caring for them is, at this stage, an unanswered question.

II. Grounds for Preserving Trees

Many of the grounds for preserving trees are also, of course, grounds for preserving wild animals and areas of wilderness as well. Of these grounds almost certainly the most important group is associated with the interests of humans. Thus it is important to preserve trees, other wild creatures and their habitats for reasons of scientific research, to retain as wide a gene pool as possible for the sake of medicine and agriculture, and for recreation, retreat and the enjoyment of natural beauty. These grounds, and the extent of their application, are well discussed by John Passmore in *Man's Responsibility for Nature,*[7] and do not need to be discussed in detail here.

Passmore correctly remarks that such considerations will often be overridden by other human interests, and sets out upon a search for other grounds for preservation. This same difficulty has been noticed by Laurence H. Tribe, who observes that, if human interests only are taken into account, the replacement of natural trees by plastic ones would often be justified.[8] His solution is to suggest that forests and other natural objects of beauty such as cliffs might be recognized as having rights which could not easily be overridden. A difficulty here, however, would be the justification of such legal or moral rights, especially where the balance of advantage would favor their disregard. As Robert Nozick[9] urges in the related matter of the treatment of animals, to justify an absolute prohibition on the infliction of pain and suffering we should need a theory of "side constraints" on which the interests of the animal concerned could not be overridden on any ground: a theory of overriding moral rights. But such a theory, requiring as it does the sacrifice on occasion of basic human needs and even of human life in the interest of non-human animals, is so counter-intuitive that it is yet less likely to command acceptance than that of Tribe. Nevertheless our inclination to accept that constraints of some kind are required in the dealings of humans with animals suggests one lesson to be learned about the preservation of wildlife: for the interests of animals, once allowed to count for something, do constitute an additional ground for preserving the plants and the habitats on which they depend; and these interests will occasionally tilt the balance of advantage in favor of preservation. . . .

One of the possible grounds for preserving both individual plants and species of plants is the desirability of diversity. The long history down from Plato's *Timaeus* of the principle that the more diverse a world is the better has been well traced by Lovejoy:[10] and in ecological connections it is an attractive principle, because of the important role played by even the humblest member of an ecosystem. But it is less easy to agree that diversity is desirable for its own sake, and that it is because of this that we are required where possible to preserve the manifold species of our planet. It is agreed on most sides that the enjoyment of sentient creatures is desirable for its own sake; and it is an important truth that delight and pleasure are usually fostered by the experience of diversities of sounds, colors, shapes and species, as well as by diversities of social traditions and individual personalities. So it may be that what makes diversity desirable is its enjoyment, together perhaps with the range of desirable activities which it facilitates.

To some, the above theory of the desirability

of diversity may seem anthropocentric: in fact, as it takes into account the experiences and activities of non-human species, this impression would be illusory. Nevertheless it makes the diversity of plant species a matter of merely derivative value, at least unless the theory is supplemented in some way: and even if it is supplemented by pointing out the importance of diversity in ecosystems for their stability, the value of diversity remains derivative, depending on the interests of those creatures such as ourselves which benefit from ecological stability.

As this may all sound unsatisfactory, it should be tested. What we have to imagine is a world in which there are no conscious experiences and no activities (at least on the part of creatures); of this imaginary world we must then ask whether it would be any the worse if it became more uniform, e.g. by coming to lack objects of one particular form or composition. Such a thought-experiment may be barely possible until we imagine the agency which might carry out the deprivation. Yet this is the sort of question which it is appropriate to ask, rather than one about, say, whether the loss of one species of plant would empoverish the world. For there may be something intrinsically desirable about plant species not because of their diversity but because they are species of living organisms: and what is at stake is whether diversity is *intrinsically* desirable, whatever its domain.

The agency which we seem to need to imagine can be introduced by a variation on Richard Routley's "last man" example.[11] The last man knows, in my version of this example, that all life on this planet is about to be terminated by multilateral nuclear warfare. He is, indeed, himself the last surviving sentient organism, and knows that he too will die within a few minutes; but he also happens himself to be possessed of a workable missile capable of destroying all the planet's remaining resources of diamond. The gesture of doing so would certainly be futile, but for himself it has a symbolical significance: and the question with which he is faced, and which we can ask about his projected act, is whether it would do any harm or destroy anything of intrinsic value. If we set aside the possibility that the planet might some day be repopulated with sentient organisms, which would, it seems to me, make a difference, the answer is surely that there is nothing wrong with this act, morally indifferent as I should certainly recognize it to be. The world would not through his act be any the poorer. (Maybe the act deprives God and the company of heaven of the experience of diversity, and is on that ground objectionable; but if so the objection arises because of the loss of valuable experiences rather than because of the value of diversity itself.)

There seems, then, no reason for preferring a slightly more diverse inanimate world to a slightly less diverse one, unless its constituents are objects of someone's or something's experience. In other words, diversity is not intrinsically desirable. If then there is something intrinsically undesirable in losses in the variety of living species, it will turn on their life and not on the loss to diversity as such.

It might here be suggested that it is rather the wrongness of vandalism which accounts for our objections to the elimination of species: indeed that his act was a piece of vandalism might be thought to show after all the wrongness of what was done by the "last man" of the recent example. Now certainly, as Passmore points out,[12] acts of destruction need justification; and certainly dispositions or policies involving the destruction of items of value for its own sake are strongly to be condemned. But even when policies and motives are bad (and this is not clearly true of the last man) the acts which stem from them are not always or necessarily wrong; and besides, vandalism is bad because of the harm habitually or usually done by vandals: so, if we are to hold that the elimination of a species is vandalism (which, I suspect, it often is) we need to show it to do harm or to be undesirable on some such more basic ground. The readiness of people to recognize vandalism may often curtail the need for further argument, as Pete Gunter reports about the tactics of some lumber companies opposed to the declaration of a National Park:[13] yet the recognition of vandalism entails the recognition of the unnecessary perpetration of evils, and it is these evils which constitute the basic objection to it. So we must continue to search for what of value is lost to the world when

plants or their species are destroyed, to see whether such losses are all ultimately losses to sentient creatures or not.

The question now becomes whether the continuation of each living species is valuable in itself. Passmore tells us that according to Aquinas this is the attitude of God, who "in the case of every other species except man . . . cares nothing for the benefit of the individual but does watch over the species as a whole."[14] A partially similar view is taken by Feinberg about animal species: "the preservation of a whole species may quite properly seem to be a morally more important matter than the preservation of an individual animal."[15] But Feinberg grounds this duty in our duty to future humans, rather than to the species concerned as such. And this is one of the grounds for preservation, or rather one class of grounds, taken account of already.

One reason for concern for species is concern for their current members: and when Stephen Clark observes that "Our distress at the destruction of a living tree is not merely at our loss of pleasure in its beauty," he expresses a sentiment which many would echo. Yet concern for species is not the same as concern for the present individual members: it involves the belief that it is desirable that *there be* elms, etc., and if it is to be an independent ground, that it is intrinsically desirable. Once a species dies out, there will be no more individual members: so either if each life of that kind is valuable in its own right, or if at least it is valuable that there be lives of that kind, the occurrence is a tragedy regardless of the circumstances or consequences.

Now the other tradition discussed by Passmore, that which enjoins reverence for life, has sometimes maintained that each life of any kind *is* valuable in its own right, and valuable just because it is a life. But, as Jonathan Glover cogently argues,[16] the belief that "all life is sacred" needs drastic modification even when applied to humans: for some lives cease to be worth living, and some never were so; and, we might add, even if some lives which are not in general worth living still include some worthwhile activities and experiences, nevertheless there are some lives which no longer do, and some which never did. And when we turn to other species we find that a great many organisms lack even the capacity to flourish after their own kind, being genetically or accidentally stunted, or having entered the phase of natural decay.

Thus, even if we agree with Feinberg that (some) animals have (some) rights, we are not obliged to hold that every animal life, let alone every vegetable life, is intrinsically valuable. Indeed there is good reason not to hold this at all. Whatever our objections to the destruction of individual trees, it is not the mere fact of their being alive which can justify our reaction: for lives can lack any features which make them worthwhile to anyone or anything, including the creature the life of which is in question.

If so, the intrinsic undesirability of the elimination of a living species cannot turn on the intrinsic value of each and every species member. It could still, in theory, turn on the intrinsic value of there being lives of that kind: but it is hard to see why we should accept this belief, granted that there is nothing intrinsically valuable about diversity in itself. Certainly most species are vital for the continued existence of many others, and certainly we enjoy their variety and might reasonably feel diminished at the extinction of any single one. But this is to acknowledge the importance of each species to other species, not their intrinsic value. It could then be that the tragedy involved in the termination of a species depends on the diminution of the worthwhile activities of members of other species or on the baneful effects is has on such individuals; and these said individuals, to be capable of worthwhile *activities,* must at least be purposive in a way in which vegetables are not.

The modern understanding of the interdependence of species supplies additional reasons why, to avert harm to humans and animals, almost all species of living creatures should be preserved, together with some of their habitats. Nevertheless the survey of the grounds for the preservation of wildlife and wilderness suggests that there are few if any grounds to be found beyond the welfare of humans and animals: for neither does mention of vandalism add to the list of basic grounds, nor is there anything intrinsically amiss in losses to diversity, in the extinction of species or in the curtailment of life rather than worthwhile life.

Moreover what is not intrinsically valuable can hardly be thought to have rights: for what has rights must be valuable in its own right. So apparently trees and plants lack rights, even though they are needed by humans many times over—and even though we should literally starve and suffocate without them.

III. The Value and Rights of Trees

The argument so far brings us to a paradox. Trees have needs and a good of their own, yet they have no intrinsic value and no rights of their own. Trees have interests, yet we have no obligation to protect those interests in themselves. And this is a position uncomfortably close to unreason: for, in other cases, what has interests of its own becomes *ipso facto* of moral concern, whereas in this case we are prepared to disregard a large set of interests and treat them as morally irrelevant.

Someone might at this point attempt to disavow the conclusion of Section I, and hold that e.g. what has no purposes has no interests: but as we there saw, this would be entirely unreasonable. The more tentative conclusions of Section II, however, could more easily be re-examined. Thus it was never established that no tree is of intrinsic value, but only that, as not all lives are worth living, it could well be that the possible objects of moral concern are confined to the class of the agents of worthwhile activities (and potential activities), and thus that the lives of non-purposive organisms are of no moral significance in themselves. But the premise only shows that *some* plants are of no intrinsic value, and that not all life is sacred. It could, then, still be true that a full-grown oak is after all morally as important as the crows and the squirrels which shelter in it.

But trees, it will be said, not only lack activity and self-motion but also beliefs, desires and feelings. Squirrels merit moral consideration because they have capacities in some way like our own: trees do not because the similarities are vanishingly few. Granted that it is the capacities of humans which make them morally significant, this analogical argument must be accepted at least as to what it affirms about animals, and as to the commended priority of animals over plants. Yet are the similarities really negligible? Trees, like humans and squirrels, have capacities for nutrition and growth, for respiration and for self-protection: and it is capacities and propensities such as these which determine their interests. If then their interests are partially similar to interests of acknowledged moral relevance (i.e. our own), can we disregard them totally? . . .

One ground [for refusing to take into account the interests of trees] might be that trees are not sentient, and thus have radically different interests: if so, the reply is that they share with sentient organisms vegetative interests which are regarded as mattering in other cases; the physical well-being of organisms which have interests is not plausibly a matter of complete indifference, even in cases where the organisms cannot suffer pain or frustration. Another ground might be that trees are not agents, because they lack purposes: if so, the reply takes the form of a request why the interests of non-purposive organisms are not as intrinsically important as the similar interests of purposive organisms, or at least why they are not intrinsically important to some degree. If the answer to this request is that only agents can exercise sanctions, it is not of an appropriate character: if it is that only agents consciously experience frustration, it can be replied that in the case of animals the stunting of natural propensities comprises harm even when it is not understood or sensed as such by the animal affected, and if this harm is an evil, so plausibly is the stunting of organisms lacking sentience.

In all this I willingly grant that the differences in potential between different species are of the very greatest importance. Thus the goods and the harms open to people because of their essential capacities vastly exceed those open to most animals, and similarly the blessings and sufferings made possible by capacities for purposiveness do indeed make the interests of non-purposive organisms count for less than those of purposive organisms and

hence of agents. But this still does not show that the interests of trees count for nothing: and even if not all lives are worthwhile lives, it still might be that many or even most vegetable lives are worthwhile and of value in themselves. After all, we have still to account for the distress which at least some of us feel at the destruction of a living tree. So the issue of whether trees have an intrinsic value remains at least an open one.

To attempt to test the issue, I revert to a form of Routley's "last man" example closer to his original. So as to discount the value of trees for people and sentient animals, we imagine once again that people and sentient animals are one and all doomed to imminent and inevitable nuclear poisoning, and that this is known to the last surviving human. But this time we imagine him considering the symbolic protest of hewing down with an axe the last tree of its kind, a hitherto healthy elm which has survived the nuclear explosions and which could propagate its kind if left unassaulted. Nothing sentient is ever likely to evolve from its descendants: so the question which he faces, and we can ask about him, is whether there is anything wrong with chopping it down and whether the world would be the poorer for the loss of it. We must suppose further, of course, that he himself will not suffer if he does not cut down the tree; he has enough timber already for firewood and shelter for his own last hours.

This question may seem to raise a problem of method: for it is asked of circumstances about which some would say that we no longer know how to apply our ordinary concepts of value. It is unclear to me how they would claim to know this: I can only invite those who nevertheless make this claim to attend instead to more ordinary cases of the uprooting of healthy trees and our reaction to it. So long, however, as the last man retains his ordinary concepts of value and his capacity to apply them, the question would seem to be both conceptually proper and apposite: and, if so, the problem of method proves illusory.

Most people who face the question would, I believe, conclude that the world would be the poorer for this act of the "last man" and that it would be wrong. He would be unnecessarily destroying a living creature which could have renewed the stock of its own species. (I suspect that a similar reaction would be the typical one to more everyday uprootings, though of course the reasons for such a reaction would often in those cases be mixed ones. I also suspect that the reaction would seldom be different even if the interests of sentient creatures are discounted.) And if, without being swayed by the interests of sentient creatures, we share in these conclusions and reactions, we must also conclude that the interests of trees are of moral significance. Although they rarely come or should come foremost in ethical deliberation, they can and in principle should be considered.

There are, of course, in practice ample grounds for disregarding the interests of trees at most junctures. Human and/or animal interests are almost always at stake, and mere vegetation can be forgotten where those interests would be imperilled. The good of trees might outweigh some of our whims: but it does not outweigh our interests except where our interests depend on it. But this is not to make trees of no ethical relevance in themselves. Very slightly, they have interests mirroring ours: at very many removes they are our living kin. But interests do, it seems, supply reasons for consideration: and there is always the residual possibility of their interests being of greater significance than any other which are at stake.

Theoretically at least, the same applies to other plants, to non-sentient animals, and to those colonies of organisms which function as individuals: although just as among sentient animals so here too there are diversities in capacities and no doubt diversities in the degree of consideration due. There again, the overall grounds for preservation and careful treatment will be supplemented in respect of value to other organisms by enormously diverse amounts, but never more, I suspect, than in the case of trees.

All the same, my conclusion is not without practical significance. It implies among other things that some degree of respect is due to almost all life, even though the main ground for the preservation of natural kinds remains human interests: and it implies that, where natural trees could be replaced without aesthetic loss or other disadvantage to humans there are

still reasons for not doing so. At the more theoretical level it suggests that nothing which has interests is to be viewed wholly instrumentally, and that things which have interests characteristically have some value in their own right. If trees have a good which is not our good, then they also *constitute* a good: if they have their own form of flourishing, they are thereby of value in themselves.

Do trees have rights? Only what is valuable in its own right has rights: but many trees do now seem to be valuable in their own right. Yet trees certainly do not have rights in Nozick's sense of their being "side-constraints" prohibiting various forms of treatment whatever the need or the benefits. At best, their interests have to be weighed with those of people and animals.

Need we, however, reject all forms of conceptual tie between interests and rights? The form of connection propounded by Feinberg is as follows. Creatures have rights if and only if they have interests, consideration is due to them, and it is due to them not for the sake of anything else but for their own sake.[17] Interests are necessary since what has rights must be capable of being represented and of being a beneficiary, having a welfare of its own. Feinberg believes, in the light of this condition, that trees lack rights, since he believes them to lack interests: but, as we have seen, he is mistaken. Now no-one would dispute that consideration is often due to trees where this just means that there are grounds for tending or preserving them. What is not usually accepted is that it is due to them for their own sake. If I am right and it is, then, granted Feinberg's conceptual connection of interests and rights, many trees have rights.

Such rights would, however, like all other rights be overridable from time to time: and the grounds for them, the intrinsic value of trees, would be so slender by comparison with the grounds of other rights as to be outweighed most of the time, so much so as to disappear into near oblivion. Yet if some trees have rights, then we should occasionally bear the fact in mind, or unsound theory will lead to misguidedness in action.

Alternatively someone who agrees that trees have interests and are of ethical relevance but cannot accept that they have rights might wish to reject or amend the conceptual tie delineated by Feinberg, such, perhaps, that only purposive or potentially purposive creatures can have rights. To such an amendment I should not object. Rights are not the sole ground of moral reasoning, and it does seem incongruous to represent the treatment of trees as a matter of justice. In any case all the *grounds* for the ascription of rights in Feinberg's unamended sense to trees would remain, and we could show concern for their needs and interests without believing them to have rights. We could, I think, still talk of obligations to them, since if it is sometimes wrong to destroy them for no reason beyond themselves then it is on those occasions obligatory not to do so,[18] and indeed the obligation is due to nothing but the tree.

"And God said, 'Let the earth put forth vegetation, plants yielding seed, and fruit trees bearing fruit in which is their seed, each according to its kind, upon the earth.' And it was so. The earth brought forth vegetation, plants yielding seed according to their own kinds, and trees bearing fruit in which is their seed, each according to its kind. And God saw that it was good."[19] Of course, in Genesis 1 *all* creation is good: be that as it may, living creatures in any case, it would seem, characteristically have a value of their own.[20]

Notes

1. Joel Feinberg, "The Rights of Animals and Unborn Generations," in *Philosophy and Environmental Crisis*, ed. William T. Blackstone (Athens: University of Georgia Press, 1974), at pp. 51–55.
2. *Summa Contra Gentiles*, translated by the English Dominican Fathers, Benziger Brothers, 1928, ch. 112, quoted in *Animal Rights and Human Obligations*, ed. Tom Regan and Peter Singer (Englewood Cliffs, NJ: Prentice-Hall, 1976), pp. 56–59.
3. See the discussion of the Stoic Balbus in Cicero's *De Natura Deorum* by John Passmore at p. 14 of *Man's Responsibility for Nature* (London: Duckworth, 1974).

4. Feinberg, op. cit., pp. 49–50.
5. Stephen R. L. Clark, *The Moral Status of Animals* (Oxford: Clarendon Press, 1977), pp. 57–58.
6. Robin Attfield, "On Being Human," *Inquiry* 17(1974):175–92.
7. Passmore, op. cit., pp. 101–110.
8. Laurence H. Tribe, "Ways not to think about plastic trees," *Yale Law Journal* 83(1974):1315–48.
9. Robert Nozick, *Anarchy, State and Utopia* (Oxford: Blackwell, 1974), pp. 28–42.
10. A. O. Lovejoy, *The Great Chain of Being* (Harvard: Harvard University Press, 1936).
11. Richard Routley, "Is There a Need for a New, an Environmental Ethic?" in *Proceedings of the Fifteenth World Congress of Philosophy* (Varna, 1973), pp. 205–10.
12. Passmore, op. cit., p. 124.
13. Pete A. Y. Gunter, "The Big Thicket," in Blackstone, op. cit., pp. 126–29.
14. Passmore, op. cit., p. 117.
15. Feinberg, op. cit., p. 56.
16. Jonathan Glover, *Causing Death and Saving Lives* (London: Penguin, 1977), ch. 3.
17. Feinberg effectively deals with the objection that right-holders must also be capable of making and of waiving claims on their own at op. cit., 46–49.
18. The claim that it is obligatory not to do what it is wrong to do and the criteria of obligation, wrongness and rightness are discussed more fully in my "Supererogation and Double Standards," *Mind* 89:481–99.
19. *Genesis*, ch. 1, vv. 11f. (Revised Standard Version).
20. I am grateful for comments and criticisms of an earlier draft of this essay from David Attfield, John Benson, Robin Downie, Robert Elliot, Thomas McPherson, Mary Midgley, Heather Milne, Peter Singer and members of the Philosophy Seminar of University College, Cardiff and for bibliographical assistance from Richard Routley. He and Val Routley (now Val Plumwood) arrive by another route at some cognate conclusions in "Against the Inevitability of Human Chauvinism," in K. E. Goodpaster and K. M. Sayre (eds.), *Ethics and Problems of the 21st Century* (Notre Dame and London: University of Notre Dame Press, 1979), pp. 36–59.

The Preservation of Species: Are They Special?

Preview

We do not seem to mourn the ceasing to exist of certain groups of biological organisms. Some we tend to view as insignificant. Recall that talk of species includes various types of animals (mammals, marsupials, insects, and so on) as well as plants. What does it matter if the earth comes to contain one less type of horned toad or one less type of mosquito? Given its role as a carrier of disease, should we regret, or should we celebrate, the extinction of the Norwegian rat? In short, what's so bad about the disappearance of certain species (other than *Homo sapiens!*)? Alternatively, are there compelling reasons to draw the moral conclusion that we ought to make strenuous efforts to preserve species? Of course, one might ask as well: What's so great about people? Why preserve *Homo sapiens*? If we could imagine things from the viewpoint of a grizzly or a coyote, perhaps we would not mourn the extinction of that Super Predator called *man*. We need to survey and reassess the reasons for and against preservation. The selections in this section will facilitate

the development of a considered view on these matters. Let us begin to orient our thoughts around four focal points:

1. the concept of species
2. empirical data about the rate of extinction, and the effects of extinction
3. arguments for and against preservation
4. proposed modes of preservation

Conceptual Twists

There are some slippery differences between considering our relations to *species* and to current *members of a species*. There is a distinction between focus on an open class (for example, a species) and a closed one (for example, the 1984 U.S. Supreme Court). Ignoring this difference is liable to generate confusion. It is of interest that a given species can continue to exist at time t^{n+1} even though all the members of that species at t^n have ceased to exist at t^{n+1} (suppose: New members are on the scene at t^{n+1}). The concept of a species, then, is unlike that of concepts designating certain groups, such as the 1984 U.S. Olympic women's volleyball team (a closed class). In contrast, the *species* designated as "the humpback whale" is not to be understood as the set of currently existing whales. Killing all such existing whales would be sufficient to extinguish the species (barring later reconstitution from residual genetic materials, e.g., frozen cells), but such an event is not necessary for the species to cease to exist. Even if there is a negative duty not to kill any whale and even if that duty is not (henceforth) violated, the whale might cease to exist. Another type of act, sterilization of all the members of a species, can cause the species to cease to exist (even though such an act would not violate any duty not to kill members of that species). There is, then, a certain asymmetry between considering relations we may have toward members of a species and relations to the species as such. Further, if there is a negative duty not to extinguish a species, this duty is not identical with a possible duty *not to kill* members of that species. In further contrast, if there is a positive duty to *preserve* a given species, the humpback whale, for example, such a duty might be carried out (in principle) by preserving only a small number of humpbacks. Some who advocate a duty to "preserve species" no doubt have in mind something stronger, that is, a duty to help *many* members of a species thrive and reproduce.

Another conceptual matter, closely related to a focus on species, concerns whether a species can have rights, moral and not merely legal rights. Even if it is clear that individuals of certain sorts (me, but not my thumb) can have rights, it is less clear that a complex entity such as a species can. Those who claim that we have duties to preserve certain species, may claim (at this juncture) that rights intelligibly and reasonably can be attributed to entities other than individuals (corporations or governments). But what sorts of complex entities can have rights? Or it may be maintained that not all duties are correlative to rights possessed by the entity to whom the duty is owed. For example, it sometimes is asserted that we have certain duties to human infants, comatose humans, and dead humans, even though they are not bearers of rights. The questions of whether a species con-ceptually *could* possess rights (as opposed to possession by individual members of the species) and whether any species *does* are questions requiring further exploration. The distinctions just noted are relevant to the larger moral issue of whether we are failing in any duties we might have to preserve any or all species. What is it, however, about the current situation and its trajectory that is thought to be deserving of great concern?

Prospective Extinction

Most in the public spotlight is the threatened extinction of certain of the "Most Impressive Creatures," for example, the tiger, the blue whale, the whooping crane, the giant panda, the orangutan, and the cheetah. Less dramatic, but of equal or greater significance, is the probable current loss of one species per day, and the probable loss of 1 million by the year 2000. Further, of the 5 to 10 million species on earth several million may be lost in a few decades. What is often not recognized—in discussions of the prospective fate of different species—is the very dramatic historical turnabout that has developed in recent years and, of course, is continuing. The facts are well documented by Norman Myers in the first essay in this section. Briefly put, due to human activity and intervention in natural processes, there is a *radical increase in the number of members of one species, Homo sapiens, and a radical increase in the rate of extinction of other species.* Again, whether this is good, bad, a reason to celebrate or mourn, is a matter of evaluation; for now we focus only on some facts. It seems fair to say that our species, counting in at about 4 billion and weighing in at 200 million tons, dominates the planet. Current population projections suggest about 8 billion people by the year 2025. Given the evident problems (say, the need for adequate food, shelter, and health care) attending large, and dense, populations of people, few today are seduced by the inference that "since human life is good, the more lives the better." Associated with this propensity of humans to "be fruitful and multiply" has been the direct destruction of many animal and plant species—as well as their indirect destruction (intentional or not; foreseen or not) by the cramping, erosion, or elimination of their habitats or food supply.

The number of identified animal types now threatened is said to be about 1,000, but many plant types and animal types simply are not yet identified. Dozens of thousands of these probably are threatened as well. Extinction of species has occurred since life began about 3.5 billion years ago. What is new under the sun is a significant increase in the rate of extinction due to human activity. Between 1600 and 1900 a species became extinct about once every 4 years. From 1900 to 1960 the rate was about one per year. Since then estimates range from 100 per year up to a projected 40,000 per year in the last quarter of this century. This last figure rests in part on the projected destruction of prairie land, wetlands, and tropical moist forests (the latter are assumed to contain 2 to 5 million species each). Even if these estimates are seriously in error, radical changes are under way.

Sketching the Arguments

As noted, one view about the demise of thousands, or even millions, of species, of habitats, and ecosystems is "So what?" Should we be concerned? Ought we to act differently? Why? And if so, how? Or why not? The reasons, or arguments in favor of the view that we ought to make efforts to preserve species or certain species, tend to fall into two broad categories— as one might surmise. First, there are purely anthropocentric considerations; other species should be preserved because they are valuable to us human beings. Some arguments maintain that for purely prudential reasons we must protect or promote *our* human interests now. It also is urged that we have duties to *other*, indeed nonexistent, humans (is it not wrong to turn the earth into a garbage dump for future generations of humans?). Second, as noted in Part I, powerful arguments can be marshalled on behalf of the view that members of at least some other species have moral standing (or are in-

trinsically valuable). If so, we owe them certain duties of nonharm—duties *not* derivative from or dependent upon *contingent* facts about whether or not the preservation of animals in the long or short run promotes human interests.

Several points are especially noteworthy here. As noted in the general introduction, criteria for possession of moral standing such as sentience, possession of consciousness, or self-consciousness will not even "confer" moral standing on all animals. Furthermore, on the standard assumption that plants lack these traits, such grounds provide no basis for concluding that direct duties are owed to plants or many animals (for example, thousands of insect species). Thus, according to such views there will be no direct duty to preserve thousands of plants and animal species. Some defenders of the "land ethic" take a contrary view, or so it appears. This type of dispute is often alluded to in terms of a tension between animal liberationists and defenders of "the land ethic" (or, in the somewhat misleading terminology, "environmental ethicists"). Closer examination of this matter is found in Part III (see Callicott's essay). If it is true that individual animals (or some) have rights, or intrinsic value, or moral standing (as the case may be), is it also the case that any *species* has rights, intrinsic value, or moral standing? In later essays, Lilly-Marlene Russow, as well as Tom Regan, defends a negative answer to this question.

Even if there are no direct duties to individual animals, to individual plants, to species, or to ecosystems, there are evident advantages to humans in preserving many species, other things being equal. The advantages accruing to humans from having certain animals and plants around to exploit are enormous. Much of this exploitation (recall the essays in Part I) may be morally unjustifiable. It is reasonable to believe, however, that much human "use" of plants and animals is, uncontroversially, permissible, for example, shearing sheep for wool, keeping dogs and cats for pets, making valuable drugs from plants, harvesting trees from farms, and so on. There is, then, a consequentialist line of argument for preserving certain species. Sometimes it may maximize utility to do so (whether the utilities accruing to sentient animals are weighed in here—as in classic utilitarianism—or not is, of course, an important matter). In some cases the benefit of preserving a species cannot be "cashed" readily in terms of the value of experimenting on its members, eating its members, or making a product of its members. Sometimes the value of preservation seems to be mainly, or solely, of an aesthetic sort. The question arises as to whether this is a rational basis for urging the preservation of the giant panda, the blue whale, the cheetah, or the penguin (or wildernesses; see next section "Wilderness: What Is It 'Good For'?"). Even if the appeal to the preservation of aesthetic values succeeds in the just mentioned cases, it is less likely to provide a plausible ground for preserving ugly, or very small, nocturnal creatures (or species). Indeed, it is hard, and perhaps impossible, to defend the preservation or conservation of certain species on the ground that they themselves are valuable as economic resources. At least some species, in short, seem to be useless as aesthetic, economic, or ecological resources. On the latter point, compare Russow's query about the ecological role of a species all of whose members are in zoos—or all of which were bred to live briefly only in a lab (such as lab rats). Still, some species, or other entities, may be part of an ecosystem or habitat that is itself valuable. If we are to preserve a certain species, then we cannot blithely, or ruthlessly, continue to destroy the habitats of such species. Analogously, it would be absurd to maintain that we cared about whooping cranes, but went ahead and destroyed all their nesting places.

There is an obvious difficulty in trying to *measure* how valuable are aesthetically valuable experiences. A standard "measuring rod," of course, is the "cash value" of a thing. How many dollars, for example, is it worth to preserve a blue whale (or heighten the probability of its preservation) so that your grandson might see it—and not just a film or a photograph? Economists have suggestions, of course, about how to assign a monetary value to things whose value we find hard to measure or even regard as incommensurable, that is, not measurable in terms of alien stuff (for example, human life in terms of dollars). What one would be willing to pay to achieve a certain lowered probability of

premature death (like giving up income to have a safer job) is often suggested to be a sort of useful measure of the cash value of "life" (or enhanced likelihood of a longer life). In spite of the frequent acceptance of current economic theory in sophomore college classes as a gospel of which the masses are ignorant, there are serious difficulties in the view that actual or hypothetical market choices properly measure certain values. These matters, however, will be explored in greater depth in Part IV.

As noted earlier, some maintain that certain species have *intrinsic value*. There are, however, various obscurities surrounding the concept of intrinsic value. Generally, it seems that when it is claimed that "X has intrinsic value" what is meant is that "X is valuable in itself and apart from whatever valuation of X is made by others" (for example, people). But sometimes an alternative interpretation seems to be employed. To say "X is intrinsically valuable" means "X is valued by others for X's own sake" (in contrast with what is often meant when philosophers claim pleasure is intrinsically good or valuable). This latter interpretation, unlike the former, requires *valuers* to be around. Would the Grand Canyon or the giant panda lack intrinsic value if people did not exist? Or if possession of the capacity to live a meaningful or worthwhile life is necessary for something to possess intrinsic value, it would seem that only sentient, or perhaps only conscious, entities could have intrinsic value. This would include most people and many animals, but little else would have intrinsic value based on this criterion for its possession.

In short there is no *smooth* path to finding a compelling ground for the conclusion that many or all species ought to be preserved—indeed for identifying a rational justification for the somewhat powerful preservationist instincts many of us share. One final item for reflection: Even if it is argued that X (a dog, say) has intrinsic value and Y (a very valuable diamond ring, for example) does not, should we automatically preserve X over Y if somehow we had to choose (imagine that a house is on fire and one can only save the dog or the diamond, but not both). Consider an alternate example. Suppose that instead of a diamond, what might be saved is the only accessible antidote for a poison that a child has just ingested. Many practical environmental problems involve a similar kind of conflict; that is, we must sacrifice one thing of value (of *some sort*) to preserve something else of value (of some sort). Just how to resolve trade-off problems in an nonarbitrary manner is an extremely recalcitrant matter. Some related issues are pursued further in Part IV.

Policy Approaches to Species Protection

Some comment is in order with regard to two broadly conceived modes of proposed protection of certain species (assuming now that we ought to do so). For convenient reference we might label them (1) the quasi-citizenship solution and (2) the private property solution. If the moral claim that a species ought to be protected can be established on other grounds, one proposed mode of protection is to place legal constraints on human dealings with creatures of that species. Thus, prohibitions on killing, hunting, experimenting on, buying, selling, hunting at certain times or places, "taking" beyond a certain number, disruption of habitat (for example, by deforestation, introduction of new predators) are all means of granting a legal status to members of a species so that they share some protections enjoyed by full citizens. Christopher Stone's recommendations, viewed in this light, are less radical than one might think. Their novel aspect, perhaps, involves extending protections to nonsentient nonhumans, for example, trees and rivers.

What we are labeling the private-property solution is explored more fully in Part IV, but we will characterize the issue here. An orthodox view of many economists is that the problem of "overuse," "exploitation," or undesirable destruction of certain species stems primarily from their status as "common property," that is, as unowned commodities or entities over which individual humans or organizations lack property rights. If plants, animals, the air, or rivers are "held in common," no one, it is claimed, will have an incentive to make any

special effort to protect, preserve, improve, or enhance the lot of such entities. As evidence of this tendency, we observe trashed public places and comparatively tidy private domains. So, if you want to save alligators, don't grant them a special protected status; rather, allow property rights in them. With the "common property" alternative, only the owner of a wetland that includes an alligator habitat will be burdened (she will be under a liability not to use her property in certain ways); hence, the property will be of less value to her. Thus, she may choose to drain the wetland to turn it toward some profitable use. Alternatively, if she can sell alligators she will have an incentive not to subvert their habitat. Hence, the species will be preserved. This line of reasoning is, and ought to be, hotly contested. One might consider how an animal liberationist would respond, as well as one who believes in conservation of species. Somewhat ironically on this view, alligators (the species or individual members?) may "owe a debt of gratitude" to those who wish to kill them and sell their hides. Similarly, must cattle owe a debt to Ray Kroc and McDonalds, chickens a debt to Colonel Sanders, or pigs a debt to those who are not orthodox Jews?

There is a modest paradox here that deserves reflection. According to the view considered, if a high (quasi-citizen–like) status is assigned to certain creatures, it is more likely that they will become extinct. If a low status (like "mere property") is assigned, the species more likely will survive. So it is claimed. The issue is an empirical one. Consider, however, this objection. Some human subgroups (such as certain tribes) may become extinct. To ensure or promote their survival, should a price tag be put on their lives? If not, why are things different with animals or plants? In Part IV we return to an exploration of "market solutions."

In passing we only note here a further, not unimportant, practical complication to both property and quasi-citizenship solutions: The habitats of certain species cut across national boundaries. Hence, international political cooperation is needed to sustain certain species—as well as in reaching agreement about controlling human impact on those great liquid and gaseous commons: the oceans and the air.

The practical, and some theoretical, issues involved in the questions of why and how to preserve cetaceans (for example, whales) are sketched in the later selection by Peter Dobra, who notes the political difficulties that persist in the light of an effective international authority and the competing interests of different nations—not to mention the widespread insensitivity to the question of whether cetaceans have moral standing.

The Sinking Ark

Norman Myers

Ask a man in the street what he thinks of the problems of disappearing species, and he may well reply that it would be a pity if the tiger or the blue whale disappeared. But he may add that it would be no big deal, not as compared with crises of energy, population, food and pollution—the "real problems." In other words, he cares about disappearing species, but he cares about many other things more: he simply does not see it as a critical issue. If the tiger were to go extinct tonight, the sun would still come up tomorrow morning.

In point of fact, by tomorrow morning we shall almost certainly have one less species on Planet Earth than we had this morning. It will not be a charismatic creature like the tiger. It could well be an obscure insect in the depths of some remote rainforest. It may even be a creature that nobody has ever heard of. But it will have gone. A unique form of life will have been driven from the face of the earth for ever.

Equally likely is that by the end of the century we shall have lost 1 million species, possibly many more. Except for the barest handful, they will have been eliminated through the hand of man.

Extinction Rates

Animal forms that have been documented and recognized as under threat of extinction now

Source: *The Sinking Ark* by Norman Myers (Oxford, England: Pergamon Press, 1980), pp. 3–13, 27–31. Reprinted by permission.

amount to over 1000. These are creatures we hear much about—the tiger and the blue whale, the giant panda and the whooping crane, the orangutan and the cheetah. Yet even though 1000 is a shockingly large number, this is only a fractionally small part of the problem. Far more important are those many species that have not even been identified by science, let alone classified as threatened. Among the plant kingdom, these could number 25,000, while among animals, notably insects, the total could run to hundreds of thousands.

Extinction of species has been a fact of life virtually right from the start of life on earth 3½ billion years ago. At least 90 percent of all species that have existed have disappeared. But almost all of them have gone under by virtue of natural processes. Only in the recent past, perhaps from around 50,000 years ago, has man exerted much influence. As a primitive hunter, man probably proved himself capable of eliminating species, albeit as a relatively rare occurrence. From the year A.D. 1600, however, he became able, through advancing technology, to over-hunt animals to extinction in just a few years, and to disrupt extensive environments just as rapidly. Between the years 1600 and 1900, man eliminated around seventy-five known species, almost all of them mammals and birds—virtually nothing has been established about how many reptiles, amphibians, fishes, invertebrates and plants disappeared. Since 1900 man has eliminated around another seventy-five known species—again, almost all of them mammals and birds, with hardly anything known about how many other creatures have faded from the scene. The rate from the year 1600 to 1900, roughly one species every 4 years, and the rate during most of the present century, about one species per year, are to be compared with a rate of possibly one per 1000 years during the "great dying" of the dinosaurs.

Since 1960, however, when growth in human numbers and human aspirations began to exert greater impact on natural environments, vast territories in several major regions of the world have become so modified as to be cleared of much of their main wildlife. The result is that the extinction rate has certainly soared, though the details mostly remain undocumented. In 1974 a gathering of scientists concerned with the problem hazarded a guess that the overall extinction rate among all species, whether known to science or not, could now have reached 100 species per year.[1]

Yet even this figure seems low. A single ecological zone, the tropical moist forests, is believed to contain between 2 and 5 million species. If present patterns of exploitation persist in tropical moist forests, much virgin forest is likely to have disappeared by the end of the century, and much of the remainder will have been severely degraded. This will cause huge numbers of species to be wiped out. Similar processes of disruption and destruction apply in other natural environments, notably grasslands and wetlands. While not so ecologically diverse as tropical moist forests, these biomes feature their own rich arrays of species—and they are likewise undergoing fundamental modification at the hand of man. The United States once featured around 1 million km^2 of pristine prairie, but now the lot has disappeared under the plough or has been otherwise transformed, except for 16,000 km^2 in Kansas. Grasslands in many parts of the world are similarly giving way to cultivated crops, to feed a hungry planet. In advanced and developing regions alike, wetlands are being drained, dug up, paved over, so that they can be converted from their present "useless" state into something more profitable for man. The result: elimination of whole communities of species, virtually overnight.

Let us suppose that, as a consequence of this man-handling of natural environments, the final one-quarter of this century witnesses the elimination of 1 million species—a far from unlikely prospect. This would work out, during the course of 25 years, at an average extinction rate of 40,000 species per year, or rather over 100 species per day. The greatest exploitation pressures will not be directed at tropical forests and other species-rich biomes until towards the end of the period. That is to say, the 1990s could see many more species accounted for than the previous several decades. But already the disruptive processes are well under way, and it is not unrealistic to suppose that, right now, at least one species is disappearing each day. By the late 1980s we could be facing a situation where one species becomes extinct each hour. By the time human communities establish ecologically sound life-styles, the fallout of species could total several million. This would amount to a biological débâcle greater than all mass extinctions of the geological past put together.

Loss to Society

We face, then, the imminent elimination of a good share of the planetary spectrum of species that have shared the common earth-home with man for millennia, but are now to be denied living space during a phase of a mere few decades. This extinction spasm would amount to an irreversible loss of unique resources. Earth is currently afflicted with other forms of environmental degradation, but, from the standpoint of permanent despoliation of the planet, no other form is anywhere so significant as the fallout of species. When water bodies are fouled and the atmosphere is treated as a garbage can, we can always clean up the pollution. Species extinction is final. Moreover, the impoverishment of life on earth falls not only on present society, but on all generations to come.

In scores of ways, the impoverishment affects everyday living right now. All around the world, people increasingly consume food, take medicines and employ industrial materials that owe their production to genetic resources and other startpoint materials of animals and plants. These pragmatic purposes served by species are numerous and growing. Given the needs of the future, species can be reckoned among society's most valuable raw materials. To consider the consequences of devastating a single biome, the tropical moist forests: elimination of these forests, with their exceptional concentrations of species, would undermine the prospects for modernized agriculture, with repercussions for the capacity of the world to feed itself. It could set back the campaign against cancer by years. Perhaps worst of all, it would eliminate one of our best bets for resolving the energy crisis: as technology develops ways to utilize the vast amounts of solar energy stored in tropical-forest plants each day, these forests could generate as much energy, in the form of methanol and other fuels, as almost half the world's energy consumption from all sources in 1970. Moreover, this energy source need never run dry like an oil well, since it can replenish itself in perpetuity.

Any reduction in the diversity of resources, including the earth's spectrum of species, narrows society's scope to respond to new problems and opportunities. To the extent that we cannot be certain what needs may arise in the future, it makes sense to keep our options open (provided that a strategy of that sort does not unduly conflict with other major purposes of society). This rationale for conservation applies to the planet's stock of species more than to virtually any other category of natural resources.

The situation has been well stated by Dr. Tom Lovejoy of the World Wildlife Fund:

If we were preparing for a new Dark Age, and could take only a limited number of books into the monasteries for the duration, we might have to determine which single branch of knowledge would have the greatest survival value for us. The outstanding candidate would be biology, including its applied forms such as medicine, agriculture, forestry and fisheries. Yet we are doing just the contrary, by busily throwing out the biology books before they have been written.

Many other biologists—switched-on scientists, not "case-hardened eco-nuts"—believe that man is permanently altering the course of evolution, and altering it for the worse. The result will be a grossly impoverished version of life's diversity on earth, from which the process of evolution will be unlikely to recover for many millions of years. And it is not going too far to say that, by eliminating an appreciable portion of earth's stock of species, humanity might be destroying life that just might save its own.

Species Conservation and Economic Advancement

There is another major dimension to the problem, the relationship between conservation of species and economic advancement for human communities.

As indicated, the prime threat to species lies with loss of habitat. Loss of habitat occurs mainly through economic exploitation of natural environments. Natural environments are exploited mainly to satisfy consumer demand for numerous products. The upshot is that species are now rarely driven extinct through the activities of a few persons with direct and deliberate intent to kill wild creatures. They are eliminated through the activities of many millions of people, who are unaware of the "spill-over" consequences of their consumerist lifestyles.

This means that species depletion can occur through a diffuse and insidious process. An American is prohibited by law from shooting a snowy egret, but, by his consumerist lifestyle, he can stimulate others to drain a marsh (for croplands, industry, highways, housing) and thereby eliminate the food supply for a whole colony of egrets. A recent advertisement by a utility corporation in the United States asserted that "Something we do today will touch your life," implying that its activities were so far-reaching that, whether the citizen was aware or not, his daily routine would be somehow affected by the corporation's multifaceted enterprise. In similar fashion, something the citizen does each day is likely to bear on the survival prospects of species. He may have no wanton or destructive intent toward wildlife.

On the contrary, he may send off a regular donation to a conservation organization. But what he contributes with his right hand he may take away with his half-dozen left hands. His desire to be consumer as well as conservationist leads him into a Jekyll-and-Hyde role. Unwitting and unmalicious as this role might be, it becomes more significant and pervasive every day.

Equally important, the impact of a consumerist lifestyle is not confined to the home country of the fat-cat citizen. Increasingly the consequences extend to lands around the back of the earth. Rich-world communities of the temperate zones, containing one-fifth of earth's population, account for four-fifths of raw materials traded through international markets. Many of these materials derive from the tropical zone, which harbors around three-quarters of all species on earth. The extraction of these materials causes disturbance of natural environments. Thus affluent sectors of the global village are responsible—unknowingly for sure, but effectively nonetheless—for disruption of myriad species' habitats in lands far distant from their own. The connoisseur who seeks out a speciality-import store in New York or Paris or Tokyo, with a view to purchasing some much-sought-after rosewood from Brazil, may be contributing to the destruction of the last forest habitat of an Amazon monkey. Few factors of the conservation scene are likely to grow so consequential in years ahead as this one of economic-ecologic linkages among the global community.

True, citizens of tropical developing countries play their part in disruption of natural environments. It is in these countries that most of the projected expansion of human numbers will take place, 85 percent of the extra 2 billion people that are likely to be added to the present world population of 4 billion by the end of the century. Of at least as much consequence as the outburst in human numbers is the outburst in human aspirations, supported by expanding technology. It is the combination of these two factors that will precipitate a transformation of most natural environments throughout the tropics. Equally to the point, impoverished citizens of developing nations tend to have more pressing concerns than conservation of species. All too often, it is as much as they can do to stay alive themselves, let alone to keep wild creatures in being.

Plainly, there is a lot of difference between the consumerdom of the world's poor majority and of the world's rich minority. For most citizens of developing countries, there is little doubt that more food available, through cultivation of virgin territories (including forests, grasslands, wetlands, etc.), would increase their levels of nutrition, just as more industrial products available would ease their struggle for existence in many ways. It is equally likely that the same cannot be said for citizens of the advanced world: additional food or material goods do not necessarily lead to any advance in their quality of life. The demand for products of every kind on the part of the 1 billion citizens of affluent nations—the most consummate consumers the world has ever known, many making Croesus and Louis XIV look like paupers by comparison—contributes a disproportionate share to the disruption of natural environments around the earth.

For example, the depletion of tropical moist forests stems in part from market demand on the part of affluent nations for hardwoods and other specialist timbers from Southeast Asia, Amazonia and West/Central Africa. In addition, the disruptive harvesting of tropical timber is often conducted by multinational corporations that supply the capital, technology and skills without which developing countries could not exploit their forest stocks at unsustainable rates. Such is the role of Georgia Pacific and Weyerhaeuser from the United States, Mitsubishi and Sumitomo from Japan and Bruynzeel and Borregaard from Europe. Similarly, the forests of Central America are being felled to make way for artificial pasturelands, in order to grow more beef. But the extra meat, instead of going into the stomachs of local citizens, makes its way to the United States, where it supplies the hamburger trade and other fast-food business. This foreign beef is cheaper than similar-grade beef from within the United States—and the American consumer, looking for a hamburger of best quality at cheapest price, is not aware of the spillover consequences of his actions. So whose hand is on the chainsaw?

A further source of destruction in tropical forests is the shifting cultivator. There are at least 140 million of these people, subsistence peasants who often have nowhere to sink a digging hoe except the virgin territories of primeval forests. Theirs is a form of agriculture that tends, by its very nature, to be inefficient: it is highly wasteful of forestlands. It could be made intensive rather than extensive, and thus relieve the pressure on virgin forests, through the perquisites of modern agriculture, notably fertilizer to make a crop patch productive year after year. But since the OPEC price hike in 1973, the cost of petroleum-based fertilizer has been driven sky-high—and has been kept sky-high through inflated demand on the part of affluent nations (Americans and Europeans use as much fertilizer on their gardens, golf courses and cemeteries as is used by all the shifting cultivators of tropical forestlands). As long as the price of fertilizer remains beyond the reach of subsistence peasants, there is less prospect that they will change their agricultural practices. Part of the responsibility for this situation lies with the OPEC cartel, part with the excessively consumerist communities of the advanced world.

An Interdependent Global Community

Looked at this way, the problem of declining tropical forests can be seen to be intimately related to other major issues of an interdependent global community: food, population, energy, plus several other problems that confront society at large. It is difficult to make progress on one front without making progress on all the others at the same time. This aspect of the plight of tropical forests—the inter-relatedness of problems—applies to the problem of disappearing species in general.

Similarly, the advanced-nation citizen can hardly support conservation of species while resisting better trade-and-aid relationships with developing nations. The decline of tropical forests could be slowed through a trade cartel of Tropical Timber Exporting Coun-

tries. If the countries in question could jack up the price of their hardwood exports, they could earn more foreign exchange from export of less timber. For importer countries of the developed world, the effect of this move would be a jump in the price of fine furniture, specialist panelling and other components of better housing. Would an affluent-world citizen respond with a cry of protest about inflation, or with a sigh of relief at improved prospects for tropical forests? For a Third-World citizen, it is difficult to see how a conservationist can be concerned with the International Union for Conservation of Nature and Natural Resources, without being equally concerned with the New International Economic Order.

A second example concerns paperpulp. There could soon be a shortage of paperpulp to match present shortages of fuel and food. The deficit could be made good through more intensive exploitation of North American forests, or through more extensive exploitation of tropical forests—both of which alternatives might prompt outcries from environmental groups. A third alternative would be for developed-world citizens, who account for five-sixths of all paperpulp consumed world-wide, to make do with inadequate supplies, in which case the cost of newsprint would rise sharply. So perhaps a definition of a conservationist could be a person who applauds when he finds that his daily newspaper has once again gone up in price.

In accord with this view of the situation, this book emphasizes that problems of threatened species and disappearing forests can be realistically viewed only within a framework of relationships between the developed world and the developing world.

A prime conservation need everywhere, and especially in tropical regions, is for countries to set aside representative examples of their ecosystems in order to protect their stocks of species. In other words, to expand their present networks of parks, such as they are, by establishing extensive systems of protected areas. However, many developing countries are in no position to designate large tracts of their territory as "off limits" to development. (Through their present efforts to safeguard the bulk of the earth's species, they in effect subsidize the rest of the global community.) If emergent regions of the tropics are to help protect the global heritage of species for the community at large, the community should see to it that their development prospects are not thereby penalized. In short, ways must be devised to make conservation programs economically acceptable and politically palatable for developing nations.

How Far Should We Go to Save Species?

Just as the whooping crane is not worth more than a mere fraction of the United States' GNP to save it, so the preservation of species in all parts of the planet, and especially in tropical regions, needs to be considered within a comprehensive context of human well-being. Anthropocentric as this approach may appear, it reflects the way the world works: few people would be willing to swap mankind, a single species, for fishkind with its thousands of species.

So the central issue is not "Let's save species, come what may." Rather we should ask whose needs are served by conservation of species, and at what cost to whose opportunities for a better life in other ways. Instead of seeking to conserve species as an over-riding objective, we should do as much as we can within a framework of trying to enhance long-term human welfare in all manner of directions.

As we have seen, people already make "choices" concerning species. Regrettably they do not make deliberate choices after careful consideration of the alternatives. Rich and poor alike, they unconsciously contribute to the decline of the species, in dozens of ways each day. Not that they have malign intentions toward wild creatures. According to a 1976 Gallup Poll, most people would like to see more done to conserve wildlife and threatened species—87 percent in the United States, 89 percent in Western Europe, 85 percent in Japan, 75 percent in Africa, and 94 percent in Latin America (though only 46 percent in crowded

India). Subsistence communities of the developing world have limited scope to change the choice they implicitly make through their ways of making a living. Rich-world people, by contrast, have more room to maneuver, and could switch toward a stronger expression of their commitment in favor of species. Meantime, through their commitment to extreme consumerism, they in effect express the view that they can do without the orangutan and the cheetah and many other species—and their descendants, for all ages to come, can likewise do without them. In theory, they would like the orangutan and the cheetah to survive in the wild, but in practice they like many other things more. However unwittingly, that is the way they are making their choice right now.

Fortunately, affluent-world citizens still have plenty of scope to make a fresh choice. They may find it turns out to be no easy choice. If they truly wish to allow living space for millions of species that existed on the planet before man got on to his hind legs, they will find that entails not only a soft-hearted feeling in support of wildlife, but a hard-nosed commitment to attempt new lifestyles. While they shed a tear over the demise of tropical moist forests with their array of species, they might go easy on the Kleenex. . . .

How Species Arrive and Disappear

The evolutionary process that throws off new species, speciation, has been under way virtually since life first appeared. As a species encounters fresh environments, brought about by factors such as climatic change, it adapts, and so alters in different ways in different parts of its range. Eventually a new form becomes differentiated enough to rank as a new species. The parent form, if unable to fit in with changed circumstances, disappears, while the genetic material persists, diversified and enriched.

By contrast, some species are not so capable at the process of adaptation and differentiation. This applies especially to those that have become so specialized in their lifestyles that they cannot cope with transformed environments. They fade away, and their distinctive genetic material is lost forever.

Since life began about 3½ billion years ago, vast amounts of unique genetic formations have been eliminated. The total number of species that is believed to have existed is put at somewhere between 100 and 250 million,[2] which means that the present stock of species, estimated at 5–10 million, represents between 2 and 10 percent of all species that have ever lived on earth. It also means that extinction is not only a biological reality, but it is a frequent phenomenon under natural circumstances. Moreover, whereas the process of speciation is limited by the rate of genetic divergence, and so generally throws up a new species only over periods of thousands or millions of years, the process of extinction is not limited by any such constraint, and can occur, through man's agency, within just a year or two, even less.

How many species have existed at each stage of evolutionary history is only roughly known. The fossil record is so limited that it is a pitiful reflection of past life. But it now appears likely that, after a gas cloud solidified into the present planet approximately 6 billion years ago, earth remained lifeless for another 2½ billion years. When life eventually appeared, it left virtually no trace of its existence for a long time, except for micro-fossils of early algae such as have been found in Swaziland. Not until about 1500 million years ago did nuclear-celled organisms appear, and not until about 700 million years ago, following an outburst of evolutionary activity during the Cambrian period, did most modern phyla become recognizable. This array of species diversified only gradually, or even remained pretty constant, for the best part of 400 million years, until it crashed spectacularly with the extinction of many marine organisms towards the end of the Permian period. Thereafter the abundance and variety of species steadily increased, until a further mass extinction during the late Cretaceous period, 70 million years ago, put an end to around one-quarter of all families, including the dinosaurs and their kin. Since that time the trend has been generally towards ever-greater diversity of species. In short, the evolutionary record does not show a steady upward climb in earth's total of species, rather a series of step-wise increases. The current stock of species is reckoned to be 10 or even 20 times larger than the stock of species inhabiting the Paleozoic seas before the Permian crash.[3]

During the past few million years, however, extinction rates seem to have speeded up. At the time of the late Pliocene, some 5 million years ago, there may have been one-third more bird species than today.[4] During the early Pleistocene, around 3 million years ago, a bird species probably had an average life expectancy of 1½ million years. This span progressively contracted until, by the end of the Pleistocene, it could have amounted to only 40,000 years.[5] Equally likely is that the pace of speciation has probably speeded up, and full speciation among certain classes of birds could now be far more rapid than the quarter of a million years once believed necessary. Indeed, it conceivably takes place in as little as 15,000 or even 10,000 years.

The house sparrow, introduced into North America in the 1850s, has thrown off a number of clear subspecies during the course of only 110–130 generations.[6] In certain circumstances, for instance when new variations are radiating from an unspecialized ancestor, a new plant species can evolve, it is estimated, in only 50–100 generations.[7] (Experiments with fruit flies, under special laboratory conditions that serve to "force the pace," show that speciation can occur in less than a dozen generations.) Among mammals, with generally slower breeding rates than birds, the average life expectancy for a species could now be, under natural circumstances, around half a million years.

Man's Impact on Extinction Rates

More recently, extinction has stemmed increasingly from the hand of man. For much of his last 50,000 years as a hunter-gatherer, primitive man, perhaps in conjunction with climatic upheavals, proved himself capable of eliminating species through over-hunting and

The Preservation of Species: Are They Special?

through habitat modification by means of fire.[8] In the main, the process was relatively rare and gradual. By around the year A.D. 1600, however, man became able, through advancing technology, to disrupt extensive environments ever more rapidly, and to employ modern weapons to over-hunt animals to extinction in just a few years. It is from this recent watershed stage that man's impact can no longer be considered on a par with "natural processes" that lead to extinction. Of course, this is not to say that natural extinction is not still taking place. The Labrador duck appears to have disappeared through no discernible fault of man, while the white-nosed saki of Brazil has been losing more of its range to other Amazon monkeys than to man.

To reduce the history of species on earth to manageable proportions, suppose the whole existence of the planet is compressed into a single year. Conditions suitable for life do not develop for certain until May, and plants and animals do not become abundant (mostly in the seas) until the end of October. In mid-December, dinosaurs and other reptiles dominate the scene. Mammals, with hairy covering and suckling their young, appear in large numbers only a little before Christmas. On New Year's Eve, at about five minutes to midnight, man emerges. Of these few moments of man's existence, recorded history represents about the time the clock takes to strike twelve. The period since A.D. 1600, when man-induced extinctions have rapidly increased, amounts to 3 seconds, and the quarter century just begun, when the fallout of species looks likely to be far greater than all mass extinctions of the past put together, takes one-eighth of a second—a twinkling of an eye in evolutionary times.

It is sometimes suggested that, as some sort of compensation for the outburst of extinctions now under way, two evolutionary processes may gather pace, one a natural process and the other contrived by man. The argument in support of the first process is that as species disappear, niches, or "ecological living-space," will open up for newly emerging species to occupy. In fact so many vacant niches could appear that they might well stimulate a spurt of speciation. Sound as this argument is in principle, it is a non-starter in practice. The present process of extinction, vastly speeded up, will not lead to anything near a similarly speeded up process of speciation. As natural environments become degraded under man's influence, there will be few areas with enough ecological diversity to encourage many new species to emerge. Furthermore, as natural environments become homogenized, there will be little geographical isolation of populations, and hence little reproductive isolation of genetic reservoirs, to enable speciation to continue as it would under less disturbed conditions.

The second argument deals with man-contrived speciation. Opportunities are now emerging to synthesize genes in the laboratory by combining segments of the master molecule of life, DNA, from different species. This opens the way to creation of forms of life distinct from any that now exist. Regrettably this argument too is not valid. Producing a new species will be costly in the extreme, far more so than conserving the gene pool of virtually any species in its natural habitats. Moreover, a synthetic species may not be adapted to conditions outside the laboratory, in which case it may either quickly be eliminated or may encounter no natural controls to restrict its increase.

Meantime, man's activities, especially his mis-use and over-use of natural environments, continue to drive species extinct at an increasing rate. From A.D. 1600 to 1900, man was certainly accounting for one species every 4 years. From the year 1900 onwards, the rate increased to an average of around one per year. These figures refer, however, almost entirely to mammals and birds; and they are limited to species which man knows have existed and which man knows have disappeared. When we consider the other 99 percent of earth's stock of species, the picture appears far different from a "mere" one species per year.

. . . it is likely that during the last quarter of this century we shall witness an extinction spasm accounting for 1 million species. The total fallout could turn out to be lower; it could also, and more probably, turn out to be higher. Taking 1 million as a "reasonable working figure," this means an average of over 100 extinctions per day. The rate of fallout will increase as habitat disruption grows worse, i.e. toward the end of the period. Already, howev er, the process is well under way. In the region where rainforest destruction is most advanced, Southeast Asia, we can expect a wave of extinctions by the mid-1980s. Thus it is not unrealistic—in fact, probably optimistic—to say that we are losing one species per day right now. Within another decade, we could be losing one every hour.

Notes

1. Anon., 1974, Scientists talk of the need for conservation and an ethic of biotic diversity to slow species extinction, *Science* 184:646–647.

2. Brodkorb, B. P., 1971, Origin and evolution of birds, *Avian Biology* 1:19–55.

3. Gould, S. J., 1975, Diversity through time, *Natural History* 84 (8):24–32; Stebbins, G. L., 1971, *Processes of Organic Evolution*, Prentice-Hall, Englewood Cliffs, New Jersey.

4. Fisher, J. and Peterson, R. J., 1964, *The World of Birds*, Macdonald Publishers, London.

5. Moreau, R. E., 1966, *The Bird Faunas of Africa and Its Islands*, Academic Press, New York.

6. Johnstone, R. F. and Selander, R. K., 1971, Evolution in the house sparrow, *Evolution* 25:1–28.

7. Huxley, A., 1974, *Plant and Planet*, Allen Lane Publisher, London.

8. Martin, P. S. and Wright, H. E. (editors), 1967, *Pleistocene Extinctions: The Search for a Cause*, Yale University Press, New Haven, Connecticut.

Why Do Species Matter?

Lilly-Marlene Russow

I. Introduction

Consider the following extension of the standard sort of objection to treating animals differently just because they are not humans: the fact that a being is or is not a member of species *S* is not a morally relevant fact, and does not justify treating that being differently from members of other species. If so, we cannot treat a bird differently *just* because it is a California condor rather than a turkey vulture. The problem, then, becomes one of determining what special obligations, if any, a person might have toward California condors, and what might account for those obligations in a way that is generally consistent with the condemnation of speciesism. Since it will turn out that the solution I offer does not admit of a direct and tidy proof, what follows comprises three sections which approach this issue from different directions. The resulting triangulation should serve as justification and motivation for the conclusion sketched in the final section.

II. Species and Individuals

Much of the discussion in the general area of ethics and animals has dealt with the rights of animals, or obligations and duties toward individual animals. The first thing to note is that some, but not all, of the actions normally thought of as obligatory with respect to the protection of vanishing species can be recast as possible duties to individual members of that species. Thus, if it could be shown that we have a *prima facie* duty not to kill a sentient being, it would follow that it would be wrong, other things being equal, to kill a blue whale or a California condor. But it would be wrong for the same reason, and to the same degree, that it

Source: *Environmental Ethics*, Vol. 3 (Summer 1981) pp. 101–12. Reprinted by permission.

would be wrong to kill a turkey vulture or a pilot whale. Similarly, if it is wrong (something which I do not think can be shown) to deprive an individual animal of its natural habitat, it would be wrong, for the same reasons and to the same degree, to do that to a member of an endangered species. And so on. Thus, an appeal to our duties toward individual animals may provide some protection, but they do not justify the claim that we should treat members of a vanishing species with *more* care than members of other species.

More importantly, duties toward individual beings (or the rights of those individuals) will not always account for all the actions that people feel obligated to do for endangered species—e.g., bring into the world as many individuals of that species as possible, protect them from natural predation, or establish separate breeding colonies. In fact, the protection of a species might involve actions that are demonstrably contrary to the interests of some or all of the individual animals: this seems true in cases where we remove all the animals we can from their natural environment and raise them in zoos, or where we severely restrict the range of a species by hunting all those outside a certain area, as is done in Minnesota to protect the timber wolf. If such efforts are morally correct, our duties to preserve a species cannot be grounded in obligations that we have toward individual animals.

Nor will it be fruitful to treat our obligations to a species as duties toward, or as arising out of the rights of, a species thought of as some special superentity. It is simply not clear that we can make sense of talk about the interests of a species in the absence of beliefs, desires, purposeful action, etc.[1] Since having interests is generally accepted as at least a necessary condition for having rights,[2] and since many of the duties we have toward animals arise directly out of the animals' interests, arguments which show that animals have rights, or that we have duties towards them, will not apply to species. Since arguments which proceed from interests to rights or from interests to obligations make up a majority of the literature on ethics and animals, it is unlikely that these arguments will serve as a key to possible obligations toward species.

Having eliminated the possibility that our obligations toward species are somehow parallel to, or similar to, our obligations not to cause unwarranted pain to an animal, there seem to be only a few possibilities left. We may find that our duties toward species arise not out of the interests of the species, but are rooted in the general obligation to preserve things of value. Alternatively, our obligations to species may in fact be obligations to individuals (either members of the species or other individuals), but obligations that differ from the ones just discussed in that they are not determined simply by the interests of the individual.

III. Some Test Cases

If we are to find some intuitively acceptable foundation for claims about our obligations to protect species, we must start afresh. In order to get clear about what, precisely, we are looking for in this context, what obligations we might think we have toward species, what moral claims we are seeking a foundation for, I turn now to a description of some test cases. An examination of these cases illustrates why the object of our search is not something as straightforward as "Do whatever is possible or necessary to preserve the existence of the species"; a consideration of some of the differences between cases will guide our search for the nature of our obligations and the underlying reasons for those obligations.

Case 1. The snail darter is known to exist only in one part of one river. This stretch of river would be destroyed by the building of the Tellico dam. Defenders of the dam have successfully argued that the dam is nonetheless necessary for the economic development and well-being of the area's population. To my knowledge, no serious or large-scale attempt has been made to breed large numbers of snail darters in captivity (for any reason other than research).

Case 2. The Pére David deer was first discovered by a Western naturalist in 1865, when Pére Armand David found herds of the deer in the Imperial Gardens in Peking: even at that time, they were only known to exist in captivity. Pére David brought several animals back to Europe, where they bred readily enough so that now there are healthy populations in several major zoos.[3] There is no reasonable hope of reintroducing the Pére David deer to its natural habitat; indeed, it is not even definitely known what its natural habitat was.

Case 3. The red wolf *(Canis rufus)* formerly ranged over the southeastern and south-central United States. As with most wolves, they were threatened, and their range curtailed, by trapping, hunting, and the destruction of habitat. However, a more immediate threat to the continued existence of the red wolf is that these changes extended the range of the more adaptable coyote, with whom the red wolf interbreeds very readily; as a result, there are very few "pure" red wolves left. An attempt has been made to capture some pure breeding stock and raise wolves on preserves.[4]

Case 4. The Baltimore oriole and the Bullock's oriole were long recognized and classified as two separate species of birds. As a result of extensive interbreeding between the two species in areas where their ranges overlapped, the American Ornithologists' Union recently declared that there were no longer two separate species; both ex-species are now called "northern orioles."

Case 5. The Appaloosa is a breed of horse with a distinctively spotted coat; the Lewis and Clark expedition discovered that the breed was associated with the Nez Percé Indians. When the Nez Percé tribe was defeated by the U.S. Cavalry in 1877 and forced to move, their horses were scattered and interbred with other horses. The distinctive coat pattern was almost lost; not until the middle of the twentieth century was a concerted effort made to gather together the few remaining specimens and reestablish the breed.

Case 6. Many strains of laboratory rats are bred specifically for a certain type of research. Once the need for a particular variety ceases— once the type of research is completed—the rats are usually killed, with the result that the variety becomes extinct.

Case 7. It is commonly known that several diseases such as sleeping sickness, malaria, and human encephalitis are carried by one variety of mosquito but not by others. Much of the disease control in these cases is aimed at exterminating the disease carrying insect; most people do not find it morally wrong to wipe out the whole species.

Case 8. Suppose that zebras were threatened solely because they were hunted for their distinctive striped coats. Suppose, too, that we could remove this threat by selectively breeding zebras that are not striped, that look exactly like mules, although they are still pure zebras. Have we preserved all that we ought to have preserved?

What does an examination of these test cases reveal? First, that our concept of what a species *is* is not at all unambiguous; at least in part, what counts as a species is a matter of current fashions in taxonomy. Furthermore, it seems that it is not the sheer diversity or number of species that matters: if that were what is valued, moral preference would be given to taxonomic schemes that separated individuals into a larger number of species, a suggestion which seems absurd. The case of the orioles suggests that the decision as to whether to call these things one species or two is not a moral issue at all.[5] Since we are not evidently concerned with the existence or diversity of species in *this* sense, there must be something more at issue than the simple question of whether we have today the same number of species represented as we had yesterday. Confusion sets in, however, when we try to specify another sense in which it is possible to speak of the "existence" of a species. This only serves to emphasize the basic murkiness of our intuitions about what the object of our concern really is.

This murkiness is further revealed by the fact that it is not at all obvious what we are trying to preserve in some of the test cases. Sometimes, as in the case of the Appaloosa or attempts to save a subspecies like the Arctic wolf or the Mexican wolf, it is not a whole species that is in question. But not all genetic subgroups are of interest—witness the case of the laboratory rat—and sometimes the preservation of the species at the cost of one of its externally obvious features (the stripes on a zebra) is not our only concern. This is not a minor puzzle which can be resolved by changing our question from "why do species matter?"

to "why do species and/or subspecies matter?" It is rather a serious issue of what makes a group of animals "special" enough or "unique" enough to warrant concern. And of course, the test cases reveal that our intuitions are not always consistent: although the cases of the red wolf and the northern oriole are parallel in important respects, we are more uneasy about simply reclassifying the red wolf and allowing things to continue along their present path.

The final point to be established is that whatever moral weight is finally attached to the preservation of a species (or subspecies), it can be overridden. We apparently have no compunction about wiping out a species of mosquito if the benefits gained by such action are sufficiently important, although many people were unconvinced by similar arguments in favor of the Tellico dam.

The lesson to be drawn from this section can be stated in a somewhat simplistic form: it is not simply the case that we can solve our problems by arguing that there is some value attached to the mere existence of a species. Our final analysis must take account of various features or properties of certain kinds or groups of animals, and it has to recognize that our concern is with the continued existence of individuals that may or may not have some distinctive characteristics.

IV. Some Traditional Answers

There are, of course, some standard replies to the question "Why do species matter?" or, more particularly, to the question "Why do we have at least a *prima facie* duty not to cause a species to become extinct, and in some cases, a duty to try actively to preserve species?" With some tolerance for borderline cases, these replies generally fall into three groups: (1) those that appeal to our role as "stewards" or "caretakers," (2) those that claim that species have some extrinsic value (I include in this group those that argue that the species is valuable as part of the ecosystem or as a link in the evolutionary scheme of things), and (3) those that appeal to some intrinsic or inherent value that is supposed to

make a species worth preserving. In this section, with the help of the test cases just discussed, I indicate some serious flaws with each of these responses.

The first type of view has been put forward in the philosophical literature by Joel Feinberg, who states that our duty to preserve whole species may be more important than any rights had by individual animals.[6] He argues, first, that this duty does not arise from a right or claim that can properly be attributed to the species as a whole (his reasons are much the same as the ones I cited in section 2 of this paper), and second, while we have some duty to unborn generations that directs us to preserve species, that duty is much weaker than the actual duty we have to preserve species. The fact that our actual duty extends beyond our duties to future generations is explained by the claim that we have duties of "stewardship" with respect to the world as a whole. Thus, Feinberg notes that his "inclination is to seek an explanation in terms of the requirements of our unique station as rational custodians of the planet we temporarily occupy."[7]

The main objection to this appeal to our role as stewards or caretakers is that it begs the question. The job of a custodian is to protect that which is deserving of protection, that which has some value or worth.[8] But the issue before us now is precisely *whether* species have value, and why. If we justify our obligations of stewardship by reference to the value of that which is cared for, we cannot also explain the value by pointing to the duties of stewardship.

The second type of argument is the one which establishes the value of a species by locating it in the "larger scheme of things." That is, one might try to argue that species matter because they contribute to, or form an essential part of, some other good. This line of defense has several variations.

The first version is completely anthropocentric: it is claimed that vanishing species are of concern to us because their difficulties serve as a warning that we have polluted or altered the environment in a way that is potentially dangerous or undesirable for us. Thus, the California condor whose eggshells are weakened due to the absorption of DDT indicates that something is wrong: presumably we are being affected in subtle ways by the absorption of DDT, and that is bad for us. Alternatively, diminishing numbers of game animals may signal overhunting which, if left unchecked, would leave the sportsman with fewer things to hunt. And, as we become more aware of the benefits that might be obtained from rare varieties of plants and animals (drugs, substitutes for other natural resources, tools for research), we may become reluctant to risk the disappearance of a species that might be of practical use to us in the future.

This line of argument does not carry us very far. In the case of a subspecies, most benefits could be derived from other varieties of the same species. More important, when faced with the loss of a unique variety or species, we may simply decide that, even taking into account the possibility of error, there is not enough reason to think that the species will ever be of use; we may take a calculated risk and decide that it is not worth it. Finally, the use of a species as a danger signal may apply to species whose decline is due to some subtle and unforeseen change in the environment, but will not justify concern for a species threatened by a known and foreseen event like the building of a dam.

Other attempts to ascribe extrinsic value to a species do not limit themselves to potential human and practical goods. Thus, it is often argued that each species occupies a unique niche in a rich and complex, but delicately balanced, ecosystem. By destroying a single species, we upset the balance of the whole system. On the assumption that the system as a whole should be preserved, the value of a species is determined, at least in part, by its contribution to the whole.[9]

In assessing this argument, it is important to realize that such a justification (a) may lead to odd conclusions about some of the test cases, and (b) allows for changes which do not affect the system, or which result in the substitution of a richer, more complex system for one that is more primitive or less evolved. With regard to the first of these points, species that exist only in zoos would seem to have no special value. In terms of our test cases, the David deer does not exist as part of a system, but only in isolation. Similarly, the Appaloosa horse, a domesticated variety which is neither better suited nor worse

than any other sort of horse, would not have any special value. In contrast, the whole cycle of mosquitoes, disease organisms adapted to these hosts, and other beings susceptible to those diseases is quite a complex and marvelous bit of systematic adaption. Thus, it would seem to be wrong to wipe out the encephalitis-bearing mosquito.

With regard to the second point, we might consider changes effected by white settlers in previously isolated areas such as New Zealand and Australia. The introduction of new species has resulted in a whole new ecosystem, with many of the former indigenous species being replaced by introduced varieties. As long as the new system works, there seems to be no grounds for objections.

The third version of an appeal to extrinsic value is sometimes presented in Darwinian terms: species are important as links in the evolutionary chain. This will get us nowhere, however, because the extinction of one species, the replacement of one by another, is as much a part of evolution as is the development of a new species.

One should also consider a more general concern about all those versions of the argument which focus on the species' role in the natural order of things: all of these arguments presuppose that "the natural order of things" is, in itself, good. As William Blackstone pointed out, this is by no means obvious: "Unless one adheres dogmatically to a position of a 'reverence for all life,' the extinction of some species or forms of life may be seen as quite desirable. (This is parallel to the point often made by philosophers that not all 'customary' or 'natural' behavior is necessarily good)."[10] Unless we have some other way of ascribing value to a system, and to the animals which actually fulfill a certain function in that system (as opposed to possible replacements), the argument will not get off the ground.

Finally, then, the process of elimination leads us to the set of arguments which point to some *intrinsic value* that a species is supposed to have. The notion that species have an intrinsic value, if established, would allow us to defend much stronger claims about human obligations toward threatened species. Thus, if a species is intrinsically valuable, we should try to preserve it even when it no longer has a place in the natural ecosystem, or when it could be replaced by another species that would occupy the same niche. Most important, we should not ignore a species just because it serves no useful purpose.

Unsurprisingly, the stumbling block is what this intrinsic value might be grounded in. Without an explanation of that, we have no nonarbitrary way of deciding whether subspecies as well as species have intrinsic value or how much intrinsic value a species might have. The last question is meant to bring out issues that will arise in cases of conflict of interests: is the intrinsic value of a species of mosquito sufficient to outweigh the benefits to be gained by eradicating the means of spreading a disease like encephalitis? Is the intrinsic value of the snail darter sufficient to outweigh the economic hardship that might be alleviated by the construction of a dam? In short, to say that something has intrinsic value does not tell us *how much* value it has, nor does it allow us to make the sorts of judgments that are often called for in considering the fate of an endangered species.

The attempt to sidestep the difficulties raised by subspecies by broadening the ascription of value to include subspecies opens a whole Pandora's box. It would follow that any genetic variation within a species that results in distinctive characteristics would need separate protection. In the case of forms developed through selective breeding, it is not clear whether we have a situation analogous to natural subspecies, or whether no special value is attached to different breeds.

In order to speak to either of these issues, and in order to lend plausibility to the whole enterprise, it would seem necessary to consider first the justification for ascribing value to whichever groups have such value. If intrinsic value does not spring from anything, if it becomes merely another way of saying that we should protect species, we are going around in circles, without explaining anything.[11] Some further explanation is needed.

Some appeals to intrinsic value are grounded in the intuition that diversity itself is a virtue. If so, it would seem incumbent upon us to create new species wherever possible, even bizarre ones that would have no purpose

other than to be different. Something other than diversity must therefore be valued.

The comparison that is often made between species and natural wonders, spectacular landscapes, or even works of art, suggest that species might have some aesthetic value. This seems to accord well with our naive intuitions, provided that *aesthetic value* is interpreted rather loosely; most of us believe that the world would be a poorer place for the loss of bald eagles in the same way that it would be poorer for the loss of the Grand Canyon or a great work of art. In all cases, the experience of seeing these things is an inherently worthwhile experience. And since diversity in some cases is a component in aesthetic appreciation, part of the previous intuition would be preserved. There is also room for degrees of selectivity and concern with superficial changes: the variety of rat that is allowed to become extinct may have no special aesthetic value, and a bird is neither more nor less aesthetically pleasing when we change its name.

There are some drawbacks to this line of argument: there are some species which, by no stretch of the imagination, are aesthetically significant. But aesthetic value can cover a surprising range of things: a tiger may be simply beautiful; a blue whale is awe-inspiring; a bird might be decorative; an Appaloosa is of interest because of its historical significance; and even a drab little plant may inspire admiration for the marvelous way it has been adapted to a special environment. Even so, there may be species such as the snail darter that simply have no aesthetic value. In these cases, lacking any alternative, we may be forced to the conclusion that such species are not worth preserving.

Seen from other angles, once again the appeal to the aesthetic value of species is illuminating. Things that have an aesthetic value are compared and ranked in some cases, and commitment of resources may be made accordingly. We believe that diminishing the aesthetic value of a thing for mere economic benefit is immoral, but that aesthetic value is not absolute—that the fact that something has aesthetic value may be overridden by the fact that harming that thing, or destroying it, may result in some greater good. That is, someone who agrees to destroy a piece of Greek statuary for personal gain would be condemned as having done something immoral, but someone who is faced with a choice between saving his children and saving a "priceless" painting would be said to have skewed values if he chose to save the painting. Applying these observations to species, we can see that an appeal to aesthetic value would justify putting more effort into the preservation of one species than the preservation of another; indeed, just as we think that the doodling of a would-be artist may have no merit at all, we may think that the accidental and unfortunate mutation of a species is not worth preserving. Following the analogy, allowing a species to become extinct for *mere* economic gain might be seen as immoral, while the possibility remains open that other (human?) good might outweigh the goods achieved by the preservation of a species.

Although the appeal to aesthetic values has much to recommend it—even when we have taken account of the fact that it does not guarantee that all species matter—there seems to be a fundamental confusion that still affects the cogency of the whole argument and its application to the question of special obligations to endangered species, for if the value of a species is based on its aesthetic value, it is impossible to explain why an endangered species should be more valuable, or more worthy of preservation, than an unendangered species. The appeal to "rarity" will not help, if what we are talking about is species: each species is unique, no more or less rare than any other species: there is in each case one and only one species that we are talking about.[12]

This problem of application seems to arise because the object of aesthetic appreciation, and hence of aesthetic value, has been misidentified, for it is not the case that we perceive, admire, and appreciate a *species*—species construed either as a group or set of similar animals or as a name that we attach to certain kinds of animals in virtue of some classification scheme. What we value is the existence of individuals with certain characteristics. If this is correct, then the whole attempt to explain why species matter by arguing that *they* have aesthetic value needs to be redirected. This is what I try to do in the final section of this paper.

V. Valuing the Individual

What I propose is that the intuition behind the argument from aesthetic value is correct, but misdirected. The reasons that were given for the value of a species are, in fact, reasons for saying that an individual has value. We do not admire the grace and beauty of the species *Panthera tigris;* rather, we admire the grace and beauty of the individual Bengal tigers that we may encounter. What we value then is the existence of that individual and the existence (present or future) of individuals like that. The ways in which other individuals should be "like that" will depend on why we value that particular sort of individual: the stripes on a zebra do not matter if we value zebras primarily for the way they are adapted to a certain environment, their unique fitness for a certain sort of life. If, on the other hand, we value zebras because their stripes are aesthetically pleasing, the stripes do matter. Since our attitudes toward zebras probably include both of these features, it is not surprising to find that my hypothetical test case produces conflicting intuitions.

The shift of emphasis from species to individuals allows us to make sense of the stronger feelings we have about endangered species in two ways. First, the fact that there are very few members of a species—the fact that we rarely encounter one—itself increases the value of those encounters. I can see turkey vultures almost every day, and I can eat apples almost every day, but seeing a bald eagle or eating wild strawberries are experiences that are much less common, more delightful just for their rarity and unexpectedness. Even snail darters, which, if we encountered them every day would be drab and uninteresting, become more interesting just because we don't—or may not—see them every day. Second, part of our interest in an individual carries over to a desire that there be future opportunities to see these things again (just as when, upon finding a new and beautiful work of art, I will wish to go back and see it again). In the case of animals, unlike works of art, I know that this animal will not live forever, but that other animals like this one will have similar aesthetic value. Thus, because I value possible future encounters, I will also want to do what is needed to ensure the possibility of such encounters—i.e., make sure that enough presently existing individuals of this type will be able to reproduce and survive. This is rather like the duty that we have to support and contribute to museums, or to other efforts to preserve works of art.

To sum up, then: individual animals can have, to a greater or lesser degree, aesthetic value: they are valued for their simple beauty, for their awesomeness, for their intriguing adaptations, for their rarity, and for many other reasons. We have moral obligations to protect things of aesthetic value, and to ensure (in an odd sense) their continued existence; thus, we have a duty to protect individual animals (the duty may be weaker or stronger depending on the value of the individual), and to ensure that there will continue to be animals of this sort (this duty will also be weaker or stronger, depending on value).

I began this paper by suggesting that our obligations to vanishing species might appear inconsistent with a general condemnation of speciesism. My proposal is not inconsistent: we value and protect animals because of their aesthetic value, not because they are members of a given species.

Notes

1. Cf. Joel Feinberg, "The Rights of Animals and Future Generations," in *Philosophy and Environmental Crisis*, ed. William Blackstone (Athens: University of Georgia Press, 1974), pp. 55–57.
2. There are some exceptions to this: for example, Tom Regan argues that some rights are grounded in the intrinsic value of a thing in "Do Animals Have a Right to Life?" in *Animal Rights and Human Obligations*, eds. Tom Regan and Peter Singer (Englewood Cliffs, N.J.: Prentice-Hall, 1975), pp. 198–203. These and similar cases will be dealt with by examining the proposed foundations of

rights; thus, the claim that species have intrinsic value will be considered in section 3.
3. The deer in China were all killed during the Boxer rebellion; recently, several pairs were sent to Chinese zoos.
4. *Predator* 7, no. 2 (1980). Further complications occur in this case because a few scientists have tried to argue that all red wolves are the result of interbreeding between grey wolves *(Canis lupus)* and coyotes *(C. latans)*. For more information, see L. David Mech, *The Wolf* (Garden City, N.Y.: Natural History Press, 1970), pp. 22–25.
5. Sometimes there are moral questions about the practical consequences of such a move. The recent decision to combine two endangered species—the seaside sparrow and the dusky seaside sparrow—aggravates the difficulties faced by attempts to protect these birds.
6. Joel Feinberg, "Human Duties and Animal Rights," in *On the Fifth Day: Animal Rights and Human Ethics*, Richard Knowles Morris and Michael W. Fox, eds. (Washington: Acropolis Books, 1978), p. 67.
7. *Ibid*, p. 68.
8. Cf. Feinberg's discussion of custodial duties in "The Rights of Animals and Future Generations," *Philosophy and Environmental Crisis*, pp. 49–50.
9. A similar view has been defended by Tom Auxter, "The Right Not to Be Eaten," *Inquiry* 22 (1979): 222–23.
10. William Blackstone, "Ethics and Ecology," *Philosophy and Environmental Crisis*, p. 25.
11. This objection parallels Regan's attack on ungrounded appeals to the intrinsic value of human life as a way of trying to establish a human right to life. Cf. Thomas Regan, "Do Animals Have a Right to Life?" *Animal Rights and Human Obligations*, p. 199.
12. There is one further attempt that might be made to avoid this difficulty: one might argue that species do not increase in value due to scarcity, but that our duties to protect a valuable species involves more when the species is more in need of protection. This goes part of the way towards solving the problem, but does not yet capture our intuition that rarity does affect the value in some way.

Cetaceans: A Litany of Cain

Peter M. Dobra

I. Introduction

Can he who has discovered only some of the values of whalebone and whale be said to have discovered the true use of a whale? Can he who slays the elephant for his ivory be said to have seen the elephant? These are petty and accidental uses; just as if a stronger race were to kill us in order to make buttons and flageolets of our bones.[1]

Man's attitude toward Cetaceans has not always been predatory. Recent conservationist demands for sea mammal protection should be seen as a rebirth of affection for these singular creatures. The ancients had a more salutary view of their relationship with nature and a particular reverence for their marine counterparts, the Cetaceans. The ancient Greek word for dolphin was closely related to *delphis*, which translates as "womb."[2] Dolphins that helped in the catch were fed a fair share by the Greek fishermen. As Pliny the Elder wrote:

[When dolphins] are aware that they have had too strenuous a task for only a single day's pay, they wait there until the following day and are given a feed of bread mash dipped in wine, in addition to the fish. Even if [the fishermen] find [the dolphins] fast in their net, yet they set them at liberty.[3]

The 2nd century A.D. Greek poet Oppian reported the symbiotic cooperation between man and dolphin:

[B]ut when the work of capture is happily accomplished, then the dolphins draw near and ask the guerdon of their friendship, even their allotted portion of the spoil. And the fishers deny them

Source: *Boston College Environmental Affairs Law Review*, Vol. 7, No. 1 (1978), pp. 165–83. Reprinted by permission.

not, but gladly give them a share of their successful fishing; for if a man sins against them in his greed, no more are the dolphins his helpers in fishing.[4]

The hunting of dolphins is immoral . . . for equally with human slaughter the gods abhor the deaths of the monarchs of the deep.[5]

Since the first Basque whalers of the 14th century, mankind has progressively reduced the whale population from about four million to approximately two million animals.[6] The numbers, however, belie the actual tragedy. All of the greater leviathian—the Blue, Fin, Right, Humpback, and Bowhead—have been ruthlessly exploited, some to within four or five percent of their natural levels.[7] Given whale sociobiology and ecology, these species may never be able to replenish themselves. With the advent in the twentieth century of such technology as the exploding harpoon and the "factory ship," as well as the recent use of helicopters and light planes, this killing has reached a frenzy. Biological extinction for several subspecies is an impending reality. While some progress has recently been made by the International Whaling Commission (IWC) to protect such mammals, the Commission's regulations do not go far enough. Moreover, a new question has arisen as to the protection of smaller Cetaceans, particularly the thousands of porpoise who die each year in the tuna industry's purse seines[8] after having led the fishermen to their prey.[9] The design of legal forms which can be effectively used to protect all cetaceans must be found in an investigation of biological, historical, economic, political, legal and ethical considerations.

II. Evolution

The other Cetacea comprises approximately seventy-eight species of dolphins, porpoise and whales. Its members are warm-blooded, air-breathing mammals. The whales are divided into two orders: the baleen, which feed on krill and other zooplankton, and the toothed whale, whose diet includes various fish and squid.[10]

Cetaceans possess highly sophisticated social instincts. They are monogamus and display nurturant and succorant behavior similar to man. Whalers have long taken advantage of this protective instinct by harpooning a baby whale, towing it alive and struggling to shore, and then exterminating the extended family which will follow the baby's cries.[11] There have been many incidents where dead whales taken by ship into port have had entire whale families wait weeks offshore for the dead whale's return. In captivity, Cetaceans have been diagnosed as suffering from certain "human" maladies such as stomach ulcers, severe depression and psychosis. Bottlenose Dolphins have even been known to commit suicide. Such behavior is strong evidence of an awareness of self. Research by neurophysiologists and behavioral scientists strongly suggests the potential intellect of these beings.

While evolution has developed the capacity of humans to formulate strategies in addressing extreme danger, group aggression and the need for communication, Cetaceans, on the other hand, have become so well adapted to their environment as to render it benign.[12] A comparison of the human and the Cetacean brain illustrates this evolutionary divergence. The human brain, which has rapidly increased in size in the last five million years from 450 cubic centimeters to 1300 cubic centimeters, contains three essential structures: the rhinicnode, the limbicnode and superlimbicnode, the latter being enveloped in a neocortical membrane.[13] Cetaceans, however, evolved brains the size of modern man's well over ten million years ago and currently possess all of the neural-structures of man, plus a fourth specialized region called the paralimbicnode.[14] Size alone, however, is only one indicator of intelligence. Anatomists have long agreed that complexity of intellect is caused by, or is at least correlative of: (1) the number of layers in the neocortex, (2) the degree of folding of the cortical surface, (3) the general area of the neocortex, (4) the degree of regional specialization and (5) the brain cell patterns of arrangement and communicative facility.[15] Little is known about what consciousness actually is, but there does appear to be at least some relation between high morphological complexity and high levels of abstract and creative thought.[16] If we accept these indications as valid, it appears that Cetaceans may be on an intellectual plane above man. Studies of the Bottlenose Dolphin (*Tursiops Truncatus*) reveal that dolphins have well-developed lamination and differentiation of the cerebral neocortex, although, as illustrated by its unique paralimbicnode, it is specialized and arranged differently than that of man.[17] Dolphins also have a higher neocortical and limbic ratio than man. In tests involving humans suffering brain damage, this ratio has been found to be proportionate to those abilities necessary for self-awareness, such as the capacity to think abstractly.[18] The dolphin brain is luxuriantly enfolded, the larger neocortical surface being more fissurated than the brain of man.[19] Such dense convolution makes for greater potentialities for neuronal communication and complexity.

Differences between the sensory modalities of man and Cetaceans have made it difficult for us to learn each other's communication systems.[20] Evolving in the absence of a dangerous and hostile environment, Cetacean intelligence has developed in response to demands for increased socialization, attended by highly complex patterns of communication and creative interplay. An analysis using a binary computer language estimates that the number of information bits in a whale song of one-half hour is between one million and one hundred million bits.[21] These songs, which may last for hours and which may be heard by other whales well over one hundred miles away, are sometimes sung, note by note, by different whales in a particular population with varying degrees of personal improvisation and embellishment.

The foregoing biological perspective evidences why halting the destruction of Cetaceans is so singular in its urgency. Although the right to exist of innumerable other species of animals has been imperiled, the case of the Cetaceans is unique. Cetaceans should not be treated as a renewable resource, but rather as a particularly exquisite life form that ought to be more fully understood. They have the potential to offer us much more than the pet food and margarine into which they continue to be processed.

While it cannot be maintained that the intellect of various Cetaceans is superior to that of man, neither can their intellectual inferiority be conclusively demonstrated. Currently, the state of the art in the fields of neurophysics and psychology does not permit definitive calibration of consciousness or creativity without tainting the conclusion with a prejudicial anthropocentrism. Despite the limitations of current scientific proof, the sophisticated social and intellectual qualities of the Cetacean demand protection. Future research may result in man's first communication with a truly alien intelligence. The potential for such an alien encounter on the planet earth should not be ignored.

The succeeding sections concern the legal, political and economic considerations complementary to the ethical imperatives offered above. The explicit policy goal these considerations serve is the significant reduction of man-induced mortality among Cetaceans.

III. Regulatory Efforts

A. Whaling Economics: The Need for Regulation

The common sense presumption that the whaling industry, if left to its own devices, would never exterminate its own means of livelihood, has underlain the International Whaling Commission's "regulation" efforts. The presumption is patently false. The peculiar economics of whaling makes it far more remunerative for whalers to hunt the species to extinction, in pursuit of short term economic profit and in disregard of non-pecuniary considerations.

In common property fishery, the depletion cost of each fisherman's catch to the basic resource is not borne by the individual fisherman, but rather by the entire industry.[22] Therefore, the individual fisherman has a vested interest in maximizing his own kill since the resource depletion costs are not internalized.[23] The result is the stimulation of sharp competition between the various whaling countries for a larger share of a finite number of animals.

In the past, fishery economics has been haphazardly applied to the management of whales. However, there are important biological differences between fish and whales which have not been incorporated into the calculus, and have led to depletion rather than management. Fishery economics is characterized by rapidly rising marginal costs as the stock is depleted.[24] Consequently, when stocks drop too low, commercial extinction is reached even though many fish still remain. Most commercial fish also have potentially astronomical reproduction rates which allow the remaining stock to replenish itself in a few years or less. In contrast, the marginal revenue from catching certain species of whales exceeds the marginal cost, even at extremely low stock levels.[25] The low marginal cost of the actual taking of a whale is the result of the capital intensive nature of whaling. An inordinantly high percentage of the cost of whaling relates to the building of ships and their positioning at the whaling sites. Once the ships are built and at sea, the cost of catching any one whale is minimal, thereby making the worth of each whale disproportionately high.[26] The result is the present situation, where the over-capitalized whaling fleets of Japan and the USSR incur little additional costs in meeting their quotas, and simultaneously exert pressure for higher quotas in order to obtain increasing marginal profits.

The fact that the whale's reproductive cycle differs from that of commercial fish also results in pressure to hunt the whale to extinction. The male Sperm Whale does not reach sexual maturity until nearly twenty years of age. Females bear only one calf at a time and not more frequently than once every two years.[27] This causes the present consumptive value of the whale to exceed the discounted future value of the whale and all its progeny. It has been estimated that the net recruitment rate, or the rate at which the whale population would naturally reproduce and grow, is about half the amount necessary to make a future kill as profitable as a current one.[28] The profit from a current kill can be invested at a rate of return in other sectors of the economy much higher than the comparable rate of return resulting from the conservation of present stocks in anticipation of larger future kills. Of course, other variables also influence the formula,[29] but the net result is a situation where it is economically advantageous to sustain high kill rates of whales, even though these rates will lead to the whale's biological extinction.

B. International Regulation Efforts

1. Efforts of the International Whaling Commission

In 1924 the League of Nations created a Committee of International Law whose chairman reported in 1925 that the whaling industry was "rapidly exterminating the whale."[30] The first attempt to regulate the taking of Cetaceans was the Whaling Convention of 1931[31] which proved to be utterly ineffectual. What the Convention did provide, however, was a centralized bank for information about whales.[32]

The International Whaling Commission (IWC), which currently has international jurisdiction over the whale, had its genesis in the Whaling Convention of 1946.[33] The Convention of 1946, however, failed to provide the IWC with any enforcement procedures. . . .

The IWC has proved ineffective in preventing the continued depletion of whales. The Baleen Whales have been the most ruthlessly hunted because their feeding and migratory patterns are strictly prescribed by the high summer concentrations of zooplankton in the polar regions.[34] Their activities are therefore easily predicted by the hunter. The toothed whales' irregular habits have saved them, until recently, from the systematic extermination suffered by the Baleen.

The complexity of whale ecology has never been fully incorporated into those IWC calculations which have been used to set kill quotas. The quotas have proven to be mere licenses for the virtual extinguishment of several whale

subspecies. For example, the Blue Whale, the largest creature to ever have existed on the face of the earth,[35] has been reduced in number from approximately 100,000 in the year 1900 to between 600 and 3000 today.

The IWC's initial regulation for the taking of whales depended on the calculation of whale capture based on the scientifically unsound Blue Whale Unit (BWU).[36] The limits imposed on each whaling company were set in BWU's which, in 1944, equaled one Blue Whale, two Fins, or two and one-half Humpback or Sei Whales.[37] Instead of protecting endangered species, these quotas simply enabled whalers to indiscriminately hunt in one geographic area, killing endangered and plentiful species alike, until the population in that geographic area was rendered economically extinct. The factory ships could then simply move on to exploit fresh populations in new geographic zones until their BWU allotment was completed.[38] Only recently have protection quotas been set by species.[39]

However, the decision to establish quotas solely by species also fails to consider the complexity of whale ecology. Species barriers are generally recognized to be absolute obstacles to interbreeding between various large Cetaceans. Yet the decision to establish quotas based solely upon the number of the species in existence ignores the findings that discrete population groups within the same species, although physiologically capable of interbreeding, do not do so because of geographical or behavioral isolation.[40] For example, North Atlantic Fin Whales apparently comprise six genetically and geographically distinct populations. None of these discrete groups interbreed among themselves or with South Atlantic Fins.[41] This lack of interbreeding necessitates the refinement of regulations so that quotas are determined on the basis of geographic location as well as by the number of the species in existence.

The IWC's failure to consider both species and geographic location has led to the depletion of the Bowhead, Right and Blue populations to such levels that replenishment may not occur for thousands of years, if ever.[42] Once the numbers are down to a few thousand, biogeographical barriers make it difficult for the members to even rendevous to mate.

A great deal of information is still needed before accurate quotas which will prevent the elimination of numerous species can be established. For example, little research or consideration has been given to such factors as the impact of the periodic extermination of individuals or groups of these highly socialized animals upon reproductive rates. There has also been no consideration of the effects of toxic industrial effluents upon those Cetaceans at the top of the food chain. Nor has the potential effect of man's competition for those resources used by whales for food been evaluated. The Japanese and Russians have recently developed techniques for the large scale harvesting of krill, the zooplankton ubiquitous to the diet of the most endangered Baleens.[43]

. . .

2. Complementary International Efforts

. . . Other national and international attempts to curtail the killing of Cetaceans has caused the IWC to strengthen its whaling regulations. In 1972 the United Nations Conference on the Human Environment in Stockholm passed a resolution calling for a ten year moratorium on commercial whaling.[44] Although the IWC formally rejected this call, it did institute some positive changes, such as the abolition of the Blue Whale Unit and the concomitant imposition of quotas by species. The United States formally protested this rejection, and most importantly, took unilateral domestic action by passing the Marine Mammal Protection Act of 1972.[45] This Act, coupled with subsequent United States legislation,[46] has had a profound impact on the attitudes within the IWC. The Act had the immediate effect of banning the importation of whale products into the United States which, until that time, had comprised 20 percent of the entire world market for such goods. . . .

C. Domestic Initiatives

Domestic legislation and litigation has focused primarily on the preservation of the small Cetaceans rather than on the preservation of whales. During the 1970's, the United States tuna industry has become the largest killer of marine mammals, particularly porpoises, incidental to the "on porpoise" purse seining[47] of White Yellow Fin and Slipjack Tuna. Since the Marine Mammal Protection Act of 1972,[48] the United States has imported no commercially appreciable quantities of whale products, nor has it whaled.[49]

The Marine Mammal Protection Act of 1972 (MMPA)[50] made it illegal for any person subject to the jurisdiction of the United States to "take any marine mammal on the high seas."[51] Furthermore, all persons are prohibited from taking marine mammals from the waters or lands under the jurisdiction of the United States[52] or importing into the United States any marine mammal taken in violation of the Act.[53] To be excepted from the prohibitions of the Act, one must obtain a special permit from the Secretary of Commerce.[54] The Act provides for criminal as well as civil liability[55] for the violation of its provisions; unfortunately, the penalty provisions of the Act have remained essentially unenforced. . . .

The Marine Mammal Commission has shown much greater concern for marine mammals, based on its scientific findings, than its parent bureaucracy, the National Marine and Fisheries Service. The Service has consistently circumscribed its own power to enforce and issue regulations pursuant to the extremely broad and powerful legislation which has been passed to protect all marine mammals. . . .

Particularly unfortunate has been the Service's disregard of the information gathered in the 1976 cruise of the *Elizabeth C.J.*, a purse seiner equipped with the most advanced net technology and employing the most sophisticated tuna seining techniques. By the Service's own conservative figures, the *Elizabeth C.J.* exhibited kill rates 175 times lower than the average for the United States tuna fleet in 1976. Instead of requirements for the phased procurement of this technology and the use of these techniques, the Service caviled, promulgating kill quotas only slightly lower than what were the current 1977 kill rates. Fishing at the *Elizabeth C.J.* rate would have led to kills appreciably under 10,000, and nowhere near the 50,000–80,000 range adopted by the Service. . . .

IV. Strategy and Policy

Domestic Powers and Prescriptions

In the near future, unilateral action, orchestrated whenever possible with international accords or goals, should prove the most effective means of protecting the large and small Cetaceans in the United States. Initial efforts should focus on maintaining the integrity of those laws that exist today, and insisting on their full implementation. One-half of the tuna consumed in the world today is consumed in the United States. Foreign vessels supply our canneries with fifty-nine percent of the raw materials they process. The American market for all types of seafood is vast, and access to it is essential for many foreign fishing interests.

Between 1960 and 1975, approximately six million dolphins and porpoises were killed by tuna fishing alone. Moreover, for many years Japanese fishermen have deliberately killed dolphins for food and other commercial uses. The first actions must be to minimize the slaughter of porpoises by our own fishermen. The National Marine and Fisheries Service should amend regulations to require the utilization of the technology and techniques developed on the *Elizabeth C.J..* This equipment, and the training needed to use it, are currently available. The integration of this technology would be facilitated by linking its adoption to various incentives for complying boats. A 1975 check of twenty-nine ships revealed that forty percent of the porpoise kills were committed by only three of the boats. Quotas allocated by vessel, retention of the proposed observer plan, vigorous exaction of the penalities the MMPA provides (but which have never been used) would reduce porpoise kills dramatically. Such vigilant enforcement of the MMPA is proposed in the new 1977 regulations. As demonstrated by the *Elizabeth C.J.,*

porpoise kills can be drastically reduced and, with further improvements, approach the goal of zero mortality. Commitment to this goal must be reincorporated into the text of the new regulations.

Next in importance to effective regulation of the domestic tuna industry is monitoring the regulation of the foreign fleet. The United States currently enjoys a virtual monopoly over purse seining technology. This will rapidly change as this technology is transferred to other countries. Purse seining without proper caution results in extremely high porpoise kills. We should discourage, not subsidize, such depredations. Those regulations that bind United States fishermen must also bind the foreign fleet. . . .

V. Conclusion

The antiquated concept of the Cetaceans and the high seas as being *res nullis* must end, and a new concept of *res communis* must take its place. Cetaceans are not "resources"—their loss touches all. Such creatures cannot be managed like the sterile extraction of raw materials for processing. Cetaceans have found particularly strong allies throughout the world, and especially here in the United States. The governmental agencies in this country must be forced to implement the legislation which exists today. These laws must then be improved to attain the explicit goal of zero domestic Cetacean mortality. These domestic initiatives must be interfaced with the concomitant and ultimate international goal of ending the slaughter of Cetaceans throughout the oceans. The recent dramatic increase in the non-consumptive use of whales and dolphins, especially for aesthetic pleasures, must be further researched and subsidized.[56] Such uses as the organization of tours to watch annual coastal migrations, the making of movies and television specials and the recording of the particularly eloquent song of the Humpback Whale are beginning to rival in worth the entire whaling industry, which in 1971 was estimated at only about $150 million.[57]

Ultimately, education and research are the tools with which to advance Cetacean rights. Scientific research has demonstrated the need for efforts to end the mass killings of Cetaceans. These beings may eventually teach us much about our own society, and our own world view.

Notes

1. Thoreau, *quoted in* McVay, *Reflections on the Management of Whaling,* in The Whale Problem 369 (W. Schevill, ed. 1974).

2. Doria, *The Dolphin Rider,* in Mind in the Waters 33 (J. McIntyre, ed. 1974).

3. *As cited* in R. Stenvit, The Dolphin: Cousin to Man 170, 171 (1971).

4. *Id.*

5. *As cited in* Reiger, *Dolphins Sacred Porpoises Profane,* 77 Audobon 3 (Jan. 1975).

6. Scheffer, *The Case for a World Moratorium on Whaling,* in Mind in the Waters 229 (J. McIntyre, ed. 1974).

7. Scarff, *The International Management of Whales, Dolphins and Porpoises: An Interdisciplinary Assessment* (Part 1), 6 Ecology L. Q. 323, 332 (1977) [hereinafter cited as Scarff].

8. Purse seines are cup-like nets with open bottoms. After encircling the fish, the open bottom of the purse seine is drawn closed in the manner of a drawstring purse, trapping the animals inside. Committee for Humane Legislation v. Richardson, 540 F.2d 1141, 1143 (D.C. Cir. 1976).

9. Tuna fishermen sight a particular species of bird which fly above porpoise schools which, in turn, swim above schools of tuna. In casting and drawing their nets or seines about the tuna, fishermen also capture the porpoises, which drown when entangled in the drawn seines.

10. *See* Scarff, *supra* note 7, at 340.

11. *Hearings on H. R. 10420 et al. Before the Subcommittee on Fisheries and Wildlife Conservation of the House Comm. on Merchant Marine and Fisheries,* 92d Cong., 1st Sess. 23 (1971) [hereinafter cited as *Hearings on H.R. 10420].*

12. Bunnell, *The Evolution of Cetacean Intelligence,* in Mind in the Waters 53, 55–58 (J. McIntyre, ed. 1974) [hereinafter cited as Bunnell]. Cetaceans have no natural enemies outside of their own genetic order. *Id.*

13. *Id.*

14. *Id.* at 57.

15. Morgane, *The Whale Brain: The Anatomical Basis of Intelligence,* in Mind in the Waters 86 (J. McIntyre, ed. 1974) [hereinafter cited as Morgane].

16. *See* Bunnell, *supra* note 12, at 57.

17. *Id.*

18. *Id.*

19. *See* Morgane, *supra* note 15, at 88.

20. Dr. Sterling Bunnell writes of these differences:

Eyesight in humans is a space-oriented distance-sense, which gives us complex simultaneous information in the form of analogic pictures but has poor time discrimination. Our auditory sense, however, has poor space perception but good time discrimination. Human languages are therefore comprised of fairly simple sounds arranged in elaborate temporal sequences. The Cetacean auditory system is predominantly spatial, like our eyesight, with much simultaneous information and poor time resolution. So dolphin language apparently consists of extremely complex sounds which are perceived as a unit. A whole paragraph's information might be conveyed in one elaborate instantaneous heirglyph. For them to follow our pattern of speech might be almost as difficult as it is for us to study the individual picture frames of a film being run at ordinary speed. It is not surprising then, that captive dolphins at first seem more interested in music than in the human voice. Our music is more similar to their voices than our speech is. Since their echolocation system gives them detailed images of objects in their world, they might even be able to recreate these sounds in their speech and thus directly project images to one another. The possible existence of digital language among dolphins is supported by known instances where complex information was transmitted among Cetaceans and also, as Bateson pointed out, by the incomprehensibility of their language to us. Analog emotional communication crosses species barriers fairly easily, while digital communication usually doesn't pass between different linguistic groups of the same species. Dolphin language may in some ways be similar to written Chinese characters, in which analog pictures are given digital functions. Perhaps future computer studies will make their linguistic patterns more recognizable to us.

Id. at 56.

21. One million bits is approximately the number of bits in Homer's Odyssey. C. Sagan, The Cosmic Connections 178 (1973).

22. Scarff, *International Management of Whales, Dolphins and Porpoises: An Interdisciplinary Assessment* (Part 2), 6 Ecology L. Q. 571, 580 (1977) [hereinafter cited as Scarff-part 2].

23. *Id.* For a more extensive treatment of the pressures for depletion inherent in the economics of whaling, *see* Gordon, *The Economic Theory of Common Property Resource: The Fishery,* 62 J. Pol. Econ. 124 (1954).

24. *See* Scarff-part 2, *supra* note 22, at 582.

25. *Id.* at 583.

26. *Id.*

27. Lockyer, *Estimates of Growth and Energy Budget for the Sperm Whale,* Doc. FAO/ACMRR/MM/SC/38 at 5 (Feb. 1976).

28. Clark, *Profit Maximization and the Extinction of Species,* 81 J. Pol. Econ. 950 (1972).

29. *Id.*

30. Suarez, *Report on the Exploitation of the Products of the Sea,* 20 A. J. I. L. 231, 235 (Supp. July 1926).

31. Convention for the Regulation of Whaling, Mar. 31, 1932, 49 Stat. 3079, T.I.A.S. No. 880.

32. *Id.*

33. Regulation of Whaling Convention, Dec. 2, 1946, 62 Stat. 1716, T.I.A.S. No. 1849.

34. Gulland, *Distribution and Abundance of Whales in Relation to Basic Productivity,* in The Whale Problem 27 (W. Scherill, ed. 1974).

35. An elephant could comfortably stand in the mouth of a Blue Whale. Matthews, The Whale 68 (1968).

36. *See* Scarff, *supra* note 7, at 350.

37. *Id.*

38. Talbot, *New Quotas Set for Whales: 1974 IWC Decisions,* 5 Mainstream 7 (Summer 1974).

39. For example, in 1972, the quotas on Antarctic Baleen Whales were set by species. *See* Scarff, *supra* note 7, at 368.

40. *Id.* at 334.

41. *Id.*

42. *Id.* In 1968, scientists realized that they had highly over-estimated the age for sexual maturity in the Fin Whale and, although quotas have been reduced, the Fin Whales have never recovered. *Id.* at 336.

43. New York Times, June 4, 1977, at 21, col. 4.

44. U.N. Doc. A/CONF. 48/14 and Corr. 1 Recommendation 33 (1972).

45. 16 U.S.C. §§ 1361 *et seq.* (Supp. III 1973).

46. See Section (III)(C), *infra.*

47. *See* Scarff, *supra* note 7, at 378–80.

48. 16 U.S.C. §§ 1361 *et seq.* (Supp. V 1975).

49. *See* Christol, *et al., The Law and the Whale,* 8 Cas. W. Res. J. Int'l. L. 157 (1976), at 156.

50. 16 U.S.C. §§ 1361 *et seq.* (Supp. V 1975).

51. *Id.* at § 1372 (a)(1).

52. *Id.* at § 1372 (a)(2)(d).

53. *Id.* at § 1372 (c)(1).

54. *Id.* at § 1374.

55. *Id.* at § 1375(b).

56. Draft Report of the working group on Low Consumptive Use of Marine Mammals, Doc. FAO/ACMRR/MM/SC/WG21 at 1 (Sept. 1970).

57. *See Hearings on H.R. 10420, supra* note 11, at 32.

Wilderness:
What Is It
"Good For"?

Preview

A Conceptual Issue: What Counts as a Wilderness?

The term *wilderness* is not easy to define, but a useful working definition is: an area of the earth substantially untrammeled or unmodified by human beings. Virtually no one suggests that an area must be entirely untouched by humans in order to qualify as wilderness. For example, in defining the content of wilderness, the Wilderness Act of 1964 recognized human beings as visitors who do not remain.[1] Val Routley, in her comment on John Passmore's remark that the presence of recreationists converts wilderness into "man-made landscape," maintains: "The occasional human presence and evidence of human activity around trails do not convert an area to a 'man-made landscape,'—anymore than the presence of a wombat trail creates a wombat-made landscape."[2]

The notion of the wild contrasts with both the domestic and the artificial. John Rodman has criticized the domestication of nonhuman animals as "a fundamentally coercive and exploitative institution."[3] Baird Callicott, in "Animal Liberation: A Triangular Affair," (Part III) questions the desirability of domesticity. Robert Elliot, in "Faking Nature," (this section) addresses questions about artificially "made to look natural" environments. Suppose we are looking at a beautiful landscape and we do not know that it is a fake. What difference does it make if we find out? if we don't find out? How should we respond to environmental engineers who claim that they can restore the environment they exploit?

Why Should We Preserve Wilderness?

What is it that is so especially valuable about wilderness? Does its existence fill a need in the human psyche? Is there some value in just knowing that it is there to go into if we should want to do that? Must its existence be *good for us* at all? Is there a moral obligation to preserve wilderness and wildness?

Many of the arguments that are given in defense of preserving the wild are labeled utilitarian. Here *utilitarian* carries one of its traditional meanings, that is, identifying as good those things that are useful or "of utility" to human beings (consider "utility companies"). For example, the scientific, recreational, aesthetic, and spiritual arguments are all utilitarian in this sense. Perhaps, according to a utilitarian view, there is an optimal amount of wilderness. For example, 80 percent may be too much, 1 percent too little.

One argument related to scientific concerns maintains that wilderness should be preserved because it contains a reservoir of genetic diversity. Wilderness is necessary (in contrast to zoos) as habitat for wild animals. Enough of it is needed to make natural evolution (sometimes called *coevolution*) possible for wild animals, as well as for most other sorts of genetic strands.[4] In all likelihood, scientists will want to conserve gene pools, but what if they could be preserved elsewhere? Suppose we could freeze genes and keep them in banks. Is the scientific argument contingent on the development of technology? Of course, wilderness may be valuable to science in many ways including undiscovered medical and other uses.

Recreational, aesthetic, and spiritual arguments for wilderness preservation center around the importance of wilderness experience. Wilderness often evokes responses of awe, wonder, even terror. In this section, René Dubos gives us a superb description of the range of possible emotional reactions to the wild. Dubos reminds us that for much of human history, wilderness denoted a harsh environment "cursed by God, and commonly occupied by foul creatures."[5] The same scenes that once elicited fear, contempt, and alienation are at other times touted as the source of inspiration, spiritual catharsis, and therapy from the stress and strain of civilized life. For example, the Derbyshire peak region in England was once considered unfit for viewing. "Travelers . . . were advised to keep their coach blinds drawn while traversing the region so as not to be shocked by its ugliness and wildness.

Within a few decades, however, the very same region came to be regarded as so attractive that it inspired lines of extravagant praise by nineteenth-century poets."[6]

Aesthetic considerations can be powerful, but they have their limitations. For example, John Rodman points out that aesthetic arguments are particularly plausible in arguing for the preservation of the Sierras and the Grand Canyons, but not with respect to saving the marshes and brushlands.[7] He further asserts that some, but not all, sacred spaces are informed by an aesthetic of the sublime and the beautiful. Thus, if we rely on aesthetic considerations, what we save depends in part on our conception of what is beautiful or ugly, awe-inspiring or threatening, clarifying or puzzling.

It is crucial to realize that not all peoples who live in a wilderness think of it as a threat. One native American, Luther Standing Bear, an Oglala Sioux, made the following remarks about the fact that different Americans have experienced wilderness differently:

We do not think of the great open plains, the beautiful rolling hills, and winding streams with tangled growth as "wild." Only to the white man was nature a "wilderness" and only to him was the land "infested" with "wild" animals and "savage" people. To us it was tame. Earth was bountiful and we were surrounded with the blessings of the Great Mystery. Not until the hairy man from the east came and with brutal frenzy heaped injustices upon us and the families we loved was it "wild" for us. When the very animals of the forest began fleeing from his approach, then it was that for us the "wild west" began.[8]

Standing Bear might find some irony in the view that wilderness symbolizes important cultural values such as freedom. Wilderness, it is claimed, has a positive influence on human character: "Wilderness can teach us moral lessons; we can learn humility and gratitude, but we also can gain self-reliance, independence, and courage in facing the challenge of the wild. Wilderness has molded us as a nation; Daniel Boone, the Oregon Trail, and the Western frontier are all part of our national heritage."[9] The loss of wilderness may mean the loss of freedom in a sense quite different from freedom as a cultural symbol. Freedom will be lost in that our choices among environments will be limited to those we create ourselves.[10] Moreover, if we continue down the road of resource depletion, pollution, and overpopulation, we may eliminate the possibility of a decent environment as one of our choices. The frontier mentality historically so influential in the United States presupposes that one can always move on, that one can foul one's nest and not live with the consequences. However, in the foreseeable future this is the only planet we've got.

Notes

1. Public Law 88-577 in U.S., *Statutes At Large*, 78, pp. 890–96.

2. Val Routley. "Critical Notice of John Pass-more's *Man's Responsibility for Nature*," *Australasian Journal of Philosophy*, 53 (1975), p. 182.

3. John Rodman. "The Liberation of Nature?" p. 127.

4. Thanks to a reviewer of *People, Penguins, and Plastic Trees* for this statement of the coevolution argument.

5. René Dubos. *The Wooing of Earth* (New York: Charles Scribners's Sons, 1980), p. 10.

6. René Dubos. *The Wooing of Earth*, p. 14.

7. John Rodman. "Four Forms of Ecological Consciousness," p. 86.

8. Luther Standing Bear. *Touch the Earth*, edited by T. Meluhan, 1971, quoted in Bill Devall, "The Deep Ecology Movements," *Natural Resources Journal* 20 (1980), p. 306.

9. Ian Barbour. *Technology, Environment, and Human Values*, p. 83.

10. See Edward B. Swain for a defense of freedom in this sense. "Wilderness and the Maintenance of Freedom," *The Humanist* (Mar./Apr. 1983).

The Wilderness Experience

René Dubos

Until the age of twenty-seven, I knew of the Earth only some of its most humanized environments, in France, Italy, England, and the eastern coast of the United States. My first direct contacts with the wilderness were during the late 1920s and the 1930s, when I drove several times across the North American continent and discovered—a true emotional discovery for me—the New Mexico mesas from the Raton Pass and the Pacific Ocean from a primeval forest in Oregon. Around 1930, these environments were still essentially wild.

I now realize how much my life would have been enriched by longer and more intimate contacts with the wilderness. The experience of nature in a native prairie, a desert, a primeval forest, or high mountains not crowded with tourists is qualitatively different from what it is in a well-tended meadow, a wheat field, an olive grove, or even in the high Alps. Humanized environments give us confidence because nature has been reduced to the human scale, but the wilderness in whatever form almost compels us to measure ourselves against the cosmos. It makes us realize how insignificant we are as biological creatures and invites us to escape from daily life into the realms of eternity and infinity.

In one of Kyoto's Zen temples, I have seen men and women who gave the impression of achieving this escape by looking at a distant hill in an attitude of reverence. We can also perceive some of the cosmic values of the wilderness by contemplating the great spectacles of nature, for example, simply by looking down into the Grand Canyon of the Colorado. But

Source: René Dubos, "The Wilderness Experience" from *René Dubos, The Wooing of Earth*. Copyright © 1980 René Dubos. Reprinted with the permission of Charles Scribner's Sons.

the real experience of the wilderness probably requires the participation of all our senses, in a manner that calls to mind Paleolithic ways of life.

The hunter-gatherers of the Old Stone Age were conditioned physically and mentally by the features of their immediate surroundings: the lay of the land, the rocks, and the soil; the springs, rivers, and lakes; the various forms of animal and plant life; the sunshine and rainfall; all the natural phenomena they experienced directly. Their bodily responses were conditioned and their mental processes were informed by the environmental stimuli they perceived through their senses. They thus acquired an empirical knowledge that was more holistic than analytic but so precise and so well fitted to their local environment that it enabled them to cope effectively with the various aspects of the wilderness in which they lived, much as wild animals do in their native habitats.

Ever since the development of agriculture in the Neolithic period, the immense majority of human beings have lived in environments they have transformed. As a result, few of us really desire to inhabit the wilderness permanently and even fewer could long survive in it. This is not because we are genetically different from the Stone Age hunter-gatherers, but because humanized environments do not provide the opportunities for the expression of certain human potentialities that are still in us but can be expressed only under conditions similar to those of Paleolithic life.

Recent observations prove that our genetic endowment would enable us, if conditions were right, to acquire the kind of organic, holistic knowledge that Stone Age people derived from their sensory experiences of the natural environments. This happened in the eighteenth and nineteenth centuries to the Europeans who became *coureurs de bois* or otherwise lived out of contact with civilization in various parts of North America. Having to function in environments that had not been domesticated and that were often very demanding, many Europeans developed within a remarkably short time the biological and psychological traits essential for life in the wilderness. These traits were the expression of fundamental human attributes

that had remained dormant during centuries of civilized life in Europe.

Even among people today, the really experienced hunters or fishermen perceive with their whole body the layout of the landscapes and waterscapes in which they practice their particular sport. They come to know almost instinctively the habits of the animals that interest them and how these habits are affected by the seasons, the vagaries of the weather, and other aspects of the environment. In *Meditations on Hunting,* José Ortega y Gasset reports how the hunter "instinctively shrinks from being seen" and "perceives all his surroundings from the point of view of the animal." For the hunter, "wind, light, temperature, ground contour, minerals, vegetation, all play a part. They are not simply there . . . as they are for the tourist or the botanist, but rather they function, they act. . . ." These words of Ortega convey how human beings can still learn to function as organic parts of a given environment instead of simply observing it passively, as do most people when looking at scenery. Human beings can even learn about nature from animals. A naturalist who had raised two wolves and was in the habit of taking long walks with them in the wilderness described how the behavior of his animal companions made him perceive aspects of Nature—smells, sounds, and sights—that he had not noticed before. Thus, although we are no longer adapted to life in the wilderness, this is not due to changes in our genetic nature but to social and cultural forces that inhibit the expression of some of our potential.

From the beginning of recorded history and even in prehistoric legends, the word *wilderness* has been used to denote barren deserts, deep forests, high mountains, and other inaccessible or harsh environments not suited to human beings, cursed by God, and commonly occupied by foul creatures. Such forms of wilderness evoked a sense of fear for a good biological reason. They are profoundly different from the environmental conditions under which our species acquired its biological and psychological characteristics during the Stone Age.

The word *wilderness* occurs approximately three hundred times in the Bible, and all its meanings are derogatory. In both the Old and New Testament, the word usually refers to parched lands with extremely low rainfall. These deserts were then as now unsuited to human life, and they were regarded as the abodes of devils and demons. After Jesus was baptized in the Jordan River, he was "led up by the Spirit into the wilderness to be tempted by the devil." The holy men of the Old Testament or of the early Christian era moved into the wilderness when they wanted to find a sanctuary from the sinful world of their times. Thus, while some great events of the Judeo-Christian tradition occurred in the desert, this environment was at best suitable for spiritual catharsis.

In Europe, the word *wilderness* applied chiefly to primeval forests, high mountains, and marshes because these parts of the continent were uninhabitable. According to Marjorie Nicolson, people until the eighteenth century regarded mountains as "nature's shames and ills . . . warts, blisters, and imposthumes" upon the otherwise fair face of the Earth. When the Puritans arrived in the New World, the huge forests that covered the Atlantic coast at that time similarly appeared to them as a "heidious and desolate wilderness full of wilde beastes and wilde men." The majority of immigrants who settled in the rest of the American continent during the following two centuries also regarded the primeval forest with fear and contempt.

Ecologists define as wilderness any environment that has not been disturbed by human activities, but in the popular mind, the word still has a deep resonance with a feeling of alienation and insecurity. It is used to denote almost any place, natural or artificial, in which people feel lost or perplexed. In the past, nature in the wild has been usually regarded as alien and cruel, the site of evil and witchcraft. Now, many people in industrialized societies use the word *wilderness* to denote huge anonymous urban agglomerations that appear to them hostile and corrupt.

Humankind has always struggled against environments to which it could not readily adapt; in particular, it has shunned the wilderness or has destroyed much of it all over the world. Contrary to what is often stated, this is just as true of Oriental as of Occidental people.

The admiration of wild landscapes expressed in Oriental arts and literature probably reflects not so much the desire to live in them as the intellectual use of them for religious or poetic inspiration. The ancient Chinese, especially the Taoists, tried to recognize in nature the unity and rhythm that they believed to pervade the universe. In Japan, the followers of Shinto deified mountains, forests, storms, and torrents and thus professed a religious veneration for these natural phenomena. Such cultural attitudes were celebrated in Chinese and Japanese landscape paintings more than a thousand years before they penetrated Western art, but this does not prove that Oriental people really identified with the wilderness. Paintings of Chinese scholars wandering thoughtfully up a lonely mountain path or meditating in a hut under the rain suggest an intellectual mood rather than life in the wilderness. The Chinese master Kuo Hsi wrote in the eleventh century that the purpose of landscape painting was to use art for making available the qualities of haze, mist, and the haunting spirits of the mountains to human beings who had little if any opportunity to experience these delights of nature. Much of the Chinese land had been grossly deforested and eroded thousands of year before, and the Taoist movement may have been generated in part by this degradation of nature and as a protest against the artificialities of Chinese social life.

In the Christian world, also, there has been a continuous succession of holy men, poets, painters, and scholars who did not live in the wilderness but praised it for its beauty and its ability to inspire noble thoughts or actions. St. Francis of Assisi was not alone among medieval Christians in admiring and loving nature. The Swiss naturalist Conrad Gessner wrote in 1541 that "he is an enemy of nature, whosoever has not deemed lofty mountains to be most worthy of great contemplation." After Jean Jacques Rousseau the many romantic writers, painters, and naturalists of Europe became more than a match for the Chinese poets and scholars of the Sung period depicted against a backdrop of mountains and torrents. But like the Chinese, they wrote of the wilderness in the comfort of their civilized homes, as intellectuals who preached rather than practiced the nature religion.

In Europe the shift from fear to admiration of the wilderness gained momentum in the eighteenth century. The shift was not brought about by a biological change in human nature but was the consequence of a new social and cultural environment. Fear of the wilderness probably began to decrease as soon as dependable roads gave confidence that safe and comfortable quarters could be reached in case of necessity. There were numerous good roads in western Europe by the time Jean Jacques Rousseau roamed through the Alps and Wordsworth through the Lake District. In the New World, access was fairly easy even to the High Sierras when John Muir reached them from San Francisco.

Appreciation of the wilderness began not among country folk who had to make a living in it, but among city dwellers who eventually came to realize that human life had been impoverished by its divorce from nature. People of culture generally wanted to experience the wilderness not for its own sake, but as a form of emotional and intellectual enrichment. In Europe, Petrarch is the first person credited with having deliberately searched mountain and primeval forest for the sheer pleasure of the experience. His account of his ascent of Mount Ventoux in 1336 is the first known written statement of the beauty of the Alps under the snow, but he reproached himself for letting the beauty of the landscape divert his mind from more important pursuits. By the early Romantic period, however, the wilderness came to be seen not only as the place in which to escape from an artificial and corrupt society but also as a place to experience the mysterious and wondrous qualities of nature. The wilderness experience became a fashionable topic of conversation as well as of literature and painting and thus rapidly changed the attitudes of the general public toward nature.

Until the eighteenth century, for example, the Derbyshire peak region in England was considered wild and unfit for human eyes. In 1681, the poet Charles Cotton described it as "a country so deformed" that it might be regarded as "Nature's pudenda." Travelers in those days were advised to keep their coach blinds drawn while traversing the region so as not to be shocked by its ugliness and wildness. Within a few decades, however, the very same region came to be regarded as so attractive that it inspired lines of extravagant praise by nineteenth-century poets. The Derbyshire hills are now considered rather tame, since they do not exceed 2,000 feet in elevation; later poets shifted their admiration to wilder and more rugged sceneries such as the Lake District, the Alps, and high mountains in general. In less than two centuries, new emotional and intellectual attitudes thus completely changed the relationships between English people and their natural environment.

People who express love for the wilderness do not necessarily practice what they preach. In 1871, Ralph Waldo Emerson refused to camp under primitive conditions when he visited John Muir in the Sierras and elected instead to spend the night in a hotel. When Thoreau delivered the lecture with the famous sentence "In Wildness is the Preservation of the World," he was living in Concord, Massachusetts, a very civilized township where the wilderness had been completely tamed. He loved the out-of-doors, but knew little of the real wilderness. His cabin by Walden Pond was only two miles from Concord; woodchucks were the wildest creatures he encountered on his way from the pond to town, where he often went for dinner. In fact, Thoreau acknowledged some disenchantment when he experienced Nature in a state approaching real wilderness during his travels through Maine.

As pointed out by Aldous Huxley in his essay "Wordsworth and the Tropics," the sceneries that inspired Thoreau and nineteenth-century Romantic poets were very different from the wilderness which has frightened people throughout the ages. "To us who live beneath a temperate sky and in the age of Henry Ford, the worship of Nature comes almost naturally. It is easy to love a feeble and already conquered enemy. . . . There are . . . wild woods and mountains, marshes and heaths, even in England. But they are there only on sufferance, because we have chosen, out of our good pleasure, to leave them their freedom." For us, now, "the corollary of mountain is tunnel, of swamp an embankment; of distance, a railway." In the real wilderness, however, "rivers imply wading, swimming, alligators. Plains mean swamps, forest, fevers."

As did their Oriental counterparts, Christian advocates of the wilderness discovered its beauty while trying to escape from their social environment in search of a better way of life. They valued it as a symbol of anticorruption at least as much as for its own sake; the European pro-wilderness movement gained momentum in the nineteenth century from the reaction against the brutalities of the Industrial Revolution.

Appreciation of the wilderness was later enriched by science. Instead of regarding deserts and marshes as the abode of evil spirits, and mountains as ugly deformities of the Earth's surface, educated people learned to look at these phenomena as expressions of a natural order different from the creations of the human order, but with a beauty of their own. Most people probably still experienced awe in the face of wilderness, but they also had a sense of sublimity at the prodigious creativeness of Nature and a feeling of reverence for the laws—divine or natural—that link humankind to the rest of creation.

Increasingly during recent years, interest in the wilderness and the desire to preserve as much of it as possible have been generated by an understanding of its ecological importance. It has been shown, for example, that the wilderness accounts for some 90 percent of the energy trapped from the sun by photosynthesis and therefore plays a crucial role in the global energy system. The wilderness, furthermore, is the habitat of countless species of animals, plants, and microbes; destroying it consequently decreases the earth's biological diversity. This in turn renders ecosystems less resistant to climatic and other catastrophes, and less able to support the various animal and plant species on which we depend. Undisturbed natural environments, including forests, prairies, wetlands, marshes, and even deserts, are the best insurance we have against the dangers inherent in the instability of the simplified ecosystems created by modern agriculture. From a purely anthropocentric point of view we must save as

much wilderness as possible because it constitutes a depository of genetic types from which we can draw to modify and improve our domesticated animals and plants.

Admiration of the wilderness can thus take different forms. It can lead to direct and prolonged experience of the natural world as in the case of John Muir. For many more people, it derives from a desire to escape from the trials and artificialities of social life, or to find a place where one can engage in a process of self-discovery. Experiencing the wilderness includes not only the love of its spectacles, its sounds, and its smells, but also an intellectual concern for the diversity of its ecological niches.

Above and beyond these considerations, however, are moral ones that also favor wilderness preservation. The statement that Earth is our mother is not a sentimental platitude. Our species has been shaped by the Earth and we feel guilty and somewhat incomplete when we lose contact with the forces of nature and with the rest of the living world. The desire to save forests, wetlands, deserts, or any other natural ecosystem is an expression of deep human values. Concern for the wilderness does not need biological justification any more than does opposing callousness and vandalism. We do not live in the wilderness but we need it for our biological and psychological welfare. The experience of the quality of wildness in the wilderness helps us to recapture some of our own wildness and authenticity. Experiencing wildness in nature contributes to our self-discovery and to the expression of our dormant potentialities.

The human species has now spread to practically all parts of the Earth. In temperate latitudes, although not in tropical or polar regions, we have enslaved much of Nature. And it is probably for this reason that we are beginning to worship the wilderness. After having for so long regarded the primeval forest as the abode of evil spirits, we have come to marvel at its eerie light and to realize that the mood of wonder it evokes cannot be duplicated in a garden, an orchard, or a park. After having been frightened by the ocean, we recognize a sensual and mystic quality in its vastness and in the endless ebb and flow of its waves. Our emotional re ponse to the thunderous silence of deep canyons, to the frozen solitude of high mountains, and to the blinding luminosity of the desert is the expression of aspects of our fundamental being that are still in resonance with cosmic forces. The experience of wilderness, even though indirect and transient, helps us to be aware of the cosmos from which we emerged, and to maintain some measure of harmonious relation to the rest of creation.

Faking Nature

Robert Elliot

I

Consider the following case. There is a proposal to mine beach sands for rutile. Large areas of dune are to be cleared of vegetation and the dunes themselves destroyed. It is agreed, by all parties concerned, that the dune area has value quite apart from a utilitarian one. It is agreed, in other words, that it would be a bad thing considered in itself for the dune area to be dramatically altered. Acknowledging this the mining company expresses its willingness, indeed its desire, to restore the dune area to its original condition after the minerals have been extracted.[1] The company goes on to argue that any loss of value is merely temporary and that full value will in fact be restored. In other words they are claiming that the destruction of what has value is compensated for by the later creation (recreation) of something of equal value. I shall call this "the restoration thesis."

In the actual world many such proposals are made, not because of shared conservationist principles, but as a way of undermining the arguments of conservationists. Such proposals are in fact effective in defeating environmentalist protest. They are also notoriously ineffective in putting right, or indeed even seeming to put right, the particular wrong that has been done to the environment. The sandmining case is just one of a number of similar cases involving such things as open-cut mining, clear-felling of forests, river diversion, and highway construction. Across a range of such cases some concession is made by way of acknowledging the value of pieces of landscape, rivers, forests and so forth, and a suggestion is made that this value can be restored once the environmentally disruptive process has been completed.

Imagine, contrary to fact, that restoration projects are largely successful; that the environment is brought back to its original condition and that even a close inspection will fail to reveal that the area has been mined, clear-felled, or whatever. If this is so then there is temptation to think that one particular environmentalist objection is defeated. The issue is by no means merely academic. I have already claimed that restoration promises do in fact carry weight against environmental arguments. Thus Mr. Doug Anthony, the Australian Deputy Prime Minister, saw fit to suggest that sand-mining on Fraser Island could be resumed once "the community becomes more informed and more enlightened as to what reclamation work is being carried out by mining companies...."[2] Or consider how the protests of environmentalists might be deflected in the light of the following report of environmental engineering in the United States.

... about 2 km of creek 25 feet wide has been moved to accommodate a highway and in doing so engineers with the aid of landscape architects and biologists have rebuilt the creek to the same stan-

Source: *Inquiry* Vol. 25, No. 1 (Mar. 1982), pp. 81–93. Reprinted by permission.

dard as before. Boulders, bends, irregularities and natural vegetation have all been designed into the new section. In addition, special log structures have been built to improve the habitat as part of a fish development program.[3]

Not surprisingly the claim that revegetation, rehabilitation, and the like restore value has been strongly contested. J. G. Mosley reports that:

The Fraser Island Environmental Inquiry Commissioners did in fact face up to the question of the relevance of successful rehabilitation to the decision on whether to ban exports (of beach sand minerals) and were quite unequivocal in saying that if the aim was to protect a natural area such success was irrelevant. . . . The Inquiry said: '. . . even if, contrary to the overwhelming weight of evidence before the Commission, successful rehabilitation of the flora after mining is found to be ecologically possible on all mined sites on the Island . . . the overall impression of a wild, uncultivated island refuge will be destroyed forever by mining'.[4]

I want to show both that there is a rational, coherent ethical system which supports decisive objections to the restoration thesis, and that that system is not lacking in normative appeal. The system I have in mind will make valuation depend, in part, on the presence of properties which cannot survive the disruption-restoration process. There is, however, one point that needs clarifying before discussion proceeds. Establishing that restoration projects, even if empirically successful, do not fully restore value does not by any means constitute a knock-down argument against some environmentally disruptive policy. The value that would be lost if such a policy were implemented may be just one value among many which conflict in this situation. Countervailing considerations may be decisive and the policy thereby shown to be the right one. If my argument turns out to be correct it will provide an extra, though by no means decisive, reason for adopting certain environmentalist policies. It will show that the resistance which environmentalists display in the face of restoration promises is not merely silly, or emotional, or irrational. This is important because so much

of the debate assumes that settling the dispute about what is ecologically possible automatically settles the value question. The thrust of much of the discussion is that if restoration is shown to be possible, and economically feasible, then recalcitrant environmentalists are behaving irrationally, being merely obstinate or being selfish.

There are indeed familiar ethical systems which will serve to explain what is wrong with the restoration thesis in a certain range of cases. Thus preference utilitarianism will support objections to some restoration proposal if that proposal fails to maximally satisfy preferences. Likewise classical utilitarianism will lend support to a conservationist stance provided that the restoration proposal fails to maximize happiness and pleasure. However, in both cases the support offered is contingent upon the way in which the preferences and utilities line up. And it is simply not clear that they line up in such a way that the conservationist position is even usually vindicated. While appeal to utilitarian considerations might be strategically useful in certain cases they do not reflect the underlying motivation of the conservationists. The conservationists seem committed to an account of what has value which allows that restoration proposals fail to compensate for environmental destruction despite the fact that such proposals would maximize utility. What then is this distinct source of value which motivates and underpins the stance taken by, among others, the Commissioners of the Fraser Island Environmental Inquiry?

II

It is instructive to list some reasons that might be given in support of the claim that something of value would be lost if a certain bit of the environment were destroyed. It may be that the area supports a diversity of plant and animal life, it may be that it is the habitat of some endangered species, it may be that it contains striking rock formations or particularly fine specimens of mountain ash. If it is only considerations such as these that contribute to the area's value then perhaps opposition to the environmentally disruptive project would be irrational provided certain firm guarantees were available; for instance that the mining company or timber company would carry out the restoration and that it would be successful. Presumably there are steps that could be taken to ensure the continuance of species diversity and the continued existence of the endangered species. Some of the other requirements might prove harder to meet, but in some sense or other it is possible to recreate the rock formations and to plant mountain ash that will turn out to be particularly fine specimens. If value consists of the presence of objects of these various kinds, independently of what explains their presence, then the restoration thesis would seem to hold. The environmentalist needs to appeal to some feature which cannot be replicated as a source of some part of a natural area's value.

Putting the point thus, indicates the direction the environmentalist could take. He might suggest that an area is valuable, partly, because it is a natural area, one that has not been modified by human hand, one that is undeveloped, unspoilt, or even unsullied. This suggestion is in accordance with much environmentalist rhetoric, and something like it at least must be at the basis of resistance to restoration proposals. One way of teasing out the suggestion and giving it a normative basis is to take over a notion from aesthetics. Thus we might claim that what the environmental engineers are proposing is that we accept a fake or a forgery instead of the real thing. If the claim can be made good then perhaps an adequate response to restoration proposals is to point out that they merely fake nature; that they offer us something less than was taken away.[5] Certainly there is a weight of opinion to the effect that, in art at least, fakes lack a value possessed by the real thing.[6]

One way in which this argument might be nipped in the bud is by claiming that it is bound to exploit an ultimately unworkable distinction between what is natural and what is not. Admittedly the distinction between the natural and the non-natural requires detailed working out. This is something I do not propose doing. However, I do think the distinction can be made good in a way sufficient to the present need. For present purposes I shall take it that "natural" means something like "unmodified by human activity." Obviously some areas will be more natural than others according to the degree to which they have been shaped by human hand. Indeed most rural landscapes will, on this view, count as non-natural to a very high degree. Nor do I intend the natural/non-natural distinction to exactly parallel some dependent moral evaluations; that is, I do not want to be taken as claiming that what is natural is good and what is non-natural is not. The distinction between natural and non-natural connects with valuation in a much more subtle way than that. This is something to which I shall presently return. My claim then is that restoration policies do not always fully restore value because part of the reason that we value bits of the environment is because they are natural to a high degree. It is time to consider some counter-arguments.

An environmental engineer might urge that the exact similarity which holds between the original and the perfectly restored environment leaves no room for a value discrimination between them. He may urge that if they are *exactly* alike, down to the minutest detail (and let us imagine for the sake of argument that this is a technological possibility), then they must be *equally* valuable. The suggestion is that value-discriminations depend on there being intrinsic differences between the states of affairs evaluated. This begs the question against the environmentalist, since it simply discounts the possibility that events temporally and spatially outside the immediate landscape in question can serve as the basis of some valuation of it. It discounts the possibility that the manner of the landscape's genesis, for example, has a legitimate role in determining its value. Here are some examples which suggest that an object's origins do affect its value and our valuations of it.

Imagine that I have a piece of sculpture in my garden which is too fragile to be moved at all. For some reason it would suit the local council to lay sewerage pipes just where the sculpture happens to be. The council engineer informs me of this and explains that my sculpture will have to go. However, I need not despair because he promises to replace it with an exactly similar artifact, one which, he assures me, not even the very best experts could tell was not the original. The example may be unlikely, but it does have some point. While I may concede that the replica would be better than nothing at all (and I may not even concede that), it is utterly improbable that I would accept it as full compensation for the original. Nor is my reluctance entirely explained by the monetary value of the original work. My reluctance springs from the fact that I value the original as an aesthetic object, as an object with a specific genesis and history.

Alternatively, imagine I have been promised a Vermeer for my birthday. The day arrives and I am given a painting which looks just like a Vermeer. I am understandably pleased. However, my pleasure does not last for long. I am told that the painting I am holding is not a Vermeer but instead an exact replica of one previously destroyed. Any attempt to allay my disappointment by insisting that there just is no difference between the replica and the original misses the mark completely. There is a difference and it is one which affects my perception, and consequent valuation, of the painting. The difference of course lies in the painting's genesis.

I shall offer one last example which perhaps bears even more closely on the environmental issue. I am given a rather beautiful, delicately constructed, object. It is something I treasure and admire, something in which I find considerable aesthetic value. Everything is fine until I discover certain facts about its origin. I discover that it is carved out of the bone of someone killed especially for that purpose. This discovery affects me deeply and I cease to value the object in the way that I once did. I regard it as in some sense sullied, spoilt by the facts of its origin. The object itself has not changed but my perceptions of it have. I now know that it is not quite the kind of thing I thought it was, and that my prior valuation of it was mistaken. The discovery is like the discovery that a painting one believed to be an original is in fact a forgery. The discovery about the object's origin changes the valuation made of it, since it reveals that the object is not of the kind that I value.

What these examples suggest is that there is at least a prima facie case for partially explaining the value of objects in terms of their origins, in terms of the kinds of processes that brought them into being. It is easy to find evidence in the writings of people who have valued nature that things extrinsic to the present, immediate environment determine valuations of it. John Muir's remarks about Hetch Hetchy Valley are a case in point.[7] Muir regarded the valley as a place where he could have direct contact with primeval nature; he valued it, not just because it was a place of great beauty, but because it was also a part of the world that had not been shaped by human hand. Muir's valuation was conditional upon certain facts about the valley's genesis; his valuation was of a, literally, natural object, of an object with a special kind of continuity with the past. The news that it was a carefully contrived elaborate *ecological* artifact would have transformed that valuation immediately and radically.

The appeal that many find in areas of wilderness, in natural forests and wild rivers depends very much on the naturalness of such places. There may be similarities between the experience one has when confronted with the multi-faceted complexity, the magnitude, the awesomeness of a very large city, and the experience one has walking through a rain forest. There may be similarities between the feeling one has listening to the roar of water over the spillway of a dam, and the feeling one has listening to a similar roar as a wild river tumbles down rapids. Despite the similarities there are also differences. We value the forest and river in part because they are representative of the world outside our dominion, because their existence is independent of us. We may value the city and the dam because of what they represent of human achievement. Pointing out the differences is not necessarily to denigrate either. However, there will be cases where we rightly judge that it is better to have the natural object than it is to have the artifact.

It is appropriate to return to a point mentioned earlier concerning the relationship between the natural and the valuable. It will not do to argue that what is natural is necessarily of value. The environmentalist can comfortably concede this point. He is not claiming that all natural phenomena have value in virtue of being natural. Sickness and disease are natural in a straightforward sense and are certainly not good. Natural phenomena such as fires, hurricanes, volcanic eruptions can totally alter landscapes and alter them for the worse. All of this can be conceded. What the environmentalist wants to claim is that, within certain constraints, the naturalness of a landscape is a reason for preserving it, a determinant of its value. Artificially transforming an utterly barren, ecologically bankrupt landscape into something richer and more subtle may be a good thing. That is a view quite compatible with the belief that replacing a rich natural environment with a rich artificial one is a bad thing. What the environmentalist insists on is that naturalness is one factor in determining the value of pieces of the environment. But that, as I have tried to suggest, is no news. The castle by the Scottish loch is a very different kind of object, value-wise, from the exact replica in the appropriately shaped environment of some Disneyland of the future. The barrenness of some Cycladic island would stand in a different, better perspective if it were not brought about by human intervention.

As I have glossed it, the environmentalist's complaint concerning restoration proposals is that nature is not replaceable without depreciation in one aspect of its value which has to do with its genesis, its history. Given this, an opponent might be tempted to argue that there is no longer any such thing as 'natural' wilderness, since the preservation of those bits of it which remain is achievable only by deliberate policy. The idea is that by placing boundaries around national parks, by actively discouraging grazing, trail-biking and the like, by prohibiting sand-mining, we are turning the wilderness into an artifact, that in some negative or indirect way we are creating an environment. There is some truth in this suggestion. In fact we need to take notice of it if we do value wilderness, since positive policies *are* required to preserve it. But as an argument against my over-all claim it fails. What is significant about wilderness is its causal continuity with the past. This is something that is not destroyed by demarcating an area and declaring it a national park. There is a distinction between the

'naturalness' of the wilderness itself and the means used to maintain and protect it. What remains within the park boundaries is, as it were, the real thing. The environmentalist may regret that such positive policy is required to preserve the wilderness against human, or even natural, assault.[8] However, the regret does not follow from the belief that what remains is of depreciated value. There is a significant difference between preventing damage and repairing damage once it is done. That is the difference that leaves room for an argument in favour of a preservation policy over and above a restoration policy.

There is another important issue which needs highlighting. It might be thought that naturalness only matters in so far as it is perceived. In other words it might be thought that if the environmental engineer could perform the restoration quickly and secretly, then there would be no room for complaint. Of course, in one sense there would not be, since the knowledge which would motivate complaint would be missing. What this shows is that there can be loss of value without the loss being perceived. It allows room for valuations to be mistaken because of ignorance concerning relevant facts. Thus my Vermeer can be removed and secretly replaced with the perfect replica. I have lost something of value without knowing that I have. This is possible because it is not simply the states of mind engendered by looking at the painting, by gloatingly contemplating my possession of it, by giving myself over to aesthetic pleasure, and so on which explain why it has value. It has value because of the kind of thing that it is, and one thing that it is is a painting executed by a man with certain intentions, at a certain stage of his artistic development, living in a certain aesthetic *milieu*. Similarly, it is not just those things which make me feel the joy that wilderness makes me feel, that I value. That would be a reason for desiring such things, but that is a distinct consideration. I value the forest because it is of a specific kind, because there is a certain kind of causal history which explains its existence. Of course I can be deceived into thinking that a piece of landscape has that kind of history, has developed in the appropriate way. The success of the deception does not elevate the restored landscape to the level of the original, no more than the success of the deception in the previous example confers on the fake the value of a real Vermeer. What has value in both cases are objects which are of the kind that I value, not merely objects which I think are of that kind. This point, it should be noted, is appropriate independently of views concerning the subjectivity or objectivity of value.

An example might bring the point home. Imagine that John is someone who values wilderness. John may find himself in one of the following situations:

1. He falls into the clutches of a utilitarian-minded super-technologist. John's captor has erected a rather incredible device which he calls an experience machine. Once the electrodes are attached and the right buttons pressed one can be brought to experience anything whatsoever. John is plugged into the machine, and, since his captor knows full well John's love of wilderness, given an extended experience as of hiking through a spectacular wilderness. This is environmental engineering at its most extreme. Quite assuredly John is being short-changed. John wants there to be wilderness and he wants to experience it. He wants the world to be a certain way and he wants to have experiences of a certain kind; veridical.

2. John is abducted, blindfolded and taken to a simulated, plastic wilderness area. When the blindfold is removed John is thrilled by what he sees around him: the tall gums, the wattles, the lichen on the rocks. At least that is what he thinks is there. We know better: we know that John is deceived, that he is once again being short-changed. He has been presented with an environment which he thinks is of value but isn't. If he knew that the leaves through which the artificially generated breeze now stirred were synthetic he would be profoundly disappointed, perhaps even disgusted at what at best is a cruel joke.

3. John is taken to a place which was once devastated by strip-mining. The forest which had stood there for some thousands

of years had been felled and the earth torn up, and the animals either killed or driven from their habitat. Times have changed, however, and the area has been restored. Trees of the species which grew there before the devastation grow there again, and the animal species have returned. John knows nothing of this and thinks he is in pristine forest. Once again, he has been short-changed, presented with less than what he values most.

In the same way that the plastic trees may be thought a (minimal) improvement on the experience machine, so too the real trees are an improvement on the plastic ones. In fact in the third situation there is incomparably more of value than in the second, but there could be more. The forest, though real, is not genuinely what John wants it to be. If it were not the product of contrivance he would value it more. It is a produce of contrivance. Even in the situation where the devastated area regenerates rather than is restored, it is possible to understand and sympathize with John's claim that the environment does not have the fullest possible value. Admittedly in this case there is not so much room for that claim, since the environment has regenerated of its own accord. Still the regenerated environment does not have the right kind of continuity with the forest that stood there initially; that continuity has been interfered with by the earlier devastation. (In actual fact the regenerated forest is likely to be perceivably quite different to the kind of thing originally there.)

III

I have argued that the causal genesis of forests, rivers, lakes, and so on is important in establishing their value. I have also tried to give an indication of why this is. In the course of my argument I drew various analogies, implicit rather than explicit, between faking art and faking nature. This should not be taken to suggest, however, that the concepts of aesthetic evaluation and judgment are to be carried straight over to evaluations of, and judgments about, the natural environment. Indeed there is good reason to believe that this cannot be done. For one thing an apparently integral part of aesthetic evaluation depends on viewing the aesthetic object as an intentional object, as an artifact, as something that is shaped by the purposes and designs of its author. Evaluating works of art involves explaining them, and judging them, in terms of their author's intentions; it involves placing them within the author's corpus of work; it involves locating them in some tradition and in some special *milieu*. Nature is not a work of art though works of art (in some suitably broad sense) may look very much like natural objects.

None of this is to deny that certain concepts which are frequently deployed in aesthetic evaluation cannot usefully and legitimately be deployed in evaluations of the environment. We admire the intricacy and delicacy of coloring in paintings as we might admire the intricate and delicate shadings in a eucalypt forest. We admire the solid grandeur of a building as we might admire the solidity and grandeur of a massive rock outcrop. And of course the ubiquitous notion of *the beautiful* has a purchase in environmental evaluations as it does in aesthetic evaluations. Even granted all this there are various arguments which might be developed to drive a wedge between the two kinds of evaluation, which would weaken the analogies between faking art and faking nature. One such argument turns on the claim that aesthetic evaluation has, as a central component, a judgmental factor, concerning the author's intentions and the like in the way that was sketched above.[9] The idea is that nature, like works of art, may elicit any of a range of emotional responses in viewers. We may be awed by a mountain, soothed by the sound of water over rocks, excited by the power of a waterfall and so on. However, the judgmental element in aesthetic evaluation serves to differentiate it from environmental evaluation and serves to explain, or so the argument would go, exactly what it is about fakes and forgeries in art which discounts their value with respect to the original. The claim is that if there is no judgmental element in environmental evaluation, then there is no rational basis to

preferring real to faked nature when the latter is a good replica. The argument can, I think, be met.

Meeting the argument does not require arguing that responses to nature count as aesthetic responses. I agree that they are not. Nevertheless there are analogies which go beyond emotional content, and which may persuade us to take more seriously the claim that faked nature is inferior. It is important to make the point that only in fanciful situations dreamt up by philosophers are there no detectable differences between fakes and originals, both in the case of artifacts and in the case of natural objects. By taking a realistic example where there are discernible, and possibly discernible, differences between the fake and the real thing, it is possible to bring out the judgmental element in responses to, and evaluations of, the environment. Right now I may not be able to tell a real Vermeer from a Van Meegaran, though I might learn to do so. By the same token I might not be able to tell apart a naturally evolved stand of mountain ash from one which has been planted, but might later acquire the ability to make the requisite judgment. Perhaps an anecdote is appropriate here. There is a particular stand of mountain ash that I had long admired. The trees were straight and tall, of uniform stature, neither densely packed nor too open-spaced. I then discovered what would have been obvious to a more expert eye, namely that the stand of mountain ash had been planted to replace original forest which had been burnt out. This explained the uniformity in size, the density and so on: it also changed my attitude to that piece of landscape. The evaluation that I make now of that landscape is to a certain extent informed, the response is not merely emotive but cognitive as well. The evaluation is informed and directed by my beliefs about the forest, the type of forest it is, its condition as a member of that kind, its causal genesis and so on. What is more, the judgmental element affects the emotive one. Knowing that the forest is not a naturally evolved forest causes me to feel differently about it: it causes me to perceive the forest differently and to assign it less value than naturally evolved forests.

Val Routley has eloquently reminded us that

people who value wilderness do not do so merely because they like to soak up pretty scenery.[10] They see much more and value much more than this. What they do see, and what they value, is very much a function of the degree to which they understand the ecological mechanisms which maintain the landscape and which determine that it appears the way it does. Similarly, knowledge of art history, of painting techniques, and the like will inform aesthetic evaluations and alter aesthetic perceptions. Knowledge of this kind is capable of transforming a hitherto uninteresting landscape into one that is compelling. Holmes Rolston has discussed at length the way in which an understanding and appreciation of ecology generates new values.[11] He does not claim that ecology reveals values previously unnoticed, but rather that the understanding of the complexity, diversity, and integration of the natural world which ecology affords us, opens up a new area of valuation. As the facts are uncovered, the values are generated. What the remarks of Routley and Rolston highlight is the judgmental factor which is present in environmental appraisal. Understanding and evaluation do go hand in hand; and the responses individuals have to forests, wild rivers, and the like are not merely raw, emotional responses.

IV

Not all forests are alike, not all rain forests are alike. There are countless possible discriminations that the informed observer may make. Comparative judgments between areas of the natural environment are possible with regard to ecological richness, stage of development, stability, peculiar local circumstance, and the like. Judgments of this kind will very often underlie hierarchical orderings of environments in terms of their intrinsic worth. Appeal to judgments of this kind will frequently strengthen the case for preserving some bit of the environment. . . .

One reason that a faked forest is not just as good as a naturally evolved forest is that there is always the possibility that the trained eye will tell the difference.[12] It takes some time to discriminate areas of Alpine plain which are naturally clear of snow gums from those that have been cleared. It takes some time to discriminate regrowth forest which has been logged from forest which has not been touched. These are discriminations which it is possible to make and which are made. Moreover, they are discriminations which affect valuations. The reasons why the "faked" forest counts for less, more often than not, than the real thing are similar to the reasons why faked works of art count for less than the real thing.

Origin is important as an integral part of the evaluation process. It is important because our beliefs about it determine the valuations we make. It is also important in that the discovery that something has an origin quite different to the origin we initially believe that it has, can literally alter the way we perceive that thing.[13] The point concerning the possibility of detecting fakes is important in that it stresses just how much detail must be written into the claim that environmental engineers can replicate nature. Even if environmental engineering could achieve such exactitude, there is, I suggest, no compelling reasons for accepting the restoration thesis. It is worth stressing though that, as a matter of strategy, environmentalists must argue the empirical inadequacy of restoration proposals. This is the strongest argument against restoration ploys, because it appeals to diverse value-frameworks, and because such proposals are promises to deliver a specific good. Showing that the good won't be delivered is thus a useful move to make.

Notes

1. In this case *full* restoration will be literally impossible because the minerals are not going to be replaced.
2. J. G. Mosley, "The Revegetation 'Debate': A Trap For Conservationists," *Australian Conservation Foundation Newsletter*, Vol. 12 (1980), No. 8, p. 1.
3. Peter Dunk, 'How New Engineering Can Work with the Environment,' *Habitat Australia*, Vol. 7 (1979), No. 5, p. 12.

4. See Mosley, op. cit., p. 1.

5. Offering something less is not, of course, always the same as offering nothing. If diversity of animal and plant life, stability of complex ecosystems, tall trees and so on are things that we value in themselves, then certainly we are offered something. I am not denying this, and I doubt that many would qualify their valuations of the above-mentioned items in a way that leaves the restored environment devoid of value. Environmentalists would count as of worth programs designed to render polluted rivers reinhabitable by fish species. The point is rather that they may, as I hope to show, rationally deem it less valuable than what was originally there.

6. See, e.g. Colin Radford, "Fakes," *Mind*, Vol. 87 (1978), No. 345, pp. 66–76, and Nelson Goodman, *Languages of Art*, Bobbs-Merrill, New York 1968, pp. 99–122, though Radford and Goodman have different accounts of why genesis matters.

7. See Ch. 10 of Roderick Nash, *Wilderness and the American Mind*, Yale University Press, New Haven 1973.

8. For example protecting the Great Barrier Reef from damage by the crown-of-thorns starfish.

9. See, e.g., Don Mannison, "A Prolegomenon to a Human Chauvinist Aesthetic," in D. S. Mannison, M. A. McRobbie, R. Routley (Eds.), *Environmental Philosophy*, Research School of Social Sciences, Australian National University, Canberra 1980, pp. 212–16.

10. Val Routley, "Critical Notice of Passmore's *Man's Responsibility for Nature*," *Australasian Journal of Philosophy*, Vol. 53 (1975), No. 2, pp. 171–85.

11. Holmes Rolston III, "Is There An Ecological Ethic," *Ethics*, Vol. 85 (1975), No. 2, pp. 93–109.

12. For a discussion of this point with respect to art forgeries, see Goodman op. cit., esp. pp. 103–12.

13. For an excellent discussion of this same point with respect to artifacts, see Radford, op. cit., esp. pp. 73–76.

Constructing an Environmental Ethic: Which Foundation?

Preview

In his essay, "Animal Liberation: A Triangular Affair," J. Baird Callicott contends that the animal liberation movement makes "no serious challenge to cherished first principles"[1] of traditional ethical theories. John Rodman makes a similar point when he characterizes the positions of Peter Singer and Christopher Stone as examples of "moral extensionism." Singer and Stone, says Rodman, "merely 'extend' (rather than seriously question or radically change) conventional anthropocentric ethics."[2] Both utilitarians and rights theorists have claimed that sentience or consciousness is of fundamental moral importance. However, some classical exponents of these theories on occasion spoke as if "human being" and "sentient being" (or "human being" and "conscious being") are synonymous terms. For example, in the early pages of his essay *On Liberty,* J. S. Mill took it for granted that the happiness referred to in the Principle of Utility is the happiness of human beings.[3] Despite Bentham's famous remark that we must take into account all who can suffer, the extension of moral standing to animals did not receive widespread attention by Western philosophers until Singer's *Animal Liberation* appeared in 1975. Moreover, classical rights theorists are notorious for their ubiquitous references to the "Rights of Man." The new literature in animal liberation and animal rights has revealed an inconsistency in traditional ethical theories: If sentience and consciousness are morally significant capacities, they must be significant wherever they are found and regardless of species.

Radical environmentalists, such as Rodman and Callicott (who take Aldo Leopold's land ethic as a model for an adequate environmental ethic), view moral extensionism as seriously inadequate for at least two reasons. First, traditional ethical theories are atomistic and remain so when extended to include nonhuman sentient beings. Moral atomism is the view that individuals (like self-contained atoms) and only individuals have moral standing. The land ethic, as explained in Part II, is "holistic"; that is, the entire biosphere as an interconnected system is claimed to have moral standing. Second, moral extensionism, Rodman says, gives us "an only slightly modified version of the conventional hierarchy of moral worth."[4] Take Singer as an example. I do nothing wrong, says Singer, if I pull a weed in my garden, for plants have no subjective experiences, no capacity to suffer and enjoy. In Singer's later work, he suggests that persons, that is, beings that are rational and self-conscious in addition to being sentient, are more valuable than beings that are merely sentient.[5] Thus, in Singer's view, a hierarchy emerges: plants, animals, persons. Plants have no moral standing, sentient animals and persons do, but persons are more valuable than sentient animals because of the additional morally significant capacities they have.

Rodman calls Singer's views *sentientist.* Sentientism, according to Rodman, is on a par with speciesism. He says, "On reflection, I find it as odd to think that the plants have value only for the happiness of the dusky-footed woodrats as to think that the dusky-footed woodrats have value only for the happiness of humans."[6]

Anthropocentrism and moral extensionism stand accused of producing a moral hierarchy of being. It is important to note that other views that do not locate moral value in species or sentience have a similar implication. For example, Paul Taylor claims that living organisms, not just sentient beings, have moral standing. This means that plants and trees as well as nonhuman animals have moral standing, but rocks and streams do not. Thus, even "respect-for-life" ethics supports a hierarchy.

Callicott claims, in an important footnote, that *moral humanism* (his term for anthropocentric ethics), *human moralism* (his term for moral extensionism), *reverence-for-life ethics* (like Schweitzer's and presumably Taylor's), and *panmoralism* (the view that "everything should be accorded moral standing")[7] "openly or implicitly espouse a pecking order model of nature."[8] The land ethic alone "abandons the 'higher/lower' ontological and axiological scheme."[9] The land ethic, Callicott claims, "is inclined to establish value distinctions not on the basis of higher and lower orders of being, but on the basis of the importance of organisms, minerals, and so on to the biotic community. Some bacteria, for example, may be of greater value to the health or economy of nature than dogs, and thus command more respect."[10]

Of all the major ethical theories in the Western tradition, natural law theory most obviously espouses a moral hierarchy of being. Contemporary philosophers such as Callicott and Rodman suggest that more modern but nonetheless traditional theories such as natural rights theory and utilitarianism have inherited this defect from the natural law and Judeo-Christian tradition. However, if the land ethic escapes this problem, it has instead, according to Tom Regan, a structural problem of equal magnitude that it shares with the theory of utilitarianism. Even as utilitarianism allows the sacrifice of individual interests for the greater good of certain social goals, the land ethic allows the sacrifice of individual interests for the greater good of the biotic whole. As Callicott's claim reveals, "In every case the effect upon ecological systems is the decisive factor in the determination of the ethical quality of actions."[11] Regan calls this view *environmental fascism*: "Like political fascism, where 'the good of the State' supercedes 'the good of the individual,' what holism gives us is a fascist understanding of the environment."[12] Regan also raises the question of the implications of holism for individual human beings: "Rare species of wild grasses doubtless contribute more to the diversity of the biosphere than do the citizens of Cleveland. But are we therefore morally obliged to 'save the wild grasses' at the expense of the life and welfare of these people?"[13] Callicott, however, is not unaware of the implications of his position.
He says, for example,

The extent of misanthropy in modern environmentalism . . . may be taken as a measure of the degree to which it is biocentric. Edward Abbey in his enormously popular *Desert Solitaire* bluntly states that he would sooner shoot a man than a snake. Abbey . . . is perhaps . . . dramatically making the point that the human population has become so disproportionate from the biological point of view that if one had to choose between a specimen of *Homo sapiens* and a specimen of a rare if unattractive species, the choice would be moot.[14]

Of course, we can adopt population policies for the future that rectify the problem of a disproportionate number of humans on earth, but the really interesting question is: What should we do about this problem *now*? What does the land ethic require us to do? What are the implications of other antisentientist views, such as Taylor's, which claim that all living things possess the same inherent worth? Peter Miller suggests that Taylor's views sanction rather nasty dealings with people. For example, he says, "I am not sure what keeps [Taylor] from advocating human genocide as the moral policy that, on balance, best respects nature."[15] Edward Johnson, however, comes to Taylor's defense. He states, "Though some thinkers *have* advocated human genocide, what keeps Taylor from agreeing with them is presumably his commitment to the attitude of respect for persons."[16] However, Johnson questions whether his attempt to rescue Taylor will work: Can Taylor's view be coherent if it entails two ultimate principles: respect for nature and respect for persons? If we abandon one of these principles, Johnson says, "it is not hard to guess which one would go."[17]

The fundamental goals of the animal liberation movement and the land ethic are in conflict. The land ethic is concerned with preserving species and ecosystems; animal liberation seeks to prevent the suffering of individual sentient animals. Mark Sagoff captures the point in the title of his recent piece, "Animal Liberation and Environmental Ethics: Bad Marriage, Quick Divorce." He says,

An environmentalist cannot be an animal liberationist; nor may animal liberationists be environmentalists. The environmentalist would sacrifice the welfare of individual creatures to preserve the authenticity, integrity, and complexity of ecological systems. The liberationist must be willing to sacrifice the authenticity, integrity, and complexity of ecosystems for the welfare of animals.[18]

The practice of certain types of hunting, for example, is perfectly consistent with and may even be necessary to the preservation of ecosystems. Callicott says, "Animal liberation, if pursued at the practical . . . level, would have ruinous consequences on plants, soils, and waters."[19] Animal liberationists typically advocate vegetarianism. Callicott says, "A vegetarian human population is . . . probably ecologically catastrophic."[20]

This conflict in fundamental goals does *not* imply that environmentalists or advocates of the land ethic approve of factory farming or animal experimentation. Callicott, for example, objects to these practices, but thinks that since the pain that results from these practices "is less than that endured by animals in the wild, the moral objection to these institutions cannot be simply that animals suffer."[21] It is at this point that Callicott develops his thesis that the real objection to these practices is that animals are turned into machines. However, if we take seriously the animal liberationist's position that factory farming and animal experimentation are wrong because animals suffer, must we not seek to alleviate animal suffering in the wild? Mark Sagoff puts the point this way:

The liberationist must ask: how can I most efficiently relieve animal suffering? The answer must be: by getting animals out of their natural environment. Starving deer in the woods might be adopted as pets; they might be fed in kennels. Birds that now kill earthworms may repair instead to birdhouses stocked with food including textured soybean protein that looks and smells like worms. And to protect the brutes from cold, we might heat their dens or provide shelter for the all too many who freeze.[22]

Sagoff concludes: "An environmentalist must take what I have said as a *reductio*."[23] This is exactly what Callicott does. Sagoff continues: "An animal liberationist must regard [what I have said] as stating a serious position."[24] Can an animal liberationist avoid adopting a position that environmentalists take to be a *reductio*? The rights view can give an answer provided we distinguish between negative and positive rights and take the position that virtually all rights are negative.[25] Negative rights, some-

times called *liberty rights,* are rights to noninterference. The core notion of liberty here is that others should leave us alone; we should be free to direct our lives as we see fit without unjustified interference. Negative rights require only that others refrain from interference. In contrast, positive rights are rights to be provided with benefits, for example, food, shelter, a university education, or a satisfying job. If animals have certain negative rights (for example, *not* to be killed prematurely or *not* to be caused to suffer), factory farming and animal experimentation violate those rights. However, according to this view we do not violate a deer's rights by our failure to provide heated dens unless deer have positive rights as well (for example, a sort of welfare right to certain amenities).

Sagoff's main target is Singer's position and not the rights view.[26] It may be that the utilitarian ethic has the implication Sagoff says it has: "We are obliged to prevent and to relieve animal suffering wherever it occurs and however it is caused."[27]

Part III begins with a piece by a British philosopher, Mary Midgley. In it, Midgley criticizes yet another traditional approach to morality known as *contractarianism.* Such an approach ignores for the most part "those who fail to clock in as normal rational agents,"[28] that is, those who cannot make contracts. Midgley graphically makes her point when she lists nineteen cases which, according to such views, fall outside the realm of moral concern. It gives one pause just to look at the length of the list about which Midgley says, "No doubt I have missed a few. . . ."[29]

All the traditional theories we have looked at—including contractarianism—presuppose an atomistic notion of human psychology. Midgley calls this notion false, and says, if true, "every member of the human race would need a separate island, and heaven knows what our ecological problems would be then."[30] However, if she is right, and if the answer lies in some kind of nonhierarchical holism, we must deal with serious trade-off problems and meet the charge of environmental fascism. The selections in Part III will help us see clearly just what the challenges are so that we can begin to articulate the best, indeed, the correct, solutions.

Notes

1. J. Baird Callicott. "Animal Liberation: A Triangular Affair," *Environmental Ethics* 2, (Winter 1980), p. 319.

2. John Rodman. "Four Forms of Ecological Consciousness Reconsidered," *Ethics and the Environment,* edited by Donald Scherer and Thomas Attig (Englewood Cliffs, N.J.: Prentice-Hall, 1983), p. 87.

3. Actually, Mill did not say "human beings," but what he did say can be construed to mean "human beings." "I regard utility as the ultimate appeal on all ethical questions, but it must be utility in the largest sense, grounded on the permanent interests of man as a progressive being." J. S. Mill. *On Liberty,* edited by Elizabeth Rapaport (Indianapolis: Hackett Publishing Company, 1978), p. 10.

4. John Rodman. "Four Forms of Ecological Consciousness Reconsidered," p. 87.

5. See Peter Singer. *Practical Ethics* (Cambridge: Cambridge University Press, 1979).

6. John Rodman. "The Liberation of Nature?" *Inquiry* 20 (Spring 1977), p. 84.

7. J. Baird Callicott. "Animal Liberation: A Triangular Affair," p. 319. Panmoralism, unlike the land ethic, is atomistic. Thus, a panmoralist must be asserting that "everything," as *individual things,* should be accorded moral standing. It is not obvious, however, why panmoralism presupposes a moral hierarchy of being.

8. J. Baird Callicott. "Animal Liberation: A Triangular Affair," p. 319.

9. J. Baird Callicott. "Animal Liberation: A Triangular Affair," p. 319.

10. J. Baird Callicott. "Animal Liberation: A Triangular Affair," p. 319.

11. J. Baird Callicott. "Animal Liberation: A Triangular Affair," p. 320.

12. Tom Regan. *The Case for Animal Rights,* (Berkeley: University of California Press, 1983), p. 372.

13. Tom Regan. *The Case for Animal Rights,* p. 372.

14. J. Baird Callicott. "Animal Liberation: A Triangular Affair," p. 326. Callicott responds to the charge of environmental fascism and defends a more moderate position in "The Search for an Environmental Ethic," *Matters of Life and Death,* edited by Tom Regan, 2d ed. (New York: Random House, 1986).

15. Peter Miller. "Value as Richness: Toward a Value Theory for the Expanded Naturalism in Environmental Ethics," *Environmental Ethics* 4 (1982), p. 113.

16. Edward Johnson. "Treating the Dirt," in *Earthbound,* p. 349. As an example of someone who has advocated human genocide, Johnson cites John Aspinal. "Man's Place in Nature" in *Animal Rights—A Symposium,* edited by David Paterson and Richard Ryder (London: Centaur Press, 1979), p. 20.

17. Edward Johnson. "Treating the Dirt" in *Earthbound,* p. 349.

18. Mark Sagoff. "Animal Liberation and Environmental Ethics: Bad Marriage, Quick Divorce," *QQ: Report from the Center for Philosophy and Public Policy* 4 (Spring 1984), p. 8.

19. J. Baird Callicott. "Animal Liberation: A Triangular Affair," p. 337.

20. J. Baird Callicott. "Animal Liberation: A Triangular Affair," p. 335.

21. J. Baird Callicott. "Animal Liberation: A Triangular Affair," p. 71.

22. Mark Sagoff. "Animal Liberation and Environmental Ethics: Bad Marriage, Quick Divorce," p. 8.

23. Mark Sagoff. "Animal Liberation and Environmental Ethics: Bad Marriage, Quick Divorce," p. 8.

24. Mark Sagoff. "Animal Liberation and Environmental Ethics: Bad Marriage, Quick Divorce," p. 8.

25. Robert Nozick, a contemporary philosopher, takes this view about natural rights.

26. Sagoff takes Henry Shue's notion of basic rights as a model of rights. These include the right to physical security and the right to minimum subsistence. No reason is given for adopting Shue's view of rights rather than, for example, Nozick's or Regan's or Tooley's.

27. Mark Sagoff. "Animal Liberation and Environmental Ethics: Bad Marriage, Quick Divorce," p. 8.

28. Mary Midgley. "Duties Concerning Islands," *Encounter* LX (Feb. 1983), p. 40.

29. Mary Midgley. "Duties Concerning Islands," p. 40.

30. Mary Midgley. "Duties Concerning Islands," p. 43.

Duties Concerning Islands

Mary Midgley

Had Robinson Crusoe any duties on his island?

When I was a philosophy student, this used to be a familiar conundrum, which was supposed to pose a very simple question: namely, can you have duties to yourself? Mill, they correctly told us, said no.

The term duty to oneself, when it means anything more than prudence, means self-respect or self-development and for none of these is anyone accountable to his fellow-creatures.[1]

Kant, on the other hand, said yes.

Duties to ourselves are of primary importance and should have pride of place . . . nothing can be expected of a man who dishonours his own person.[2]

There is a serious disagreement here, not to be sneezed away just by saying—"it depends on what you mean by duty." Much bigger issues are involved. But quite how big has, I think, not yet been fully realized. To grasp this, I suggest that we rewrite a part of Crusoe's story, so as to bring in sight a different range of concerns, thus:

"*Sept. 19, 1685.* This day I set aside to devastate my island. My pinnace being now ready on the shore, and all things prepared for my departure, Friday's people also expecting me, and the wind blowing fresh away from my little harbour, I had in mind to see how all would burn. So then, setting sparks and powder craftily among certain dry spinneys which I had chosen, I soon had it ablaze, nor was there left, by the next dawn, any green stick among the ruins. . . ."

Now, work on the style how you will, you cannot make that into a convincing paragraph. Crusoe was not the most scrupulous of men, but he would have felt an invincible objection to

Source: *Encounter* LX (Feb. 1983), pp. 36–43. Reprinted by permission.

this senseless destruction. So would the rest of us. Yet the language of our moral tradition has tended strongly, ever since the Enlightenment, to make that objection unstateable. All the terms which express that a claim is serious or binding—duty, right, law, morality, obligation, justice—have been deliberately narrowed in their use so as to apply only within the framework of contract, to describe only relations holding between free and rational agents. Since it has been decided *a priori* that rationality has no degrees and that cetaceans are not rational, it follows that, unless you take either religion or science fiction seriously, we can only have duties to humans, and sane, adult, fully responsible humans at that.

Now the morality we live by certainly does not accept this restriction. In common life we recognize many other duties as serious and binding, though of course not necessarily overriding. If philosophers want to call these something else instead of "duties," they must justify their move. We have here one of these clashes between the language of common morality (which is of course always to some extent confused and inarticulate) and an intellectual scheme which arose in the first place from a part of that morality, but has now taken off on its own and claims authority to correct other parts of its source.

There are always real difficulties here. As ordinary citizens we have to guard against dismissing such intellectual schemes too casually; we have to do justice to the point of them. But as philosophers, we have to resist the opposite temptation of taking the intellectual scheme as decisive, just because it is elegant and satisfying, or because the moral insight which is its starting-point is specially familiar to us. Today, this intellectualist bias is often expressed by calling the insights of common morality mere "intuitions." This is quite misleading, since it gives the impression that they have been reached without thought, and that there is, by contrast, a scientific solution somewhere else to which they ought to bow as there might be if we were contrasting commonsense "intuitions" about the physical world with physics or astronomy. Even when they do not use that word, however, philosophers often manage to give the impression that whenever our moral views clash with any simple, convenient scheme, it is our *duty* to abandon them. Thus G. R. Grice:

It is an inescapable consequence of the thesis presented in these pages that certain classes cannot have natural rights: animals, the human embryo, future generations, lunatics and children under the age of, say, ten. In the case of young children at least, my experience is that this consequence is found hard to accept. But it is a consequence of the theory; it is, I believe, true; and I think we should be willing to accept it. At first sight it seems a harsh conclusion, but it is not nearly so harsh as it appears. . . . (*Grounds of Moral Judgment,* 1967, pp. 146–47)

But it is in fact extremely harsh, since what he is saying is that the treatment of children ought not to be determined by their interests, but by the interests of the surrounding adults capable of contract, which of course can easily conflict with them.

In our own society, he explains, this does not actually make much difference, because parents here are so benevolent that they positively want to benefit their children: and accordingly here "the interests of children are reflected in the interests of their parents." But this, he adds, is just a contingent fact about us. "It is easy to imagine a society where this is not so," where, that is, parents are entirely exploitative. "In this circumstance, the morally correct treatment of children would no doubt be harsher than it is in our society. But the conclusion has to be accepted." Grice demands that we withdraw our objections to harshness, in deference to theoretical consistency. But "harsh" here does not mean just "brisk and bracing" like cold baths and a plain diet. (There might well be more of those where parents do feel bound to consider their children's interests.) It means unjust.

Our objection to unbridled parental selfishness is not a mere matter of tone or taste; it

is a moral one. It therefore requires a moral answer, an explanation of the contrary value which the contrary theory expresses. Grice and those who argue like him take the ascetic, disapproving tone of people who have already displayed such a value, and who are met by a slovenly reluctance to rise to it. But they have not displayed that value. The ascetic tone cannot be justified merely by an appeal to consistency. An ethical theory which, when consistently followed through, has iniquitous consequences is a bad theory and must be changed. Certainly we can ask whether these consequences really are iniquitous; but this question must be handled seriously. We cannot directly conclude that the consequences cease to stink the moment they are seen to follow from our theory.

The theoretical model which has spread blight in this area is, of course, that of social contract, to fit which the whole cluster of essential moral terms which I mentioned—right, duty, justice, and the rest—has been progressively narrowed. This model shows human society as a spread of standard social atoms, originally distinct and independent, each of which combines with others only at its own choice and in its own private interest. This model is drawn from physics, and from 17th-century physics at that, where the ultimate particles of matter were conceived as hard, impenetrable, homogeneous little billiard-balls, with no hooks or internal structure. To see how such atoms could combine at all was very hard. Physics, accordingly, moved on from this notion to one which treats atoms and other particles as complex items, describable mainly in terms of forces, and those the same kind of forces which operate outside them. It has abandoned the notion of ultimate, solitary, independent individuals.

Social contract theory, however, retains it. On this physical—or archaeophysical—model, all significant moral relations between individuals are the symmetrical ones expressed by contract. If, on the other hand, we use a biological or "organic" model, we can talk also of a variety of asymmetrical relations found within a whole. Leaves relate not only to other leaves, but to fruit, twigs, branches, and the whole tree. People appear not only as individuals, but as members of their groups, families, tribes, species, ecosystems and biosphere, and have moral relations, as parts, to these various wholes.

The choice between these two ways of thinking is not, of course, a simple once-for-all affair. Different models are useful for different purposes. We can, however, reasonably point out, first, that the old physical pattern makes all attempts to explain combination extremely difficult. Second, that since human beings actually are living creatures, not crystals or galaxies, it is reasonable to expect that biological ways of thinking will be useful in understanding them.

In its own sphere, the social contract model has of course been of enormous value. Where we deal with clashes of interest between free and rational agents already in existence, and particularly where we want to disentangle a few of them from some larger group which really does not suit them, it is indispensable. And for certain political purposes during the last three centuries these clashes have been vitally important. An obsession with contractual thinking and a conviction that it is a cure-all are therefore understandable. But the trouble with such obsessions is that they distort the whole shape of thought and language in a way which makes them self-perpetuating, and constantly extends their empire. Terms come to be defined in a way which leaves only certain moral views expressible. This can happen without any clear intention on the part of those propagating them, and even contrary to their occasional declarations, simply from mental inertia.

Thus, John Rawls, having devoted most of his long book to his very subtle and exhaustive contractual view of justice, remarks without any special emphasis near the end that,

We should recall here the limits of a theory of justice. Not only are many aspects of morality left aside, but no account can be given of right conduct in regard to animals and the rest of nature. (*A Theory of Justice*, p. 512)

He concedes that these are serious matters.

Certainly it is wrong to be cruel to animals and the destruction of a whole species can be a great evil. The capacity for feelings of pleasure and pain and for the forms of life of which animals are capable clearly impose duties of compassion and humanity in their case.

All this is important, he says, and it calls for a wider metaphysical enquiry, but it is not his subject. Earlier in the same passage he touches on the question of permanently irrational human beings, and remarks that it "may present a difficulty. I cannot examine this problem here, but I assume that the account of equality would not be materially affected."

Won't it though? It is a strange project to examine a single virtue—justice—without at least sketching in one's view of the vast background of general morality which determines its shape and meaning, including, of course, such awkward and non-contractual virtues as "compassion and humanity." It isolates the duties which people owe each other *merely as thinkers* from those deeper and more general ones which they owe each other as beings who feel. It cannot, therefore, fail both to split man's nature and to isolate him from the rest of the creation to which he belongs. Such an account may not be *Hamlet* without the prince, but it is *Hamlet* with half the cast missing, and without the state of Denmark. More exactly, it is like a history of Poland which regards Russia, Germany, Europe, and the Roman Church as not part of its subject.

I am not attacking John Rawls' account on its own ground. I am simply pointing out what the history of ethics shows all too clearly how much our thinking is shaped by what our sages *omit* to mention. The Greek philosophers never really raised the problem of slavery till towards the end of their epoch, and then few of them did so with conviction. This happened even though it lay right in the path of their enquiries into political justice and the value of the individual soul. Christianity did raise that problem, because its social background was different, and because the world was in the Christian era already in turmoil, so that men were not presented with the narcotic of happy stability. But Christianity itself did not, until quite recently, raise the problem of the morality of punishment, and particularly of eternal punishment.

This failure to raise central questions was not in either case complete. One can find very intelligent and penetrating criticisms of slavery occurring from time to time in Greek writings—even in Aristotle's defence of that institution.[3] But they are mostly like Rawls's remark here. They conclude "this should be investigated some day." The same thing happens with Christian writings concerning punishment, except that the consideration "this is a great mystery" acts as an even more powerful paralytic to thought. Not much more powerful, however. Natural inertia, when it coincides with vested interest or the illusion of vested interest, is as strong as gravitation.

It is important that Rawls does not (like Grice) demand that we toe a line which would make certain important moral views impossible. Like Hume, who similarly excluded animals from justice, he simply leaves them out of his discussion. This move ought in principle to be harmless. But when it is combined with an intense concentration of discussion on contractual justice, and a corresponding neglect of compassion and humanity, it inevitably suggests that the excluded problems are relatively unimportant.

This suggestion is still more strongly conveyed by rulings which exclude the non-human world from rights, duties, and morality. Words like *rights* and *duties* are awkward because they do indeed have narrow senses approximating to the legal, but they also have much wider ones in which they cover the whole moral sphere. To say "They do not have rights" or "You do not have duties to them" conveys to any ordinary hearer a very simple message, namely, "They do not matter. . . ." This is an absolution, a removal of blame for ill-treatment of "them," whoever they may be.

To see how strong this informal, moral usage of "rights" is, we need only look at the history of that powerful notion, "the Rights of Man." These rights were not supposed to be ones conferred by law, since the whole point of appealing to them was to change laws so as to embody them. They were vague, but vast. They did not arise, as rights are often said to do, only within a community, since they were taken to apply in principle everywhere. The immense,

and on the whole coherent, use which has been made of this idea by reforming movements shows plainly that the tension between the formal and the informal idea of *right* is part of the word's meaning, a fruitful connection of thought, not just a mistake. It is therefore hard to adopt effectively the compromise which some philosophers now favor, of saying that it is indeed wrong to treat animals in certain ways, but that we have no duties to them or that they have no rights.[4] "Animal rights" may be hard to formulate, as indeed are the rights of man. But "no rights" will not do.[5] The word may need to be dropped entirely.

The compromise is still harder with the word *duty,* which is rather more informal, and is more closely wedded to a private rather than political use. Where the realm of right and duty stops, there, to ordinary thinking, begins the realm of the optional. What is not a duty may be a matter of taste, style or feeling, of aesthetic sensibility, of habit and nostalgia, of etiquette and local custom; but it cannot be something which demands our attention whether we like it or not. When claims get into this area, they can scarcely be taken seriously.

This becomes clear when Kant tries to straddle the border. He says that we have no direct duties to animals, because they are not rational, but that we should treat them properly all the same because of "indirect duties" which are really duties to our own humanity.[6] This means that ill-treating them might lead us to ill-treat humans, and is also a sign of a bad or inhumane disposition. The whole issue thus becomes a contingent one of spiritual style or training, like contemplative exercises, intellectual practice, or indeed refined manners.[7] Some might need practice of this kind to make them kind to people; others might not and indeed might get on better without it. (Working off one's ill-temper on animals might make one treat people *better.*) But the question of cruelty to animals cannot be like this, because it is of the essence of such training exercises that they are internal. Anything that affects some other being is not just practice, it is real action. Anyone who refrained from cruelty *merely* from a wish not to sully his own character, without any direct consideration for the possible victims, would be frivolous and narcissistic.

A similar trivialization follows where theorists admit duties of compassion and humanity to noncontractors, but deny duties of justice. Hume and Rawls, in making this move, do not explicitly subordinate these other duties, or say that they are less binding. But because they make the contract element so central to morality, this effect seems to follow. The priority of justice is expressed in such everyday proverbs as "Be just before you're generous." We are therefore rather easily persuaded to think that compassion, humanity, and so forth are perhaps emotional luxuries, to be indulged only after all debts are paid.

A moment's thought will show that this is wrong. Someone who receives simultaneously a request to pay a debt and another to comfort somebody bereaved or on their death-bed is not, as a matter of course, under obligation to pay the debt first. He has to look at circumstances on both sides; but in general we should probably expect the other duties to have priority. This is still more true if, on his way to pay the debt, he encounters a stranger in real straits, drowning or lying injured in the road. To give the debt priority, we probably need to think of his creditor as also being in serious trouble—which brings compassion and humanity in on both sides of the case.

What makes it so hard to give justice a different clientele from the other virtues—as Hume and Rawls do—is simply the fact that justice is such a pervading virtue. In general, all serious cases of cruelty, meanness, inhumanity, and the like are also cases of injustice. If we are told that a certain set of these cases does not involve injustice, our natural thought is that these cases must be *trivial*. Officially, Hume's and Rawls's restriction is not supposed to mean this. What, however, is it supposed to mean? It is forty years since I first read David Hume's text, and I find his thought as obscure now as I did then. I well remember double-taking then, and going back over the paragraph for a point which I took it I must have missed. Can anyone see it?

Were there [Hume says] a species of creature intermingled with men, which, though rational, were possessed of such inferior strength, both of body and mind, that they were incapable of all resistance, and could never, upon the highest provocation, make us feel the effects of their resentment; the necessary consequence, I think, is that we should be bound by the laws of humanity to give gentle usage to these creatures, but should not, properly speaking, lie under any restraint of justice with regard to them, nor could they possess any right or property, exclusive of such arbitrary lords. Our intercourse with them could not be called society, which supposes a degree of equality, but absolute command on one side and servile obedience on the other. This is plainly the situation of men with regard to animals. (*Enquiry Concerning the Principles of Morals*, para 152)

I still think that the word justice, so defined, has lost its normal meaning. In ordinary life we think that duties of justice become *more* pressing, not less so, when we are dealing with the weak and inarticulate, who cannot argue back. It is the boundaries of prudence which depend on power, not those of justice.

Historically, Hume's position becomes more understandable when one sees its place in the development of social-contract thinking. The doubtful credit for confining justice to the human species seems to belong to Grotius, who finally managed to ditch the Roman notion of *ius naturale*, natural right or law common to all species. I cannot here discuss his remarkably unimpressive arguments for this.[8] The point I want to make here is simply the effect of these restrictive definitions of terms like justice on people's view of the sheer size of the problems raised by what falls outside them.

Writers who treat morality as primarily contractual tend to discuss non-contractual cases briefly, casually, and parenthetically, as though they were rather rare. (Rawls's comments on the problem of mental defectives are entirely typical here.) We have succeeded, they say, in laying most of the carpet; why are you making this fuss about those little wrinkles behind the sofa?

This treatment confirms a view, already suggested by certain aspects of contemporary politics in the United States, that those who fail to clock in as normal rational agents and make their contracts are just occasional exceptions, constituting one more "minority" group—worrying no doubt to the scrupulous, but not a central concern of any society. Let us, then, glance briefly at their scope, by roughly listing some cases which seem to involve us in non-contractual duties. (The order is purely provisional and the numbers are added just for convenience.)

Human Sector

1. The dead
2. Posterity
3. Children
4. The senile
5. The temporarily insane
6. The permanently insane
7. Defectives, ranging down to "human vegetables"
8. Human embryos

Animal Sector

9. Sentient animals
10. Non-sentient animals

Inanimate Sector

11. Plants of all kinds
12. Artifacts, including works of art
13. Inanimate but structured objects—crystals, rivers, rocks, etc.

Comprehensive

14. Unchosen human groups of all kinds, including families, villages, cities and the species
15. Unchosen multi-species groups, such as ecosystems, forests, and countries
16. The biosphere

Miscellaneous

17. Arts and sciences
18. Oneself
19. God

No doubt I have missed a few, but that will do to go on with.

The point is this. If we look only at a few of these groupings, and without giving them full attention, it is easy to think that we can include one or two as honorary contracting members, by a slight stretch of our conceptual scheme, and find arguments for excluding the others from serious concern entirely. But if we keep our eye on the size of the range, this stops being plausible.

As far as sheer numbers go, this is no minority of the beings with whom we have to deal. We are a small minority of them. As far as importance goes, it is certainly possible to argue that some of these sorts of being should concern us more and others less; we need a priority system. But to build it, *moral* arguments are required. The various kinds of claims have to be understood and compared, not written off in advance. We cannot rule that those who, in our own, and other cultures, suppose that there is a direct objection to injuring or destroying some of them, are always just confused, and mean only, in fact, that this item will be needed for rational human consumption.

The blank antithesis which Kant made between rational persons (having value) and mere things (having none) cannot serve us to map out this vast continuum. And the idea that, starting at some given point on this list, we have a general licence for destruction, is itself a moral view which would have to be justified.

Our culture differs from most others in the breadth of destructive licence which it does allow itself, and from the 17th century onwards, that licence has been greatly extended. Scruples about rapine have been continually dismissed as irrational, but it is not always clear what the rational principles are supposed to be with which they conflict. Western destructiveness has not in fact developed in response to a new set of disinterested intellectual principles, demonstrating the need for more people and less redwoods, but mainly as a by-product of greed and increasing commercial confidence.

Humanistic hostility to superstition has certainly played some part in the process, because respect for the non-human items on our list is often taken to be religious. But it does not have to be. Many scientists who are card-carrying atheists can still see the point of preserving the biosphere. So can the rest of us, religious or otherwise. It is the whole of which we are parts, and its other parts concern us for that reason.

But the language of rights is rather ill-suited for expressing this, because it has been developed mainly for the protection of people who, though oppressed, are in principle articulate. This makes it quite reasonable for theorists to say that rights belong only to those who understand them and can claim them. When confronted with the Human Sector of our list, these theorists can either dig themselves in like Grice and exclude the lot, or stretch the scheme like Rawls, by including the hypothetical rational choices which these honorary members *would* make if they were not unfortunately prevented.

Since many of these people seem less rational than many animals, zoophiles like Peter Singer have then a good case for calling this second device arbitrary and specious, and extending rights to the border of sentience.[9] Here, however, the meaning of the term does become thin, and when we reach the inanimate area, usage will scarcely cover it.[10] There may be a point in campaigning to extend usage. But to me it seems wiser on the whole not to waste energy on this verbal point, but instead to insist on the immense variety of kinds of being with which we have to deal. Once we grasp this, we ought not to be surprised that we are involved in many different kinds of claim or duty. The dictum that "rights and duties are correlative" is quite misleading, because the two words keep different company, and one may be narrowed without affecting the other.

What, then, about duties? I believe that this term can properly be used over the whole range. We have quite simply got many kinds of duties, including those to animals, to plants, and to the biosphere. But to speak in this way we must free the term once and for all from its restrictive contractual use, or irrelevant doubts will still haunt us. If we cannot do this, we shall have to exclude the word *duty,* along with *right* (as a noun) from all detailed discussion, using wider words like *wrong, right* (adjectival), and *ought* instead. This gymnastic would be possible but inconvenient.

The issue about duty becomes clear as soon as we look at the controversy from which I started, between Kant's and Mill's views on duties to oneself. What do we think about this? Are there duties of integrity, autonomy, self-knowledge, self-respect? It seems that there are.

Mill was right, of course, to point out that they are not duties *to* someone in the ordinary sense. The divided self is a metaphor. It is as natural and necessary a metaphor here as it is over, say, self-deception or self-control; but it certainly is not literal truth. The form of the requirement is different. Rights, for instance, certainly do not seem to come in here as they often would with duties to other persons; we shall scarcely say, "I have a right to my own respect." And the *kind* of things which we can owe ourselves are distinctive. It is not just chance who they are owed to. You cannot owe it to somebody else, as you can to yourself, to force him to act freely or with integrity. He owes that to himself; the rest of us can only remove outside difficulties.

As Kant justly said, our business is to promote our own perfection and the happiness of others; the perfection of others is an aim which belongs to them.[11] *Respect* indeed we owe both to ourselves and to others, but Kant may well be right to say that *self-respect* is really a different and deeper requirement, something without which all outward duties would become meaningless. (This may explain the paralyzing effect of depression.)

Duties to oneself, in fact, are duties with a different *form.* They are far less close than outward duties to the literal model of debt, especially money debt. Money is a thing which can be owed in principle to anybody; it is the same whoever you owe it to; and if by chance you come to owe it to yourself, the debt vanishes. Not many of our duties are really of this impersonal kind; the attempt to commute other sorts of duty into money is a notorious form of evasion. Utilitarianism, however, wants to make all duties as homogeneous as possible, and that is the point of Mill's position. He views all our self-concerning motives as parts of the desire for happiness. Therefore he places all duty, indeed, all morality, in the outside world, as socially required restriction of that desire—

an expression, that is, of other people's desire for happiness.

We do not call anything wrong, unless we mean that a person ought to be punished in some way or another for doing it; if not by law, by the opinion of his fellow-creatures; if not by opinion, by the reproaches of his own conscience. This seems the real turning-point of the distinction between morality and simple expediency. It is a part of the notion of Duty in every one of its forms, that a person may rightly be compelled to fulfill it. Duty is a thing which may be *exacted* from a person, as one exacts a debt.[12]

But to make the notion of wrongness depend on punishment and public opinion in this way instead of the other way round is wild.

Mill never minded falling flat on his face from time to time in trying out a new notion for the public good. He did it for us here—and we should, I think, take proper advantage of his generosity, and accept the impossibility which he demonstrates. The concepts cannot be connected up this way round. Unless you think of certain facts as wrong, it makes no sense to talk of punishment. "Punishing" alcoholics with aversion therapy, or experimental rats with electric shocks, is not really punishing at all; it is just deterrence. This "punishment" will not make their previous actions wrong, nor has it anything to do with morality. The real point of morality returns into Mill's scheme in the Trojan horse of "the reproaches of his own conscience." Why do *they* matter? Unless the conscience is talking sense—that is, on Utilitarian principles, unless it is delivering the judgment of society—it should surely be silenced? Mill, himself a man of enormous integrity and deeply concerned about autonomy, would never have agreed to silence it. But unless we do so, we shall have to complicate his scheme.

It may well be true that, in the last resort and at the deepest level, conscience and the desire for happiness converge. We do want to be honest. But in ordinary life and at the everyday level they can diverge amazingly. We do not want to be put out. What we know we ought to do is often most unwelcome to us, which is why we call it *duty*. And whole sections of that duty do not concern other people directly at all.

A good example is the situation in *Brave New World* where a few dissident citizens have grasped the possibility of a fuller and freer life. Nobody else wants this. Happiness is already assured. If there is a duty of change here, it must be first of all that of each to himself. True, they may feel bound also to help others to change, but hardly in a way which those others would *exact*. In fact, we may do better here by dropping the awkward second party altogether and saying that they all have a duty *of* living differently—one which will affect both themselves and others, but which does not require, as a debt does, a named person or people *to* whom it must be paid. Wider models like "the whole duty of man" may be more relevant.

This one example from my list will, I hope, be enough to explain the point. I cannot go through all of them, nor ought it to be necessary. Duties need not be quasi-contractual relations holding between symmetrical pairs of rational human agents. There are all kind of other obligations holding between asymmetrical pairs, or involving, as in this case, no outside beings at all.

To speak of duties *to* things in the inanimate and comprehensive sectors of my list is not necessarily to personify them superstitiously, or to indulge in chatter about "the secret life of plants."[13] It expresses merely that there are suitable and unsuitable ways of behaving in given situations. People have duties *as* farmers, parents, consumers, forest-dwellers, colonists, species-members, ship-wrecked mariners, tourists, potential ancestors and actual descendants, etc. As such, it is the business of each not to forget his transitory and dependent position, the rich gifts which he has received, and the tiny part he plays in a vast, irreplaceable and fragile whole.

It is remarkable that we nowadays have to state this obvious truth as if it were new, and invent words like "ecological" to describe a whole vast class of duties. Most peoples are used to the idea. In stating it, and getting it back into the center of our moral stage, we meet various difficulties, of which the most insidious is possibly the temptation to feed this issue as fuel to long-standing controversies about religion. Is concern for the nonhuman aspects of our biosphere necessarily superstitious and therefore to be resisted tooth-and-nail?

I have pointed out that it need not be religious at all. Certified rejectors of all known religions can share it. No doubt there is a wider sense in which any deep and impersonal concern can be called religious—one in which Marxism also is a religion. No doubt too all such deep concerns have their dangers, but certainly the complete absence of them has worse ones. Moreover, anyone wishing above all to avoid the religious dimension should consider that the intense individualism which has focused our attention exclusively on the social-contract model is itself thoroughly mystical. It has glorified the individual human soul as an object having infinite and transcendent value, has hailed it as the only real creator, and has bestowed on it much of the panoply of God.

Nietzsche, who was responsible for much of this new theology,[14] took over from the old Thomistic theology which he plundered the assumption that all the rest of creation mattered only as a frame for man. This is not an impression which any disinterested observer would get from looking round at it, nor do we need it in order to take our destiny sufficiently seriously.

Robinson Crusoe then, I conclude, did have duties concerning his island, and with the caution just given we can reasonably call them duties *to* it.

They were not very exacting, and were mostly negative. They differed, of course, from those which a long-standing inhabitant of a country has. Here the language of *fatherland* and *motherland*, which is so widely employed, indicates rightly a duty of care and responsibility which can go very deep, and which long-settled people commonly do feel strongly. To insist that it is really only a duty to the exploiting human beings is not consistent with the emphasis often given to reverence for the actual trees, mountains, lakes, rivers, and the like which are found there. A decision to inhibit all this rich area of human love is a special maneuver for which reasons would need to be given, not a dispassionate analysis of existing duties and feelings.

What happens, however, when you are shipwrecked on an entirely strange island? As the history of colonization shows, there is a tendency for people so placed to drop any reverence and become more exploitative. But it is not irresistible. Raiders who settle down can quite soon begin to feel at home, as the Vikings did in East Anglia, and can after a while become as possessive, proud, and protective towards their new land as old inhabitants. Crusoe from time to time shows this pride rather touchingly, and it would, I think, certainly have inhibited any moderate temptation such as that which I mentioned to have a good bonfire. What keeps him sane through his stay, however, is in fact his duty to God. If that had been absent, I should rather suppose that sanity would depend on a stronger and more positive attachment to the island itself and its creatures.

It is interesting, however, that Crusoe's story played its part in developing that same unrealistic, icy individualism which has gone so far towards making both sorts of attachment seem corrupt or impossible. Rousseau delighted in Defoe's *Robinson Crusoe*, and praised it as the only book fit to be given to a child, *not* because it showed a man in his true relation to animal and vegetable life, but because it was the bible of individualism.

The surest way to raise him [the child] above prejudice and to base his judgments on the true relations of things, is to put him in the place of a solitary man, and to judge all things as they would be judged by such a man in relation to their own utility. . . . So long as only bodily needs are recognised, man is self-sufficing . . . the child knows no other happiness but food and freedom! (*Emile*, Everyman ed, pp. 147–8)

That false atomic notion of human psychology—a prejudice above which nobody ever raised Rousseau—is the flaw in all social-contract thinking. If he were right, every member of the human race would need a separate island, and heaven knows what our ecological problems would be then.

Perhaps, after all, we had better count our blessings.

Notes

1. J. S. Mill, *Essay on Liberty,* Ch. IV (Everyman ed.), p. 135.

2. Immanuel Kant, "Duties to Oneself," in *Lectures on Ethics* (tr. Infield, 1930), p. 118.

3. Aristotle, *Politics* I, 3–8, cf. *Nicomachean Ethics* VII, 11.

4. E.g. John Passmore, *Man's Responsibility for Nature* (1974). pp. 116–117; H. J. McCloskey, "Rights," *Philosophical Quarterly* (No. 15), 1965.

5. Nor will it help for philosophers to say "it is not the case that they have rights." Such pompous locutions have either no meaning at all, or the obvious one.

6. Kant, "Duties towards Animals and Spirits," *Lectures on Ethics,* p. 240.

7. A point well discussed by Stephen Clark, *The Moral Status of Animals* (1977), pp. 12–13.

8. For details see John Rodman, "Animal Justice; The Counter-Revolution in Natural Right and Law," *Inquiry* (Vol. 22, nos. 1–2), Summer 1979.

9. A case first made by Jeremy Bentham, *Introduction to the Principles of Morals and Legislation,* Ch. 17, and ably worked out by Peter Singer in *Animal Liberation* (1976), Chs. 1, 5 and 6.

10. It is worth noticing that long before this, when dealing merely with "the Rights of Man," the term often seems obscure, because to list and specify these rights is so much harder than to shout for them. The phrase is probably more useful as a slogan, indicating a general direction, than as a detailed conceptual tool.

11. Kant, "Preface to the Metaphysical Elements of Ethics," *Introduction to Ethics,* Chs. 4 and 5.

12. J. S. Mill, *Utilitarianism* (Everyman ed.), Ch. 5, p. 45.

13. The book so titled, by Peter Tompkins and Christopher Bird (1973), claimed to show, by various experiments involving electrical apparatus, that plants can feel. Attempts to duplicate their experiments have, however, totally failed to produce any similar results. See A. W. Galson and C. L. Slayman, "The Not So Secret Life of Plants," *American Scientist* (No. 67 p. 337). It seems possible that the original results were due to a fault in the electrical apparatus.

The attempt shows, I think, one of the confusions which continually arise from insisting that all duties must be of the same form. We do not need to prove that plants are animals in order to have reason to spare them. This point is discussed by Marian Dawkins in her book *Animal Suffering* (Chapman and Hall, 1981), pp. 117–119.

14. See particularly *Thus Spake Zarathustra,* part 3, "Of Old and New Tables," and *The Joyful Wisdom* (otherwise called *The Gay Science*), p. 125 (the Madman's Speech). I have discussed this rather mysterious appointment of man to succeed God in a paper called "Creation and Originality," published in a volume of my essays called *Heart & Mind: The Varieties of Moral Experience* (Harvester Press, 1981).

Ecological Sensibility

John Rodman

. . . The term "sensibility" is chosen to suggest a complex pattern of perceptions, attitudes, and judgments which, if fully developed, would constitute a disposition to appropriate conduct that would make talk of rights and duties un-

Source: *Ethics and the Environment,* edited by Donald Scherer and Thomas Attig (Englewood Cliffs, N.J.: Prentice-Hall, 1983), pp. 88–92. Reprinted by permission.

necessary under normal conditions. At this stage of development, however, we can analytically distinguish three major components of an Ecological Sensibility: a theory of value that recognizes *intrinsic value in nature* without (hopefully) engaging in mere extensionism; . . . a metaphysics that takes account of the reality and importance of relationships and systems as well as of individuals; and an ethics that includes such duties as noninterference with natural processes, resistance to human acts and policies that violate the noninterference principle, limited intervention to repair environmental damage in extreme circumstances, and a style of coinhabitation that involves the knowledgeable, respectful, and restrained use of nature. Since there is not space to discuss all these components here, and since I have sketched some of them elsewhere,[1] I shall focus here on two basic dimensions of the theory of value, drawing primarily upon the writings of Leopold,[2] the Routleys,[3] and Rodman.

The first dimension is simple but sweeping in its implications. It is based upon the obligation principle that one ought not to treat with disrespect or use as a mere means anything that has a *telos* or end of its own—anything that is autonomous in the basic sense of having a capacity for internal self-direction and self-regulation. This principle is widely accepted but has been mistakenly thought (e.g., by Kant and others) to apply only to persons. Unless one engages in a high redefinition of terms, however, it more properly applies to (at least) all living natural entities and natural systems. (I leave aside in this essay the difficult and important issue of physical systems.) The vision of a world composed of many things and many kinds of things, all having their own *telē*, goes back (except for the recognition of ecosystems) to Aristotle's metaphysics and philosophy of nature and does therefore not involve us in the kinds of problems that arise from extending the categories of modern Liberal ethics to a natural world made up of the dead "objects" of modern thought. (To mention Aristotle is not, of course, to embrace all of his opinions, especially the very anthropocentric *obiter dicta*—e.g., that plants exist for the sake of animals, animals for humans, etc.—that can be found in his *Ethics* and *Politics*.) This notion of natural entities and natural systems as having intrinsic value in the specific and basic form, of having *telē* of their own, having their own characteristic patterns of behavior, their own stages of development, their own business (so to speak), is the basic ground in which is rooted the attitude of respect, the obligation of noninterference, etc. In it is rooted also the indictment of the Resource Conservation standpoint as being, at bottom, an ideology of human chauvinism and human imperialism.

It may be objected that our paradigmatic notion of a being having a *telos* is an individual human being or a person, so that viewing nature in terms of *telē* involves merely another extension of an all-too-human quality to (part of) nature, retaining the conventional atomistic metaphysics and reinstating the conventional moral pecking order. I do not think that this is the case. It seems to me an observable fact that thistles, oak trees, and wombats, as well as rainforests and chaparral communities, have their own characteristic structures and potentialities to unfold, and that it is as easy to see this in them as it is in humans, if we will but look.

For those unaccustomed to looking, Aldo Leopold's *Sand County Almanac* provides, in effect, a guidebook. Before the reader is introduced to the "land ethic" chapter (which is too often read out of the context of the book as a whole), (s)he is invited to accompany Leopold as he follows the tracks of the skunk in the January snow, wondering where the skunk is heading and why; speculating on the different meanings of a winter thaw for the mouse whose snow burrow has collapsed and for the owl who has just made dinner of the mouse; trying to understand the honking of the geese as they circle the pond; and wondering what the world must look like to a muskrat eye-deep in the swamp. By the time one reaches Leopold's discussion of the land ethic, one has grown accustomed to thinking of different animals—and (arguably), by extension, different natural entities in general—as subjects rather than objects, as beings that have their own purposes, their own perspectives on the world, and their own goods that are differentially affected by events. While we can never get inside a muskrat's head and know exactly what the world looks like from that angle, we can be pretty certain that the view is different from ours. What melts away as we become intrigued with this plurality of perspectives is the assumption that any one of them (for example, ours) is privileged. So we are receptive when the "land ethic" chapter suggests that other natural beings deserve respect and should be treated as if they had a "right" in the most basic sense of being entitled to continue existing in a natural state. To want from Leopold a full-scale theory of the rights of nature, however, would be to miss the point, since the idea of rights has only a limited application. Moreover, Leopold does not present logical arguments for the land ethic in general, because such arguments could not persuade anyone who still looked at nature as if it were comprised of objects or mere resources, and such arguments are unnecessary for those who have come to perceive nature as composed of subjects. When perception is sufficiently changed, respectful types of conduct seem "natural," and one does not have to belabor them in the language of rights and duties. Here, finally, we reach the point of "paradigm change."[4] What brings it about is not exhortation, threat, or logic, but a rebirth of the sense of wonder that in ancient times gave rise to philosophers but is now more often found among field naturalists.

In further response to the objection that viewing nature in terms of *telē* is simply another version of anthropocentric Moral Extensionism, consider that a forest may be in some ways more nearly paradigmatic than an individual human for illustrating what it means to have a *telos*. A tropical rainforest may take 500 years to develop to maturity and may then maintain a dynamic, steady-state indefinitely (for millions of years, judging from fossils) if not seriously interfered with. It exhibits a power of self-regulation that may have been shared to some extent by millennia of hunter-gatherer societies but is not an outstanding characteristic of modern humans, taken either as individuals or as societies. While there may therefore be some differences in the degree to which certain aspects of what it means to have a *telos* are present in one organism or one system compared with another, the basic principle is that all items having a *telos* are entitled to respectful treatment. Comparisons are more fruitfully made in terms of the second dimension of the theory of value.

The second dimension incorporates a cluster of value-giving characteristics that apply both to natural entities and (even more) to natural systems: diversity, complexity, integrity, harmony, stability, scarcity, etc. While the *telos*

principle serves primarily to provide a common basic reason for respectful treatment of natural entities and natural systems (ruling out certain types of exploitative acts on deontological grounds), and to provide a criterion for drawing morally relevant distinctions between natural trees and plastic trees, natural forests and timber plantations, etc., this cluster of value-giving qualities provides criteria for evaluating alternative courses of permissible action in terms of optimizing the production of good effects, the better action being the one that optimizes the qualities taken as an interdependent, mutually constraining cluster. Aldo Leopold seems to have had something like this model in mind when he stated the land ethic in these terms:

A thing is right when it tends to preserve the integrity, stability, and beauty of the biotic community. It is wrong when it tends otherwise.

(We may wish to modify Leopold's statement, omitting reference to beauty and adding additional criteria, especially diversity [which stands as a principle in its own right, not merely as a means to stability]; moreover, an action can be right or wrong in reference to individuals as well as communities—but Leopold was redressing an imbalance, calling our attention to the supra-individual level, and can be forgiven for overstating his case.) More controversially, the cluster of ecological values can also be used to appraise the relative value of different ecosystems when priorities must be set (given limits on time, energy, and political influence) by environmentalists working to protect nature against the bulldozer and the chain saw. The criteria of diversity, complexity, etc., will sometimes suggest different priorities than would result from following the esthetic of the sublime or a criterion such as sentience, while a fully pantheistic philosophy of preservation provides no criteria at all for discriminating cases.

What can be said in justification of this cluster of ecological values? It is possible for human beings to hold such values. Those who do not, and those who are not sure whether they do or not, may wish to imagine alternative worlds, asking whether they prefer the diverse world to the monocultural world, and so forth. But it would be naive to assume that such thought experiments are conducted without any significant context. For example, I am aware that my preference for diverse, complex, and stable systems occurs in a time that I perceive as marked by an unprecedentedly high rate of species extinction and ecosystem simplification. In this situation, diversity has scarcity value in addition to its intrinsic value, in addition to its instrumental value as conducive to stability. This illustrates a general characteristic of the cluster of ecological values: the balance is not static but fluctuates in response to changes in the environment, so that different principles are more or less prominent at different times.

Since the cluster of value-giving principles applies generally throughout the world to living natural entities and systems, it applies to human beings and human societies as well as to the realm of nonhuman nature. To the extent that diversity on an individual human level is threatened by the pressures of conformity in mass society, and diversity of social ways of life is threatened by the pressures of global resource exploitation and an ideology of worldwide "development" in whose name indigenous peoples are being exterminated along with native forests, it would be short-sighted to think of "ecological issues" as unrelated to "social issues." From an ecological point of view, one of the most striking socio-political phenomena of the twentieth century—the rise of totalitarian dictatorships that forcibly try to eliminate the natural condition of human

diversity in the name of some monocultural ideal (e.g., an Aryan Europe or a classless society)—is not so much a freakish aberration from modern history as it is an intensification of the general spirit of the age. Ecological Sensibility, then is "holistic" in a sense beyond that usually thought of: it grasps the underlying principles that manifest themselves in what are ordinarily perceived as separate "social" and "environmental" issues.[5]

Notes

1. "Ecological Resistance: John Stuart Mill and the Case of the Kentish Orchid," paper presented at the annual meeting of the American Political Science Association, 1977.
2. Aldo Leopold, *A Sand County Almanac* (New York: Oxford University Press, 1949).
3. Richard and Val Routley, "Human Chauvinism and Environmental Ethics," in *Environmental Philosophy*, eds. Don Mannison, Michael McRobbie, and Richard Routley (Department of Philosophy, Research School of Social Sciences, The Australian National University, 1980); Val and Richard Routley, "Social Theories, Self Management, and Environmental Problems," in ibid.
4. Obviously, I believe that those who see Leopold's land ethic as a mere extension of conventional ethics are radically mistaken.
5. See also Rodman, "Paradigm Change in Political Science," *American Behavioral Scientist* 21, 1 (September–October 1980): 67–69.

The Ethics of Respect for Nature

Paul W. Taylor

I. Human-centered and Life-centered Systems of Environmental Ethics

In this paper I show how the taking of a certain ultimate moral attitude toward nature, which I call "respect for nature," has a central place in the foundations of a life-centered system of environmental ethics. I hold that a set of moral norms (both standards of character and rules of conduct) governing human treatment of the natural world is a rationally grounded set if and only if, first, commitment to those norms is a practical entailment of adopting the attitude of respect for nature as an ultimate moral attitude, and second, the adopting of that attitude on the part of all rational agents can itself be justified. When the basic characteristics of the attitude of respect for nature are made clear, it will be seen that a life-centered system of environmental ethics need not be holistic or organicist in its conception of the kinds of entities that are deemed the appropriate objects of moral concern and consideration. Nor does such a system require that the concepts of ecological homeostasis, equilibrium, and integrity provide us with normative principles from which could be derived (with the addition of factual knowledge) our obligations with regard to natural ecosystems. The "balance of nature" is not itself a moral norm, however important may be the role it plays in our general outlook on the natural world that underlies the attitude of respect for nature. I argue that finally it is the good (well-being, welfare) of individual organisms, considered as entities having inherent worth, that determines our moral relations with the Earth's wild communities of life.

Source: *Environmental Ethics*, Vol. 3 (Fall 1981), pp. 197–218. Reprinted by permission.

In designating the theory to be set forth as life-centered, I intend to contrast it with all anthropocentric views. According to the latter, human actions affecting the natural environment and its nonhuman inhabitants are right (or wrong) by either of two criteria: they have consequences which are favorable (or unfavorable) to human well-being, or they are consistent (or inconsistent) with the system of norms that protect and implement human rights. From this human-centered standpoint it is to humans and only to humans that all duties are ultimately owed. We may have responsibilities *with regard to* the natural ecosystems and biotic communities of our planet, but these responsibilities are in every case based on the contingent fact that our treatment of those ecosystems and communities of life can further the realization of human values and/or human rights. We have no obligation to promote or protect the good of nonhuman living things, independently of this contingent fact.

A life-centered system of environmental ethics is opposed to human-centered ones precisely on this point. From the perspective of a life-centered theory, we have prima facie moral obligations that are owed to wild plants and animals themselves as members of the Earth's biotic community. We are morally bound (other things being equal) to protect or promote their good for *their* sake. Our duties to respect the integrity of natural ecosystems, to preserve endangered species, and to avoid environmental pollution stem from the fact that these are ways in which we can help make it possible for wild species populations to achieve and maintain a healthy existence in a natural state. Such obligations are due those living things out of recognition of their inherent worth. They are entirely additional to and independent of the obligations we owe to our fellow humans. Although many of the actions that fulfill one set of obligations will also fulfill the other, two different grounds of obligation are involved. Their well-being, as well as human well-being, is something to be realized *as an end in itself*.

If we were to accept a life-centered theory of environmental ethics, a profound reordering of our moral universe would take place. We would begin to look at the whole of the Earth's biosphere in a new light. Our duties with respect to the "world" of nature would be seen as making prima facie claims upon us to be balanced against our duties with respect to the "world" of human civilization. We could no longer simply take the human point of view and consider the effects of our actions exclusively from the perspective of our own good.

II. The Good of a Being and the Concept of Inherent Worth

What would justify acceptance of a life-centered system of ethical principles? In order to answer this it is first necessary to make clear the fundamental moral attitude that underlies and makes intelligible the commitment to live by such a system. It is then necessary to examine the considerations that would justify any rational agent's adopting that moral attitude.

Two concepts are essential to the taking of a moral attitude of the sort in question. A being which does not "have" these concepts, that is, which is unable to grasp their meaning and conditions of applicability, cannot be said to have the attitude as part of its moral outlook. These concepts are, first, that of the good (well-being, welfare) of a living thing, and second, the idea of an entity possessing inherent worth. I examine each concept in turn.

1. Every organism, species population, and community of life has a good of its own which moral agents can intentionally further or damage by their actions. To say that an entity has a good of its own is simply to say that, without reference to any *other* entity, it can be benefited or harmed. One can act in its overall interest or contrary to its overall interest, and environmental conditions can be good for it (advantageous to it) or bad for it (disadvantageous to it).

What is good for an entity is what "does it good" in the sense of enhancing or preserving its life and well-being. What is bad for an entity is something that is detrimental to its life and well-being.[1]

We can think of the good of an individual nonhuman organism as consisting in the full development of its biological powers. Its good is realized to the extent that it is strong and healthy. It possesses whatever capacities it needs for successfully coping with its environment and so preserving its existence throughout the various stages of the normal life cycle of its species. The good of a population or community of such individuals consists in the population or community maintaining itself from generation to generation as a coherent system of genetically and ecologically related organisms whose average good is at an optimum level for the given environment. (Here *average good* means that the degree of realization of the good of *individual organisms* in the population or community is, on average, greater than would be the case under any other ecologically functioning order of interrelations among those species populations in the given ecosystem.)

The idea of a being having a good of its own, as I understand it, does not entail that the being must have interests or take an interest in what affects its life for better or for worse. We can act in a being's interest or contrary to its interest without its being interested in what we are doing to it in the sense of wanting or not wanting us to do it. It may, indeed, be wholly unaware that favorable and unfavorable events are taking place in its life. I take it that trees, for example, have no knowledge or desires or feelings. Yet it is undoubtedly the case that trees can be harmed or benefited by our actions. We can crush their roots by running a bulldozer too close to them. We can see to it that they get adequate nourishment and moisture by fertilizing and watering the soil around them. Thus we can help or hinder them in the realization of their good. It is the good of trees themselves that is thereby affected. We can similarly act so as to further the good of an entire tree population of a certain species (say, all the redwood trees in a California valley) or the good of a whole community of plant life in a given wilderness area, just as we can do harm to such a population or community.

When construed in this way, the concept of a being's good is not coextensive with sentience or the capacity for feeling pain. William Frankena has argued for a general theory of environmental ethics in which the ground of a creature's being worthy of moral consideration is its sentience. I have offered some criticisms of this view elsewhere, but the full refutation of such a position, it seems to me, finally depends on the positive reasons for accepting a life-centered theory of the kind I am defending in this essay.[2]

It should be noted further that I am leaving open the question of whether machines—in particular, those which are not only goal-directed, but also self-regulating—can properly be said to have a good of their own.[3] Since I am concerned only with human treatment of wild organisms, species populations, and communities of life as they occur in our planet's natural ecosystems, it is to those entities alone that the concept "having a good of its own" will here be applied. I am not denying that other living things, whose genetic origin and environmental conditions have been produced, controlled, and manipulated by humans for human ends, do have a good of their own in the same sense as do wild plants and animals. It is not my purpose in this essay, however, to set out or defend the principles that should guide our conduct with regard to their good. It is only insofar as their production and use by humans have good or ill effects upon natural ecosystems and their wild inhabitants that the ethics of respect for nature comes into play.

2. The second concept essential to the moral attitude of respect for nature is the idea of inherent worth. We take that attitude toward wild living things (individuals, species populations, or whole biotic communities) when and only when we regard them as entities possessing inherent worth. Indeed, it is only because they are conceived in this way that moral agents can think of themselves as having validly binding duties, obligations, and responsibilities that are *owed* to them as their *due*. I am not at this juncture arguing why they *should* be so regarded; I consider it at length below. But so regarding them is a presupposition of our taking the attitude of respect toward

them and accordingly understanding ourselves as bearing certain moral relations to them. This can be shown as follows:

What does it mean to regard an entity that has a good of its own as possessing inherent worth? Two general principles are involved: the principle of moral consideration and the principle of intrinsic value.

According to the principle of moral consideration, wild living things are deserving of the concern and consideration of all moral agents simply in virtue of their being members of the Earth's community of life. From the moral point of view their good must be taken into account whenever it is affected for better or worse by the conduct of rational agents. This holds no matter what species the creature belongs to. The good of each is to be accorded some value and so acknowledged as having some weight in the deliberations of all rational agents. Of course, it may be necessary for such agents to act in ways contrary to the good of this or that particular organism or group of organisms in order to further the good of others, including the good of humans. But the principle of moral consideration prescribes that, with respect to each being an entity having its own good, every individual is deserving of consideration.

The principle of intrinsic value states that, regardless of what kind of entity it is in other respects, if it is a member of the Earth's community of life, the realization of its good is something *intrinsically* valuable. This means that its good is prima facie worthy of being preserved or promoted as an end in itself and for the sake of the entity whose good it is. Insofar as we regard any organism, species population, or life community as an entity having inherent worth, we believe that it must never be treated as if it were a mere object or thing whose entire value lies in being instrumental to the good of some other entity. The well-being of each is judged to have value in and of itself.

Combining these two principles, we can now define what it means for a living thing or group of living things to possess inherent worth. To say that it possesses inherent worth is to say that its good is deserving of the concern and consideration of all moral agents, and that the realization of its good has intrinsic value, to be pursued as an end in itself and for the sake of the entity whose good it is.

The duties owed to wild organisms, species populations, and communities of life in the Earth's natural ecosystems are grounded on their inherent worth. When rational, autonomous agents regard such entities as possessing inherent worth, they place intrinsic value on the realization of their good and so hold themselves responsible for performing actions that will have this effect and for refraining from actions having the contrary effect.

III. The Attitude of Respect for Nature

Why should moral agents regard wild living things in the natural world as possessing inherent worth? To answer this question we must first take into account the fact that, when rational, autonomous agents subscribe to the principles of moral consideration and intrinsic value and so conceive of wild living things as having that kind of worth, such agents are *adopting a certain ultimate moral attitude toward the natural world.* This is the attitude I call "respect for nature." It parallels the attitude of respect for persons in human ethics. When we adopt the attitude of respect for persons as the proper (fitting, appropriate) attitude to take toward all persons as persons, we consider the fulfillment of the basic interests of each individual to have intrinsic value. We thereby make a moral commitment to live a certain kind of life in relation to other persons. We place ourselves under the direction of a system of standards and rules that we consider validly binding on all moral agents as such.[4]

Similarly, when we adopt the attitude of respect for nature as an ultimate moral attitude we make a commitment to live by certain normative principles. These principles constitute the rules of conduct and standards of character that are to govern our treatment of the natural world. This is, first, an *ultimate* commitment because it is not derived from any higher norm. The attitude of respect for nature is not grounded on some other, more

general, or more fundamental attitude. It sets the total framework for our responsibilities toward the natural world. It can be justified, as I show below, but its justification cannot consist in referring to a more general attitude or a more basic normative principle.

Second, the commitment is a *moral* one because it is understood to be a disinterested matter of principle. It is this feature that distinguishes the attitude of respect for nature from the set of feelings and dispositions that comprise the love of nature. The latter stems from one's personal interest in and response to the natural world. Like the affectionate feelings we have toward certain individual human beings, one's love of nature is nothing more than the particular way one feels about the natural environment and its wild inhabitants. And just as our love for an individual person differs from our respect for all persons as such (whether we happen to love them or not), so love of nature differs from respect for nature. Respect for nature is an attitude we believe all moral agents ought to have simply as moral agents, regardless of whether or not they also love nature. Indeed, we have not truly taken the attitude of respect for nature ourselves unless we believe this. To put it in a Kantian way, to adopt the attitude of respect for nature is to take a stance that one wills it to be a universal law for all rational beings. It is to hold that stance categorically, as being validly applicable to every moral agent without exception, irrespective of whatever personal feelings toward nature such an agent might have or might lack.

Although the attitude of respect for nature is in this sense a disinterested and universalizable attitude, anyone who does adopt it has certain steady, more or less permanent dispositions. These dispositions, which are themselves to be considered disinterested and universalizable, comprise three interlocking sets: dispositions to seek certain ends, dispositions to carry on one's practical reasoning and deliberation in a certain way, and dispositions to have certain feelings. We may accordingly analyze the attitude of respect for nature into the following components. (a) The disposition to aim at, and to take steps to bring about, as final and disinterested ends, the promoting and protecting of the good of organisms, species populations, and life communities in natural ecosystems. (These ends are "final" in not being pursued as means to further ends. They are "disinterested" in being independent of the self-interest of the agent.) (b) The disposition to consider actions that tend to realize those ends to be prima facie obligatory *because* they have that tendency. (c) The disposition to experience positive and negative feelings toward states of affairs in the world *because* they are favorable or unfavorable to the good of organisms, species populations, and life communities in natural ecosystems.

The logical connection between the attitude of respect for nature and the duties of a life-centered system of environmental ethics can now be made clear. Insofar as one sincerely takes that attitude and so has the three sets of dispositions, one will at the same time be disposed to comply with certain rules of duty (such as nonmaleficence and noninterference) and with standards of character (such as fairness and benevolence) that determine the obligations and virtues of moral agents with regard to the Earth's wild living things. We can say that the actions one performs and the character traits one develops in fulfilling these moral requirements are the way one *expresses* or *embodies* the attitude in one's conduct and character. In his famous essay, "Justice as Fairness," John Rawls describes the rules of the duties of human morality (such as fidelity, gratitude, honesty, and justice) as "forms of conduct in which recognition of others as persons is manifested."[5] I hold that the rules of duty governing our treatment of the natural world and its inhabitants are forms of conduct in which the attitude of respect for nature is manifested.

IV. The Justifiability of the Attitude of Respect for Nature

I return to the question posed earlier, which has not yet been answered: why *should* moral agents regard wild living things as possessing inherent worth? I now argue that the only way we can answer this question is by showing how adopting the attitude of respect for nature is justified for all moral agents. Let us suppose that we were able to establish that there are good reasons for adopting the attitude, reasons which are intersubjectively valid for every rational agent. If there are such reasons, they would justify anyone's having the three sets of dispositions mentioned above as constituting what it means to have the attitude. Since these include the disposition to promote or protect the good of wild living things as a disinterested and ultimate end, as well as the disposition to perform actions for the reason that they tend to realize that end, we see that such dispositions commit a person to the principles of moral consideration and intrinsic value. To be disposed to further, as an end in itself, the good of any entity in nature just because it is that kind of entity, is to be disposed to give consideration to *every* such entity and to place intrinsic value on the realization of its good. Insofar as we subscribe to these two principles we regard living things as possessing inherent worth. Subscribing to the principle is what it *means* to so regard them. To justify the attitude of respect for nature, then, is to justify commitment to these principles and thereby to justify regarding wild creatures as possessing inherent worth.

We must keep in mind that inherent worth is not some mysterious sort of objective property belonging to living things that can be discovered by empirical observation or scientific investigation. To ascribe inherent worth to an entity is not to describe it by citing some feature discernible by sense perception or inferable by inductive reasoning. Nor is there a logically necessary connection between the concept of a being having a good of its own and the concept of inherent worth. We do not contradict ourselves by asserting that an entity that has a good of its own lacks inherent worth. In order to show that such an entity "has" inherent worth we must give good reasons for ascribing that kind of value to it (placing that kind of value upon it, conceiving of it to be valuable in that way). Although it is humans (persons, valuers) who must do the valuing, for the ethics of respect for nature, the value so ascribed is not a human value. That is to say, it is not a value derived from considerations regarding human well-being or human rights. It is a value that is ascribed to nonhuman animals and plants themselves, independently of their relationship to what humans judge to be conducive to their own good.

Whatever reasons, then, justify our taking the attitude of respect for nature as defined above are also reasons that show why we *should* regard the living things of the natural world as possessing inherent worth. We saw earlier that, since the attitude is an ultimate one, it cannot be derived from a more fundamental attitude nor shown to be a special case of a more general one. On what sort of grounds, then, can it be established?

The attitude we take toward living things in the natural world depends on the way we look at them, on what kind of beings we conceive them to be, and on how we understand the relations we bear to them. Underlying and supporting our attitude is a certain *belief system* that constitutes a particular world view or outlook on nature and the place of human life in it. To give good reasons for adopting the attitude of respect for nature, then, we must first articulate the belief system which underlies and supports that attitude. If it appears that the belief system is internally coherent and well-ordered, and if, as far as we can now tell, it is consistent with all known scientific truths relevant to our knowledge of the object of the attitude (which in this case includes the whole set of the Earth's natural ecosystems and their communities of life), then there remains the task of indicating why scientifically informed and rational thinkers with a developed capacity of reality awareness can find it acceptable as a way of conceiving of the natural world and our place in it. To the extent we can do this we provide at least a reasonable argument for accepting the belief system and the ultimate moral attitude it supports.

I do not hold that such a belief system can be *proven* to be true, either inductively or deductively. As we shall see, not all of its components can be stated in the form of empirically verifiable propositions. Nor is its internal order governed by purely logical relationships. But the system as a whole, I contend, constitutes a coherent, unified, and rationally acceptable "picture" or "map" of a total world. By examining each of its main components and seeing how they fit together, we obtain a scientifically informed and well-ordered conception of nature and the place of humans in it.

This belief system underlying the attitude of respect for nature I call (for want of a better name) "the biocentric outlook on nature." Since it is not wholly analyzable into empirically confirmable assertions, it should not be thought of as simply a compendium of the biological sciences concerning our planet's ecosystems. It might best be described as a philosophical world view, to distinguish it from a scientific theory or explanatory system. However, one of its major tenets is the great lesson we have learned from the science of ecology: the interdependence of all living things in an organically unified order whose balance and stability are necessary conditions for the realization of the good of its constituent biotic communities.

Before turning to an account of the main components of the biocentric outlook, it is convenient here to set forth the overall structure of my theory of environmental ethics as it has now emerged. The ethics of respect for nature is made up of three basic elements: a belief system, an ultimate moral attitude, and a set of rules of duty and standards of character. These elements are connected with each other in the following manner. The belief system provides a certain outlook on nature which supports and makes intelligible an autonomous agent's adopting, as an ultimate moral attitude, the attitude of respect for nature. It supports and makes intelligible the attitude in the sense that, when an autonomous agent understands its moral relations to the natural world in terms of this outlook, it recognizes the attitude of respect to be the only *suitable* or *fitting* attitude to take toward all wild forms of life in the Earth's biosphere. Living things are now viewed as *the appropriate objects of the attitude of respect* and are accordingly regarded as entities possessing inherent worth. One then places intrinsic value on the promotion and protection of their good. As a consequence of this, one makes a moral commitment to abide by a set of rules of duty and to fulfill (as far as one can by one's own efforts) certain standards of good character. Given one's adoption of the attitude of respect, one makes that moral commitment because one considers those rules and standards to be validly binding on all moral agents. They are seen as embodying forms of conduct and character structures in which the attitude of respect for nature is manifested.

This three-part complex which internally orders the ethics of respect for nature is symmetrical with a theory of human ethics grounded on respect for persons. Such a theory includes, first, a conception of oneself and others as persons, that is, as centers of autonomous choice. Second, there is the attitude of respect for persons as persons. When this is adopted as an ultimate moral attitude it involves the disposition to treat every person as having inherent worth or "human dignity." Every human being, just in virtue of her or his humanity, is understood to be worthy of moral consideration, and intrinsic value is placed on the autonomy and well-being of each. This is what Kant meant by conceiving of persons as ends in themselves. Third, there is an ethical system of duties which are acknowledged to be owed by everyone to everyone. These duties are forms of conduct in which public recognition is given to each individual's inherent worth as a person.

This structural framework for a theory of human ethics is meant to leave open the issue of consequentialism (utilitarianism) versus non-consequentialism (deontology). That issue concerns the particular kind of system of rules defining the duties of moral agents toward persons. Similarly, I am leaving open in this paper the question of what particular kind of system of rules defines our duties with respect to the natural world.

V. The Biocentric Outlook on Nature

The biocentric outlook on nature has four main components. (1) Humans are thought of as members of the Earth's community of life, holding that membership on the same terms as apply to all the nonhuman members. (2) The Earth's natural ecosystems as a totality are seen as a complex web of interconnected elements,

with the sound biological functioning of each being dependent on the sound biological functioning of the others. (This is the component referred to above as the great lesson that the science of ecology has taught us.) (3) Each individual organism is conceived of as a teleological center of life, pursuing its own good in its own way. (4) Whether we are concerned with standards of merit or with the concept of inherent worth, the claim that humans by their very nature are superior to other species is a groundless claim and, in the light of elements (1), (2), and (3) above, must be rejected as nothing more than an irrational bias in our own favor.

The conjunction of these four ideas constitutes the biocentric outlook on nature. In the remainder of this paper I give a brief account of the first three components, followed by a more detailed analysis of the fourth. I then conclude by indicating how this outlook provides a way of justifying the attitude of respect for nature.

VI. Humans as Members of the Earth's Community of Life

We share with other species a common relationship to the Earth. In accepting the biocentric outlook we take the fact of our being an animal species to be a fundamental feature of our existence. We consider it an essential aspect of "the human condition." We do not deny the differences between ourselves and other species, but we keep in the forefront of our consciousness the fact that in relation to our planet's natural ecosystems we are but one species population among many. Thus we acknowledge our origin in the very same evolutionary process that gave rise to all other species and we recognize ourselves to be confronted with similar environmental challenges to those that confront them. The laws of genetics, of natural selection, and of adaptation apply equally to all of us as biological creatures. In this light we consider ourselves as one with them, not set apart from them. We, as well as they, must face certain basic conditions of existence that impose requirements on us for our survival and well-being. Each animal and plant is like us in having a good of its own. Although our human good (what is of true value in human life, including the exercise of individual autonomy in choosing our own particular value systems) is not like the good of a nonhuman animal or plant, it can no more be realized than their good can without the biological necessities for survival and physical health.

When we look at ourselves from the evolutionary point of view, we see that not only are we very recent arrivals on Earth, but that our emergence as a new species on the planet was originally an event of no particular importance to the entire scheme of things. The Earth was teeming with life long before we appeared. Putting the point metaphorically, we are relative newcomers, entering a home that has been the residence of others for hundreds of millions of years, a home that must now be shared by all of us together.

The comparative brevity of human life on Earth may be vividly depicted by imagining the geological time scale in spatial terms. Suppose we start with algae, which have been around for at least 600 million years. (The earliest protozoa actually predated this by several *billion* years.) If the time that algae have been here were represented by the length of a football field (300 feet), then the period during which sharks have been swimming in the world's oceans and spiders have been spinning their webs would occupy three quarters of the length of the field; reptiles would show up at about the center of the field; mammals would cover the last third of the field; hominids (mammals of the family *Hominidae*) the last two feet; and the species *Homo sapiens* the last six inches.

Whether this newcomer is able to survive as long as other species remains to be seen. But there is surely something presumptuous about the way humans look down on the "lower" animals, especially those that have become extinct. We consider the dinosaurs, for example, to be biological failures, though they existed on our planet for 65 million years. One writer has made the point with beautiful simplicity:

We sometimes speak of the dinosaurs as failures; there will be time enough for that judgment when we have lasted even for one tenth as long. . . .[6]

The possibility of the extinction of the human species, a possibility which starkly confronts us in the contemporary world, makes us aware of another respect in which we should not consider ourselves privileged beings in relation to other species. This is the fact that the well-being of humans is dependent upon the ecological soundness and health of many plant and animal communities, while their soundness and health does not in the least depend upon human well-being. Indeed, from their standpoint the very existence of humans is quite unnecessary. Every last man, woman, and child could disappear from the face of the Earth without any significant detrimental consequence for the good of wild animals and plants. On the contrary, many of them would be greatly benefited. The destruction of their habitats by human "developments" would cease. The poisoning and polluting of their environment would come to an end. The Earth's land, air, and water would no longer be subject to the degradation they are now undergoing as the result of large-scale technology and uncontrolled population growth. Life communities in natural ecosystems would gradually return to their former healthy state. Tropical forests, for example, would again be able to make their full contribution to a life-sustaining atmosphere for the whole planet. The rivers, lakes, and oceans of the world would (perhaps) eventually become clean again. Spilled oil, plastic trash, and even radioactive waste might finally, after many centuries, cease doing their terrible work. Ecosystems would return to their proper balance, suffering only the disruptions of natural events such as volcanic eruptions and glaciation. From these the community of life could recover, as it has so often done in the past. But the ecological disasters now perpetrated on it by humans—disasters from which it might never recover—these it would no longer have to endure.

If, then, the total, final, absolute extermination of our species (by our own hands?) should take place and if we should not carry all the others with us into oblivion, not only would the Earth's community of life continue to exist, but in all probability its well-being would be enhanced. Our presence, in short, is not needed. If we were to take the standpoint of the community and give voice to its true interest, the ending of our six-inch epoch would most likely be greeted with a hearty "Good riddance!"

VII. The Natural World as an Organic System

To accept the biocentric outlook and regard ourselves and our place in the world from its perspective is to see the whole natural order of the Earth's biosphere as a complex but unified web of interconnected organisms, objects, and events. The ecological relationships between any community of living things and their environment form an organic whole of functionally interdependent parts. Each ecosystem is a small universe itself in which the interactions of its various species populations comprise an intricately woven network of cause-effect relations. Such dynamic but at the same time relatively stable structures as food chains, predator-prey relations, and plant succession in a forest are self-regulating, energy-recycling mechanisms that preserve the equilibrium of the whole.

As far as the well-being of wild animals and plants is concerned, this ecological equilibrium must not be destroyed. The same holds true of the well-being of humans. When one views the realm of nature from the perspective of the biocentric outlook, one never forgets that in the long run the integrity of the entire biosphere of our planet is essential to the realization of the good of its constituent communities of life, both human and nonhuman.

Although the importance of this idea cannot be overemphasized, it is by now so familiar and so widely acknowledged that I shall not further elaborate on it here. However, I do wish to point out that this "holistic" view of the Earth's ecological systems does not itself constitute a moral norm. It is a factual aspect of biological reality, to be understood as a set of causal connections in ordinary empirical terms. Its significance for humans is the same as its significance for nonhumans, namely, in setting basic conditions for the realization of the good of living things. Its ethical implications for our treatment of the natural environment lie en-

tirely in the fact that our *knowledge* of these causal connections is an essential *means* to fulfilling the aims we set for ourselves in adopting the attitude of respect for nature. In addition, its theoretical implications for the ethics of respect for nature lie in the fact that it (along with the other elements of the biocentric outlook) makes the adopting of that attitude a rational and intelligible thing to do.

VIII. Individual Organisms as Teleological Centers of Life

As our knowledge of living things increases, as we come to a deeper understanding of their life cycles, their interactions with other organisms, and the manifold ways in which they adjust to the environment, we become more fully aware of how each of them is carrying out its biological functions according to the laws of its species-specific nature. But besides this, our increasing knowledge and understanding also develop in us a sharpened awareness of the uniqueness of each individual organism. Scientists who have made careful studies of particular plants and animals, whether in the field or in laboratories, have often acquired a knowledge of their subjects as identifiable individuals. Close observation over extended periods of time has led them to an appreciation of the unique "personalities" of their subjects. Sometimes a scientist may come to take a special interest in a particular animal or plant, all the while remaining strictly objective in the gathering and recording of data. Nonscientists may likewise experience this development of interest when, as amateur naturalists, they make accurate observations over sustained periods of close acquaintance with an individual organism. As one becomes more and more familiar with the organism and its behavior, one becomes fully sensitive to the particular way it is living out its life cycle. One may become fascinated by it and even experience some involvement with its good and bad fortunes (that is, with the occurrence of environmental conditions favorable or unfavorable to the realization of its good). The organism comes to mean something to one as a unique, irreplaceable individual. The final culmination of this process is the achievement of a genuine understanding of its point of view and, with that understanding, an ability to "take" that point of view. *Conceiving of it as a center of life, one is able to look at the world from its perspective.*

This development from objective knowledge to the recognition of individuality, and from the recognition of individuality to full awareness of an organism's standpoint, is a process of heightening our consciousness of what it means to be an individual living thing. We grasp the particularity of the organism as a teleological center of life, striving to preserve itself and to realize its own good in its own unique way.

It is to be noted that we need not be falsely anthropomorphizing when we conceive of individual plants and animals in this manner. Understanding them as teleological centers of life does not necessitate "reading into" them human characteristics. We need not, for example, consider them to have consciousness. Some of them may be aware of the world around them and others may not. Nor need we deny that different kinds and levels of awareness are exemplified when consciousness in some form is present. But conscious or not, all are equally teleological centers of life in the sense that each is a unified system of goal-oriented activities directed toward their preservation and well-being.

When considered from an ethical point of view, a teleological center of life is an entity whose "world" can be viewed from the perspective of *its* life. In looking at the world from that perspective we recognize objects and events occurring in its life as being beneficent, maleficent, or indifferent. The first are occurrences which increase its powers to preserve its existence and realize its good. The second decrease or destroy those powers. The third have neither of these effects on the entity. With regard to our human role as moral agents, we can conceive of a teleological center of life as a being whose standpoint we can take in making judgments about what events in the world are good or evil, desirable or undesirable. In making those judgments it is what promotes or protects the being's own good, not what benefits moral agents themselves, that sets the standard

of evaluation. Such judgments can be made about anything that happens to the entity which is favorable or unfavorable in relation to its good. As was pointed out earlier, the entity itself need not have any (conscious) *interest* in what is happening to it for such judgments to be meaningful and true.

It is precisely judgments of this sort that we are disposed to make when we take the attitude of respect for nature. In adopting that attitude those judgments are given weight as reasons for action in our practical deliberation. They become morally relevant facts in the guidance of our conduct.

IX. The Denial of Human Superiority

This fourth component of the biocentric outlook on nature is the single most important idea in establishing the justifiability of the attitude of respect for nature. Its central role is due to the special relationship it bears to the first three components of the outlook. This relationship will be brought out after the concept of human superiority is examined and analyzed.[7]

In what sense are humans alleged to be superior to other animals? We are different from them in having certain capacities that they lack. But why should these capacities be a mark of superiority? From what point of view are they judged to be signs of superiority and what sense of superiority is meant? After all, various nonhuman species have capacities that humans lack. There is the speed of a cheetah, the vision of an eagle, the agility of a monkey. Why should not these be taken as signs of *their* superiority over humans?

One answer that comes immediately to mind is that these capacities are not as *valuable* as the human capacities that are claimed to make us superior. Such uniquely human characteristics as rational thought, aesthetic creativity, autonomy and self-determination, and moral freedom, it might be held, have a higher value than the capacities found in other species. Yet we must ask: valuable to whom, and on what grounds?

The human characteristics mentioned are all valuable to humans. They are essential to the preservation and enrichment of our civilization and culture. Clearly it is from the human standpoint that they are being judged to be desirable and good. It is not difficult here to recognize a begging of the question. Humans are claiming human superiority from a strictly human point of view, that is, from a point of view in which the good of humans is taken as the standard of judgment. All we need to do is to look at the capacities of nonhuman animals (or plants, for that matter) from the standpoint of *their* good to find a contrary judgment of superiority. The speed of the cheetah, for example, is a sign of its superiority to humans when considered from the standpoint of the good of its species. If it were as slow a runner as a human, it would not be able to survive. And so for all the other abilities of nonhumans which further their good but which are lacking in humans. In each case the claim to human superiority would be rejected from a nonhuman standpoint.

When superiority assertions are interpreted in this way, they are based on judgments of *merit*. To judge the merits of a person or an organism one must apply grading or ranking standards to it. (As I show below, this distinguishes judgments of merit from judgments of inherent worth.) Empirical investigation then determines whether it has the "good-making properties" (merits) in virtue of which it fulfills the standards being applied. In the case of humans, merits may be either moral or nonmoral. We can judge one person to be better than (superior to) another from the moral point of view by applying certain standards to their character and conduct. Similarly, we can appeal to nonmoral criteria in judging someone to be an excellent piano player, a fair cook, a poor tennis player, and so on. Different social purposes and roles are implicit in the making of such judgments, providing the frame of reference for the choice of standards by which the nonmoral merits of people are determined. Ultimately such purposes and roles stem from a society's way of life as a whole. Now a society's way of life may be thought of as the cultural form given to the realization of human values. Whether moral or nonmoral standards are being applied, then, all judgments of people's merits finally depend on human values. All are made from an exclusively human standpoint.

The question that naturally arises at this juncture is: why should standards that are based on human values be assumed to be the only valid criteria of merit and hence the only true signs of superiority? This question is especially pressing when humans are being judged superior in merit to nonhumans. It is true that a human being may be a better mathematician than a monkey, but the monkey may be a better tree climber than a human being. If we humans value mathematics more than tree climbing, that is because our conception of civilized life makes the development of mathematical ability more desirable than the ability to climb trees. But is it not unreasonable to judge nonhumans by the values of human civilization, rather than by values connected with what it is for a member of *that* species to live a good life? If all living things have a good of their own, it at least makes sense to judge the merits of nonhumans by standards derived from *their* good. To use only standards based on human values is already to commit oneself to holding that humans are superior to nonhumans, which is the point in question.

A further logical flaw arises in connection with the widely held conviction that humans are *morally* superior beings because they possess, while others lack, the capacities of a moral agent (free will, accountability, deliberation, judgment, practical reason). This view rests on a conceptual confusion. As far as moral standards are concerned, only beings that have the capacities of a moral agent can properly be judged to be *either* moral (morally good) *or* immoral (morally deficient). Moral standards are simply not applicable to beings that lack such capacities. Animals and plants cannot therefore be said to be morally inferior in merit to humans. Since the only beings that can have moral merits *or be deficient in such merits* are moral agents, it is conceptually incoherent to judge humans as superior to nonhumans on the ground that humans have moral capacities while nonhumans don't.

Up to this point I have been interpreting the claim that humans are superior to other living things as a grading or ranking judgment regarding their comparative merits. There is, however, another way of understanding the idea of human superiority. According to this interpretation, humans are superior to nonhumans not as regards their merits but as regards their inherent worth. Thus the claim of human superiority is to be understood as asserting that all humans, simply in virtue of their humanity, have *a greater inherent worth* than other living things.

The inherent worth of an entity does not depend on its merits.[8] To consider something as possessing inherent worth, we have seen, is to place intrinsic value on the realization of its good. This is done regardless of whatever particular merits it might have or might lack, as judged by a set of grading or ranking standards. In human affairs, we are all familiar with the principle that one's worth as a person does not vary with one's merits or lack of merits. The same can hold true of animals and plants. To regard such entities as possessing inherent worth entails disregarding their merits and deficiencies, whether they are being judged from a human standpoint or from the standpoint of their own species.

The idea of one entity having more merit than another, and so being superior to it in merit, makes perfectly good sense. Merit is a grading or ranking concept, and judgments of comparative merit are based on the different degrees to which things satisfy a given standard. But what can it mean to talk about one thing being superior to another in inherent worth? In order to get at what is being asserted in such a claim it is helpful first to look at the social origin of the concept of degrees of inherent worth.

The idea that humans can possess different degrees of inherent worth originated in societies having rigid class structures. Before the rise of modern democracies with their egalitarian outlook, one's membership in a hereditary class determined one's social status. People in the upper classes were looked up to, while those in the lower classes were looked down upon. In such a society one's social superiors and social inferiors were clearly defined and easily recognized.

Two aspects of these class-structured societies are especially relevant to the idea of degrees of inherent worth. First, those born into the upper classes were deemed more worthy of respect than those born into the lower orders. Second, the superior worth of upper class people had nothing to do with their merits nor did the inferior worth of those in the lower classes rest on their lack of merits. One's superiority or inferiority entirely derived from a social position one was born into. The modern concept of a meritocracy simply did not apply. One could not advance into a higher class by any sort of moral or nonmoral achievement. Similarly, an aristocrat held his title and all the privileges that went with it just because he was the eldest son of a titled nobleman. Unlike the bestowing of knighthood in contemporary Great Britain, one did not earn membership in the nobility by meritorious conduct.

We who live in modern democracies no longer believe in such hereditary social distinctions. Indeed, we would wholeheartedly condemn them on moral grounds as being fundamentally unjust. We have come to think of class systems as a paradigm of social injustice, it being a central principle of the democratic way of life that among humans there are no superiors and no inferiors. Thus we have rejected the whole conceptual framework in which people are judged to have different degrees of inherent worth. That idea is incompatible with our notion of human equality based on the doctrine that all humans, simply in virtue of their humanity, have the same inherent worth. (The belief in universal human rights is one form that this egalitarianism takes.)

The vast majority of people in modern democracies, however, do not maintain an egalitarian outlook when it comes to comparing human beings with other living things. Most people consider our own species to be superior to all other species and this superiority is understood to be a matter of inherent worth, not merit. There may exist thoroughly vicious and depraved humans who lack all merit. Yet because they are human they are thought to belong to a higher class of entities than any plant or animal. That one is born into the species *Homo sapiens* entitles one to have lordship over those who are one's inferiors, namely, those born into other species. The parallel with hereditary social classes is very close. Implicit in this view is a hierarchical conception of nature according to which an organism has a position of superiority or inferiority in the Earth's community of life simply on the basis of its genetic background. The "lower" orders of life are looked down upon and it is considered perfectly proper that they serve the interests of those belonging to the highest order, namely humans. The intrinsic value we place on the well-being of our fellow humans reflects our recognition of their rightful position as our equals. No such intrinsic value is to be placed on the good of other animals, unless we choose to do so out of fondness or affection for them. But their well-being imposes no moral requirement on us. In this respect there is an absolute difference in moral status between ourselves and them.

This is the structure of concepts and beliefs that people are committed to insofar as they regard humans to be superior in inherent worth to all other species. I now wish to argue that this structure of concepts and beliefs is completely groundless. If we accept the first three components of the biocentric outlook and from that perspective look at the major philosophical traditions which have supported that structure, we find it to be at bottom nothing more than the expression of an irrational bias in our own favor. The philosophical traditions themselves rest on very questionable assumptions or else simply beg the question. I briefly consider three of the main traditions to substantiate the point. These are classical Greek humanism, Cartesian dualism, and the Judeo-Christian concept of the Great Chain of Being.

The inherent superiority of humans over other species was implicit in the Greek definition of man as a rational animal. Our animal nature was identified with "brute" desires that need the order and restraint of reason to rule them (just as reason is the special virtue of those who rule in the ideal state). Rationality was then seen to be the key to our superiority over animals. It enables us to live on a higher plane and endows us with a nobility and worth that other creatures lack. This familiar way of comparing humans with other species is deeply ingrained in our Western philosophical outlook. The point to consider here is that this view does not actually provide an argument *for* hu-

man superiority but rather makes explicit the framework of thought that is implicitly used by those who think of humans as inherently superior to nonhumans. The Greeks who held that humans, in virtue of their rational capacities, have a kind of worth greater than that of any nonrational being, never looked at rationality as but one capacity of living things among many others. But when we consider rationality from the standpoint of the first three elements of the ecological outlook, we see that its value lies in its importance for *human* life. Other creatures achieve their species-specific good without the need of rationality, although they often make use of capacities that humans lack. So the humanistic outlook of classical Greek thought does not give us a neutral (nonquestion-begging) ground on which to construct a scale of degrees of inherent worth possessed by different species of living things.

The second tradition, centering on the Cartesian dualism of soul and body, also fails to justify the claim to human superiority. That superiority is supposed to derive from the fact that we have souls while animals do not. Animals are mere automata and lack the divine element that makes us spiritual beings. I won't go into the now familiar criticisms of this two-substance view. I only add the point that, even if humans are composed of an immaterial, unextended soul and a material, extended body, this in itself is not a reason to deem them of greater worth than entities that are only bodies. Why is a soul substance a thing that adds value to its possessor? Unless some theological reasoning is offered here (which many, including myself, would find unacceptable on epistemological grounds), no logical connection is evident. An immaterial something which thinks is better than a material something which does not think only if thinking itself has value, either intrinsically or instrumentally. Now it is intrinsically valuable to humans alone, who value it as an end in itself, and it is instrumentally valuable to those who benefit from it, namely humans.

For animals that neither enjoy thinking for its own sake nor need it for living the kind of life for which they are best adapted, it has no value. Even if "thinking" is broadened to include all forms of consciousness, there are still many living things that can do without it and yet live what is for their species a good life. The anthropocentricity underlying the claim to human superiority runs throughout Cartesian dualism.

A third major source of the idea of human superiority is the Judeo-Christian concept of the Great Chain of Being. Humans are superior to animals and plants because their Creator has given them a higher place on the chain. It begins with God at the top, and then moves to the angels, who are lower than God but higher than humans, then to humans, positioned between the angels and the beasts (partaking of the nature of both), and then on down to the lower levels occupied by nonhuman animals, plants, and finally inanimate objects. Humans, being "made in God's image," are inherently superior to animals and plants by virtue of their being closer (in their essential nature) to God.

The metaphysical and epistemological difficulties with this conception of a hierarchy of entities are, in my mind, insuperable. Without entering into this matter here, I only point out that if we are unwilling to accept the metaphysics of traditional Judaism and Christianity, we are again left without good reasons for holding to the claim of inherent human superiority.

The foregoing considerations (and others like them) leave us with but one ground for the assertion that a human being, regardless of merit, is a higher kind of entity than any other living thing. This is the mere fact of the genetic makeup of the species *Homo sapiens*. But this is surely irrational and arbitrary. Why should the arrangement of genes of a certain type be a mark of superior value, especially when this fact about an organism is taken by itself, unrelated to any other aspect of its life? We might just as well refer to any other genetic makeup as a ground of superior value. Clearly we are confronted here with a wholly arbitrary claim that can only be explained as an irrational bias in our own favor.

That the claim is nothing more than a deep-seated prejudice is brought home to us when we look at our relation to other species in the light of the first three elements of the biocentric outlook. Those elements taken conjointly give us a certain overall view of the natural world and of the place of humans in it. When we take

this view we come to understand other living things, their environmental conditions, and their ecological relationships in such a way as to awake in us a deep sense of our kinship with them as fellow members of the Earth's community of life. Humans and nonhumans alike are viewed together as integral parts of one unified whole in which all living things are functionally interrelated. Finally, when our awareness focuses on the individual lives of plants and animals, each is seen to share with us the characteristic of being a teleological center of life striving to realize its own good in its own unique way.

As this entire belief system becomes part of the conceptual framework through which we understand and perceive the world, we come to see ourselves as bearing a certain moral relation to nonhuman forms of life. Our ethical role in nature takes on a new significance. We begin to look at other species as we look at ourselves, seeing them as beings which have a good they are striving to realize just as we have a good we are striving to realize. We accordingly develop the disposition to view the world from the standpoint of their good as well as from the standpoint of our own good. Now if the groundlessness of the claim that humans are inherently superior to other species were brought clearly before our minds, we would not remain intellectually neutral toward that claim but would reject it as being fundamentally at variance with our total world outlook. In the absence of any good reasons for holding it, the assertion of human superiority would then appear simply as the expression of an irrational and self-serving prejudice that favors one particular species over several million others.

Rejecting the notion of human superiority entails its positive counterpart: the doctrine of species impartiality. One who accepts that doctrine regards all living things as possessing inherent worth—the *same* inherent worth, since no one species has been shown to be either "higher" or "lower" than any other. Now we saw earlier that, insofar as one thinks of a living thing as possessing inherent worth, one considers it to be the appropriate object of the attitude of respect and believes that attitude to be the only fitting or suitable one for all moral agents to take toward it.

Here, then, is the key to understanding how the attitude of respect is rooted in the biocentric outlook on nature. The basic connection is made through the denial of human superiority. Once we reject the claim that humans are superior either in merit or in worth to other living things, we are ready to adopt the attitude of respect. The denial of human superiority is itself the result of taking the perspective on nature built into the first three elements of the biocentric outlook.

Now the first three elements of the biocentric outlook, it seems clear, would be found acceptable to any rational and scientifically informed thinker who is fully "open" to the reality of the lives of nonhuman organisms. Without denying our distinctively human characteristics, such a thinker can acknowledge the fundamental respects in which we are members of the Earth's community of life and in which the biological conditions necessary for the realization of our human values are inextricably linked with the whole system of nature. In addition, the conception of individual living things as teleological centers of life simply articulates how a scientifically informed thinker comes to understand them as the result of increasingly careful and detailed observations. Thus, the biocentric outlook recommends itself as an acceptable system of concepts and beliefs to anyone who is clear-minded, unbiased, and factually enlightened, and who has a developed capacity of reality awareness with regard to the lives of individual organisms. This, I submit, is as good a reason for making the moral commitment involved in adopting the attitude of respect for nature as any theory of environmental ethics could possibly have.

X. Moral Rights and the Matter of Competing Claims

I have not asserted anywhere in the foregoing account that animals or plants have moral rights. This omission was deliberate. I do not think that the reference class of the concept, bearer of moral rights, should be extended to include nonhuman living things. My reasons for taking this position, however, go beyond the scope of this paper. I believe I have been able to accomplish many of the same ends which those who ascribe rights to animals or plants wish to accomplish. There is no reason, moreover, why plants and animals, including whole species populations and life communities, cannot be accorded *legal* rights under my theory. To grant them legal protection could be interpreted as giving them legal entitlement to be protected, and this, in fact, would be a means by which a society that subscribed to the ethics of respect for nature could give public recognition to their inherent worth.

There remains the problem of competing claims, even when wild plants and animals are not thought of as bearers of moral rights. If we accept the biocentric outlook and accordingly adopt the attitude of respect for nature as our ultimate moral attitude, how do we resolve conflicts that arise from our respect for persons in the domain of human ethics and our respect for nature in the domain of environmental ethics? This is a question that cannot adequately be dealt with here. My main purpose in this paper has been to try to establish a base point from which we can start working toward a solution to the problem. I have shown why we cannot just begin with an initial presumption in favor of the interests of our own species. It is after all within our power as moral beings to place limits on human population and technology with the deliberate intention of sharing the Earth's bounty with other species. That such sharing is an ideal difficult to realize even in an approximate way does not take away its claim to our deepest moral commitment.

Notes

1. The conceptual links between an entity *having* a good, something being good *for* it, and events doing good *to* it are examined by G. H. Von Wright in *The Varieties of Goodness* (New York: Humanities Press, 1963), chaps. 3 and 5.
2. See W. K. Frankena, "Ethics and the Environment," in K. E. Goodpaster and K. M. Sayre, eds., *Ethics and Problems of the 21st Century* (Notre Dame,

University of Notre Dame Press, 1979), pp. 3–20. I critically examine Frankena's views in "Frankena on Environmental Ethics," *Monist*, forthcoming.

3. In the light of considerations set forth in Daniel Dennett's *Brainstorms: Philosophical Essays on Mind and Psychology* (Montgomery, Vermont: Bradford Books, 1978), it is advisable to leave this question unsettled at this time. When machines are developed that function in the way our brains do, we may well come to deem them proper subjects of moral consideration.

4. I have analyzed the nature of this commitment of human ethics in "On Taking the Moral Point of View," *Midwest Studies in Philosophy*, vol. 3, *Studies in Ethical Theory* (1978), pp. 35–61.

5. John Rawls, "Justice As Fairness," *Philosophical Review* 67 (1958): 183.

6. Stephen R. L. Clark, *The Moral Status of Animals* (Oxford: Clarendon Press, 1977), p. 112.

7. My criticisms of the dogma of human superiority gain independent support from a carefully reasoned essay by R. and V. Routley showing the many logical weaknesses in arguments for human-centered theories of environmental ethics. R. and V. Routley, "Against the Inevitability of Human Chauvinism," in K. E. Goodpaster and K. M. Sayre, eds., *Ethics and Problems of the 21st Century* (Notre Dame: University of Notre Dame Press, 1979), pp. 36–59.

8. For this way of distinguishing between merit and inherent worth, I am indebted to Gregory Vlastos, "Justice and Equality," in R. Brandt, ed., *Social Justice* (Englewood Cliffs, N.J.: Prentice-Hall, 1962), pp. 31–72.

Animal Liberation: A Triangular Affair*

J. Baird Callicott

Environmental Ethics and Animal Liberation

Partly because it is so new to Western philosophy (or at least heretofore only scarcely represented) *environmental ethics* has no precisely fixed conventional definition in glossaries of philosophical terminology. Aldo Leopold, however, is universally recognized as the father or founding genius of recent environmental ethics. His "land ethic" has become a modern classic and may be treated as the standard example, the paradigm case, as it were, of what an environmental ethic is. *Environmental ethics* then can be defined ostensively by using Leopold's land ethic as the exemplary type. I do not mean to suggest that all environmental ethics should necessarily conform to Leopold's paradigm, but the extent to which an ethical system resembles Leopold's land ethic might be used, for want of anything better, as a criterion to measure the extent to which it is or is not of the environmental sort.

It is Leopold's opinion, and certainly an overall review of the prevailing traditions of Western ethics, both popular and philosophical, generally confirms it, that traditional Western systems of ethics have not accorded moral standing to nonhuman beings.[1] Animals and plants, soils and waters, which Leopold includes in his community of ethical beneficiaries, have traditionally enjoyed no moral standing, no rights, no respect, in sharp contrast to human persons whose rights and interests ideally must be fairly and equally considered if our actions are to be considered "ethical" or "moral." One fundamental and novel feature

*The author expresses his appreciation to Richard A. Watson for helpful comments on the final version of this paper.

Source: *Environmental Ethics* Vol. 2, No. 4 (Winter 1980), pp. 311–38. Reprinted by permission.

of the Leopold land ethic, therefore, is the extension of *direct* ethical considerability from people to nonhuman natural entities.

At first glance, the recent ethical movement usually labeled "animal liberation" or "animal rights" seems to be squarely and centrally a kind of environmental ethics.[2] The more uncompromising among the animal liberationists have demanded equal moral consideration on behalf of cows, pigs, chickens, and other apparently enslaved and oppressed nonhuman animals.[3] The theoreticians of this new hyper-egalitarianism have coined such terms as *speciesism* (on analogy with *racism* and *sexism*) and *human chauvinism* (on analogy with *male chauvinism*), and have made animal liberation seem, perhaps not improperly, the next and most daring development of political liberalism.[4] Aldo Leopold also draws upon metaphors of political liberalism when he tells us that his land ethic "changes the role of *Homo sapiens* from conqueror of the land community to plain member and citizen of it."[5] For animal liberationists it is as if the ideological battles for equal rights and equal consideration for women and for racial minorities have been all but won, and the next and greatest challenge is to purchase equality, first theoretically and then practically, for all (actually only *some*) animals, regardless of species. This more rhetorically implied than fully articulated historical progression of moral rights from fewer to greater numbers of "persons" (allowing that animals may also be persons) as advocated by animal liberationists, also parallels Leopold's scenario in "The Land Ethic" of the historical extension of "ethical criteria" to more and more "fields of conduct" and to larger and larger groups of people during the past three thousand or so years.[6] As Leopold develops it, the land ethic is a cultural "evolutionary possibility," the next "step in a sequence."[7] For Leopold, however, the next step is much more sweeping, much more inclusive than the animal liberationists envision, since it "enlarges the boundaries of the [moral] community to include soils, waters, [and] plants . . ." as well as animals.[8] Thus, the animal liberation movement *could* be construed as partitioning Leopold's perhaps undigestable and totally inclusive environmental ethic into a series of

more assimilable stages: today animal rights, tomorrow equal rights for plants, and after that full moral standing for rocks, soil, and other earthy compounds, and perhaps sometime in the still more remote future, liberty and equality for water and other elementary bodies.

Put just this way, however, there is something jarring about such a graduated progression in the exfoliation of a more inclusive environmental ethic, something that seems absurd. A more or less reasonable case might be made for rights for some animals, but when we come to plants, soils, and waters, the frontier between plausibility and absurdity appears to have been crossed. Yet, there is no doubt that Leopold sincerely proposes that *land* (in his inclusive sense) be ethically regarded. The beech and chestnut, for example, have in his view as much "biotic right" to life as the wolf and the deer, and the effects of human actions on mountains and streams for Leopold is an ethical concern as genuine and serious as the comfort and longevity of brood hens.[9] In fact, Leopold to all appearances never considered the treatment of brood hens on a factory farm or steers in a feed lot to be a pressing moral issue. He seems much more concerned about the integrity of the farm *wood lot* and the effects of clear-cutting steep slopes on neighboring *streams*.

Animal liberationists put their ethic into practice (and display their devotion to it) by becoming vegetarians, and the moral complexities of vegetarianism have been thoroughly debated in the recent literature as an adjunct issue to animal rights.[10] (No one however has yet expressed, as among Butler's Erewhonians, qualms about eating plants, though such sentiments might be expected to be latently present, if the rights of plants are next to be defended.) Aldo Leopold, by contrast did not even condemn hunting animals, let alone eating them, nor did he personally abandon hunting, for which he had had an enthusiasm since boyhood, upon becoming convinced that his ethical responsibilities extended beyond the human sphere.[11] There are several interpretations for this behavioral peculiarity. One is that Leopold did not see that his land ethic actually ought to prohibit hunting, cruelly killing, and eating animals. A corollary of this interpretation is that Leopold was so un-perspicacious as deservedly to be thought stu-pid—a conclusion hardly comporting with the intellectual subtlety he usually evinces in most other respects. If not stupid, then perhaps Leopold was hypocritical. But if a hypocrite, we should expect him to conceal his proclivity for blood sports and flesh eating and to treat them as shameful vices to be indulged secretively. As it is, bound together between the same covers with "The Land Ethic" are his unabashed rem-iniscences of killing and consuming *game*.[12] This term (like *stock*) when used of animals, moreover, appears to be morally equivalent to referring to a sexually appealing young woman as a "piece" or to a strong, young black man as a "buck"—if animal rights, that is, are to be con-sidered as on a par with women's rights and the rights of formerly enslaved races. A third in-terpretation of Leopold's approbation of reg-ulated and disciplined sport hunting (and *a fortiori* meat eating) is that it is a form of human/ animal behavior not inconsistent with the land ethic as he conceived it. A corollary of this in-terpretation is that Leopold's land ethic and the environmental ethic of the animal liberation movement rest upon very different theoretical foundations, and that they are thus two very different forms of environmental ethics.

The urgent concern of animal liberationists for the suffering of *domestic* animals, toward which Leopold manifests an attitude which can only be described as indifference, and the ur-gent concern of Leopold, on the other hand, for the disappearance of *species* of plants as well as animals and for soil erosion and stream pollution, appear to be symptoms not only of very different ethical perspectives, but pro-foundly different cosmic visions as well. The neat similarities, noted at the beginning of this discussion, between the environmental ethic of the animal liberation movement and the classi-cal Leopoldian land ethic appear in light of these observations to be rather superficial and to conceal substrata of thought and value which are not at all similar. The theoretical founda-tions of the animal liberation movement and those of the Leopoldian land ethic may even turn out not to be companionable, com-plementary, or mutually consistent. The an-imal liberationists may thus find themselves not only engaged in controversy with the many conservative philosophers upholding *apartheid* between man and "beast," but also faced with an unexpected dissent from another, very dif-ferent, system of environmental ethics.[13] An-imal liberation and animal rights may well prove to be a triangular rather than, as it has so far been represented in the philosophical com-munity, a polar controversy.

Ethical Humanism and Humane Moralism

The orthodox response of "ethical humanism" (as this philosophical perspective may be styled) to the suggestion that nonhuman animals should be accorded moral standing is that such animals are not worthy of this high perquisite. Only human beings are rational, or capable of having interests, or possess *self*-awareness, or have linguistic abilities, or can represent the future, it is variously argued.[14] These essential attributes taken singly or in various com-binations make people somehow exclusively deserving of moral consideration. The so-called "lower animals," it is insisted, lack the crucial qualification for ethical considerabili-ty and so may be treated (albeit humanely, according to some, so as not to brutalize man) as things or means, not as persons or as ends.[15]

The theoreticians of the animal liberation movement ("humane moralists" as they may be called) typically reply as follows.[16] Not all hu-man beings qualify as worthy of moral regard, according to the various criteria specified. Therefore, by parity of reasoning, human per-sons who do not so qualify as moral patients may be treated, as animals often are, as mere things or means (e.g., used in vivisection ex-periments, disposed of if their existence is in-convenient, eaten, hunted, etc., etc.). But the ethical humanists would be morally outraged if irrational and inarticulate infants, for example, were used in painful or lethal medical ex-periments, or if severely retarded people were hunted for pleasure. Thus, the double-dealing, the hypocrisy, of ethical humanism appears to be exposed.[17] Ethical humanism, though claiming to discriminate between worthy and unworthy ethical patients on the basis of objective criteria impartially applied, turns out after all, it seems, to be *speciesism*, a philosophically indefensible prejudice (analogous to racial prejudice) against animals. The tails side of this argument is that some animals, usually the "higher" lower animals (cetaceans, other primates, etc.), as ethological studies seem to indicate, may meet the criteria specified for moral worth, although the ethical humanists, even so, are not prepared to grant them full dignity and the rights of persons. In short, the ethical humanists' various criteria for moral standing do not include all or only human beings, humane moralists argue, although in practice ethical humanism wishes to make the class of morally considerable beings coextensive with the class of human beings.

The humane moralists, for their part, insist upon *sentience* (*sensibility* would have been a more precise word choice) as the only relevant capacity a being need possess to enjoy full moral standing. If animals, they argue, are conscious entities who, though deprived of reason, speech, forethought or even *self*-awareness (however that may be judged), are capable of suffering, then their suffering should be as much a matter of ethical concern as that of our fellow human beings, or strictly speaking, as our very own. What, after all, has rationality or any of the other allegedly uniquely human capacities to do with ethical standing? Why, in other words, should beings who reason or use speech (etc.) qualify for moral status, and those who do not fail to qualify?[18] Isn't this just like saying that only persons with white skin should be free, or that only persons who beget and not those who bear should own property? The criterion seems utterly unrelated to the benefit for which it selects. On the other hand, the capacity to suffer is, it seems, a more relevant criterion for moral standing because—as Bentham and Mill, notable among modern philosophers, and Epicurus, among the ancients, aver—pain is evil, and its opposite, pleasure and freedom from pain, good. As moral agents (and this

seems axiomatic), we have a duty to behave in such a way that the effect of our actions is to promote and procure good, so far as possible, and to reduce and minimize evil. That would amount to an obligation to produce pleasure and reduce pain. Now pain is pain wherever and by whomever it is suffered. As a *moral* agent, I should not consider my pleasure and pain to be of greater consequence in determining a course of action than that of other persons. Thus, by the same token, if animals suffer pain—and among philosophers only strict Cartesians would deny that they do—then we are morally obliged to consider their suffering as much an evil to be minimized by conscientious moral agents as human suffering.[19] Certainly actions of ours which contribute to the suffering of animals, such as hunting them, butchering and eating them, experimenting on them, etc., are on these assumptions morally reprehensible. Hence, a person who regards himself or herself as not aiming in life to live most selfishly, conveniently, or profitably, but rightly and in accord with practical principle, if convinced by these arguments, should, among other things, cease to eat the flesh of animals, to hunt them, to wear fur and leather clothing and bone ornaments and other articles made from the bodies of animals, to eat eggs and drink milk, if the animal producers of these commodities are retained under inhumane circumstances, and to patronize zoos (as sources of psychological if not physical torment of animals). On the other hand, since certain very simple animals are almost certainly insensible to pleasure and pain, they may and indeed should be treated as morally inconsequential. Nor is there any *moral* reason why trees should be respected or rivers or mountains or anything which is, though living or tributary to life processes, unconscious. The humane moralists, like the moral humanists, draw a firm distinction between those beings worthy of moral consideration and those not. They simply insist upon a different but quite definite cut-off point on the spectrum of natural entities, and accompany their criterion with arguments to show that it is more ethically defensible (granting certain assumptions) and more consistently applicable than that of the moral humanists.[20]

The First Principle of the Land Ethic

The fundamental principle of humane moralism, as we see, is Benthamic. Good is equivalent to pleasure and, more pertinently, evil is equivalent to pain. The presently booming controversy between moral humanists and humane moralists appears, when all the learned dust has settled, to be esentially internecine; at least, the lines of battle are drawn along familiar watersheds of the conceptual terrain.[21] A classical ethical theory, Bentham's, has been refitted and pressed into service to meet relatively new and unprecedented ethically relevant situations—the problems raised especially by factory farming and ever more exotic and frequently ill-conceived scientific research employing animal subjects. Then, those with Thomist, Kantian, Lockean, Moorean (etc.) ethical affiliation have heard the bugle and have risen to arms. It is no wonder that so many academic philosophers have been drawn into the fray. The issues have an apparent newness about them; moreover, they are socially and politically *avant garde*. But there is no serious challenge to cherished first principles.[22] Hence, without having to undertake any creative ethical reflection or exploration, or any reexamination of historical ethical theory, a fresh debate has been stirred up. The familiar historical positions have simply been retrenched, applied, and exercised.

But what about the third (and certainly minority) party to the animal liberation debate? What sort of reasonable and coherent moral theory would at once urge that animals (and plants and soils and waters) be included in the same class with people as beings to whom ethical consideration is owed and yet not object to some of them being slaughtered (whether painlessly or not) and eaten, others hunted, trapped, and in various other ways seemingly cruelly used? Aldo Leopold provides a concise statement of what might be called the categorical imperative or principal precept of the land ethic: "A thing is right when it tends to preserve the integrity, stability, and beauty of the biotic community. It is wrong when it tends otherwise."[23] What is especially note-worthy, and that to which attention should be directed in this proposition, is the idea that the good of the biotic *community* is the ultimate measure of the moral value, the rightness or wrongness, of actions. Thus, to hunt and kill a white-tailed deer in certain districts may not only be ethically permissible, it might actually be a moral requirement, necessary to protect the local environment, taken as a whole, from the disintegrating effects of a cervid population explosion. On the other hand, rare and endangered animals like the lynx should be especially nurtured and preserved. The lynx, cougar, and other wild feline predators, from the neo-Benthamite perspective (if consistently and evenhandedly applied) should be regarded as merciless, wanton, and incorrigible murderers of their fellow creatures, who not only kill, it should be added, but cruelly toy with their victims, thus increasing the measure of pain in the world. From the perspective of the land ethic, predators generally should be nurtured and preserved as critically important members of the biotic communities to which they are native. Certain plants, similarly, may be overwhelmingly important to the stability, integrity, and beauty of biotic communities, while some animals, such as domestic sheep (allowed perhaps by egalitarian and humane herdspersons to graze freely and to reproduce themselves without being harvested for lamb and mutton) could be a pestilential threat to the natural floral community of a given locale. Thus, the land ethic is logically coherent in demanding at once that moral consideration be given to plants as well as to animals and yet in permitting animals to be killed, trees felled, and so on. In every case the effect upon ecological systems is the decisive factor in the determination of the ethical quality of actions. . . .

The Land Ethic and the Ecological Point of View

. . . Since ecology focuses upon the relationships between and among things, it inclines its students toward a more holistic vision of the world. Before the rather recent emergence of ecology as a science the landscape appeared to be, one might say, a collection of objects, some of them alive, some conscious, but all the same, an aggregate, a plurality of separate individuals. With this "atomistic" representation of things it is no wonder that moral issues might be understood as competing and mutually contradictory clashes of the "rights" of separate individuals, each separately pursuing its "interests." Ecology has made it possible to apprehend the same landscape as an articulate unity (without the least hint of mysticism or ineffability). Ordinary organic bodies have articulated and discernible parts (limbs, various organs, myriad cells); yet, because of the character of the network of relations among those parts, they form in a perfectly familiar sense a second-order whole. Ecology makes it possible to see land, similarly, as a unified system of integrally related parts, as, so to speak, a third-order organic whole.[24]

Another analogy that has helped ecologists to convey the particular holism which their science brings to reflective attention is that land is integrated as a human community is integrated. The various parts of the "biotic community" (individual animals and plants) depend upon one another *economically* so that the system as such acquires distinct characteristics of its own. Just as it is possible to characterize and define collectively peasant societies, agrarian communities, industrial complexes, capitalist, communist, and socialist economic systems, and so on, ecology characterizes and defines various biomes as desert, savanna, wetland, tundra, wood land, etc., communities, each with its particular "professions," "roles," or "niches."

Now we may think that among the duties we as moral agents have toward ourselves is the duty of self-preservation, which may be interpreted as a duty to maintain our own organic integrity. It is not uncommon in historical moral theory, further, to find that in addition to those peculiar responsibilities we have in relation both to ourselves and to other persons severally, we also have a duty to behave in ways that do not harm the fabric of society *per se*. The land ethic, in similar fashion, calls our attention to the recently discovered integrity—in other

words, the unity—of the biota and posits duties binding upon moral agents in relation to that whole. Whatever the strictly formal logical connections between the concept of a social community and moral responsibility, there appears to be a strong psychological bond between that idea and conscience. Hence, the representation of the natural environment as, in Leopold's terms, "one humming community" (or, less consistently in his discussion, a third-order organic being) brings into play, whether rationally or not, those stirrings of conscience which we feel in relation to delicately complex, functioning social and organic systems.[25]

The neo-Benthamite humane moralists have, to be sure, digested one of the metaphysical implications of modern biology. They insist that human beings must be understood continuously with the rest of organic nature. People are (and are only) animals, and much of the rhetorical energy of the animal liberation movement is spent in fighting a rear guard action for this aspect of Darwinism against those philosophers who still cling to the dream of a special metaphysical status for people in the order of "creation." To this extent the animal liberation movement is biologically enlightened and argues from the taxonomical and evolutionary continuity of man and beast to moral standing for some nonhuman animals. Indeed, pain, in their view the very substance of evil, is something that is conspicuously common to people and other sensitive animals, something that we as people experience not in virtue of our metasimian cerebral capabilities, but because of our participation in a more generally animal, limbic-based consciousness. *If* it is pain and suffering that is the ultimate evil besetting human life, and this not in virtue of our humanity but in virtue of our animality, then it seems only fair to promote freedom from pain for those animals who share with us in this mode of experience and to grant them rights similar to ours as a means to this end.

Recent ethological studies of other primates, ceteceans, and so on, are not infrequently cited to drive the point home, but the biological information of the animal liberation movement seems to extend no further than this—the continuity of human with other animal life forms. The more recent ecological perspective especially seems to be ignored by humane moralists. The holistic outlook of ecology and the associated value premium conferred upon the biotic community, its beauty, integrity, and stability may simply not have penetrated the thinking of the animal liberationists, or it could be that to include it would involve an intolerable contradiction with the Benthamite foundations of their ethical theory. Bentham's view of the "interests of the community" was bluntly reductive. With his characteristic bluster, Bentham wrote, "The community is a fictitious *body* composed of the individual persons who are considered as constituting as it were its *members*. The interest of the community then is, what?—the sum of the interests of the several members who compose it."[26] Bentham's very simile—the community is like a body composed of members—gives the lie to his reduction of its interests to the sum of its parts taken severally. The interests of a person are not those of his or her cells summed up and averaged out. Our organic health and well-being, for example, require vigorous exercise and metabolic stimulation which cause stress and often pain to various parts of the body and a more rapid turnover in the life cycle of our individual cells. For the sake of the person taken as whole, some parts may be, as it were, unfairly sacrificed. On the level of social organization, the interests of society may not always coincide with the sum of the interests of its parts. Discipline, sacrifice, and individual restraint are often necessary in the social sphere to maintain social integrity as within the bodily organism. A society, indeed, is particularly vulnerable to disintegration when its members become preoccupied totally with their own particular interest, and ignore those distinct and independent interests of the community as a whole. One example, unfortunately, our own society, is altogether too close at hand to be examined with strict academic detachment. The United States seems to pursue uncritically a social policy of reductive utilitarianism, aimed at promoting the happiness of all its members severally. Each special interest accordingly clamors more loudly to be satisfied while the community as a whole becomes noticeably more and more infirm economically, environmentally, and politically.

The humane moralists, whether or not they are consciously and deliberately following Bentham on this particular, nevertheless, in point of fact, are committed to the welfare of certain kinds of animals distributively or reductively in applying their moral concern for nonhuman beings.[27] They lament the treatment of animals, most frequently farm and laboratory animals, and plead the special interests of these beings. We might ask, from the perspective of the land ethic, what the effect upon the natural environment taken as whole would be if domestic animals were actually liberated? There is, almost certainly, very little real danger that this might actually happen, but it would be instructive to speculate on the ecological consequences.

Ethical Holism

Before we take up this question, however, some points of interest remain to be considered on the matter of a holistic versus a reductive environmental ethic. To pit the one against the other as I have done without further qualification would be mistaken. A society is constituted by its members, an organic body by its cells, and the ecosystem by the plants, animals, minerals, fluids, and gases which compose it. One cannot affect a system as a whole without affecting at least some of its components. An environmental ethic which takes as its *summum bonum* the integrity, stability, and beauty of the biotic community is not conferring moral standing on something *else* besides plants, animals, soils, and waters. Rather, the former, the good of the community as a whole, serves as a standard for the assessment of the relative value and relative ordering of its constitutive parts and therefore provides a means of adjudicating the often mutually contradictory demands of the parts considered separately for *equal* consideration. If diversity does indeed contribute to stability (a classical "law" of ecology), then *specimens* of rare and endangered species, for example, have a *prima facie* claim to preferential consideration from the perspective of the land ethic. Animals of those species, which, like the honey bee, function in ways critically important to the economy of nature, moreover, would be granted a greater claim to moral attention than psychologically more complex and sensitive ones, say, rabbits and moles, which seem to be plentiful, globally distributed, reproductively efficient, and only routinely integrated into the natural economy. Animals and plants, mountains, rivers, seas, the atmosphere are the *immediate* practical beneficiaries of the land ethic. The well-being of the biotic community, the biosphere as a whole, cannot be logically separated from their survival and welfare.

Some suspicion may arise at this point that the land ethic is ultimately grounded in *human* interests, not in those of nonhuman natural entities. Just as we might prefer a sound and attractive house to one in the opposite condition so the "goodness" of a whole, stable, and beautiful environment seems rather to be of the instrumental, not the autochthonous, variety. The question of ultimate value is a very sticky one for environmental as well as for all ethics and cannot be fully addressed here. It is my view that there can be no value apart from an evaluator, that all value is as it were in the eye of the beholder. The value that is attributed to the ecosystem, therefore, is humanly dependent or (allowing that other living things may take a certain delight in the well-being of the whole of things, or that the gods may) at least dependent upon some variety of morally and aesthetically sensitive consciousness. Granting this, however, there is a further, very crucial distinction to be drawn. It is possible that while things may only have value because we (or someone) values them, they may nonetheless be valued for themselves as well as for the contribution they might make to the realization of our (or someone's) interests. Children are valued for themselves by most parents. Money, on the other hand, has only an instrumental or indirect value. Which sort of value has the health of the biotic community and its members severally for Leopold and the land ethic? It is especially difficult to separate these two general sorts of value, the one of moral significance, the other merely selfish, when something that may be valued in *both ways at once* is the subject of consideration. Are pets, for example, well-treated, like children, for the sake of themselves, or, like mechanical ap-

pliances, because of the sort of services they provide their owners? Is a healthy biotic community something we value because we are so utterly and (to the biologically well-informed) so obviously dependent upon it not only for our happiness but for our very survival, or may we also perceive it disinterestedly as having an independent worth? Leopold insists upon a noninstrumental value for the biotic community and *mutatis mutandis* for its constituents. According to Leopold, collective enlightened self-interest on the part of human beings does not go far enough; the land ethic in his opinion (and no doubt this reflects his own moral intuitions) requires "love, respect, and admiration for land, and a high regard for its value." The land ethic, in Leopold's view, creates "obligations over and above self-interest." And, "obligations have no meaning without conscience, and the problem we face is the extension of the social conscience from people to land."[28] If, in other words, any genuine ethic is possible, if it is possible to value *people* for the sake of themselves, then it is equally possible to value *land* in the same way.

Some indication of the genuinely biocentric value orientation of ethical environmentalism is indicated in what otherwise might appear to be gratuitous misanthropy. The biospheric perspective does not exempt *Homo sapiens* from moral evaluation in relation to the well-being of the community of nature taken as a whole. The preciousness of individual deer, as of any other specimen, is inversely proportional to the population of the species. Environmentalists, however reluctantly and painfully, do not omit to apply the same logic to their own kind. As omnivores, the population of human beings should, perhaps, be roughly twice that of bears, allowing for differences of size. A global population of more than four billion persons and showing no signs of an orderly decline presents an alarming prospect to humanists, but it is at present a global disaster (the more *per capita* prosperity, indeed, the more disastrous it appears) for the biotic community. If the land ethic were only a means of managing nature for the sake of man, misleadingly phrased in moral terminology, then man would be considered as having an ultimate value essentially different from that of his "resources." The extent of misanthropy in modern environmentalism thus may be taken as a measure of the degree to which it is biocentric. Edward Abbey in his enormously popular *Desert Solitaire* bluntly states that he would sooner shoot a man than a snake.[29] Abbey may not be simply depraved; this is perhaps only his way of dramatically making the point that the human population has become so disproportionate from the biological point of view that if one had to choose between a specimen of *Homo sapiens* and a specimen of a rare even if unattractive species, the choice would be moot. Among academicians, Garret Hardin, a human ecologist by discipline who has written extensively on ethics, environmental and otherwise, has shocked philosophers schooled in the preciousness of human life with his "lifeboat" and "survival" ethics and his "wilderness economics." In context of the latter, Hardin recommends limiting access to wilderness by criteria of hardiness and woodcraft and would permit no emergency roads or airborne rescue vehicles to violate the pristine purity of wilderness areas. If a wilderness adventurer should have a serious accident, Hardin recommends that he or she get out on his or her own or die in the attempt. Danger, from the strictly human-centered, psychological perspective, is part of the wilderness experience, Hardin argues, but in all probability his more important concern is to protect from mechanization the remnants of wild country that remain even if the price paid is the incidental loss of human life which, from the perspective once more of the biologist, is a commodity altogether too common in relation to wildlife and to wild landscapes.[30] . . .

. . . Modern systems of ethics have, it must be admitted, considered the principle of the equality of persons to be inviolable. This is true, for example, of both major schools of modern ethics, the utilitarian school going back to Bentham and Mill, and the deontological, originating with Kant. The land ethic manifestly does not accord equal moral worth to each and every member of the biotic community; the moral worth of individuals (including, n.b., human individuals) is relative, to be assessed in accordance with the particular relation of each to the collective entity which Leopold called "land."

There is, however, a classical Western ethic, with the best philosophical credentials, which assumes a similar holistic posture (with respect to the social moral sphere). I have in mind Plato's moral and social philosophy. Indeed, two of the same analogies figuring in the conceptual foundations of the Leopold land ethic appear in Plato's value theory.[31] From the ecological perspective, according to Leopold as I have pointed out, land is like an organic body or like a human society. According to Plato, body, soul, and society have similar structures and corresponding virtues.[32] The goodness of each is a function of its structure or organization and the relative value of the parts or constituents of each is calculated according to the contribution made to the integrity, stability, and beauty of each whole.[33] In the *Republic*, Plato, in the very name of virtue and justice, is notorious for, among other things, requiring infanticide for a child whose only offense was being born without the sanction of the state, making presents to the enemy of guardians who allow themselves to be captured alive in combat, and radically restricting the practice of medicine to the dressing of wounds and the curing of seasonal maladies on the principle that the infirm and chronically ill not only lead miserable lives but contribute nothing to the good of the polity.[34] Plato, indeed, seems to regard individual human life and certainly human pain and suffering with complete indifference. On the other hand, he shrinks from nothing so long as it seems to him to be in the interest of the community. Among the apparently inhuman recommendations that he makes to better the community are a program of eugenics involving a phony lottery (so that those whose natural desires are frustrated, while breeding proceeds from the best stock as in a kennel or stable, will blame chance, not the design of the rulers), the destruction of the pair bond and nuclear family (in the interests of greater military and bureaucratic efficiency and group solidarity), and the utter abolition of private property.[35]

When challenged with the complaint that he is ignoring individual human happiness (and the happiness of those belonging to the most privileged class at that), he replies that it is the well-being of the community as a whole, not that of any person or special class at which his legislation aims.[36] This principle is readily accepted, first of all, in our attitude toward the body, he reminds us—the separate interests of the parts of which we acknowledge to be subordinate to the health and well-being of the whole—and secondly, assuming that we accept his faculty psychology, in our attitude toward the soul—whose multitude of desires must be disciplined, restrained, and, in the case of some, altogether repressed in the interest of personal virtue and a well-ordered and morally responsible life.

Given these formal similarities to Plato's moral philosophy, we may conclude that the land ethic—with its holistic good and its assignment of differential values to the several parts of the environment irrespective of their intelligence, sensibility, degree of complexity, or any other characteristic discernible in the parts considered separately—is somewhat foreign to modern systems of ethical philosophy, but perfectly familiar in the broader context of classical Western ethical philosophy. If, therefore, Plato's system of public and private justice is properly an "ethical" system, then so is the land ethic in relation to environmental virtue and excellence.[37]

Reappraising Domesticity

Among the last philosophical remarks penned by Aldo Leopold before his untimely death in 1948 is the following: "Perhaps such a shift of values [as implied by the attempt to weld together the concepts of ethics and ecology] can be achieved by reappraising things unnatural, tame, and confined in terms of things natural, wild, and free."[38] John Muir, in a similar spirit of reappraisal, had noted earlier the difference between the wild mountain sheep of the Sierra and the ubiquitous domestic variety. The latter, which Muir described as "hooved locusts," were only, in his estimation, "half alive" in comparison with their natural and autonomous counterparts.[39] One of the more distressing aspects of the animal liberation movement is the failure of almost all its exponents to draw a

sharp distinction between the very different plights (and rights) of wild and domestic animals.[40] But this distinction lies at the very center of the land ethic. Domestic animals are creations of man. They are living artifacts, but artifacts nevertheless, and they constitute yet another mode of extension of the works of man into the ecosystem. From the perspective of the land ethic a herd of cattle, sheep, or pigs is as much or more a ruinous blight on the landscape as a fleet of four-wheel drive off-road vehicles. There is thus something profoundly incoherent (and insensitive as well) in the complaint of some animal liberationists that the "natural behavior" of chickens and bobby calves is cruelly frustrated on factory farms. It would make almost as much sense to speak of the natural behavior of tables and chairs.

Here a serious disanalogy (which no one to my knowledge has yet pointed out) becomes clearly evident between the liberation of blacks from slavery (and more recently, from civil inequality) and the liberation of animals from a similar sort of subordination and servitude. Black slaves remained, as it were, metaphysically autonomous: they were by nature if not by convention free beings quite capable of living on their own. They could not be enslaved for more than a historical interlude, for the strength of the force of their freedom was too great. They could, in other words, be retained only by a continuous counterforce, and only temporarily. This is equally true of caged wild animals. African cheetas in American and European zoos are captive, not indentured, beings. But this is not true of cows, pigs, sheep, and chickens. They have been bred to docility, tractability, stupidity, and dependency. It is literally meaningless to suggest that they be liberated. It is, to speak in hyperbole, a logical impossibility.

Certainly it is a practical impossibility. Imagine what would happen if the people of the world became morally persuaded that domestic animals were to be regarded as oppressed and enslaved persons and accordingly *set free*. In one scenario we might imagine that like former American black slaves they would receive the equivalent of forty acres and a mule and be turned out to survive on their own. Feral cattle and sheep would hang around farm outbuildings waiting forlornly to be sheltered and fed, or would graze aimlessly through their abandoned and deteriorating pastures. Most would starve or freeze as soon as winter settled in. Reproduction which had been assisted over many countless generations by their former owners might be altogether impossible in the feral state for some varieties, and the care of infants would be an art not so much lost as never acquired. And so in a very short time, after much suffering and agony, these species would become abruptly extinct. Or, in another scenario beginning with the same simple emancipation from human association, survivors of the first massive die-off of untended livestock might begin to recover some of their remote wild ancentral genetic traits and become smaller, leaner, heartier, and smarter versions of their former selves. An actual contemporary example is afforded by the feral mustangs ranging over parts of the American West. In time such animals as these would become (just as the mustangs are now) competitors both with their former human masters and (with perhaps more tragic consequences) indigenous wildlife for food and living space.

Foreseeing these and other untoward consequences of immediate and unplanned liberation of livestock, a human population grown morally more perfect than at present might decide that they had a duty, accumulated over thousands of years, to continue to house and feed as before their former animal slaves (whom they had rendered genetically unfit to care for themselves), but not to butcher them or make other ill use of them, including frustrating their "natural" behavior, their right to copulate freely, reproduce, and enjoy the delights of being parents. People, no longer having meat to eat, would require more vegetables, cereals, and other plant foods, but the institutionalized animal incompetents would still consume all the hay and grains (and more since they would no longer be slaughtered) than they did formerly. This would require clearing more land and bringing it into agricultural production with further loss of wildlife habitat and ecological destruction. Another possible scenario might be a decision on the part of people not literally to liberate domestic animals but simply to cease to breed and raise them. When

the last livestock have been killed and eaten (or permitted to die "natural" deaths), people would become vegetarians and domestic livestock species would thus be rendered deliberately extinct (just as they had been deliberately created). But there is surely some irony in an outcome in which the beneficiaries of a humane extension of conscience are destroyed in the process of being saved.[41]

The land ethic, it should be emphasized, as Leopold has sketched it, provides for the *rights* of nonhuman natural beings to a share in the life processes of the biotic community. The conceptual foundation of such rights, however, is less conventional than natural, based upon, as one might say, evolutionary and ecological entitlement. Wild animals and native plants have a particular place in nature, according to the land ethic, which domestic animals (because they are products of human art and represent an extended presence of human beings in the natural world) do not have. The land ethic, in sum, is as much opposed, though on different grounds, to commercial traffic in wildlife, zoos, the slaughter of whales and other marine mammals, etc., as is the humane ethic. Concern for animal (and plant) rights and well-being is as fundamental to the land ethic as to the humane ethic, but the difference between naturally evolved and humanly bred species is an essential consideration for the one, though not for the other.

The "shift of values" which results from our "reappraising things unnatural, tame, and confined in terms of things natural, wild, and free" is especially dramatic when we reflect upon the definitions of *good* and *evil* espoused by Bentham and Mill and uncritically accepted by their contemporary followers. Pain and pleasure seem to have nothing at all to do with good and evil if our appraisal is taken from the vantage point of ecological biology. Pain in particular is primarily information. In animals, it informs the central nervous system of stress, irritation, or trauma in outlying regions of the organism. A certain level of pain under optimal organic circumstances is indeed desirable as an indicator of exertion—of the degree of exertion needed to maintain fitness, to stay "in shape," and of a level of exertion beyond which it would be dangerous to go. An arctic wolf in pursuit of a caribou may experience pain in her feet or chest because of the rigors of the chase. There is nothing bad or wrong in that. Or, consider a case of injury. Suppose that a person in the course of a wilderness excursion sprains an ankle. Pain informs him or her of the injury and by its intensity the amount of further stress the ankle may endure in the course of getting to safety. Would it be better if pain were not experienced upon injury or, taking advantage of recent technology, anaesthetized? Pleasure appears to be, for the most part (unfortunately it is not always so) a reward accompanying those activities which contribute to organic maintenance, such as the pleasures associated with eating, drinking, grooming, and so on, or those which contribute to social solidarity like the pleasures of dancing, conversation, teasing, etc., or those which contribute to the continuation of the species, such as the pleasures of sexual activity and of being parents. The doctrine that life is the happier the freer it is from pain and that the happiest life conceivable is one in which there is continuous pleasure uninterrupted by pain is biologically preposterous. A living mammal which experienced no pain would be one which had a lethal dysfunction of the nervous system. The idea that pain is evil and ought to be minimized or eliminated is as primitive a notion as that of a tyrant who puts to death messengers bearing bad news on the supposition that thus his well-being and security is improved.[42]

More seriously still, the value commitments of the humane movement seem at bottom to betray a world-denying or rather a life-loathing philosophy. The natural world as actually constituted is one in which one being lives at the expense of others.[43] Each organism, in Darwin's metaphor, struggles to maintain its own organic integrity. The more complex animals seem to experience (judging from our own case, and reasoning from analogy) appropriate and adaptive psychological accompaniments to organic existence. There is a palpable passion for self-preservation. There are desire, pleasure in the satisfaction of desires, acute agony attending injury, frustration, and chronic dread of death. But these experiences are the psychological substance of living. To live *is* to be anxious about life, to feel pain and pleasure in a

fitting mixture, and sooner or later to die. That is the way the system works. If nature as a whole is good, then pain and death are also good. Environmental ethics in general require people to play fair in the natural system. The neo-Benthamites have in a sense taken the uncourageous approach. People have attempted to exempt themselves from the life/death reciprocities of natural processes and from ecological limitations in the name of a prophylactic ethic of maximizing rewards (pleasure) and minimizing unwelcome information (pain). To be fair, the humane moralists seem to suggest that we should attempt to project the same values into the nonhuman animal world and to widen the charmed circle—no matter that it would be biologically unrealistic to do so or biologically ruinous if, per impossible, such an environmental ethic were implemented.

There is another approach. Rather than imposing our alienation from nature and natural processes and cycles of life on other animals, we human beings could reaffirm our participation in nature by accepting life as it is given without a sugar coating. Instead of imposing artificial legalities, rights, and so on on nature, we might take the opposite course and accept and affirm natural biological laws, principles, and limitations in the human personal and social spheres. Such appears to have been the posture toward life of tribal peoples in the past. The chase was relished with its dangers, rigors, and hardships as well as its rewards: animal flesh was respectfully consumed; a tolerance for pain was cultivated; virtue and magnanimity were prized; lithic, floral, and faunal spirits were worshipped; population was routinely optimized by sexual continency, abortion, infanticide, and stylized warfare; and other life forms, although certainly appropriated, were respected as fellow players in a magnificent and awesome, if not altogether idyllic, drama of life. It is impossible today to return to the symbiotic relationship of Stone Age man to the natural environment, but the ethos of this by far the longest era of human existence could be abstracted and integrated with a future human culture seeking a viable and mutually beneficial relationship with nature. Personal, social, and environmental *health* would, accordingly, receive a premium value rather than comfort, self-indulgent pleasure, and anaesthetic insulation from pain. Sickness would be regarded as a worse evil than death. The pursuit of health or wellness at the personal, social, and environmental levels would require self-discipline in the form of simple diet, vigorous exercise, conservation, and social responsibility.

Leopold's prescription for the realization and implementation of the land ethic—the reappraisal of things unnatural, tame, and confined in terms of things natural, wild, and free—does not stop, in other words, with a reappraisal of nonhuman domestic animals in terms of their wild (or willed) counterparts; the human ones should be similarly reappraised. This means, among other things, the reappraisal of the comparatively recent values and concerns of "civilized" *Homo sapiens* in terms of those of our "savage" ancestors.[44] Civilization has insulated and alienated us from the rigors and challenges of the natural environment. The hidden agenda of the humane ethic is the imposition of the anti-natural prophylactic ethos of comfort and soft pleasure on an even wider scale. The land ethic, on the other hand, requires a shrinkage, if at all possible, of the domestic sphere; it rejoices in a recrudescence of wilderness and a renaissance of tribal cultural experience.

The converse of those goods and evils, axiomatic to the humane ethic, may be illustrated and focused by the consideration of a single issue raised by the humane morality: a vegetarian diet. Savage people seem to have had, if the attitudes and values of surviving tribal cultures are representative, something like an intuitive grasp of ecological relationships and certainly a morally charged appreciation of eating. There is nothing more intimate than eating, more symbolic of the connectedness of life, and more mysterious. What we eat and how we eat is by no means an insignificant ethical concern.

From the ecological point of view, for human beings universally to become vegetarians is tantamount to a shift of trophic niche from omnivore with carnivorous preferences to herbivore. The shift is a downward one on the trophic pyramid, which in effect shortens those food chains terminating with man. It represents an increase in the efficiency of the conversion of solar energy from plant to human biomass, and thus, by bypassing animal intermediates, increases available food resources for human beings. The human population would probably, as past trends overwhelmingly suggest, expand in accordance with the potential thus afforded. The net result would be fewer nonhuman beings and more human beings, who, of course, have requirements of life far more elaborate than even those of domestic animals, requirements which would tax other "natural resources" (trees for shelter, minerals mined at the expense of topsoil and its vegetation, etc.) more than under present circumstances. A vegetarian human population is therefore *probably* ecologically catastrophic.

Meat eating as implied by the foregoing remarks may be more *ecologically* responsible than a wholly vegetable diet. Meat, however, purchased at the supermarket, externally packaged and internally laced with petrochemicals, fattened in feed lots, slaughtered impersonally, and, in general, mechanically processed from artificial insemination to microwave roaster, is an affront not only to physical metabolism and bodily health but to conscience as well. From the perspective of the land ethic, the immoral aspect of the factory farm has to do far less with the suffering and killing of nonhuman animals than with the monstrous transformation of living things from an organic to a mechanical mode of being. Animals, beginning with the Neolithic Revolution, have been debased through selective breeding, but they have nevertheless remained animals. With the Industrial Revolution an even more profound and terrifying transformation has overwhelmed them. They have become, in Ruth Harrison's most apt description, "animal machines." The very presence of animals, so emblematic of delicate, complex organic tissue, surrounded by machines, connected to machines, penetrated by machines in research laboratories or crowded together in space-age "production facilities" is surely the more real and visceral source of our outrage at vivisection and factory farming than the contemplation of the quantity of pain that these unfortunate beings experience. I wish to denounce as loudly as the neo-Benthamites this ghastly abuse of animal life, but also to stress that the pain and suffering of research and agribusiness animals is not greater than that endured by free-living wildlife as a consequence of predation, disease, starvation, and cold—indicating that there is something immoral about vivisection and factory farming which is not an ingredient in the natural lives and deaths of wild beings. That immoral something is the transmogrification of organic to mechanical processes.

Ethical vegetarianism to all appearances insists upon the human consumption of plants (in a paradoxical moral gesture toward those animals whose very existence is dependent upon human carnivorousness), even when the tomatoes are grown hydroponically, the lettuce generously coated with chlorinated hydrocarbons, the potatoes pumped up with chemical fertilizers, and the cereals stored with the help of chemical preservatives. The land ethic takes as much exception to the transmogrification of plants by mechanicochemical means as to that of animals. The important thing, I would think, is not to eat vegetables as opposed to animal flesh, but to resist factory farming in all its manifestations, including especially its liberal application of pesticides, herbicides, and chemical fertilizers to maximize the production of *vegetable* crops.

The land ethic, with its ecological perspective, helps us to recognize and affirm the organic integrity of self and the untenability of a firm distinction between self and environment. On the ethical question of what to eat, it answers, not vegetables instead of animals, but organically as opposed to mechanicochemically produced food. Purists like Leopold prefer, in his expression, to get their "meat from God," i.e., to hunt and consume wildlife and to gather wild plant foods, and thus to live within the parameters of the aboriginal human ecological niche.[45] Second best is eating from one's own orchard, garden, henhouse, pigpen, and barnyard. Third best is buying or bartering organic foods from one's neighbors and friends.

Conclusion

Philosophical controversy concerning animal liberation/rights has been most frequently represented as a polar dispute between traditional moral humanists and seemingly *avant garde* humane moralists. Further, animal liberation has been assumed to be closely allied with environmental ethics, possibly because in Leopold's classical formulation moral standing and indeed rights (of some unspecified sort) is accorded nonhuman beings, among them animals. The purpose of this discussion has been to distinguish sharply environmental ethics from the animal liberation/rights movement both in theory and practical application and to suggest, thereupon, that there is an underrepresented, but very important, point of view respecting the problem of the moral status of nonhuman animals. The debate over animal liberation, in short, should be conceived as triangular, not polar, with land ethics or environmental ethics, the third and, in my judgment, the most creative, interesting, and practicable alternative. Indeed, from this third point of view moral humanism and humane moralism appear to have much more in common with one another than either have with environmental or land ethics. On reflection one might even be led to suspect that the noisy debate between these parties has served to drown out the much deeper challenge to "business-as-usual" ethical philosophy represented by Leopold and his exponents, and to keep ethical philosophy firmly anchored to familiar modern paradigms.

Moral humanism and humane moralism, to restate succinctly the most salient conclusions of this essay, are *atomistic* or distributive in their theory of moral value, while environmental ethics (again, at least, as set out in Leopold's outline) is *holistic* or collective. Modern ethical theory, in other words, has consistently located moral value in individuals and set out certain metaphysical reasons for including some individuals and excluding others. Humane moralism remains firmly within this modern convention and centers its attention on the competing criteria for moral standing and rights holding, while environmental ethics locates ultimate value in the "biotic community" and assigns differential moral value to the constitutive individuals relatively to that standard. This is perhaps the most fundamental theoretical difference between environmental ethics and the ethics of animal liberation.

Allied to this difference are many others.

One of the more conspicuous is that in environmental ethics, plants are included within the parameters of the ethical theory as well as animals. Indeed, inanimate entities such as oceans and lakes, mountains, forests, and wetlands are assigned a greater value than individual animals and in a way quite different from systems which accord them moral considerability through a further multiplication of competing individual loci of value and holders of rights.

There are intractable practical differences between environmental ethics and the animal liberation movement. Very different moral obligations follow in respect, most importantly, to domestic animals, the principal beneficiaries of the humane ethic. Environmental ethics sets a very low priority on domestic animals as they very frequently contribute to the erosion of the integrity, stability, and beauty of the biotic communities into which they have been insinuated. On the other hand, animal liberation, if pursued at the practical as well as rhetorical level, would have ruinous consequences on plants, soils, and waters, consequences which could not be directly reckoned according to humane moral theory. As this last remark suggests, the animal liberation/animal rights movement is in the final analysis utterly unpracticable. An imagined society in which all animals capable of sensibility received equal consideration or held rights to equal consideration would be so ludicrous that it might be more appropriately and effectively treated in satire than in philosophical discussion. The land ethic, by contrast, even though its ethical purview is very much wider, is nevertheless eminently practicable, since, by reference to a single good, competing individual claims may be adjudicated and relative values and priorities assigned to the myriad components of the biotic community. This is not to suggest that the implementation of environmental ethics as social policy would be easy. Implementation of the land ethic would require discipline, sacrifice, retrenchment, and massive economic reform, tantamount to a virtual revolution in prevailing attitudes and life styles. Nevertheless, it provides a unified and coherent practical principle and thus a decision procedure at the practical level which a distributive or atomistic ethic may achieve only

artificially and so imprecisely as to be practically indeterminate.

Notes

1. Aldo Leopold, *A Sand County Almanac* (New York: Oxford University Press, 1949), pp. 202–3. Some traditional Western systems of ethics, however, have accorded moral standing to non-human beings. The Pythagorean tradition did, followed by Empedocles of Acragas; Saint Francis of Assisi apparently believed in the animal soul; in modern ethics Jeremy Bentham's hedonic utilitarian system is also an exception to the usual rule. John Passmore ("The Treatment of Animals," *Journal of the History of Ideas* 36 [1975]: 196–218) provides a well-researched and eye-opening study of historical ideas about the moral status of animals in Western thought. Though exceptions to the prevailing attitudes have existed, they are exceptions indeed and represent but a small minority of Western religious and philosophical points of view.
2. The tag "animal liberation" for this moral movement originates with Peter Singer whose book *Animal Liberation* (New York: New York Review, 1975) has been widely influential. "Animal rights" have been most persistently and unequivocally championed by Tom Regan in various articles, among them: "The Moral Basis of Vegetarianism," *Canadian Journal of Philosophy* 5 (1975): 181–214; "Exploring the Idea of Animal Rights" in *Animal Rights: A Symposium*, eds. D. Patterson and R. Ryder (London: Centaur, 1979); "Animal Rights, Human Wrongs," *Environmental Ethics* 2 (1980): 99–120. A more complex and qualified position respecting animal rights has been propounded by Joel Feinberg, "The Rights of Animals and Unborn Generations" in *Philosophy and Environmental Crisis*, ed. William T. Blackstone (Athens: University of Georgia Press, 1974), pp. 43–68, and "Human Duties and Animal Rights," in *On the Fifth Day*, eds. R. K. Morris and M. W. Fox (Washington: Acropolis Books, 1978), pp. 45–69. Lawrence Haworth ("Rights, Wrongs and Animals," *Ethics* 88 [1978]: 95–105), in the context of the contemporary debate, claims limited rights on behalf of animals. S. R. L. Clark's

The Moral Status of Animals (Oxford: Clarendon Press, 1975) has set out arguments which differ in some particulars from those of Singer, Regan, and Feinberg with regard to the moral considerability of some nonhuman animals. In this discussion, as a tribute to Singer, I use the term *animal liberation* generically to cover the several philosophical rationales for a humane ethic. Singer has laid particular emphasis on the inhumane usage of animals in agribusiness and scientific research. Two thorough professional studies from the humane perspective of these institutions are Ruth Harrison's *Animal Machines* (London: Stuart, 1964) and Richard Ryder's *Victims of Science* (London: Davis-Poynter, 1975), respectively.

3. Peter Singer and Tom Regan especially insist upon *equal* moral *consideration* for nonhuman animals. Equal moral *consideration* does not necessarily imply equal *treatment*, however, as Singer insists. Cf. Singer, *Animal Liberation*, pp. 3, 17–24, and Singer, "The Fable of the Fox and the Unliberated Animals," *Ethics* 88 (1978): 119–20. Regan provides an especially clear summary of both his position and Singer's in "Animal Rights, Human Wrongs," pp. 108–12.

4. We have Richard Ryder to thank for coining the term *speciesism*. See his *Speciesism: The Ethics of Vivisection* (Edinburgh: Scottish Society for the Prevention of Vivisection, 1974). Richard Routley introduced the term *human chauvinism* in "Is There a Need for a New, an Environmental Ethic?" *Proceedings of the Fifteenth World Congress of Philosophy 1* (1973): 205–10. Peter Singer ("All Animals Are Equal," in *Animal Rights and Human Obligations*, eds. Tom Regan and Peter Singer [Englewood Cliffs, N.J.: Prentice-Hall, 1976], pp. 148–62) developed the egalitarian comparison of speciesism with racism and sexism in detail. To extend the political comparison further, animal liberation is also a reformist and activist movement. We are urged to act, to become vegetarians, to boycott animal products, etc. The concluding paragraph of Regan's "Animal Rights, Human Wrongs," (p. 120) is especially zealously hortatory.

5. Leopold, *Sand County Almanac*, p. 204.

6. Ibid, pp. 201–3. A more articulate historical representation of the parallel expansion of legal rights appears in C. D. Stone's *Should Trees Have Standing?* (Los Altos: William Kaufman, 1972),

pp. 3–10, however without specific application to animal liberation.

7. Leopold, *Sand County Almanac*, p. 203.

8. Ibid., p. 204.

9. Ibid., p. 221 (trees); pp. 129–133 (mountains); p. 209 (streams).

10. John Benson ("Duty and the Beast," *Philosophy* 53 [1978]: 547–48) confesses that in the course of considering issues raised by Singer et al he was "obliged to change my own diet as a result." An elaborate critical discussion is Philip E. Devine's "The Moral Basis of Vegetarianism" (*Philosophy* 53 [1978]: 481–505).

11. For a biography of Leopold including particular reference to Leopold's career as a "sportsman," see Susan L. Flader, *Thinking Like a Mountain* (Columbia: University of Missouri Press, 1974).

12. See especially, Leopold, *Sand County Almanac*, pp. 54–58; 62–66; 120–22; 149–54; 177–87.

13. A most thorough and fully argued dissent is provided by John Rodman in "The Liberation of Nature," *Inquiry* 20 (1977): 83–131. It is surprising that Singer, whose book is the subject of Rodman's extensive critical review, or some of Singer's philosophical allies, has not replied to these very penetrating and provocative criticisms. Another less specifically targeted dissent is Paul Shepard's "Animal Rights and Human Rites" (*North American Review* [Winter, 1974]: 35–41). More recently Kenneth Goodpaster ("From Egoism to Environmentalism" in *Ethics and Problems of the 21st Century*, eds. K. Goodpaster and K. Sayre [Notre Dame: Notre Dame University Press, 1979], pp. 21–35) has expressed complaints about the animal liberation and animal rights movement in the name of environmental ethics. "The last thing we need," writes Goodpaster, "is simply another 'liberation movement' " (p. 29).

14. Singer, "All Animals are Equal" (p. 159), uses the term *humanist* to convey a speciesist connotation. Rationality and future-conceiving capacities as criteria for rights holding have been newly revived by Michael E. Levin with specific reference to Singer in "Animal Rights Evaluated," *The Humanist* (July/August, 1977): 12; 14–15. John Passmore, in *Man's Responsibility for Nature* (New York: Charles Scribner's Sons, 1974), cf., p. 116, has recently insisted upon having interests as a criterion for having rights and denied that nonhuman beings have interests. L. P. Francis

and R. Norman ("Some Animals are More Equal than Others," *Philosophy* 53 [1978]: 507–27) have argued, again with specific reference to animal liberationists, that linguistic abilities are requisite for moral status. H. J. McCloskey ("The Right to Life," *Mind* 84 [1975]: 410–13, and "Moral Rights and Animals," *Inquiry* 22 [1979]: 23–54), adapting an idea of Kant's, defends *autonomy* as the main ingredient of human nature which entitles human beings to rights. Michael Fox ("Animal Liberation: A Critique," *Ethics* 88 [1978]: 106–18) defends, among other exclusively human qualifications for rights holding, *self*-awareness. Richard A. Watson ("Self-Consciousness and the Rights of Nonhuman Animals and Nature," *Environmental Ethics* 1 [1979]: 99–129) also defends self-consciousness as a criterion for rights holding, but allows that some nonhuman animals also possess it.

15. In addition to the historical figures, who are nicely summarized and anthologized in *Animal Rights and Human Obligations*, John Passmore has recently defended the reactionary notion that cruelty towards animals is morally reprehensible for reasons independent of any obligation or duties people have to animals as such (*Man's Responsibility*, cf., p. 117).

16. "Humane moralists" is perhaps a more historically accurate designation than "animal liberationists." John Rodman, "The Liberation of Nature" (pp. 88–89), has recently explored in a programmatic way the connection between the contemporary animal liberation/rights movements and the historical humane societies movement.

17. Tom Regan styles more precise formulations of this argument, "the argument from marginal cases," in "An Examination and Defense of One Argument Concerning Animal Rights," *Inquiry* 22 (1979): 190. Regan directs our attention to Andrew Linzey, *Animal Rights* (London: SCM Press, 1976) as well as to Singer, *Animal Liberation*, for paradigmatic employment of this argument on behalf of moral standing for animals (p. 144).

18. A particularly lucid advocacy of this notion may be found in Feinberg, "Human Duties and Animal Rights," especially p. 53ff.

19. Again, Feinberg in "Human Duties and Animal Rights" (pp. 57–59) expresses this point especially forcefully.

20. John Rodman's comment in "The Liberation of Nature" (p. 91) is worth repeating here since it has to all appearances received so little attention elsewhere: "If it would seem arbitrary . . . to find one species claiming a monopoly on intrinsic value by virtue of its allegedly exclusive possession of reason, free will, soul, or some other occult quality, would it not seem almost as arbitrary to find that same species claiming a monopoly of intrinsic value for itself and those species most resembling it (e.g. in type of nervous system and behavior) by virtue of their common and allegedly exclusive possession of sentience [i.e., sensibility]?" Goodpaster ("From Egoism to Environmentalism," p. 29) remarks that in modern moral philosophy "a fixation on egoism and a consequent loyalty to a model of moral sentiment or reason which in essence generalizes or universalizes that egoism . . . makes it particularly inhospitable to our recent felt need for an environmental ethic. . . . For such an ethic does not readily admit of being reduced to 'humanism'—nor does it sit well with any class or generalization model of moral concern."

21. John Rodman, "The Liberation of Nature" (p. 95), comments: "Why do our 'new ethics' seem so old? . . . Because the attempt to produce a 'new ethics' by the process of 'extension' perpetuates the basic assumptions of the conventional modern paradigm, however much it fiddles with the boundaries." When the assumptions remain conventional, the boundaries are, in my view, scalar, but triangular when both positions are considered in opposition to the land ethic. The scalar relation is especially clear when two other positions, not specifically discussed in the text, the reverence-for-life ethic and pan-moralism, are considered. The reverence-for-life ethic (as I am calling it in deference to Albert Schweitzer) seems to be the next step on the scale after the humane ethic. William Frankena considers it so in "Ethics and the Environment," *Ethics and Problems of the 21st Century*, pp. 3–20. W. Murry Hunt ("Are *Mere Things* Morally Considerable," *Environmental Ethics* 2 [1980]: 59–65) has gone a step past Schweitzer, and made the bold suggestion that *everything* should be accorded moral standing, pan-moralism. Hunt's discussion shows clearly that there is a similar logic ("slippery slope" logic) involved in taking each downward step, and thus a certain commonality of underlying assumptions among all the ethical types to which the land ethic stands in opposition. Hunt is not unaware that his

suggestion may be interpreted as a *reductio ad absurdum* of the whole matter, but insists that that is not his intent. The land ethic is not part of this linear series of steps and hence may be represented as a point off the scale. The principal difference, as I explain below, is that the land ethic is collective or "holistic" while the others are distributive or "atomistic." Another relevant difference is that moral humanism, humane moralism, reverence-for-life ethics, and the limiting case, pan-moralism, either openly or implicitly espouse a pecking-order model of nature. The land ethic, founded upon an ecological model of nature emphasizing the contributing roles played by various species in the economy of nature, abandons the "higher"/"lower" ontological and axiological schema, in favor of a functional system of value. The land ethic, in other words, is inclined to establish value distinctions not on the basis of higher and lower orders of being, but on the basis of the importance of organisms, minerals, and so on to the biotic community. Some bacteria, for example, may be of greater value to the health or economy of nature than dogs, and thus command more respect.

22. Rodman, "The Liberation of Nature" (p. 86), says in reference to Singer's humane ethic that "the weakness . . . lies in the limitation of its horizon to the late eighteenth and early nineteenth century Utilitarian humane movement [and] its failure to live up to its own noble declaration that 'philosophy ought to question the basic assumptions of the age'. . . ."

23. Leopold, *Sand County Almanac*, pp. 224–25.

24. By "first," "second," and "third" order wholes I intend paradigmatically single cell organisms, multicell organisms, and biocoenoses, respectively.

25. "Some Fundamentals of Conservation in the Southwest," composed in the 1920s but unpublished until it appeared last year (*Environmental Ethics* 1 [1979]: 131–41), shows that the organic analogy, conceptually representing the nature of the whole resulting from ecological relationships, antedates the community analogy in Leopold's thinking, so far at least as its moral implications are concerned. "The Land Ethic" of *Sand County Almanac* employs almost exclusively the community analogy but a rereading of "The Land Ethic" in the light of "Some Fundamentals" reveals that Leopold did not entirely abandon the organic

analogy in favor of the community analogy. For example, toward the end of "The Land Ethic" Leopold talks about "land health" and "land the collective organism" (p. 258). William Morton Wheeler, *Essays in Philosophical Biology* (New York: Russell and Russell, 1939), and Lewis Thomas, *Lives of a Cell* (New York: Viking Press, 1974), provide extended discussions of holistic approaches to social, ethical, and environmental problems. Kenneth Goodpaster, almost alone among academic philosophers, has explored the possibility of a holistic environmental ethical system in "From Egoism to Environmentalism."

26. *An Introduction to the Principles of Morals and Legislation* (Oxford: Oxford University Press, 1823), chap. 1, sec. 4.

27. This has been noticed and lamented by Alistair S. Gunn ("Why Should We Care About Rare Species?" *Environmental Ethics* 2 [1980]: 36) who comments, "Environmentalism seems incompatible with the 'Western' obsession with individualism, which leads us to resolve questions about our treatment of animals by appealing to the essentially atomistic, competitive notion of rights. . . ." John Rodman, "The Liberation of Nature" (p. 89), says practically the same thing: "The moral atomism that focuses on individual animals and their subjective experiences does not seem well adapted to coping with ecological systems." Peter Singer has in fact actually stressed the individual focus of his humane ethic in "Not for Humans Only: The Place of Nonhumans in Environmental Issues" (*Ethics and Problems of the 21st Century*, pp. 191–206) as if it were a virtue! More revealingly, the only grounds that he can discover for moral concern over species, since species are *per se* not sensible entities (and that is the extent of his notion of an ethically relevant consideration), are anthropocentric grounds, human aesthetics, environmental integrity for humans, etc.

28. Leopold, *Sand County Almanac*, pp. 223 and 209.

29. Edward Abbey, *Desert Solitaire* (New York: Ballantine Books, 1968), p. 20.

30. Garrett Hardin, "The Economics of Wilderness," *Natural History* 78 [1969]: 173–77. Hardin is blunt: "Making great and spectacular efforts to save the life of an individual makes sense only when there is a shortage of people. I have not lately heard that there is a shortage of people" (p. 176).

31. In *Republic* 5 Plato directly says that "the best governed state most nearly resembles an organism" (462D) and that there is no "greater evil for a state than the thing that distracts it and makes it many instead of one, or a greater good than that which binds it together and makes it one" (462A). Goodpaster in "From Egoism to Environmentalism" (p. 30) has in a general way anticipated this connection: "The oft-repeated plea by some ecologists and environmentalists that our thinking needs to be less atomistic and more 'holistic' translates in the present context into a plea for a more embracing object of moral consideration. In a sense it represents a plea to return to the richer Greek conception of man by nature social and not intelligibly removable from his social and political context though it goes beyond the Greek conception in emphasizing that societies too need to be understood in a context, an ecological context, and that it is this larger whole that is the 'bearer of value.' "

32. See especially *Republic* 4.444A–E.

33. For a particularly clear statement by Plato of the idea that the goodness of anything is a matter of the fitting order of the parts in relation to respective wholes see *Gorgias* 503D–507A.

34. Cf., *Republic* 5.461C (infanticide); 468A (disposition of captives); *Republic* 3.405D–406E (medicine).

35. Cf., *Republic* 5.459A–460E (eugenics, non-family life and child rearing), *Republic* 3.416D–417B (private property).

36. Cf., *Republic* 4.419A–421C and *Republic* 7.419D–521B.

37. After so much strident complaint has been registered here about the lack of freshness in self-proclaimed "new" environmental ethics (which turn out to be "old" ethics retreaded) there is surely an irony in comparing the (apparently brand new) Leopoldian land ethic to Plato's ethical philosophy. There is, however, an important difference. The humane moralists have simply revived and elaborated Bentham's historical application of hedonism to questions regarding the treatment of animals with the capacity of sensibility. There is nothing new but the revival and elaboration. Plato, on the other hand, never develops anything faintly resembling an *environmental* ethic. Plato never reached an ecological view of living nature. The wholes of his universe are body, soul, society, and cosmos. Plato is large-

ly, if not exclusively, concerned with moral problems involving individual human beings in a political context and he has the temerity to insist that the good of the whole transcends individual claims. (Even in the *Crito* Plato is sympathetic to the city's claim to put *Socrates* to death however unjust the verdict against him.) Plato thus espouses a holistic ethic which is valuable as a (very different) paradigm to which the Leopoldian *land* ethic, which is also holistic but in relation to a very different whole, may be compared. It is interesting further that some (but not all) of the analogies which Plato finds useful to convey his holistic social values are also useful to Leopold in his effort to set out a land ethic.

38. Leopold, *Sand County Almanac*, p. ix.

39. See John Muir, "The Wild Sheep of California," *Overland Monthly* 12 (1874): 359.

40. Roderick Nash (*Wilderness and the American Mind*, rev. ed. [New Haven and London: Yale University Press, 1973], p. 2) suggests that the English word *wild* is ultimately derived from *will*. A wild being is thus a willed one—"self-willed, willful, or uncontrollable." The humane moralists' indifference to this distinction is rather dramatically represented in Regan's "Animal Rights, Human Wrongs" (pp. 99–104) which begins with a bid for the reader's sympathy through a vivid description of four concrete episodes of human cruelty toward animals. I suspect that Regan's intent is to give examples of four principal categories of animal abuse at the hands of man: whaling, traffic in zoo captives, questionable scientific experimentation involving unquestionable torture, and intensive meat production. But his illustration, divided according to precepts central to land ethics, concern two episodes of wanton slaughter of *wild* animals, a blue whale and a gibbon, aggravated by the consideration that both are specimens of disappearing species, and two episodes of routine cruelty toward *domestic* animals, a "bobby calf" (destined to become veal) and a laboratory rabbit. The misery of the calf and the agony of the rabbit are, to be sure, reprehensible, from the perspective of the land ethic, for reasons I explain shortly, but it is, I think, a trivialization of the deeper environmental and ecological issues involved in modern whaling and wildlife traffic to discuss the exploitation and destruction of blue whales and gibbon apes as if they are wrong for the same reasons that the treatment of laboratory

rabbits and male dairy calves is wrong. The inhumane treatment of penned domestics should not be, I suggest, even discussed in the same context as whaling and wildlife traffic; it is a disservice to do so.

41. John Rodman, "The Liberation of Nature" (p. 101), castigates Singer for failing to consider what the consequences of wholesale animal liberation might be. With tongue in cheek he congratulates Singer for taking a step toward the elimination of a more subtle evil, the genetic debasement of other animal beings, i.e., domestication *per se*.

42. A particularly strong statement of the ultimate value commitment of the neo-Benthamites is found in Feinberg's "Human Duties and Animal Rights" (p. 57): "We regard pain and suffering as an intrinsic evil . . . simply because they are pain and suffering. . . . The question 'What's wrong with pain anyway?' is never allowed to arise." I shall raise it. I herewith declare in all soberness that I see nothing wrong with pain. It is a marvelous method, honed by the evolutionary process, of conveying important organic information. I think it was the late Alan Watts who somewhere remarks that upon being asked if he did not think there was too much pain in the world replied, "No, I think there's just enough."

43. Paul Shepard, "Animal Rights and Human Rites" (p. 37), comments that "the humanitarian's projection onto nature of illegal murder and the rights of civilized people to safety not only misses the point but is exactly contrary to fundamental ecological reality: the structure of nature is a sequence of killings."

44. This matter has been ably and fully explored by Paul Shepard, *The Tender Carnivore and the Sacred Game* (New York: Scribner's Sons, 1973). A more empirical study has been carried out by Marshall Sahlins, *Stone Age Economics* (Chicago: Aldine/Atherton, 1972).

45. The expression "our meat from God" is found in Leopold, *Sand County Almanac*, p. viii. Leopold mentions "organic farming" as something intimately connected with the land ethic; in the same context he also speaks of "biotic farming" (p. 222).

The Rights View

Tom Regan

. . . The rights view is not opposed to efforts to save endangered species. It only insists that we be clear about the reasons for doing so. On the rights view, the reason we ought to save the members of endangered species of animals is not because the species is endangered but because the individual animals have valid claims and thus rights against those who would destroy their natural habitat, for example, or who would make a living off their dead carcasses through poaching and traffic in exotic animals, practices that unjustifiably override the rights of these animals. But though the rights view must look with favor on any attempt to protect the rights of any animal, and so supports efforts to protect the members of endangered species, these very efforts, aimed specifically at protecting the members of species that are endangered, can foster a mentality that is antagonistic to the implications of the rights view. If people are encouraged to believe that the harm done to animals matters morally *only when* these animals belong to endangered species, then these same people will be encouraged to regard the harm done to *other* animals as morally acceptable. In this way people may be encouraged to believe that, for example, the trapping of plentiful animals raises no serious moral question, whereas the trapping of rare animals does. This is not what the rights view implies. The mere size of the relative population of the species to which a given animal belongs makes no moral difference to the grounds for attributing rights to that individual animal or to the basis for determining when

Source: *The Case for Animal Rights*, by Tom Regan (Berkeley: The University of California Press, 1983), pp. 360–63. Reprinted by permission.

that animal's rights may be justifiably over-ridden or protected.

Though said before, it bears repeating: *the rights view is not indifferent to efforts to save endangered species. It supports these efforts.* It supports them, however, not because these animals are few in number; primarily it supports them because they are equal in value to all who have inherent value, ourselves included, sharing with us the fundamental right to be treated with respect. Since they are not mere receptacles or renewable resources placed here for our use, the harm done to them as individuals cannot be justified merely by aggregating the disparate benefits derived by commercial developers, poachers, and other interested third parties. That is what makes the commercial exploitation of endangered species wrong, not that the species are endangered. On the rights view, the same principles apply to the moral assessment of rare or endangered animals as apply to those that are plentiful, and the same principles apply whether the animals in question are wild or domesticated.

The rights view does not deny, nor is it antagonistic to recognizing, the importance of human aesthetic, scientific, sacramental, and other interests in rare and endangered species or in wild animals generally. What it denies is that (1) the value of these animals is reducible to, or is interchangeable with, the aggregate satisfaction of these human interests, and that (2) the determination of how these animals should be treated, including whether they should be saved in preference to more plentiful animals, is to be fixed by the yardstick of such human interests, either taken individually or aggregatively. Both points cut both ways, concerning, as they do, both how animals may and how they may not be treated. In particular, any and all harm done to rare or endangered animals, done in the name of aggregated human interests, is wrong, according to the rights view, because it violates the individual animal's right to respectful treatment. With regard to wild animals, the general policy recommended by the rights view is: *let them be!* Since this will require increased human intervention in *human* practices that threaten rare or endangered species (e.g., halting the destruction of natural

habitat and closer surveillance of poaching, with much stiffer fines and longer prison sentences), the rights view sanctions this intervention, assuming that those humans involved are treated with the respect they are due. Too little is not enough.

. . . The difficulties and implications of developing a rights-based environmental ethic . . . should be abundantly clear by now and deserve brief comment before moving on. The difficulties include reconciling the *individualistic* nature of moral rights with the more *holistic* view of nature emphasized by many of the leading environmental thinkers. Aldo Leopold is illustrative of this latter tendency. "A thing is right," he states, "when it tends to preserve the integrity, stability, and beauty of the biotic community. It is wrong when it tends otherwise."[1] The implications of this view include the clear prospect that the individual may be sacrificed for the greater biotic good, in the name of "the integrity, stability, and beauty of the biotic community." It is difficult to see how the notion of the rights of the individual could find a home within a view that, emotive connotations to one side, might be fairly dubbed "environmental fascism." To use Leopold's telling phrase, man is "*only* a member of the biotic team,"[2] and as such has the same moral standing as any other "member" of "the team." If, to take an extreme, fanciful but, it is hoped, not unfair example, the situation we faced was either to kill a rare wildflower or a (plentiful) human being, and if the wildflower, as a "team member," would contribute more to "the integrity, stability, and beauty of the biotic community" than the human, then presumably we would not be doing wrong if we killed the human and saved the wildflower. The rights view cannot abide this position, not because the rights view categorically denies that inanimate objects can have rights (more on this momentarily) but because it denies the propriety of deciding what should be done to individuals who have rights by appeal to aggregative considerations, including, therefore, computations about what will or will not maximally "contribute to the integrity, stability, and beauty of the biotic community." Individual rights are not to be outweighed by such considerations (which is not to say that they are never to be outweighed). Environmental fascism and the rights view are like oil and water: they don't mix.

The rights view does not deny the possibility that collections or systems of natural objects might have inherent value—that is, might have a kind of value that is not the same as, is not reducible to, and is incommensurate with any one individual's pleasures, preference-satisfactions, and the like, or with the sum of such goods for any number of individuals. The beauty of an undisturbed, ecologically balanced forest, for example, might be conceived to have value of this kind. The point is certainly arguable. What is far from certain is how moral rights could be meaningfully attributed to the *collection* of trees or the ecosystem. Since neither is an individual, it is unclear how the notion of moral rights can be meaningfully applied. Perhaps this difficulty can be surmounted. It is fair to say, however, that no one writing in this important area of ethics has yet done so.[3]

Because paradigmatic right-holders are individuals, and because the dominant thrust of contemporary environmental efforts (e.g., wilderness preservation) is to focus on the whole rather than on the part (i.e., the individual), there is an understandable reluctance on the part of environmentalists to "take rights seriously," or at least a reluctance to take them as seriously as the rights view contends we should. But this may be a case of environmentalists not seeing the forest for the trees—or, more accurately, of not seeing the trees for the forest. The implications of the successful development of a rights-based environmental ethic, one that made the case that individual inanimate natural objects (e.g., *this* redwood) have inherent value and a basic moral right to treatment respectful of that value, should be welcomed by environmentalists. If individual trees have inherent value, they have a kind of value that is not the same as, is not reducible to, and is incommensurate with the intrinsic values of the pleasures, preference-satisfactions, and

the like, of others, and since the rights of the individual never are to be overridden merely on the grounds of aggregating such values for all those affected by the outcome, a rights-based environmental ethic would bar the door to those who would uproot wilderness in the name of "human progress," whether this progress be aggregated economic, educational, recreational, or other human interests. On the rights view, assuming this could be successfully extended to inanimate natural objects, our general policy regarding wilderness would be precisely what the preservationists want—namely, let it be! Before those who favor such preservation dismiss the rights view in favor of the holistic view more commonly voiced in environmental circles, they might think twice about the implications of the two. There is the danger that the baby will be thrown out with the bath water. A rights-based environmental ethic remains a live option, one that, though far from being established, merits continued exploration. It ought not to be dismissed out of hand by environmentalists as being in principle antagonistic to the goals for which they work. It isn't. Were we to show proper respect for the rights of the individuals who make up the biotic community, would not the *community* be preserved? And is not that what the more holistic, systems-minded environmentalists want? . . .

Notes

1. Aldo Leopold, *A Sand County Almanac* (New York: Oxford University Press, 1949), p. 217.
2. Aldo Leopold, *A Sand County Almanac*, p. 209, emphasis added.
3. For further remarks on these matters, see my "What Sorts of Beings Can Have Rights?" and "The Nature and Possibility of an Environmental Ethic," both in Regan, *All That Dwell Therein* (Berkeley: University of California Press, 1982).

Economics, Ethics, and Ecology: How Much Common Ground?

Letting the Market Decide: Is Efficiency Overrated?

Preview

Many people probably share the sentiments of
two writers who, in commenting on the despoliation of "our natural heritage" and the
poisoning of the environment with the use of
pesticides, stated that "although, it is obvious
that what we are doing is wrong, it is by no
means obvious what would be right."[1] Indeed,
the perplexities are deep. There is disagreement about whether certain practices are
wrong, what proper policies would be, and,
importantly, the grounds for deciding such
matters. As noted in the General Introduction,
one source of dispute concerns what sorts of
things have moral standing. Even if that difficult question were resolved, there are other
sources of perplexity. Although the following
suggestion deserves critical reflection and continued reassessment, one way of categorizing
competing approaches to deciding an important range of environmental disputes is to divide them crudely into (a) those that assume
that the mechanism of the market place is the
proper means of determining both the allocation of resources to different productive uses
and the distribution of benefits and burdens
across the relevant populations, and (b) those
which assume that these matters should not be
left much, or at all, to the contingencies of the
marketplace (that is, certain matters should be
decided politically and certain protections or
constraints on the market must be politically
enforced in order to avoid certain failures or
abuses to which unconstrained markets lead).

We need to think about the effects of the
market mechanism on the environment and
assess the arguments for claiming that the environmental effects of the market mechanism
are tolerable or desirable. Markets, of course,
existed long before economists or ecologists
did. A major source of defense of the desirability of the market mechanism comes, however,
from economists. For this reason and because
economists, more than any other group of social scientists, have explored environmental
issues in considerable detail, it is important to
identify and examine some fundamental
strands in economic theory and also to see how
economists tend to approach particular current

problems, for example, pollution, predicted species extinction, or the question whether we should save for the sake of future generations. It seems fair to say that "economic reasoning," indeed the economic point of view, is extremely influential in policy making and, for a number of reasons, inviting. Shortly, we shall note a number of objections to orthodox economic theory; so, we should make it quite clear that economists deserve special praise for paying careful attention to consequences and to related trade-off problems. In short, the "economic approach" is sensitive to particular facts; it is specific; it suggests a method for resolving questions of trade-offs between competing and valued ends. It seems, then, "practical," "hard-nosed," and "realistic," as well as holding out the allure of employing precise, formal modes of quantification and calculation.

In recent years there has developed a more concentrated effort to identify the points of agreement and disagreement between economic theory, ethical theory, and the outlook of the ecologists. This effort (of which some essays in this volume are examples) promises to be an important and revealing one for developing an adequate view of our environment and a reasonable approach to setting policy on environmental matters. Here there is room only to touch on a few central matters.

On the one hand, markets seem terribly useful. They provide us (or many of us) with all sorts of "goodies," including decent shelter, nutrition, medical care, and transportation—to consider some "items" that few fail to value. The market in a decentralized fashion, without the (maligned) "government bureaucrats" deciding for the rest of us, allocates the use of resources to myriad productive functions and provides a mode for distributing benefits (as well as the burdens of work, risk-taking, and so on). That the market mechanism has all sorts of wonderful results is not subverted by the disdain we may feel rightly for certain insipid, tasteless, defective products that the market also generates. Sometimes, one person's junk is another's treasure; sometimes it is just another's junk as well.

The main defense of the market mechanism appeals to the value of efficiency; it can be characterized as follows. In the best, perhaps idealized, case, two parties, for example, are mature, have settled preferences, are well-informed, and with no undue pressure or misrepresentation, agree to exchange goods or services. Perhaps I agree to paint your house in exchange for your old car. I value the car more than the labor-effort I must make, and you value having your house painted more than the car. After the exchange we are both better off. Other things being equal, our welfare is enhanced, our respective utility levels raised. Thus, the sum of (your and my) utilities is increased. The pretrade situation was one in which at least one (of us) could be better off and no one worse off. It was, in the technical sense in which economists use the term, an inefficient situation. The posttrade situation is more efficient. Someone has become better off and no one is worse off. Is efficiency valuable *in itself*? The answer from orthodox economic theory is "no"; rather, *moving toward more efficient arrangements is viewed as desirable because to do so is to increase the sum of utilities or welfares* (to take a step toward "maximization of total net expected utility" to put matters more carefully). To understand the argument for adopting or perpetuating the use of the market mechanism, it is crucial to note these assumptions—ones that too often are in the background and that, hence, frequently escape the scrutiny of philosophical and moral appraisal.

To highlight some crucial assumptions and to emphasize which values or principles are being treated as basic, or alternatively, derivative ones, it is useful to set out certain elements of economic reasoning more explicitly and systematically. Standardly, what is implicit is the anthropocentric view that all and only humans morally count; thus, only benefits (utilities) or harms (disutilities) to humans have weight in evaluating actions or policies. For example consider this representative remark:

To assert that there is a pollution problem or an environmental problem is to assert, at least implicitly, that one or more resources is not being used so as to maximize human satisfactions.[2]

Thus what is *conceptually* to *count* (for example) as pollution, directly or indirectly, must involve harm to humans; if penguins are poisoned by an industrial chemical but no humans (now or in the future?) are affected, that is not "pollution" (or, at least, morally significant pollution). Representative are the remarks of William Baxter (from the later selection "People or Penguins"):

My criteria are oriented to people, not penguins. Damage to penguins, or sugar pines, or geological marvels is, without more, simply irrelevant. One must . . . say: Penguins are important because people enjoy seeing them walk about rocks. . . .

I reject the proposition that we *ought* to respect the "balance of nature" or to "preserve the environment" unless the reason for doing so, express or implied, is the benefit of man. Every man is entitled to his own definition of Walden Pond, but there is no definition that has any moral superiority over another, except by reference to the selfish needs of the human race.[3]

To make an important point briefly, if the anthropocentric assumption embodied in orthodox economic theory is indefensible, then the theory as it stands is unacceptable—as would be a theory that regarded only benefits and harms to white people as having moral significance. A theory that is not anthropocentric will be a theoretically more complex one. But simplicity is not the sole determinant of rationality.

The modern economic approach also assumes and accepts (however inexplicitly) a distribution of legally protected property rights. Implicit are certain assumptions. For example, human beings can be owners but cannot be owned. Any nonhuman can be owned. This view reflects the anthropocentric criterion of moral standing. Legal property in an object X is best understood as possession of a package of rights over what is owned, often a right to use X, to exclude others from doing so, to authorize others to use X, to be compensated for unauthorized uses, and, sometimes, to destroy X if one wishes. There is a moral question whether anyone should have a legal right to kill (or torture) his or her animals. The "it's my property to do with as I please" mentality implies an affirmative answer. The main point here, however, is just that orthodox economists typically assume the moral legitimacy of *some* set of well-defined property rights. Further, it is

assumed that these will foster certain sorts of exchanges, for example, voluntary, nonfraudulent ones between competent persons. Thus, the core of the market mechanism, exchanges of goods or services (actually rights to such), is understood to go on against the background of morally acceptable *norms and institutions;* these latter constitute "the rules of the game" as it were.

Economists often insist that they engage in *value-free* inquiry, that they are impotent (as economists) to say whether the rules are good or right. Some deny that evaluative claims are rationally decidable or are any more than expressions of emotion. For example, McKenzie and Tullock claim that "the approach of the economist is amoral" and that "as economists we cannot say what is 'just' or 'fair'."[4] Paul Heyne and Thomas Johnson maintain that "we do not have any (means) of resolving ethical disagreements, they are ultimately judgments of value . . . and cannot finally be proved or disproved."[5] These stances are questionable (and have been explored systematically and in detail in the philosophical literature for years) but many economists seem oblivious to this fact, and to the fact that their own implicit or explicit commitment to the value of the market mechanism or to efficiency or to maximizing utility (or aggregate human want-satisfaction) suggests, to the contrary, that the discipline of economics rests, in part, on evaluative assumptions. One who thought that only benefits or harms *to penguins* was significant would be making an important evaluative assumption. So also for one who says "Aryans count; Jews do not." The question rather would seem to be which view is rationally superior; we simply cannot avoid evaluations.

The concept of efficiency, and its assumed high value (or possibly, overriding value), is so central in economic approaches to environmental matters that we should dissect it more thoroughly. To do so requires a bit of technical terminology, but one will be helpless in trying to assess the economic approach unless one masters a few concepts.

In ordinary (nontechnical) talk, there is a tendency to use *efficient* as an honorific term; thus, if X is efficient, X is thought good (in a respect). Conversely, if X is inefficient, X is thought bad (in a respect). *Given* such usage, it seems perverse to question or oppose the efficient course, and unobjectionable or "nice" to urge efficient policies. All this can mislead us, however. The term *efficient* has a technical sense in economics; further, we should distinguish (1) what it *means* to say that some state of affairs is efficient, and (2) whether efficiency is a valuable goal that we ought to pursue. And importantly, is efficiency valuable in itself or only as a means? First, we have noted, in so many words, that a standard implicit assumption is, not surprisingly, that efficiency is understood as efficiency for humans. Modern factory farms that raise veal calves may be quite efficient for humans, but hardly so, let us assume, for the calves.[6] Let us return to (1). The standard *criterion of efficiency* employed is called the *Pareto criterion* (after the early twentieth century economist-sociologist Vilfredo Pareto). If a situation in which parties possessing various goods is such that at least one party could be better off (in his or her own estimation) *without* making any one worse off, it is said to be one which is inefficient (or not maximally efficient). A "*Pareto improvement*" could be made; that is, at least one party could be better off without worsening another's situation. In our earlier tale, in which I get your car and you get your house painted, a Pareto improvement was made. Voluntary exchanges are thought to generate Pareto improvements, that is, to increase efficiency. If a situation is one in which it is not possible for anyone to become better off without worsening another's circumstance, it is said to be *Pareto-optimal* (or maximally efficient). As noted before, the core idea is that in a more efficient situation the sum of the welfares of the relevant parties is greater than in the less efficient one. Moving toward more efficient circumstances *seems* desirable since it moves things closer to utility maximization. If in fact the sketched mechanism is the best means of arriving at maximization of the sum of welfares, that seems to be a strong reason to employ it. Thus, the market is defended often on grounds that it best maximizes utility (quite apart from or in addition to appeals to implementation of, or respecting, some sort of human right to choose). Although we may give three cheers for the marketplace, critical reflection

may make us wonder whether it deserves three, or even two. Much depends on how much we should value utility maximization, or efficiency as a means of fostering it—and whether voluntary exchanges invariably or usually increase efficiency.

It is easy to overlook some crucial points. We may have serious moral reservations about even maximally efficient situations. For example, suppose I am your master and you are my slave. There may be no way to alter this arrangement so that one of us can be better off and no one worse off. That is, it may be *Pareto-optimal*—or maximally efficient. The criterion focuses on a given situation and prospective departures from it, not on how it came about. As noted, a distribution of goods between master and slave may be Pareto-optimal or maximally efficient (in the Paretian sense)—but morally indefensible. In short it seems absurd to believe that whatever is efficient is right or permissible. If so, then we must conclude that although efficiency is desirable, it only is desirable *other things being equal*.

In the exchange of old car for painting your house there was a gain from trade, both parties were better off, and aggregate welfare increased. In applying the Pareto criterion, economists standardly assume that the proper way of determining whether the parties to the transaction are better off or not is according to the judgment of the parties themselves—(usually) post-trade. Several comments are relevant here; all of them may reduce one's enthusiasm for thinking that the market is invariably the proper vehicle (or an effective one) to enhance social (human) welfare. First, in idealized models, the traders may possess "complete information." In fact, actual traders are ignorant to a degree (sometimes victimized by self-interested, or profit-maximizing, individuals or corporations). We may *believe*, prior to trading, that acquiring a widget (the product most discussed in economics texts, but hard to find) and forgoing some money may improve our lot. On getting the widget, the car, the meal, or the record, we often regard ourselves as worse off. In fact, voluntary exchanges do not always (often?) yield a Pareto improvement over the preexchange situation because one party *is* worse off postexchange. This point tends to get overlooked or discounted by some ostensibly empirical scientists.

To avoid, so it would seem, this awkward result of observing what actually happens with some actual transactions, some economists seem to *stipulatively define* "voluntary exchange" as one an individual would engage in if and only if beneficial to that individual. Thus, with this conceptual sleight of hand, it becomes analytically true (roughly, true by definition) that "all voluntary exchanges benefit the parties who engage in them." But then this use of *voluntary exchange* does *not* refer to what most of us mean by such an expression.

A brief comment that may provide food for thought is this. We desire things *under-a-description* (at least often). Thus Oedipus wanted to marry Jocasta. He got "what he wanted." Was he better off? He did not want to marry his mother, but since Jocasta was his mother, he also got what, in one sense, he did *not* want. The economists' model of human psychology and choice seems a mite too simple.

Another feature of the market mechanism worth noting concerns *who* participates in market transactions, either small or large. It is worth observing that only those who are *willing and able* to pay have access to markets, that is, can participate in market transactions. It may not be far wrong to estimate that of the world's (almost) 5 billion members of *Homo sapiens* at least a billion or so are unable to cast, or are radically hindered from casting, an effective vote in the economic marketplace, for example, the extremely poor, the very young, the severely retarded, the seriously (mentally) disturbed. Not only do nonhumans have no say about the distribution of benefits and burdens generated by market transactions but also a large number of existing humans are in this way, voiceless—not to mention future generations.

For the reasons mentioned it is doubtful that voluntary, "informed" exchanges invariably benefit *existing human participants* in the exchange. Even if they did, much of the world's population effectively is excluded from participation in market transactions. In spite of the incautious praise heaped upon capitalism by some ideologues, the proper assessment of markets (and especially commercial practices and environmental effects) must involve consideration of the alternatives to a given market system. Large questions of political philosophy and economics arise that cannot be explored here. However, there are two basic alternatives to a comparatively unconstrained market system. If a given system seems intolerable in some respect, it may be possible to add a new constraint to it in order to remedy the problem. This is the alternative of *setting appropriate constraints* on the market. Thus if we judge that blood (or bodily parts, or babies) ought not to be bought and sold (to the highest bidder?), we can legally prohibit the practice—and let the distribution be determined by nonmarket procedures. Similarly, if we judge that a corporation's self-interest in a good reputation is not an adequate safeguard to prevent it from selling defective products or polluting the environment, we can require governmental testing and set stringent liability rules that function as a disincentive to corporate distribution of dangerous products or polluting. Defenders of the market are fond of pointing out that it is not the baker's altruism but his self-interest that makes bread available for purchase. Perhaps, but this same motive also can lead to industrial spying, theft of trade secrets, corporate bribery, and "coverups" of dangerous products.

We have noted some important criticisms of letting the market mechanism determine allocation and distribution questions. The alleged efficiency of the market process seems a means to maximizing utility. For reasons discussed in the General Introduction, utility maximization is hardly an uncontroversial goal. There are powerful philosophical arguments in favor of the view that maximizing utility allows or requires unjust distributions of benefits and burdens. As we have noted, to assume the value of maximizing only human utility is to beg the question against anti-anthropocentric counter arguments. Further, even if those difficulties were not serious, there are reasons (as noted) to doubt that all (most?) voluntary participants in market exchanges are better off as a result. If they are not, there may be no increase in efficiency (increase in the sum of utilities). We have observed also that much of the world's population is disenfranchised from casting an effective monetary vote in the market decision process.

This brief survey of moral and other worries

about the market has omitted a concern that economists rightly and increasingly have stressed in recent decades: the fact that many parties who are not participants to voluntary, informed exchanges are made worse off as a result of the exchanges. These are what are called *negative externalities*. The focus here is on the generation of unconsented-to-harms to some individuals, "costs" generated for which compensation is not paid. Thus, much pollution of the air or water is a prime example of negative externalities. Because only some of the costs to all parties are borne by the "private parties," the "social costs" exceed the "private costs." It commonly is held that if external costs only could be "internalized" (borne by those who seek to benefit from activities that generate them) there would be no problem (no moral complaint?). Thus, it is claimed that we ought to prevent or minimize externalities (some economists might be uncomfortable with this blatantly normative mode of speaking). How can we do that? To oversimplify, three basic alternatives present themselves: (1) persuade people or corporations or nations not to generate externalities, that is, appeal to voluntary self-restraint, (2) coerce by attaching criminal penalties to violations of publicly set standards, or (3) coerce by attaching "taxes" or charges to each additional unit of pollution emitted beyond a certain amount. Economists have a sufficiently low estimate of human nature so as to dismiss (1) rather quickly. One well may agree even if one regards the picture of people embodied in *homo economicus* as a serious distortion and simplistic psychology.

The current debate between defenders of (2) and (3) is important, intriguing, and embodies notable psychological and moral assumptions. Once more, the focus on *unconsented-to harm to others* is viewed anthropocentrically. Only harms to humans count. The English hunter W. D. M. Bell is reported to have killed 1,011 elephants in his lifetime.[7] This slaughter, if involving no unconsented-to harm to humans, fails to count as an externality needing any internalizing—according to the orthodox economic view. The term *social costs* means costs to human society. An obvious question is whether a cost-benefit accounting can be thought thorough when "costs to nonhumans" are either tacitly treated as nonsensical or rec-

ognized but treated as irrelevant. These matters will be taken up in the next section.

It should not go unnoticed that many economists would object to labeling negative externalities as "instances of market failure." Instead, they would maintain that unconsented-to harms ("negative externalities," "overexploitations of resources," "pollution," and so on) result from the *failure to have a market*. As some have argued, the solution is to allow property rights in them. The "tragedy of the commons" is that "goods" unowned (except "owned by all") get misused in one fashion or another. Since "chunks" of air or water rarely can be partitioned off so that particular individuals have a right to them, such persons may have little self-interested incentive to preserve, respect, or ration consumption of such things. According to the view being considered, it is better to allow the market to operate more broadly (by creating a more extensive distribution of property rights) rather than to restrict the market's scope of operation. Having been somewhat grumpy about much in economic theory in these introductory remarks, we will let the reader critically appraise this proposal— as well as the criticisms we have set forth.

The first selection to follow, by William Baxter, expresses, in no uncertain terms, an anthropocentric approach to environmental trade-offs. As Baxter states, "[d]amage to penguins, or sugar pines, or geological marvels is, without more, simply irrelevant." Baxter optimistically believes that what is good for people, often at least, is good for the environment. One might question whether "maximize human satisfaction" underlies Baxter's economic viewpoint. A more qualified, more cautious, and more sophisticated effort at setting out fundamental, theoretic assumptions of modern economics (such as Pareto considerations) and applying them to environmental questions (for example, what to do about pollution) is found in A. Myrick Freeman's essay. It is not easy reading, but it is a rich summary and deserves careful study. Part of a critique of "the economic viewpoint" is set out in Mark Sagoff's essay. Sagoff calls attention to where market decision making (or "the cult of Pareto optimality") has led us. He is not enamored with the resulting gas stations, tract developments, strip mines, pizza stands, beach condos, and snowmobiles in the mountains. Importantly, he questions the tendency of economists to view citizens' expressions of *ideals* (such as "we ought to preserve dolphins") as just another consumer *preference*—as just another consumer vote in the economic marketplace—to be taken seriously only if backed by the willingness and ability to pay.

Notes

1. Robert and Nancy Dorfman, eds. *Economics and the Environment* (New York: W.W. Norton & Company, 1972), p. XIX.

2. William Baxter. *People or Penguins: The Case for Optimal Pollution* (New York: Columbia University Press, 1974), p. 17.

3. William Baxter. *People or Penguins*, p. 5.

4. Richard B. McKenzie and Gordon Tullock. *The New World of Economics* (Homewood, Illinois: Richard D. Irwin, 1978), p. 7.

5. Paul Heyne and Thomas Johnson, *Toward Economic Understanding* (Chicago: Science Research Associates, 1976), p. 767.

6. See Peter Singer, *Animal Liberation* (New York: Avon Books, 1975).

7. Bell's act is reported in Cleveland Amory, *Man Kind?* (New York: Dell Publishing Co., 1974), p. 30.

People or Penguins

William F. Baxter

I start with the modest proposition that, in dealing with pollution, or indeed with any problem, it is helpful to know what one is attempting to accomplish. Agreement on how and whether to pursue a particular objective, such as pollution control, is not possible unless some more general objective has been identified and stated with reasonable precision. We talk loosely of having clean air and clean water, of preserving our wilderness areas, and so forth. But none of these is a sufficiently general objective: each is more accurately viewed as a means rather than as an end.

With regard to clean air, for example, one may ask, "how clean?" and "what does clean mean?" It is even reasonable to ask, "why have clean air?" Each of these questions is an implicit demand that a more general community goal be stated—a goal sufficiently general in its scope and enjoying sufficiently general assent among the community of actors that such "why" questions no longer seem admissible with respect to that goal.

Source: *People or Penguins: The Case for Optimal Pollution*, by William F. Baxter (New York: Columbia University Press, © 1974), pp. 1–13. Reprinted by permission.

If, for example, one states as a goal the proposition that "every person should be free to do whatever he wishes in contexts where his actions do not interfere with the interests of other human beings," the speaker is unlikely to be met with a response of "why." The goal may be criticized as uncertain in its implications or difficult to implement, but it is so basic a tenet of our civilization—it reflects a cultural value so broadly shared, at least in the abstract—that the question "why" is seen as impertinent or imponderable or both.

I do not mean to suggest that everyone would agree with the "spheres of freedom" objective just stated. Still less do I mean to suggest that a society could subscribe to four or five such general objectives that would be adequate in their coverage to serve as testing criteria by which all other disagreements might be measured. One difficulty in the attempt to construct such a list is that each new goal added will conflict, in certain applications, with each prior goal listed; and thus each goal serves as a limited qualification on prior goals.

Without any expectation of obtaining unanimous consent to them, let me set forth four goals that I generally use as ultimate testing criteria in attempting to frame solutions to problems of human organization. My position regarding pollution stems from these four criteria. If the criteria appeal to you and any part of what appears hereafter does not, our disagreement will have a helpful focus: which of us is correct, analytically, in supposing that his position on pollution would better serve these general goals. If the criteria do not seem acceptable to you, then it is to be expected that our more particular judgments will differ, and the task will then be yours to identify the basic set of criteria upon which your particular judgments rest.

My criteria are as follows:

1. The spheres of freedom criterion stated above.

2. Waste is a bad thing. The dominant feature of human existence is scarcity—our available resources, our aggregate labors, and our skill in employing both have always been, and will continue for some time to be, inadequate to yield to every man all the tangible and intangible satisfactions he would like to have. Hence, none of those resources, or labors, or skills, should be wasted—that is, employed so as to yield less than they might yield in human satisfactions.

3. Every human being should be regarded as an end rather than as a means to be used for the betterment of another. Each should be afforded dignity and regarded as having an absolute claim to an evenhanded application of such rules as the community may adopt for its governance.

4. Both the incentive and the opportunity to improve his share of satisfactions should be preserved to every individual. Preservation of incentive is dictated by the "no-waste" criterion and enjoins against the continuous, totally egalitarian redistribution of satisfactions, or wealth; but subject to that constraint, everyone should receive, by continuous redistribution if necessary, some minimal share of aggregate wealth so as to avoid a level of privation from which the opportunity to improve his situation becomes illusory.

The relationship of these highly general goals to the more specific environmental issues at hand may not be readily apparent, and I am not yet ready to demonstrate their pervasive implications. But let me give one indication of their implications. Recently scientists have informed us that use of DDT in food production is causing damage to the penguin population. For the present purposes let us accept that assertion as an indisputable scientific fact. The scientific fact is often asserted as if the correct implication—that we must stop agricultural use of DDT—followed from the mere statement of the fact of penguin damage. But plainly it does not follow if my criteria are employed.

My criteria are oriented to people, not penguins. Damage to penguins, or sugar pines, or geological marvels is, without more, simply irrelevant. One must go further, by my criteria, and say: Penguins are important because people enjoy seeing them walk about rocks; and furthermore, the well-being of people would be less impaired by halting use of DDT than by giving up penguins. In short, my observations about environmental problems will be people-oriented, as are my criteria. I have no interest in preserving penguins for their own sake.

It may be said by way of objection to this position, that it is very selfish of people to act as if each person represented one unit of importance and nothing else was of any importance. It is undeniably selfish. Nevertheless I think it is the only tenable starting place for analysis for several reasons. First, no other position corresponds to the way most people really think and act—i.e., corresponds to reality.

Second, this attitude does not portend any massive destruction of nonhuman flora and fauna, for people depend on them in many obvious ways, and they will be preserved because and to the degree that humans do depend on them.

Third, what is good for humans is, in many respects, good for penguins and pine trees—clean air for example. So that humans are, in these respects, surrogates for plant and animal life.

Fourth, I do not know how we could administer any other system. Our decisions are either private or collective. Insofar as Mr. Jones is free to act privately, he may give such preferences as he wishes to other forms of life: he may feed birds in winter and do with less himself, and he may even decline to resist an advancing polar bear on the ground that the bear's appetite is more important than those portions of himself that the bear may choose to eat. In short my basic premise does not rule out private altruism to competing life-forms. It does rule out, however, Mr. Jones' inclination to feed Mr. Smith to the bear, however hungry the bear, however despicable Mr. Smith.

Insofar as we act collectively on the other hand, only humans can be afforded an opportunity to participate in the collective decisions. Penguins cannot vote now and are unlikely subjects for the franchise—pine trees more unlikely still. Again each individual is free to cast his vote so as to benefit sugar pines if that is his inclination. But many of the more extreme assertions that one hears from some conservationists amount to tacit assertions that they are specially appointed representatives of sugar pines, and hence that their preferences should be weighted more heavily than the preferences of other humans who do not enjoy equal rapport with "nature." The simplistic assertion that agricultural use of DDT must stop at once because it is harmful to penguins is of that type.

Fifth, if polar bears or pine trees or penguins, like men, are to be regarded as ends rather than means, if they are to count in our calculus of social organization, someone must tell me how much each one counts, and someone must tell me how these life-forms are to be permitted to express their preferences, for I do not know either answer. If the answer is that certain people are to hold their proxies, then I want to know how those proxy-holders are to be selected: self-appointment does not seem workable to me.

Sixth, and by way of summary of all the foregoing, let me point out that the set of environmental issues under discussion—although they raise very complex technical questions of how to achieve any objective—ultimately raise a normative question: what *ought* we to do. Questions of *ought* are unique to the human mind and world—they are meaningless as applied to a nonhuman situation.

I reject the proposition that we *ought* to respect the "balance of nature" or to "preserve the environment" unless the reason for doing so, express or implied, is the benefit of man.

I reject the idea that there is a "right" or "morally correct" state of nature to which we should return. The word "nature" has no normative connotation. Was it "right" or "wrong" for the earth's crust to heave in contortion and create mountains and seas? Was it "right" for the first amphibian to crawl up out of the primordial ooze? Was it "wrong" for plants to reproduce themselves and alter the atmospheric composition in favor of oxygen? For animals to alter the atmosphere in favor of carbon dioxide both by breathing oxygen and eating plants? No answers can be given to these questions because they are meaningless questions.

All this may seem obvious to the point of being tedious, but much of the present controversy over environment and pollution rests on tacit normative assumptions about just such nonnormative phenomena: that it is "wrong" to impair penguins with DDT, but not to slaughter cattle for prime rib roasts. That it is wrong to kill stands of sugar pines with industrial fumes, but not to cut sugar pines and build housing for the poor. Every man is entitled to his own preferred definition of Walden Pond, but there is no definition that has any moral superiority over another, except by reference to the selfish needs of the human race.

From the fact that there is no normative definition of the natural state, it follows that there is no normative definition of clean air or pure water—hence no definition of polluted air—or of pollution—except by reference to the needs of man. The "right" composition of the atmosphere is one which has some dust in it and some lead in it and some hydrogen sulfide in it—just those amounts that attend a sensibly organized society thoughtfully and knowledgeably pursuing the greatest possible satisfaction for its human members.

The first and most fundamental step toward solution of our environmental problems is a clear recognition that our objective is not pure air or water but rather some optimal state of pollution. That step immediately suggests the question: How do we define and attain the level of pollution that will yield the maximum possible amount of human satisfaction?

Low levels of pollution contribute to human satisfaction but so do food and shelter and education and music. To attain ever lower levels of pollution, we must pay the cost of having less of these other things. I contrast that view of the cost of pollution control with the more popular statement that pollution control will "cost" very large numbers of dollars. The popular statement is true in some senses, false in others; sorting out the true and false senses is of some importance. The first step in that sorting process is to achieve a clear understanding of the difference between dollars and resources. Resources are the wealth of our nation; dollars are merely claim checks upon those resources. Resources are of vital importance; dollars are comparatively trivial.

Four categories of resources are sufficient for our purposes: At any given time a nation, or a planet if you prefer, has a stock of labor, of technological skill, of capital goods, and of natural resources (such as mineral deposits, timber, water, land, etc.). These resources can be used in various combinations to yield goods and services of all kinds—in some limited quantity. The quantity will be larger if they are combined efficiently, smaller if combined inefficiently. But in either event the resource stock is limited, the goods and services that they can be made to yield are limited; even the most efficient use of them will yield less than our population, in the aggregate, would like to have.

If one considers building a new dam, it is appropriate to say that it will be costly in the sense that it will require x hours of labor, y tons of steel and concrete, and z amount of capital goods. If these resources are devoted to the dam, then they cannot be used to build hospitals, fishing rods, schools, or electric can openers. That is the meaningful sense in which the dam is costly.

Quite apart from the very important question of how wisely we can combine our resources to produce goods and services, is the very different question of how they get distributed—who gets how many goods? Dollars constitute the claim checks which are distributed among people and which control their share of national output. Dollars are nearly valueless pieces of paper except to the extent that they do represent claim checks to some fraction of the output of goods and services. Viewed as claim checks, all the dollars outstanding during any period of time are worth, in the aggregate, the goods and services that are available to be claimed with them during that period—neither more nor less.

It is far easier to increase the supply of dollars than to increase the production of goods and services—printing dollars is easy. But printing more dollars doesn't help because each dollar then simply becomes a claim to fewer goods, i.e., becomes worth less.

The point is this: many people fall into error upon hearing the statement that the decision to build a dam, or to clean up a river, will cost $X million. It is regrettably easy to say: "It's only money. This is a wealthy country, and we have lots of money." But you cannot build a dam or clean a river with $X million—unless you also have a match, you can't even make a fire. One builds a dam or cleans a river by diverting labor and steel and trucks and factories from making one kind of goods to making another. The cost in dollars is merely a shorthand way of describing the extent of the diversion necessary. If we build a dam for $X million, then we must recognize that we will have $X million less housing and food and medical care and electric can openers as a result.

Similarly, the costs of controlling pollution are best expressed in terms of the other goods we will have to give up to do the job. This is not to say the job should not be done. Badly as we need more housing, more medical care, and more can openers, and more symphony orchestras, we could do with somewhat less of them, in my judgment at least, in exchange for somewhat cleaner air and rivers. But that is the nature of the trade-off, and analysis of the problem is advanced if that unpleasant reality is kept in mind. Once the trade-off relationship is clearly perceived, it is possible to state in a very general way what the optimal level of pollution is. I would state it as follows:

People enjoy watching penguins. They enjoy relatively clean air and smog-free vistas. Their health is improved by relatively clean water and air. Each of these benefits is a type of good or service. As a society we would be well advised to give up one washing machine if the resources that would have gone into that washing machine can yield greater human satisfaction when diverted into pollution control. We should give up one hospital if the resources thereby freed would yield more human satisfaction when devoted to elimination of noise in our cities. And so on, trade-off by trade-off, we should divert our productive capacities from the production of existing goods and services to the production of a cleaner, quieter, more pastoral nation up to—and no further than—the point at which we value more highly the next washing machine or hospital that we would have to do without than we value the next unit

of environmental improvement that the diverted resources would create.

Now this proposition seems to me unassailable but so general and abstract as to be unhelpful—at least unadministerable in the form stated. It assumes we can measure in some way the incremental units of human satisfaction yielded by very different types of goods. The proposition must remain a pious abstraction until I can explain how this measurement process can occur. . . . But I insist that the proposition stated describes the result for which we should be striving—and again, that it is always useful to know what your target is even if your weapons are too crude to score a bull's eye.

The Ethical Basis of the Economic View
of the Environment

A. Myrick Freeman III

I. Introduction

At least in some circles, economists' recommendations for a policy concerning pollution and other environmental problems are regarded with a good deal of skepticism and perhaps even distrust.[1] For example, when we suggest that economic factors such as cost should be taken into account in setting ambient air quality standards, we are told that it is wrong to put a price on human life or beauty. And when we argue that placing a tax or charge on the emissions of pollutants would be more effective than the present regulatory approach, we are told that this would simply create "licenses to pollute" and pollution is wrong.

I am not sure how much of this type of reaction stems from a misunderstanding or lack of familiarity with the arguments for the economists' policy recommendations, and how much is due to a rejection of the premises, analysis, and value judgments on which these recommendations are based. And I will not attempt to answer that question here. Rather, I will limit myself to making clear the rationale for some of our recommendations concerning policy and the value judgments on which they are based.

To the economist, the environment is a scarce resource which contributes to human welfare. The economic problem of the environment is a small part of the overall economic problem: how to manage our activities so as to meet our material needs and wants in the face of scarcity. The economists' recommendations concerning the environment flow out of our analysis of the overall economic problem. It will be useful to begin with a brief review of the principal conclusions of economic reasoning concerning the allocation of scarce resources to

Source: Center for the Study of Value and Social Policy at the University of Colorado at Boulder (1983). Reprinted by permission.

essentially unlimited needs and wants. After reviewing some basic economic principles and the criteria that economists have used in the evaluation of alternative economic outcomes, I will explain the economic view of the environment and some of the major policy recommendations which follow from that view. I will conclude by identifying some of the major questions and possible sources of disagreement about the validity and usefulness of economic reasoning as a way of looking at environmental problems.

II. Some Basic Economics

We begin with the basic premises that the purpose of economic activity is to increase the well-being of the individuals who make up the society, and that each individual is the best judge of how well off he or she is in a given situation. To give this premise some operational content, we assume that each individual has preferences over alternative bundles of economic goods and services. In other words, the individual can rank all of the alternative combinations of goods and services he can consume from most preferred to least preferred. Of course there may be ties in this ranking.[2] We assume that individuals act so as to obtain the most preferred (to them) bundles given the constraints imposed by technology and the availability of the means of production.

These preferences of individuals are assumed to have two properties which are important for our purposes: substitutability among the components of bundles, and the absence of limits on wants. Substitutability simply means that preferences are not lexicographic. Consider a consumption bundle labeled A with specified quantities of food, clothing, shelter, and so forth. Now consider alternative bundle B which contains 10 percent less clothing and the same quantities of all other goods. Since B contains less clothing, it is less desirable to the individual. In other words, bundle A is preferred to bundle B. But substitutability means that it is possible to alter the composition of bundle B by increasing the quantities of one or more of the other goods in the bundle to the point where the individual will consider A and B as equally preferred. That is to say, the individual can be compensated for the loss of some quantity of one good by increases in the quantities of one or more of the other goods. The value of the lost clothing to this individual can be expressed in terms of the quantities of the other goods which must be added to the bundle to substitute for it. This principle is the basis of the economic theory of value. In a market economy where all goods and services can be bought and sold at given prices in markets, the necessary amount of substitution can be expressed in money terms.

The significance of the substitution principle for the economic view of the environment should be apparent. If the substitution principle applies to good things that are derived from a clean environment, then it is possible to put a price on those things. The price is the money value of the quantities of other goods that must be substituted to compensate for the loss of the environmental good. Whether the substitution principle applies to those things derived from the environment is essentially an empirical question about human behavior. It is possible to think of examples that violate the substitution principle. The slogan printed on all license plates issued in New Hampshire ("Live Free or Die") shows a lexicographic preference for freedom. If the statement is believed, there is no quantity of material goods that can compensate for the loss of freedom. It is not clear that all individuals have lexicographic preferences for freedom. And the question for our purpose is whether there are similar examples in the realm of environmental goods.

By unlimited wants, I mean that for any conceivable bundle A, it is possible to describe another bundle B with larger quantities of one or more goods such that an individual would prefer B to A. Is this property plausible? It is possible to imagine some upper limit on the gross consumption of food as measured by calories or weight. But quality and variety are also goods over which individuals have preferences. And it may always be possible to conceive of a bundle containing a more exotic dish or one with more careful preparation with higher quality ingredients. Again, whether this property is plausible is an empirical question about human behavior. But its significance for anti-growth arguments is apparent.

Much of economic theory is concerned with understanding how individuals with given preferences interact as they seek to attain the highest level of satisfaction. Many societies have developed systems of markets for guiding this interaction; and historically the bulk of economists' effort has gone to the study of market systems. In part this can be explained by the historic fact that economics as a separate discipline emerged during a period of rapid industrialization, economic change, and growth in the extent of the market system. But it is also true that as early as Adam Smith's time, it was recognized that a freely functioning market system had significant advantages over alternative means of organizing and coordinating economic activity. Even in more primitive societies, markets facilitate exchange whereby an individual can attain a more preferred bundle by giving up less preferred goods in exchange for more preferred goods. And in more developed economies, markets also facilitate the specialization of productive activities and the realization of economies of scale in production.

A market system can be said to have advantages only in terms of some criterion and in comparison with some alternative set of economic institutions. It is time now to make the criterion explicit. The criterion is economic efficiency, or after the man who first developed the concept in formal terms, Pareto Optimality. An economy has reached a state of economic efficiency if it is not possible to rearrange production and consumption activity so as to make at least one person better off except by making one or more other individuals worse off. To put it differently, an economy is in an inefficient position if it is possible to raise at least one individual to a more preferred consumption bundle while hurting no one. If an economy is in an inefficient position, it is possible to achieve a sort of "free lunch" in the form of an improvement for at least one individual *at no cost* to anyone.

One of the fundamental conclusions of economic reasoning is that given certain conditions a market system will always reach a position of economic efficiency. The conditions are

that: *(a)* all goods that matter to individuals (that is, all goods over which individuals have preference orderings) must be capable of being bought and sold in markets; and *(b)* all such markets must be perfectly competitive in the sense that there are large numbers of both buyers and sellers no one of which has any influence over market price.[3] The extensiveness and competitiveness of markets are sufficient to assure that economic efficiency in the allocation of resources will be achieved. This conclusion provides much of the intellectual rationale for *laissez faire* capitalism as well as the justification for many forms of government intervention in the market, for example, anti-monopoly policies, the regulation of the prices charged by monopolies such as electric utilities, and, as we shall see, the control of pollution.

The ideal of efficiency and the perfectly competitive market economy which guarantees its attainment acts as a yardstick by which the performance of real world economies can be measured. If there is monopoly power in a market, the yardstick shows that there is a shortfall in the performance of the economy. It would be possible by eliminating monopoly and restoring perfect competition to the market to increase output in such a way that no one would be made worse off and at least one person would be made better off. How monopoly power is to be eliminated without making at least the monopolist worse off is a difficult question in practice. But I will return to this point below.

The ideal of perfect competition and economic efficiency is a powerful one. But it is not without its limitations. Perhaps the most important of these is that there is no single, unique Pareto Optimum position. Rather there is an infinite number of alternative Pareto Optimums, each different from the others in the way in which it distributes economic well-being among the members of the society.

A society in which one individual owned all of the capital, land, and resources could achieve a Pareto Optimum position. It would likely be one in which all but one of the individuals lived in relative poverty. But it would not be possible to make any of the workers better off without making the rich person worse off. This Pareto Optimum position would be quite different from the Pareto Optimum which would be achieved by an economy in which each individual owned equal shares of the land, capital, and so forth. Which Pareto Optimum position is attained by an economy depends upon the initial distribution of the entitlements to receive income from the ownership of factor inputs such as land and capital. Each conceivable distribution of rights of ownership has associated with it a different Pareto Optimum. And each Pareto Optimum position represents the best that can be done for the members of society *conditioned* upon acceptance of the initial distribution of entitlements. Since the ranking of different Pareto Optimums requires the comparison of alternative distributions of well-being, it is inherently an ethical question. There is nothing more that economic reasoning can contribute to this issue.

III. Policy Evaluation

Given the fact that the real world economy is characterized by many market imperfections and failures and that for a variety of reasons it is not possible to create the perfect, all encompassing market system of the Pareto ideal, we must consider piecemeal efforts to make things better at the margin. The question is: what criterion should be used to evaluate policy proposals which would alter the outcomes of existing market processes?

The Pareto Criterion says to accept only those policies that benefit some people while harming no one. In other words, this criterion rules out any policy which imposes costs on any individual, no matter how small the cost and no matter how large the benefits to any other members of the society. This is a very stringent criterion in practice. There are very few policy proposals which do not impose some costs on some members of the society. For example, a policy to curb pollution reduces the incomes and welfares of those who find it more profitable to pollute than to control their waste. The Pareto Criterion is not widely accepted by economists as a guide to policy. And it plays no role in what might be called "mainstream" environmental economics.[4]

The most widely accepted criterion asks whether the aggregate of the gains to those made better off measured in money terms is greater than the money value of the losses of those made worse off. If the gains exceed the losses, the policy is accepted by this criterion. The gains and losses are to be measured in terms of each individual's willingness-to-pay to receive the gains or to prevent the policy-imposed losses. Thus this criterion draws on the substitutability principle discussed earlier. If the gains or losses came in the form of goods over which individuals have lexicographic preferences, this criterion could not be utilized.

This criterion is justified on ethical grounds by observing that if the gains outweigh the losses, it would be possible for the gainers to compensate fully the losers with money payments and still themselves be better off with the policy. Thus if the compensation were actually paid, there would be no losers, only gainers. This criterion is sometimes referred to as the potential compensation criterion. This criterion is the basis of the benefit-cost analysis of public policy. Benefits are the money values of the gains to individuals and costs are the money values of the losses to individuals. If benefits exceed costs, the gainers could potentially compensate the losers.

There are two observations concerning the potential compensation criterion. First, the criterion is silent on the question of whether compensation should be paid or not. If society decides that compensation shall always be paid, compensation becomes a mechanism for assuring that there are never any losers and that all adopted policies pass the Pareto Criterion. On the other hand, if society decides that compensation should never be paid, the potential compensation criterion becomes a modern form of utilitarianism in which the aggregate of utilities is measured by the sum of the money values of all goods consumed by all individuals. Finally, society may decide that whether compensation should be paid or not depends upon the identity and relative deservingness of the gainers and losers. If this is the case, then society must adopt some basis for determining relative deservingness, that is, some ethical rule concerning the justness of creating gains and imposing losses on individuals.

The second observation concerns the measurement of gains and losses in money terms.

Willingness to pay for a good is constrained by ability to pay. Economic theory shows that an individual's willingness to pay for a good depends on his income and that for most goods, higher income means higher willingness to pay, other things equal. As a consequence, the potential compensation criterion has a tendency to give greater weight to the preferences of those individuals with higher incomes. As a practical matter there are reasons to doubt that this bias is quantitatively significant in most cases. But the question is often raised when benefit-cost analysis is applied to environmental goods. And it is well to keep this point in mind.

IV. Environmental Economics

The environment is a resource which yields a variety of valuable services to individuals in their roles as consumers and producers. The environment is the source of the basic means of life support—clean air and clean water. It provides the means for growing food. It is a source of minerals and other raw materials. It can be used for recreation. It is the source of visual amenities. And it can be used as a place to deposit the wastes from production and consumption activities. The economic problem of the environment is that it is a scarce resource. It cannot be called upon to provide all of the desired quantities of all of the services at the same time. Greater use of one type of environmental service usually means that less of some other type of service is available. Thus the use of the environment involves trade-offs. And the environment must be managed as an economic resource. But unlike other resources such as land, labor, or capital, the market does not perform well in allocating the environment to its highest valued uses. This is primarily because individuals do not have effective property rights in units of the environment.

For example, if a firm wishes to use one hour of labor time in production, it must find an individual who is willing to provide one hour of labor and it must pay that individual an amount at least equal to the value to the individual of

that time in an alternative use. If a voluntary exchange of labor for money takes place, it is presumed that neither party is made worse off, and it is likely that both parties benefit from the exchange. Otherwise they would not have agreed to it. But if a firm wishes to dump a ton of sulfur dioxide into the atmosphere, it is under no obligation to determine whose health or whose view might be impaired by this use of the environment and to obtain their voluntary agreement through the payment of money. Thus firms need not take into account the costs imposed on others by their uses of the environment. Because there is no market for environmental services, the decentralized decision making of individuals and firms will result in a misallocation of environmental resources. The market fails. And the economy does not achieve a Pareto Optimum allocation.

Where markets have failed, economists have made two kinds of suggestions for dealing with market failure. The first is to see if markets can be established through the creation of legally transferable property rights in certain environmental services. If such property rights can be created, then markets can assume their proper role in achieving an efficient allocation of environmental services. Because of the indivisible nature of many aspects of the environment, for example, the urban air shed, there is limited scope for this solution. The second approach is to use various forms of government regulations, taxes, and subsidies to create incentives which replicate the incentives and outcomes that a perfectly functioning market would produce. Activities under this approach could include the setting of ambient air quality standards, placing limits on discharges from individual polluters, imposing taxes on pollution, and so forth. In the next section, I take up several specific applications of this approach to dealing with the environment in an economically rational manner.

V. Applications

Environment Quality Standards

An environmental quality standard is a legally established minimum level of cleanliness or maximum level of pollution in some part of the environment, for example, an urban air shed or a specific portion of a river. A standard, once established, can be the basis for enforcement actions against a polluter whose discharges cause the standard to be violated. The principle of Pareto Optimality provides a basis for determining at what level an environmental quality standard should be set. In general, Pareto Optimality requires that each good be provided at the level for which the marginal willingness to pay for the good (the maximum amount that an individual would be willing to give up to get one more unit of the good) is just equal to the cost of providing one more unit of the good (its marginal cost).

Consider for example an environment which is badly polluted because of existing industrial activity. Consider making successive one unit improvements in some measure of environment quality. For the first unit, individuals' marginal willingnesses to pay for a small improvement are likely to be high. The cost of the first unit of clean-up is likely to be low. The difference between them is a net benefit. Further increases in cleanliness bring further net benefits as long as the marginal willingness to pay is greater than the marginal cost. But as the environment gets cleaner, the willingness to pay for additional units of cleanliness decreases, while the additional cost of further cleanliness rises. At that point where the marginal willingness to pay just equals the marginal cost, the net benefit of further cleanliness is zero, and the total benefits of environmental improvement are at a maximum. This is the point at which the environmental quality standard should be set, if economic reasoning is followed.

There are two points to make about this approach to standard setting. First, an environmental quality standard set by this rule will almost never call for complete elimination of pollution. As the worst of the pollution is cleaned up, the willingness to pay for additional cleanliness will be decreasing, while the extra cost of further clean-up will be increasing. The extra cost of going from 95 percent clean-up to 100 percent clean-up may often be several times larger than the total cost of obtaining the first 95 percent clean-up. And it will seldom be

worth it in terms of willingness to pay. Several economists have argued that the air quality standards for ozone that were first established in 1971 were too stringent in terms of the relationship between benefits and costs. If this is true, then the resources devoted to controlling ozone could be put to better use in some other economic activity. Many economists have urged Congress to require that costs be compared with benefits in the setting of ambient air quality standards.

The second point is that the logic of benefit-cost analysis does not require that those who benefit pay for those benefits or that those who ultimately bear the cost of meeting a standard be compensated for those costs. It is true that if standards are set so as to maximize the net benefits, then the gainers could fully compensate the losers and still come out ahead. But when beneficiaries do not compensate losers, there is a political asymmetry. Those who benefit call for ever more strict standards and clean-up, because they obtain the gross benefits and bear none of the costs. While those who must control pollution call for less strict standards.

Charging for Pollution

One way to explain the existence of pollution is in terms of the incentives faced by firms and others whose activities generate waste products. Each unit of pollution discharged imposes costs or damages on other individuals. But typically the dischargers are not required to compensate the losers for these costs. Thus there is no economic incentive for the discharger to take those costs into account. This is the essence of the market failure argument.

If it is impractical to establish a private market in rights to clean air, it may be possible to create a pseudo-market by government regulation. Suppose that the government imposed a charge or tax on each unit of pollution discharged and set the tax equal to the money value of the damage that pollution caused to others. Then each discharger would compare the tax cost of discharging a unit of pollution with the cost of controlling or preventing that discharge. As long as the cost of control were less than the tax or charge, the firm would prevent the discharge. In fact it would control pollution back to the point where its marginal cost of control was just equal to the marginal tax and by indirection equal to the marginal damage the pollution would cause. The properly set tax or charge would cause the firm to undertake on its own accord the optimum amount of pollution control. By replicating a market incentive, the government regulation would bring about an efficient allocation of resources.

Since the firm would likely find that some level of discharges would be more preferred to a zero discharge level, it would be paying taxes to the government equal to the damages caused by the remaining discharges. In principle, the government could use the tax revenues to compensate those who are damaged by the remaining discharges.

Risk and the Value of Life

Because some forms of pollution are harmful to human health and may increase mortality, economists have had to confront the question of the economic value of life. It turns out that the "value of life" is an unfortunate phrase which does not really reflect the true nature of the question at hand. This is because pollutants do not single out and kill readily identifiable people. Rather, they result in usually small increases in the *probability* of death to exposed *groups* of individuals. So what is really at issue is the economic value of reductions in the risk of death. This is a manageable question and one on which we have some evidence.

People in their daily lives make a variety of choices that involve trading off changes in the risk of death with other economic goods whose values we can measure in money terms. For example, some people travel to work in cars rather than by bus or by walking because of the increased convenience and lower travel time, even though they increase the risk of dying prematurely. Also, some people accept jobs with known higher risks of accidental death because those jobs pay higher wages. The "value" of saving a life can be calculated from information on individuals' trade-offs between risk and money.

Suppose there were a thousand people each of whom has a probability of .004 of dying during this next year. Suppose an environmental change would reduce that probability to .003, a change of .001. Let us ask each individual to state his or her maximum willingness to pay for that reduction in risk. Suppose for simplicity that each person states the same willingness to pay, $100. The total willingness to pay of the group is $100,000. If the policy is adopted, there will on average be one less death during this next year, (.001 × 1000). The total willingness to pay for a change that results in one fewer deaths is $100,000. This is the "value of life" that is revealed from individual preferences. Efforts to estimate the value of life from data on wage premiums for risky jobs have led to values in the range of $500,000 to $5 million.

If an economic approach is to be used in setting standards for toxic chemicals, hazardous air pollutants, and so forth, then some measure of the value of reductions in risk must be the basis for computing the benefits of pollution control. There are immense practical difficulties in providing accurate, refined estimates of this value. But these are not my concern here. Rather I am concerned with the ethical issues of even attempting to employ this approach to environmental decision making.

I think that the principal ethical issue here is compensation. Suppose that a standard has been set for an air pollutant such that even with the standard being met the population has a higher probability of death than if the pollutant were fully controlled. The standard was presumably set at this level because the cost of eliminating the remaining risk exceeded the individuals' willingness to pay to eliminate the risk. Many people would argue that the risk should be reduced to zero regardless of cost. After all, some people are being placed at risk while others are benefiting by avoiding the cost of controlling pollution. But suppose the population is compensated for bearing this risk with money from, for example, a charge on the polluting substance. Is there then any reason to argue for reducing pollution to zero? If the pollution were reduced to zero and the compensation withdrawn, the people at risk would be no better off in their own eyes than they are with the pollution and compensation. But some people would be made worse off because of the additional costs of eliminating the pollution.[5]

Future Generations

Some environmental decisions impose risks on future generations in order to achieve present benefits. In standard benefit-cost analysis based on the economic efficiency criterion, a social rate of discount is used to weight benefits and costs occurring at different points in time.[6] There have been long debates about the appropriateness of applying a discount rate to effects on future generations. It is argued that ethically unacceptable damage imposed on future generations may be made to appear acceptably small, from today's perspective, by discounting.

Consider the case where this generation wishes to do something which will yield benefits today worth \$B. This act will also set in motion some physical process which will cause \$D of damages 100,000 years from now. Assume that the events are certain and that the values of benefits and damages based on individual preferences can be accurately measured.

In brief, the argument against discounting is: at any reasonable (nonzero) discount rate, r, the present value of damages

$$\$P = \frac{\$D}{(1 + r)100,000}$$

will be trivial and almost certainly will be outweighed by present benefits. The implication of discounting is that we care virtually nothing about the damages that we inflict on future generations provided that they are postponed sufficiently far into the future. Therefore, the argument goes, we should discard the discounting procedure. Instead, since the real issue is intergenerational equity, a zero discount rate should be used. This would represent the most appropriate value judgment about the relative weights to be attached to the consumption of present and future generations.

I believe this argument is confused. Certainly, the problem is equity; but that has nothing to do with discounting. Rather, the equity question revolves around the distinction between actual and potential compensation.

In order to separate the compensation and discounting issues, consider a project for which both benefits and costs are realized today. Whenever benefits are greater than costs, the efficiency criterion says that the project should be undertaken, even if the benefits and costs accrue to different groups. This is because there is at least the *possibility* of compensation. Whether compensation should be paid or not is a value judgment hinging on equity considerations.

Now consider the intergenerational case. If \$B is greater than \$P (the discounted present value of future damages), the project is worthwhile and should be undertaken if the objective is economic efficiency. If the trivial sum of \$P is set aside now at interest, it will grow to

$$(1+r)100,000 \ \$P$$

which of course is the same as \$D and therefore by definition will just compensate the future generation for the damages our actions will have imposed on them. If actual compensation is provided for, no one, present or future, will be made worse off, and some will benefit.

Some may wish to adhere to the principle that compensation should *always* be paid. The principle would apply to losers in the present as well as future generations. The discount rate would help them to calculate the amount to be set aside for future payment. Others may wish to say that whether compensation should be paid or not depends on the relative positions of potential gainers and losers. Finally some will choose to ignore the compensation question entirely. But no matter how they resolve the compensation question, they should discount future damages.

Ecological Effects

Suppose that an accidental spill of a toxic chemical or crude oil wipes out the population of some marine organism in a certain area. What is the economic value of this damage? If the organism is a fish that is sought by sports or commercial fishermen, then there are standard economic techniques for determining the willingness to pay for or value of fish in the water. If the organism is part of the food chain which supports a commercially valuable fishery, then it is also possible, at least conceptually, to establish the biological link between the organism and the economic system. The value of the organism is based on its contribution to maintaining the stock of the commercially valued fish. But if there is no link between the organism and human production or consumption activity, there is no basis for establishing an economic value. Those species that lie completely outside of the economic system also are beyond the reach of the economic rubric for establishing value.

Some people have suggested alternative bases for establishing values, for example, cost of replacing the organisms, or cost of replacing biological functions such as photosynthesis and nitrogen fixation. But if those functions have no economic value to man, for example, because there are substitute organisms to perform them, then we would not be willing to pay the full cost of replacement. And this signifies that the economic value is less, perhaps much less, than replacement cost.

Rather than introduce some arbitrary or biased method for imputing a value to such organisms, I prefer to be honest about the limitations of the economic approach to determining values. This means that we should acknowledge that certain ecological effects are not commensurable with economic effects measured in dollars. Where trade-offs between noncommensurable magnitudes are involved, choices must be made through the political system.

VI. Conclusions

The argument for the adoption of the economists' point of view concerning environmental policy can be summarized as follows. Given the premises about individual preferences and the value judgment that satisfying these preferences should be the objective of policy, the adoption of the economists' recommendations concerning environmental policy will always lead to a potential Pareto improvement, that is, it will always be possible through taxes and compensating payments to make sure that at least some people are better off and that no one loses. Society could choose not to make these compensating payments; but this choice should

be on the basis of some ethical judgment concerning the deservingness of the gainers and losers from the policy.

It might be helpful at this point to review and summarize these premises and value judgments so that they might be in the focus of discussion:

1. Should individual preferences matter? If not individual preferences, then whose preferences should matter? What about ecological effects that have no perceptible effect on human welfare, that is, that lie outside of the set of things over which individuals have preferences?

2. Does the substitution principle hold for environmental services? Or are individuals' preferences for environmental goods lexicographic? This is an empirical question. Economists have developed a substantial body of evidence that people are willing to make trade-offs between environmental goods such as recreation, visual amenities, and healthful air and other economic goods.

3. Are preferences characterized by unlimited wants? This is also an empirical question. But I think that most economists would agree that if there are such limits, we have not begun to approach them for the vast bulk of the citizens of this world. A related question is whether it should be the objective of economic activity to satisfy wants without limits? But this question is more closely related to question (1) concerning the role of individual preferences.

4. Is achieving an efficient allocation of resources that important? Or, as Kelman (1981) has argued, should we be willing to accept less economic efficiency in order to preserve the idea that environmental values are in some sense superior to economic values? An affirmative answer to the latter question implies a lexicographic preference system and a rejection of the substitution principle for environmental goods.

5. Should compensation always be paid? Paid sometimes? Never? This is an ethical question. But as I have indicated, I think it plays a central role in judging the ethical im-

plications of economists' environmental policy recommendations. Not only is there the question of whether compensation should be paid, but also the question of who should be compensated. For example, should compensation be paid to those who are damaged by the optimal level of pollution? Or should compensation be paid to those who lose because of the imposition of pollution control requirements?

References

Freeman, A. Myrick, III. "Equity, Efficiency, and Discounting: The Reasons for Discounting Intergenerational Effects," *Futures* (October, 1977), 375–376.

Kelman, Steven. "Economists and the Environmental Muddle," *The Public Interest* 641 (Summer, 1981), 106–123.

Peacock, Alan T. and Charles K. Rowley. *Welfare Economics: A Liberal Restatement*, London, M. Robertson, 1975.

Notes

1. For some empirical evidence in support of this assertion, see Kelman (1981).
2. This is equivalent to saying that the individual has a utility function which assigns utility numbers to all possible consumption bundles. More preferred bundles have higher utility numbers.
3. There are other more technical conditions which need not concern us here.
4. For a different view of the Pareto Criterion and public policy, see Peacock and Rowley (1975).
5. In discussions of the use of risk-benefit analysis in policy making, the distinction is sometimes made between voluntary and involuntary risk. The argument being made is that involuntary risks are somehow worse. But I think that this misses the point. The real distinction is between compensated and uncompensated risk. A compensated risk is one, by the definition of compensation, that the individual would bear voluntarily.
6. The following argument is based on Freeman (1977).

At the Shrine of Our Lady of Fàtima, or Why Political Questions Are Not All Economic

Mark Sagoff

Lewiston, New York, a well-to-do community near Buffalo, is the site of the Lake Ontario Ordinance Works, where the federal government, years ago, disposed of the residues of the Manhattan Project. These radioactive wastes are buried but are not forgotten by the residents, who say that when the wind is southerly radon gas blows through the town. Several parents at a recent conference I attended there described their terror on learning that cases of leukemia had been found among area children. They feared for their own lives as well. At the other sides of the table, officials from New York State and from local corporations replied that these fears were ungrounded. People who smoke, they said, take greater risks than people who live close to waste disposal sites. One speaker talked in terms of "rational methodologies of decisionmaking." This aggravated the parents' rage and frustration.

The speaker suggested that the townspeople, were they to make their decision in a free market, would choose to live near the hazardous waste facility, if they knew the scientific facts. He told me later they were irra-

Source: *Arizona Law Review* Vol. 23, pp. 1283–1298. Copyright © 1981 by the Arizona Board of Regents. Reprinted by permission.

tional—he said, "neurotic"—because they refused to recognize or to act upon their own interests. The residents of Lewiston were unimpressed with his analysis of their "willingness to pay" to avoid this risk or that. They did not see what risk-benefit analysis had to do with the issues they raised.

If you take the Military Highway (as I did) from Buffalo to Lewiston, you will pass through a formidable wasteland. Landfills stretch in all directions, where enormous trucks—tiny in that landscape—incessantly deposit sludge which great bulldozers, like yellow ants, then push into the ground. These machines are the only signs of life, for in the miasma that hangs in the air, no birds, not even scavengers, are seen. Along colossal power lines which criss-cross this dismal land, the dynamos at Niagara send electric power south, where factories have fled, leaving their remains to decay. To drive along this road is to feel, oddly, the mystery and awe one experiences in the presence of so much power and decadence.

Henry Adams had a similar response to the dynamos on display at the Paris Exposition of 1900. To him "the dynamo became a symbol of infinity."[1] To Adams, the dynamo functioned as the modern equivalent of the Virgin, that is, as the center and focus of power. "Before the end, one began to pray to it; inherited instinct taught the natural expression of man before silent and infinite force."[2]

Adams asks in his essay "The Dynamo and the Virgin" how the products of modern industrial civilization will compare with those of the religious culture of the Middle Ages. If he could see the landfills and hazardous waste facilities bordering the power stations and honeymoon hotels of Niagara Falls he would know the answer. He would understand what happens when efficiency replaces infinity as the central conception of value. The dynamos at Niagara will not produce another Mont-Saint-Michel. "All the steam in the world," Adams wrote, "could not, like the Virgin, build Chartres."[3]

At the Shrine of Our Lady of Fàtima, on a plateau north of the Military Highway, a larger than life sculpture of Mary looks into the chemical air. The original of this shrine stands in central Portugal, where in May, 1917, three children said they saw a Lady, brighter than the sun, raised on a cloud in an evergreen tree.[4] Five months later, on a wet and chilly October day, the Lady again appeared, this time before a large crowd. Some who were skeptical did not see the miracle. Others in the crowd reported, however, that "the sun appeared and seemed to tremble, rotate violently and fall, dancing over the heads of the throng. . . ."[5]

The Shrine was empty when I visited it. The cult of Our Lady of Fàtima, I imagine, has only a few devotees. The cult of Pareto optimality, however, has many. Where some people see only environmental devastation, its devotees perceive efficiency, utility, and the maximization of wealth. They see the satisfaction of wants. They envision the good life. As I looked over the smudged and ruined terrain I tried to share that vision. I hoped that Our Lady of Fàtima, worker of miracles, might serve, at least for the moment, as the Patroness of cost-benefit analysis. I thought of all the wants and needs that are satisfied in a landscape of honeymoon cottages, commercial strips, and dumps for hazardous waste. I saw the miracle of efficiency. The prospect, however, looked only darker in that light.

I

This essay concerns the economic decisions we make about the environment. It also concerns our political decisions about the environment. Some people have suggested that ideally these should be the same, that all environmental problems are problems in distribution. According to this view there is an environmental problem only when some resource is not allocated in equitable and efficient ways.[6]

This approach to environmental policy is pitched entirely at the level of the consumer. It is his or her values that count, and the measure of these values is the individual's willingness to pay. The problem of justice or fairness in society becomes, then, the problem of distributing goods and services so that more people get more of what they want to buy. A condo on the beach. A snowmobile for the mountains. A tank full of gas. A day of labor. The only values we have, on this view, are those which a market can price.[7]

How much do you value open space, a stand of trees, an "unspoiled" landscape? Fifty dollars? A hundred? A thousand? This is one way to measure value. You could compare the amount consumers would pay for a townhouse or coal or a landfill and the amount they would pay to preserve an area in its "natural" state. If users would pay more for the land with the house, the coal mine, or the landfill, than without—less construction and other costs of development—then the efficient thing to do is to improve the land and thus increase its value. That is why we have so many tract developments. And pizza stands. And gas stations. And strip mines. And landfills. How much did you spend last year to preserve open space? How much for pizza and gas? "In principle, the ultimate measure of environmental quality," as one basic text assures us, "is the value people place on these . . . services or their *willingness to pay*."[8]

Willingness to pay. What is wrong with that? The rub is this: not all of us think of ourselves simply as *consumers*. Many of us regard ourselves *as citizens* as well. We act as consumers to get what we want *for ourselves*. We act as citizens to achieve what we think is right or best *for the community*. The question arises, then, whether what we want for ourselves individually as consumers is consistent with the goals we would set for ourselves collectively as citizens. Would I vote for the sort of things I shop for? Are my preferences as a consumer consistent with my judgments as a citizen?

They are not. I am schizophrenic. Last year, I fixed a couple of tickets and was happy to do so since I saved fifty dollars. Yet, at election time, I helped to vote the corrupt judge out of office. I speed on the highway; yet I want the police to enforce laws against speeding. I used to buy mixers in returnable bottles—but who can bother to return them? I buy only disposables now, but, to soothe my conscience, I urge my state senator to outlaw one-way containers. I love my car; I hate the bus. Yet I vote for candidates who promise to tax gasoline to pay for public transportation. I send my dues to the Sierra Club to protect areas in Alaska I shall never visit. And I support the work of the American League to Abolish Capital Punishment although, personally, I have nothing to gain one way or the other. (When I hang, I will hang myself.) And of course I applaud the Endangered Species Act, although I have no earthly use for the Colorado squawfish or the Indiana bat. I support almost any political cause that I think will defeat my consumer interests. This is because I have contempt for—although I act upon—those interests. I have an "Ecology Now" sticker on a car that leaks oil everywhere it's parked.

The distinction between consumer and citizen preferences has long vexed the theory of public finance. Should the public economy serve the same goals as the household economy? May it serve, instead, goals emerging from our association as citizens? The question asks if we may collectively strive for and achieve only those items we individually compete for and consume. Should we aspire, instead, to public goals we may legislate as a nation?

The problem, insofar as it concerns public finance, is stated as follows by R. A. Musgrave, who reports a conversation he had with Gerhard Colm.

He [Colm] holds that the individual voter dealing with political issues has a frame of reference quite distinct from that which underlies his allocation of income as a consumer. In the latter situation the voter acts as a private individual determined by self-interest and deals with his personal wants; in the former, he acts as a political being guided by his image of a good society. The two, Colm holds, are different things.[9]

Are these two different things? Stephen Marglin suggests that they are. He writes:

The preferences that govern one's unilateral market actions no longer govern his actions when the form of reference is shifted from the market to the political arena. The Economic Man and the Citizen are for all intents and purposes two different individuals. It is not a question, therefore, of rejecting individual . . . preference maps; it is, rather, that market and political preference maps are inconsistent.[10]

Marglin observes that if this is true, social choices optimal under one set of preferences will not be optimal under another. What, then, is the meaning of "optimality"? He notices that if we take a person's true preferences to be those expressed in the market, we may, then, neglect or reject the preferences that person reveals in advocating a political cause or position. "One might argue on welfare grounds," Marglin speculates, "for authoritarian rejection of individuals' politically revealed preferences in favor of their market revealed preferences!"

II

On February 19, 1981, President Reagan published Executive Order 12,291 requiring all administrative agencies and departments to support every new major regulation with a cost-benefit analysis establishing that the benefits of the regulation to society outweigh its costs.[11] The Order directs the Office of Management and Budget (OMB) to review every such regulation on the basis of the adequacy of the cost-benefit analysis supporting it. This is a departure from tradition. Traditionally, regulations have been reviewed not by OMB but by the courts on the basis of their relation not to cost-benefit analysis but to authorizing legislation.

A month earlier, in January 1981, the Supreme Court heard lawyers for the American Textile Manufacturers Institute argue against a proposed Occupational Safety and Health Administration (OSHA) regulation which would have severely restricted the acceptable levels of cotton dust in textile plants.[12] The lawyers for industry argued that the benefits of the regulation would not equal the costs. The lawyers for the government contended that the law required the tough standard. OSHA, acting consistently with Executive Order 12,291, asked the Court not to decide the cotton dust case, in order to give the agency time to complete the cost-benefit analysis required by the textile industry. The Court declined to accept OSHA's request and handed down its opinion on June 17, 1981.[13]

The Supreme Court, in a 5–3 decision,

found that the actions of regulatory agencies which conform to the OSHA law need not be supported by cost-benefit analysis. In addition, the Court asserted that Congress in writing a statute, rather than the agencies in applying it, has the primary responsibility for balancing benefits and costs. The Court said:

When Congress passed the Occupational Health and Safety Act in 1970, it chose to place pre-eminent value on assuring employees a safe and healthful working environment, limited only by the feasibility of achieving such an environment. We must measure the validity of the Secretary's actions against the requirements of that Act.[14]

The opinion upheld the finding of the Appeals Court that "Congress itself struck the balance between costs and benefits in the mandate to the agency."[15]

The Appeals Court opinion in *American Textile Manufacturers* vs. *Donovan* supports the principle that legislatures are not necessarily bound to a particular conception of regulatory policy. Agencies that apply the law, therefore, may not need to justify on cost-benefit grounds the standards they set. These standards may conflict with the goal of efficiency and still express our political will as a nation. That is, they may reflect not the personal choices of self-interested individuals, but the collective judgments we make on historical, cultural, aesthetic, moral, and ideological grounds.

The appeal of the Reagan Administration to cost-benefit analysis, however, may arise more from political than economic considerations. The intention, seen in the most favorable light, may not be to replace political or ideological goals with economic ones but to make economic goals more apparent in regulation. This is not to say that Congress should function to reveal a collective willingness-to-pay just as markets reveal an individual willingness-to-pay. It is to suggest that Congress should do more to balance economic with ideological, aesthetic, and moral goals. To think that environmental or worker safety policy can be based exclusively on aspiration for a "natural" and "safe" world is as foolish as to hold that environmental law can be reduced to cost-benefit accounting. The more we move to one extreme, as I found in Lewiston, the more likely we are to hear from the other.

III

The labor unions won an important political victory when Congress passed the Occupational Safety and Health Act of 1970.[16] That Act, among other things, severely restricts worker exposure to toxic substances. It instructs the Secretary of Labor to set "the standard which most adequately assures, to the extent feasible . . . that no employee will suffer material impairment of health or functional capacity even if such employee has regular exposure to the hazard . . . for the period of his working life."[17]

Pursuant to this law, the Secretary of Labor, in 1977, reduced from ten to one part per million (ppm) the permissible ambient exposure level for benzene, a carcinogen for which no safe threshold is known. The American Petroleum Institute thereupon challenged the new standard in court.[18] It argued, with much evidence in its favor, that the benefits (to workers) of the one ppm standard did not equal the costs (to industry). The standard, therefore, did not appear to be a rational response to a market failure in that it did not strike an efficient balance between the interests of workers in safety and the interests of industry and consumers in keeping prices down.

The Secretary of Labor defended the tough safety standard on the ground that the law demanded it. An efficient standard might have required safety until it cost industry more to prevent a risk than it cost workers to accept it. Had Congress adopted this vision of public policy—one which can be found in many economics texts[19]—it would have treated workers not as ends-in-themselves but as means for the production of overall utility. And this, as the Secretary saw it, was what Congress refused to do.

The United States Court of Appeals for the Fifth Circuit agreed with the American Petroleum Institute and invalidated the one ppm benzene standard.[20] On July 2, 1980, the Supreme Court affirmed remanding the benzene

standard back to OSHA for revision.[21] The narrowly based Supreme Court decision was divided over the role economic considerations should play in judicial review. Justice Marshall, joined in dissent by three other justices, argued that the Court had undone on the basis of its own theory of regulatory policy an act of Congress inconsistent with that theory. He concluded that the plurality decision of the Court "requires the American worker to return to the political arena to win a victory that he won before in 1970."[22]

To reject cost-benefit analysis, as Justice Marshall would, as a basis for public policy making is not necessarily to reject cost-effectiveness analysis, which is an altogether different thing. "*Cost-benefit analysis,*" one commentator points out, "is used by the decision maker to establish societal goals as well as the means for achieving these goals, whereas *cost-effectiveness analysis* only compares alternative means for achieving 'given' goals."[23] Justice Marshall's dissent objects to those who would make efficiency the goal of public policy. It does not necessarily object to those who would accomplish as efficiently as possible the goals Congress sets.[24]

IV

When efficiency is the criterion of public safety and health one tends to conceive of social relations on the model of a market, ignoring competing visions of what we as a society should be like. Yet it is obvious that there are competing conceptions of how we should relate to one other. There are some who believe, on principle, that worker safety and environmental quality ought to be protected only insofar as the benefits of protection balance the costs. On the other hand, people argue, also on principle, that neither worker safety nor environmental quality should be treated merely as a commodity, to be traded at the margin for other commodities, but should be valued for its own sake. The conflict between these two principles is logical or moral, to be resolved by argument or debate. The question whether cost-benefit analysis should play a decisive role in policymaking is not to be decided by cost-benefit analysis. A contradiction between principles—between contending visions of the good society—cannot be settled by asking how much partisans are willing to pay for their beliefs.

The role of the *legislator,* the political role, may be more important to the individual than the role of *consumer.* The person, in other words, is not to be treated as merely a bundle of preferences to be juggled in cost-benefit analyses. The individual is to be respected as an advocate of ideas which are to be judged in relation to the reasons for them. If health and environmental statutes reflect a vision of society as something other than a market by requiring protections beyond what are efficient, then this may express not legislative ineptitude but legislative responsiveness to public values. To deny this vision because it is economically inefficient is simply to replace it with another vision. It is to insist that the ideas of the citizen be sacrificed to the psychology of the consumer.

We hear on all sides that government is routinized, mechanical, entrenched, and bureaucratized; the jargon alone is enough to dissuade the most mettlesome meddler. Who can make a difference? It is plain that for many of us the idea of a national political community has an abstract and suppositious quality. We have only our private conceptions of the good, if no way exists to arrive at a public one. This is only to note the continuation, in our time, of the trend Benjamin Constant described in the essay, *De La Liberte des Anciens Comparee a Celle des Modernes.*[25] Constant observes that the modern world, as opposed to the ancient, emphasizes civil over political liberties, the rights of privacy and property over those of community and participation. "Lost in the multitude," Constant writes, "the individual rarely perceives the influence that he exercises," and, therefore, must be content with "the peaceful enjoyment of private independence."[26] The individual asks only to be protected by laws common to all in his pursuit of his own self-interest. The citizen has been replaced by the consumer; the tradition of Rousseau has been supplanted by that of Locke and Mill.

Nowhere are the rights of the moderns, particularly the rights of privacy and property, less helpful than in the area of the natural environment. Here the values we wish to protect—cultural, historical, aesthetic, and moral—are public values; they depend not so much upon what each person wants individually as upon what he or she believes we stand for collectively. We refuse to regard worker health and safety as commodities; we regulate hazards as a matter of right. Likewise, we refuse to treat environmental resources simply as public goods in the economist's sense. Instead, we prevent significant deterioration of air quality not only as a matter of individual self-interest but also as a matter of collective self-respect. How shall we balance efficiency against moral, cultural, and aesthetic values in policy for the workplace and the environment? No better way has been devised to do this than by legislative debate ending in a vote. This is not the same thing as a cost-benefit analysis terminating in a bottom line.

V

It is the characteristic of cost-benefit analysis that it treats all value judgments other than those made on its behalf as nothing but statements of preference, attitude, or emotion, insofar as they are value judgments. The cost-benefit analyst regards as true the judgment that we should maximize efficiency or wealth. The analyst believes that this view can be backed by reasons;[27] the analyst does not regard it as a preference or want for which he or she must be willing to pay. The cost-benefit analyst, however, tends to treat all other normative views and recommendations as if they were nothing but subjective reports of mental states. The analyst supposes in all such cases that "this is right" and "this is what we ought to do" are equivalent to "I want this" and "this is what I prefer." Value judgments are beyond criticism if, indeed, they are nothing but expressions of personal preference; they are incorrigible since every person is in the best position to know what he or she wants. All valuation, according to this approach, happens *in foro interno;* debate *in foro publico* has no point. On this approach, the reasons that people give for their views, unless these people are welfare economists, do not count; what counts is how much they are willing to pay to satisfy their wants. Those who are willing to pay the most, for all intents and purposes, have the right view; theirs is the more informed opinion, the better aesthetic judgment, and the deeper moral insight.

The assumption that valuation is subjective, that judgments of good and evil are nothing but expressions of desire and aversion, is not unique to economic theory.[28] There are psychotherapists—Carl Rogers is an example—who likewise deny the objectivity or cognitivity of valuation.[29] For Rogers, there is only one criterion of worth: it lies in "the subjective world of the individual. Only he knows it fully."[30] The therapist shows his or her client that a "value system is not necessarily something imposed from without, but is something experienced."[31] Therapy succeeds when the client "perceives himself in such a way that no self-experience can be discriminated as more or less worthy of positive self-regard than any other...."[32] The client then "tends to place the basis of standards within himself, recognizing that the 'goodness' or 'badness' of any experience or perceptual object is not something inherent in that object, but is a value placed in it by himself."[33]

Rogers points out that "some clients make strenuous efforts to have the therapist exercise the valuing function, so as to provide them with guides for action."[34] The therapist, however, "consistently keeps the locus of evaluation with the client."[35] As long as the therapist refuses to "exercise the valuing function" and as long as he or she practices an "unconditional positive regard"[36] for all the affective states of the client, then the therapist remains neutral among the client's values or "sensory and visceral experiences."[37] The role of the therapist is legitimate, Rogers suggests, because of this value neutrality. The therapist accepts all felt preferences as valid and imposes none on the client.

Economists likewise argue that their role as

policymakers is legitimate because they are neutral among competing values in the client society. The political economist, according to James Buchanan, "is or should be ethically neutral: the indicated results are influenced by his own value scale only insofar as this reflects his membership in a larger group."[38] The economist might be most confident of the impartiality of his or her policy recommendations if he or she could derive them formally or mathematically from individual preferences. If theoretical difficulties make such a social welfare function impossible,[39] however, the next best thing, to preserve neutrality, is to let markets function to transform individual preference orderings into a collective ordering of social states. The analyst is able then to base policy on preferences that exist in society and are not necessarily his own.

Economists have used this impartial approach to offer solutions to many outstanding social problems, for example, the controversy over abortion. An economist argues that "there is an optimal number of abortions, just as there is an optimal level of pollution, or purity. . . . Those who oppose abortion could eliminate it entirely, if their intensity of feeling were so strong as to lead to payments that were greater at the margin than the price anyone would pay to have an abortion."[40] Likewise economists, in order to determine whether the war in Vietnam was justified, have estimated the willingness to pay of those who demonstrated against it.[41] Likewise it should be possible, following the same line of reasoning, to decide whether Creationism should be taught in the public schools, whether black and white people should be segregated, whether the death penalty should be enforced, and whether the square root of six is three. All of these questions depend upon how much people are willing to pay for their subjective preferences or wants—or none of them do. This is the beauty of cost-benefit analysis: no matter how relevant or irrelevant, wise or stupid, informed or uninformed, responsible or silly, defensible or indefensible wants may be, the analyst is able to derive a policy from them—a policy which is legitimate because, in theory, it treats all of these preferences as equally valid and good.

VI

Consider, by way of contrast, a Kantian conception of value.[42] The individual, for Kant, is a judge of values, not a mere haver of wants, and the individual judges not for himself or herself merely, but as a member of a relevant community or group. The central idea in a Kantian approach to ethics is that some values are more reasonable than others and therefore have a better claim upon the assent of members of the community as such.[43] The world of obligation, like the world of mathematics or the world of empirical fact, is intersubjective, it is public not private, so that objective standards of argument and criticism apply. Kant recognizes that values, like beliefs, are subjective states of mind, but he points out that like beliefs they have an objective content as well; therefore they are either correct or mistaken. Thus Kant discusses valuation in the context not of psychology but of cognition. He believes that a person who makes a value judgment—or a policy recommendation—claims to know what is *right* and not just what is *preferred*. A value judgment is like an empirical or theoretical judgment in that it claims to be *true*, not merely to be *felt*.

We have, then, two approaches to public policy before us. The first, the approach associated with normative versions of welfare economics, asserts that the only policy recommendation that can or need be defended on objective grounds is efficiency or wealth-maximization. Every policy decision after that depends only on the preponderance of feeling or preference, as expressed in willingness to pay. The Kantian approach, on the other hand, assumes that many policy recommendations other than that one may be justified or refuted on objective grounds. It would concede that the approach of welfare economics applies adequately to some questions, e.g., those which ordinary consumer markets typically settle. How many yo-yos should be produced as compared to how many frisbees? Shall pens have black ink or blue? Matters such as these are so trivial it is plain that markets should handle them. It does not follow, however, that we

should adopt a market or quasi-market approach to every public question.

A market or quasi-market approach to arithmetic, for example, is plainly inadequate. No matter how much people are willing to pay, three will never be the square root of six. Similarly, segregation is a national curse and the fact that we are willing to pay for it does not make it better but only makes us worse. Similarly, the case for abortion must stand on the merits; it cannot be priced at the margin. Similarly, the war in Vietnam was a moral debacle and this can be determined without shadow-pricing the willingness to pay of those who demonstrated against it. Similarly, we do not decide to execute murderers by asking how much bleeding hearts are willing to pay to see a person pardoned and how much hard hearts are willing to pay to see him hanged. Our failures to make the right decisions in these matters are failures in arithmetic, failures in wisdom, failures in taste, failures in morality—but not market failures. There are no relevant markets to have failed. What separates these questions from those for which markets are appropriate is this. They involve matters of knowledge, wisdom, morality, and taste that admit of better or worse, right or wrong, true or false—and these concepts differ from that of economic optimality. Surely environmental questions—the protection of wilderness, habitats, water, land, and air as well as policy toward environmental safety and health—involve moral and aesthetic principles and not just economic ones. This is consistent, of course, with cost-effectiveness and with a sensible recognition of economic constraints.

The neutrality of the economist, like the neutrality of Rogers' therapist, is legitimate if private preferences or subjective wants are the only values in question. A person should be left free to choose the color of his or her necktie or necklace—but we cannot justify a theory of public policy or private therapy on that basis. If the patient seeks moral advice or tries to find reasons to justify a choice, the therapist, according to Rogers' model, would remind him or her to trust his visceral and sensory experiences. The result of this is to deny the individual status as a cognitive being capable of responding intelligently to reasons; it reduces him or her to a bundle of affective states. What Rogers' therapist does to the patient the cost-benefit analyst does to society as a whole. The analyst is neutral among our "values"—having first imposed a theory of what value is. This is a theory that is impartial among values and for that reason fails to treat the persons who have them with respect or concern. It does not treat them even as persons but only as locations at which wants may be found. And thus we may conclude that the neutrality of economics is not a basis for its legitimacy. We recognize it as an indifference toward value—an indifference so deep, so studied, and so assured that at first one hesitates to call it by its right name.

VII

The residents of Lewiston at the conference I attended demanded to know the truth about the dangers that confronted them and the reasons for these dangers. They wanted to be convinced that the sacrifice asked of them was legitimate even if it served interests other than their own. One official from a large chemical company dumping wastes in the area told them, in reply, that corporations were people and that people could talk to people about their feelings, interests, and needs. This sent a shiver through the audience. Like Joseph K. in *The Trial*,[44] the residents of Lewiston asked for an explanation, justice, and truth, and they were told that their wants would be taken care of. They demanded to know the reasons for what was continually happening to them. They were given a personalized response instead.

This response, that corporations are "just people serving people" is consistent with a particular view of power. This is the view that identified power with the ability to get what one wants as an individual, that is, to satisfy one's personal preferences. When people in official positions in corporations or in the government put aside their personal interests, it would follow that they put aside their power as well. Their neutrality then justifies them in directing the resources of society in ways they determine to be best. This managerial role serves not their own interests but those of their clients. Cost-benefit analysis may be seen as a pervasive form of this paternalism. Behind this paternalism, as William Simon observes of the lawyer-client relationship, lies a theory of value that tends to personalize power. "It resists understanding power as a product of class, property, or institutions and collapses power into the personal needs and dispositions of the individuals who command and obey."[45] Once the economist, the therapist, the lawyer, or the manager abjures his own interests and acts wholly on behalf of client individuals, he appears to have no power of his own and thus justifiably manipulates and controls everything. "From this perspective it becomes difficult to distinguish the powerful from the powerless. In every case, both the exercise of power and submission to it are portrayed as a matter of personal accommodation and adjustment."[46]

The key to the personal interest or emotive theory of value, as one commentator has rightly said, "is the fact that emotivism entails the obliteration of any genuine distinction between manipulative and non-manipulative social relations."[47] The reason is that once the effective self is made the source of all value, the public self cannot participate in the exercise of power. As Philip Reiff remarks, "the public world is constituted as one vast stranger who appears at inconvenient times and makes demands viewed as purely external and therefore with no power to elicit a moral response."[48] There is no way to distinguish tyranny from the legitimate authority that public values and public law create.[49]

"At the rate of progress since 1900," Henry Adams speculates in his *Education*, "every American who lived into the year 2000 would know how to control unlimited power."[50] Adams thought that the Dynamo would organize and release as much energy as the Virgin. Yet in the 1980s, the citizens of Lewiston, surrounded by dynamos, high tension lines, and nuclear wastes, are powerless. They do not know how to criticize power, resist power, or justify power—for to do so depends on making distinctions between good and evil, right and wrong, innocence and guilt, justice and injustice, truth and lies. These distinctions cannot be made out and have no significance within an emotive or psychological theory of value. To adopt this theory is to imagine society as a market in which individuals trade voluntarily and without coercion. No individual, no belief, no faith has authority over them. To have power to act as a nation, however, we must be able to act, at least at times, on a public philosophy, conviction, or faith. We cannot replace with economic analysis the moral function of public law. The antinomianism of cost-benefit analysis is not enough.

Notes

---

1. H. Adams, *The Education of Henry Adams* 380 (1970, 1961).
2. *Id.*
3. *Id.* at 388.
4. For an account, see J. Pelletier, *The Sun Danced At Fatima* (1951).
5. *New Catholic Encyclopedia* 856 (1967).
6. See, e.g., W. Baxter, *People or Penguins: The Case For Optimal Pollution* chap. 1 (1974). See generally A. Freeman III, R. Haveman, A. Kneese, *The Economics of Environmental Policy* (1973).
7. R. Posner puts this point well in discussing wealth maximization as an ethical concept. "The only kind of preference that counts in a system of wealth-maximization," he writes, "is ... one that is backed up by money—in other words, that is registered in a market." Posner, "Utilitarianism, Economics, and Legal Theory," 8 *J. Legal Stud.* 119 (1979).
8. Freeman et al., note 6 *supra* at 23.
9. R. Musgrave, *The Theory of Public Finance* 87–88 (1959).
10. Marglin, "The Social Rate of Discount and the Optimal Rate of Investment," 77 *Q. J. of Econ.* 98 (1963).
11. See 46 *Fed. Reg.* 13193 (February 19, 1981). The Order specifies that the cost-benefit requirement shall apply "to the extent permitted by law."
12. *American Textile Mfgrs. Inst.* v. *Bingham*, 617 F.2d 636 (D.C. Cir. 1979) *cert.* granted *sub nom.* [1980]; *American Textile Mfgrs.* v. *Marshall*, 49 U.S.L.W. 3208.
13. *Textile Mfgrs.* v. *Donovan*, 101 S.Ct. 2478 (1981).
14. *Id.* U.S.L.W. (1981), 4733–34.
15. *Ibid.*, 4726–29.
16. Pub. L. No. 91-596, 84 Stat. 1596 (codified at 29 U.S.C. 651-78) (1970).
17. 29 U.S.C., 655(b) (5).
18. *American Petroleum Institute* v. *Marshall*, 581 F.2d 493 (1978) (5th Cir.), aff'd 100 S. Ct. 2844 (1980).
19. See, e.g., R. Posner, *Economic Analysis of Law*, parts I, II (1972, 1973). In *The Costs of Accidents* (1970), G. Calabresi argues that accident law balances two goals, "efficiency" and "equality" or "justice."
20. 581 F.2d 493 (1978).
21. 100 S.Ct. 2844 (1980).
22. *Id.* at 2903.
23. M. Baram, "Cost-Benefit Analysis: An Inadequate Basis for Health, Safety and Environmental Regulatory Decision Making" 8 *Ecological Law Quarterly* 473 (1980).
24. See 49 U.S.L.W. 4724–29 for this reasoning applied in the cotton dust case.
25. *De la Liberte des Anciens Comparee a Celle des Modernes* (1819).
26. *Oeuvres Politiques de Benjamin Constant*, ed. C. Luandre 269 (Paris, 1874); quoted in S. Wolin, *Politics and Vision* 281 (1960).
27. There are arguments that whatever reasons may be given are no good. See, e.g., Dworkin, "Why Efficiency?" 8 *Hofstra L. Rev.* 563 (1980); Dworkin, "Is Wealth a Value?" 9 *J. Legal Stud.* 191 (1980); Kennedy, "Cost-Benefit Analysis of Entitlement Problems: A Critique" 33 *Stan L. Rev.* 387 (1980); Rizzo, "The Mirage of Efficiency" 8 *Hofstra L. Rev.* 641 (1980); Sagoff, "Economic Theory and Environmental Law" 79 *Mich L. Rev.* 1393 (1981).
28. This is the emotive theory of value. For the classic statement, see C. Stevenson, *Ethics and Language* chaps. 1, 2 (1944). For criticism, see Blanshard, "The New Subjectivism in Ethics" 9 *Philosophy and Phenomenological Research* 504 (1949). For a statement of the related interest theory of value, see E. Westermarck, *Ethical Relativity* chaps. 3, 4, 5 (1932); R. Perry, *General Theory of Value* (1926). For criticisms of subjectivism in ethics and a case for the objective theory presupposed here, see generally, P. Edwards, *The Logic of Moral Discourse* (1955) and W. Ross, *The Right and the Good* (1930).
29. My account is based on C. Rogers, *On Becoming*

a Person (1961); C. Rogers, *Client Centered Therapy* (1965); and Rogers, "A Theory of Therapy, Personality, and Interpersonal Relationships, as Developed in the Client Centered Framework" 3 *Psychology: A Study of a Science* 184 (S. Koch ed., 1959). For a similar account used as a critique of the lawyer-client relation, see Simon, "Homo Psychologious: Notes on a New Legal Formalism" 32 *Stan. L. Rev.* 487 (1980).

30. Rogers, note 29 *supra* at 210.

31. C. Rogers, *Client Centered Therapy* 150 (1965).

32. Rogers, note 29 *supra* at 208.

33. Rogers, note 31 *supra* at 139.

34. *Id.* at 150.

35. *Id.*

36. Rogers, note 29 *supra* at 208.

37. *Id.* at 523–24.

38. Buchanan, "Positive Economics, Welfare Economics, and Political Economy" 2 *J. L. and Econ.* 124, 127 (1959).

39. K. Arrow, *Social Choice and Individual Values* i–v (2d ed., 1963).

40. H. Macaulay and B. Yandle, *Environmental Use and the Market* 120–21 (1978).

41. Cicchetti, Freeman, Haveman, and Knetsch, "On the Economics of Mass Demonstrations: A Case Study of the November 1969 March on Washington, 61 *Am. Econ. Rev.* 719 (1971).

42. I. *Kant, Foundations of the Metaphysics of Morals* (R. Wolff, ed., L. Beck trans., 1969). I follow the interpretation of Kantian ethics of W. Sellars, *Science and Metaphysics* chap. VII (1968) and Sellars, "On Reasoning about Values" 17 *Am. Phil. Q.* 81 (1980).

43. See A. Macintyre, *After Virtue* 22 (1981).

44. F. Kafka, *The Trial* (rev. ed. trans. 1957). Simon (note 29 *supra*) at 524 applies this analogy to the lawyer-client relationship.

45. Simon, note 29 *supra* at 495.

46. *Id.*

47. Macintyre, note 43 *supra* at 22.

48. P. Reiff, *The Triumph of the Therapeutic: Uses of Faith after Freud* 52 (1966).

49. That public law regimes inevitably lead to tyranny seems to be the conclusion of H. Arendt, *The Human Condition* (1958); K. Popper, *The Open Society and Its Enemies* (1966); L. Strauss, *Natural Right and History* (1953). For an important criticism of this conclusion in these authors, see Holmes, "Aristippus In and Out of Athens" 73 *Am. Pol. Sci. Rev.* 113 (1979).

50. H. Adams, note 1 *supra* at 476.

Cost-Benefit Analysis: Are We Bewitched by Numbers?

Preview

As noted earlier, it is widely agreed that markets as they exist are thought to fail in various respects. Unowned, or "commonly held," resources are overused or "exploited." Some goods such as fossil fuels, clean air, or water are thought to be used up too quickly or in the wrong manner. Burdens are imposed on parties who do not consent to them (hence, "negative externalities"). It is often held that government intervention in certain cases is appropriate, such as prohibiting certain activities by regulation (and perhaps criminal penalties) or placing charges on certain activities (for example, through licensing, or effluent charges). In some cases a government agency decides whether to undertake a project such as building a dam. If the aggregate costs were to exceed the aggregate benefit, it would be foolish to proceed. It is reasonable to claim *(a)* if a policy is adopted, then the costs must not exceed the benefits. We should distinguish this claim and the following two claims from one another: *(b)* if a policy, P, ought to be carried out for whatever are the relevant reasons, P
should be done in the way that maximizes benefits minus costs, and *(c)* if a policy, P, maximizes benefits minus costs, then P ought to be carried out (call this the *maximization principle*). The major controversy surrounds *(c)*. Specifically, those who argue for the adoption of a particular policy (such as flooding a valley and building a dam) may do so by arguing as follows:

1. We (or a governmental agency) ought to do whatever maximizes benefits-minus-costs.
2. Policy P maximizes benefits-minus-costs.

Hence,

3. We ought to carry out P.

Two basic questions are (1) why should we do whatever maximizes benefits-minus-cost, and (2) is it ever possible to know or reasonably believe of some (or any) policy that it maximizes benefits-minus-costs. Further, in a given case is it reasonable to believe that a particular policy does so? The essays that follow explore these matters (for example, the proper way to think about and deal with pollution) and in some cases how they bear on a particular dispute.

Here we begin to lay out the Pandora's box of puzzles that arise when one sets out to identify and reassess what is presupposed by the sort of normative cost-benefit approach identified above (whose core is [c] that the policy that maximizes benefits-minus-costs is right and therefore ought to be adopted). What seems at first only a simple truism like "don't be wasteful" is not so at all; rather, the presuppositions are many, hard to unearth, entrenched, and extremely influential.

The concepts of cost and benefit are not as straightforward as is often implied. What is to count as a cost? A number of possibilities come to mind: premature death, injury, pain, (felt) frustration of preferences, or nonfulfillment of preferences. Such suggestions may focus only on costs to humans. There are reasons to reject such anthropocentrism. Should we not include what economists almost invariably exclude, such as pain or premature death to animals, or destruction of a river or forest if there is no loss to humans? Analogously, what is to count as a benefit? Is pure life prolongation of humans a benefit (eternal life *as such* might be boring!). Are all instances of human preference-satisfaction to be weighed positively in a cost-benefit calculation? There is a tendency to equate "benefit," "good," "welfare," "satisfaction," "utility," and "preference fulfillment," but should we regard the fulfillment of "anti-social preferences" (such as, sadistic, envious, jealous ones) as a benefit?

Orthodox economists, perhaps in an excess of antipaternalism, antimoralism, or uncritical acceptance of moral subjectivism, tend not to pass judgment on existing preferences—acting as if they (the preferences) all had an equal right to be fulfilled (what of Hitler's high-ranking preference to exterminate Jews—or a hunter's intense preference to maximize his kill of baby seals or whales?). Further, such preferences tend to be regarded as "given"—falling from the sky like theoretical manna. Needless to say, the assumption is doubtful.

Similarly, little gets said about the connection between *beliefs* and *preferences* (as if preferences were like itches unconnected with cognition). However, it is clear that one's preferences are heavily dependent on one's beliefs. Compare preferences for and against slavery, polygamy, the use of DDT, killing

whales, or Oedipus's preference for Jocasta when he believed, and when he did not believe, Jocasta to be his mother. If preferences (such as for destroying all Jews, keeping women barefoot and pregnant, nuking the Russians) are based on irrational beliefs (Jews are vermin, women rightly are property of males—God's designated "helpmates" for men, Russian retaliation would be minor), it is not at all clear why satisfaction of such preferences is a benefit to be weighed positively in some C-B (cost benefit) calculus. Thus, aside from the fact that only effects on humans are to get weight in the calculus, it seems doubtful that all instances of preference fulfillment should be conceptualized as benefits. If so, why maximize them? Further, it is not obvious that all harms to humans ("costs") can be viewed as frustration of wants. When urban children suffer brain damage (and consequent retardation) from exposure to lead (from our use of leaded gasoline), what preference of the child is frustrated? Suppose the child is only a year old. If acid rain destroys many of our forests, is there no cost if and when people do not care, if we come (as a result of indoctrination) to prefer plastic trees?

A different, competing, analysis of welfare/illfare, benefit/cost, gain/loss is in terms of promoting or subverting the *interests* of a person or other organism, in terms of what is *in the interest* of, or subversive of, a being. When one takes into account children, the comatose, or the severely retarded—as philosophers and social theorists sometimes forget to do, it is especially clear that *what people want* and *what is in their interest* only overlap. Those who identify benefit with want-satisfaction need to give reasons for rejecting a competing analysis of benefit. The person on the street probably takes cost-benefit techniques to be aimed at promoting welfare, but it does not go without argument that promoting want-satisfaction is the same thing as promoting welfare.

Even if it were unproblematic that benefit equals want-satisfaction, it is questionable whether all benefits (so understood) can be identified and measured. There is no established market in some goods. Thus, economists seek to infer by indirect means how much people ("consumers") "value" (*value* in economics equals *prefer* in English) a good or a service. There are two main approaches: *(a)* see what people are willing to pay for packages of goods for which there is a market, and *(b)* ask them direct or indirect questions. Consider *(a)* first. It should not go unnoticed that what people are *willing* to pay is, in part, a function of how much they are *able* to pay. If willingness to pay for car safety devices is the criterion, then it may be thought that the rich value their lives more than the poor value theirs. Should we believe as much? Suppose Jones is out of work and starving on Monday, and takes a highly risky job on Tuesday (washing windows on the fifth floor). He may "demand" only a modest premium to compensate for the extra risk to his life (suppose he could have had the first floor job for a slightly smaller salary). Should we infer that the value of Jones's life is small—or that he values it not so much? According to another approach, it sometimes is said that the value (or "economic value"?) of a person's life is equivalent to his or her foregone earnings. Perhaps, this is a suitable criterion for determining how much compensation there should be to a person's estate when that person wrongfully is killed. As a measure of the value of that person's life or the amount that should be spent to prevent premature death, the monetary measure seems dubious. Happenstance affects earnings (as do preferences for leisure time, and moral convictions). Would Wilt Chamberlain's life be worth less if there were no market for basketball players? Is a ditchdigger's life at twenty-one worth less than that of the twenty-one-year-old computer wizard?

Years ago the Ford motor company did a cost-benefit analysis on the policy of adding certain devices in order to prevent gas tanks on automobiles from rupturing. In brief, one of the prospective benefits was saving a certain number of lives. How valuable is one life? Can that rationally be assigned a monetary value? Ford figured $200,000 (for 1971!) as the cost of a death. Presumably this figure largely reflects costs to others; only $10,000 of the amount was designated as the cost (value?) of the victim's pain and suffering. Why not $50,000 or $100,000? Is the benefit of preserving a life equal to avoiding the cost of death (which is assumed to be a function of wages forgone)? What figure is assigned here directly affects, of course, the outcome of the C-B calculation and policy determination. We are noting here the obvious questions that arise about the reasonableness of assigning monetary values to certain "goods and bads." For reasons discussed there are important questions about the way "cost" and "benefit" are conceptualized, problems in attempting to identify all the costs and benefits, and difficulties in rationally assigning a monetary measure to many costs and benefits—even when one takes an anthropocentric approach. This fact, of course, is not by itself a reason to do so; our cost-benefit calculations also would be comparatively simpler if we did not count the well-being of children or the severely retarded.

The Matter of Consent

In law and in common sense, whether another (voluntarily and knowingly) consents to the imposition of a harm is thought morally significant in deciding on the permissibility or desirability of generating the harm. The surgeon and the mugger may make similar "incisions," perhaps with similar results, but we view the unconsented-to cutting as wrong but not the one to which there is consent. It is striking that, in some discussions in defense of cost-benefit analysis (in contrast, see the Leonard and Zeckhauser selection), there is little attention as to whether those who are harmed, or subjected to risks, consent or not. It is clear that (more or less) voluntary smoking results in great harms (on average and in the aggregate) to smokers. A cost-benefit analysis of smoking (or alcohol usage) might (we conjecture) suggest strongly that the practice fails to maximize benefits-minus-costs. It is natural to wonder, however, whether the burdens on the smokers (aside from associated "indirect" burdens on nonsmokers) should be counted as a cost in a C-B calculation. At the least we raise here the question of whether *imposed* costs and *voluntarily absorbed* costs should be viewed similarly. As frequently discussed, no discrimination is required on a C-B approach.

The Maximization Principle

Although an analyst may only purport to identify costs and benefits (and thus remain untainted by ethical commitments) and not subscribe to the maximization principle (we ought to do whatever maximizes benefits-minus-costs), further questions arise for anyone who accepts the (normative) maximization principle. If the prior difficulties cannot be overcome, the principle may be inapplicable. Also, the principle seems subject to the well-known difficulties with the principle of utility; on one construal "maximize benefits-minus-costs" just *is* the principle of utility (except that the classic utilitarians Jeremy Bentham and John Stuart Mill were not anthropocentric in their conception of "cost" and "benefit." Both Bentham and Mill explicitly maintained that the suffering of animals must be given weight in deciding what to do). The main objection to be noted here concerns whether a policy of maximizing the balance of benefits over costs is defensible when it gives no direct weight to how those benefits and costs are *distributed* among the relevant population.

The policy that maximizes benefits-minus-costs may make some worse off. Thus, adopting the policy may not be an efficient step in the sense of making a Pareto improvement (see the preceding preview for an explanation). The gains to the "winners," however, may be sufficiently great that they outbalance the losses to the losers. If so, it would be *possible* in principle for the gainers to *compensate* the losers—thus, making the latter "nonlosers" (no worse off). The costs of making the transfer (information costs, and so on) may make full compensation impossible. If, however, full compensation were made, a Pareto improvement would occur, there would be no losers on balance, and one sort of complaint regarding injustice could not be made, namely, that some suffered an unconsented to, on balance, harm. (Note, however, that some might be relatively, if not absolutely, worse off—on one "objective" measure, at least.) Some economists and others, however, believe a "potential compensation

principle" (or potential Pareto criterion) is satisfactory: The results of a policy must make full compensation *possible,* but it need not be paid. This view is puzzling. To accept the potential compensation principle is to set aside an intuitively attractive feature of the strict Pareto principle (that no one will lose), one that sidesteps important moral objections based on considerations of justice. If salesman A steals salesman B's $5,000 car, and as a result earns an extra $50,000 a year, perhaps A could compensate B for his losses. If A does not, there is ground for serious moral complaint. We do not pursue the point here, but there may be ground for complaint *even if* compensation is made (assuming it can be).

Simply to maximize benefits-minus-costs without compensating losers looks suspiciously like merely maximizing total net utility. Uncompensated losses look like "market failures" or negative externalities. Supposedly, an attraction of cost-benefit analysis is to help patch up the market, that is, to eliminate or reduce such externalities. Pure maximization policies (whether what is to be maximized is GNP, utility, wealth, or "benefits-minus-costs") seem to give no direct weight to concerns about how benefits and costs are distributed. This seems morally intolerable.

Perhaps, however, a coupling (somehow) of cost-benefit analysis and principles of just distribution may be more attractive. If so, one may have to surrender the unqualified maximization principle. Further, one may have to drop the pervasive metaethical assumption seemingly made by many environmental economists that "the proper use of environmental resources is more a matter of economics than of morals."[1] This last assumption is plausible only if we should accept the maximization principle and the assumption that we can measure all the relevant benefits and costs, but these claims cannot be decided apart from careful ethical inquiry.

Matters are not all this simple, of course. The claims that some "environmentalists," some philosophers, and some ecologists have proposed as guides to environmental decision making (maxims such as "nature knows best," "a thing is right when it tends to preserve the integrity, stability, and beauty of the biotic community," "maximize utility" [again], "preserve endangered species," "everything has a right to exist") seem to be either too vague and indeterminate as guides, to be analytic truisms, or otherwise objectionable. The essays that follow survey the attractions of efficiency and cost-benefit considerations—as well as the persistent reservations about their invocation and employment (especially as a ground for *policy selection*—as opposed to their use to foster cheap implementation of an already selected policy such as *cost-effectiveness*).

To speak at length of these matters is not to talk directly of rain forests, blue whales, acid rain, marshlands, or estuaries; rather it is to explore grounds for choices that will determine their destiny as well as that of those superpredators called humans. To ignore such matters, if one is concerned with the fate of our planet, is to choose to be a naive environmentalist.

In the first selection to follow, Steven Kelman, *apart from* considering questions about the anthropocentric nature of cost-benefit analysis, argues that a policy might be right even if it does *not* maximize benefits-minus-costs. Further, he questions the attempt to assign monetary values to nonmarketed benefits and costs. Kelman's critique, in short, is important and provocative. Against at least some of the current criticisms of C-B analysis, Herman Leonard and Richard Zeckhauser respond. In particular they argue that C-B analysis is sensitive to distributional worries, and need not go astray in its assignment of monetary values. The conflict with Kelman's view is not always direct, but the pair of essays is instructive. The last essay, by Laurence Tribe, envisions the possibility of a morally enriched (nonanthropocentric) set of analytic tools (like C-B techniques) to decide tough environmental questions. If Tribe is wrong on this point, and if anthropocentrism is wrong, the only alternative is a radical rejection of traditional analytic methods. However, we already know how to put certain matters largely beyond the grasp of economic calculations. We no longer allow human beings to be bought and sold. We know how, by political means, to make the costs of the destruction of life if not irrelevant, then at least, forbiddingly high. Still fundamental, then, are the questions concerning moral standing and determining appropriate trade-off principles.

Note

1. Robert and Nancy Dorfman, eds. *Economics of the Environment* (New York: W. W. Norton Company, 1972), p. XL.

Cost-Benefit Analysis: An Ethical Critique

Steven Kelman

At the broadest and vaguest level, cost-benefit analysis may be regarded simply as systematic thinking about decision-making. Who can oppose, economists sometimes ask, efforts to think in a systematic way about the consequences of different courses of action? The alternative, it would appear, is unexamined decision-making. But defining cost-benefit analysis so simply leaves it with few implications for actual regulatory decision-making. Presumably, therefore, those who urge regulators to make greater use of the technique have a more extensive prescription in mind. I assume here that their prescription includes the following views:

1. There exists a strong presumption that an act should not be undertaken unless its benefits outweigh its costs.

2. In order to determine whether benefits outweigh costs, it is desirable to attempt to ex-

Source: *Regulation* (Jan., Feb. 1981), pp. 74–82. Reprinted by permission of the American Enterprise Institute.

press all benefits and costs in a common scale or denominator, so that they can be compared with each other, even when some benefits and costs are not traded on markets and hence have no established dollar values.

3. Getting decision-makers to make more use of cost-benefit techniques is important enough to warrant both the expense required to gather the data for improved cost-benefit estimation and the political efforts needed to give the activity higher priority compared to other activities, also valuable in and of themselves.

My focus is on cost-benefit analysis as applied to environmental, safety, and health regulation. In that context, I examine each of the above propositions from the perspective of formal ethical theory, that is, the study of what actions it is morally right to undertake. My conclusions are:

1. In areas of environmental, safety, and health regulation, there may be many instances where a certain decision might be right even though its benefits do not outweigh its costs.

2. There are good reasons to oppose efforts to put dollar values on non-marketed benefits and costs.

3. Given the relative frequency of occasions in the areas of environmental, safety, and health regulation where one would not wish to use a benefits-outweigh-costs test as a decision rule, and given the reasons to oppose the monetizing of nonmarketed benefits or costs that is a prerequisite for cost-benefit analysis, it is not justifiable to devote major resources to the generation of data for cost-benefit calculations or to undertake efforts to "spread the gospel" of cost-benefit analysis further.

I

How do we decide whether a given action is morally right or wrong and hence, assuming the desire to act morally, why it should be un-

dertaken or refrained from? Like the Molière character who spoke prose without knowing it, economists who advocate use of cost-benefit analysis for public decisions are philosophers without knowing it: the answer given by cost-benefit analysis, that actions should be undertaken so as to maximize net benefits, represents one of the classic answers given by moral philosophers—that given by utilitarians. To determine whether an action is right or wrong, utilitarians tote up all the positive consequences of the action in terms of human satisfaction. The act that maximizes attainment of satisfaction under the circumstances is the right act. That the economists' answer is also the answer of one school of philosophers should not be surprising. Early on, economics was a branch of moral philosophy, and only later did it become an independent discipline.

Before proceeding further, the subtlety of the utilitarian position should be noted. The positive and negative consequences of an act for satisfaction may go beyond the act's immediate consequences. A facile version of utilitarianism would give moral sanction to a lie, for instance, if the satisfaction of an individual attained by telling the lie was greater than the suffering imposed on the lie's victim. Few utilitarians would agree. Most of them would add to the list of negative consequences the effect of the one lie on the tendency of the person who lies to tell other lies, even in instances when the lying produced less satisfaction for him than dissatisfaction for others. They would also add the negative effects of the lie on the general level of social regard for truth-telling, which has many consequences for future utility. A further consequence may be added as well. It is sometimes said that we should include in a utilitarian calculation the feeling of dissatisfaction produced in the liar (and perhaps in others) because, by telling a lie, one has "done the wrong thing." Correspondingly, in this view, among the positive consequences to be weighed into a utilitarian calculation of truth-telling is satisfaction arising from "doing the right thing." This view rests on an error, however, because it *assumes* what it is the purpose of the calculation to *determine*— that telling the truth in the instance in question is indeed the right thing to do. Economists are likely to object to this point, arguing that no feeling ought "arbitrarily" to be excluded from a complete cost-benefit calculation, including a feeling of dissatisfaction at doing the wrong thing. Indeed, the economists' cost-benefit calculations would, at least ideally, include such feelings. Note the difference between the economist's and the philosopher's cost-benefit calculations, however. The economist may choose to include feelings of dissatisfaction in his cost-benefit calculation, but what happens if somebody asks the economist, "Why is it right to evaluate an action on the basis of a cost-benefit test?" If an answer is to be given to that question (which does not normally preoccupy economists but which does concern both philosophers and the rest of us who need to be persuaded that cost-benefit analysis is right), then the circularity problem reemerges. And there is also another difficulty with counting feelings of dissatisfaction at doing the wrong thing in a cost-benefit calculation. It leads to the perverse result that under certain circumstances a lie, for example, might be morally right if the individual contemplating the lie felt no compunction about lying and morally wrong only if the individual felt such a compunction!

This error is revealing, however, because it begins to suggest a critique of utilitarianism. Utilitarianism is an important and powerful moral doctrine. But it is probably a minority position among contemporary moral philosophers. It is amazing that economists can proceed in unanimous endorsement of cost-benefit analysis as if unaware that their conceptual framework is highly controversial in the discipline from which it arose—moral philosophy.

Let us explore the critique of utilitarianism. The logical error discussed before appears to suggest that we have a notion of certain things being right or wrong that *predates* our calculation of costs and benefits. Imagine the case of an old man in Nazi Germany who is hostile to the regime. He is wondering whether he should speak out against Hitler. If he speaks out, he will lose his pension. And his action will have done nothing to increase the chances that the Nazi regime will be overthrown: he is regarded as somewhat eccentric by those around him, and nobody has ever consulted his views

on political questions. Recall that one cannot add to the benefits of speaking out any satisfaction from doing "the right thing," because the purpose of the exercise is to determine whether speaking out *is* the right thing. How would the utilitarian calculation go? The benefits of the old man's speaking out would, as the example is presented, be nil, while the costs would be his loss of his pension. So the costs of the action would outweigh the benefits. By the utilitarians' cost-benefit calculation, it would be *morally wrong* for the man to speak out.

To those who believe that it would not be morally wrong for the old man to speak out in Nazi Germany, utilitarianism is insufficient as a moral view. We believe that some acts whose costs are greater than their benefits may be morally right and, contrariwise, some acts whose benefits are greater than their costs may be morally wrong.

This does not mean that the question whether benefits are greater than costs is morally irrelevant. Few would claim such. Indeed, for a broad range of individual and social decisions, whether an act's benefits outweigh its costs is a sufficient question to ask. But not for all such decisions. These may involve situations where certain duties—duties not to lie, break promises, or kill, for example—make an act wrong, even if it would result in an excess of benefits over costs. Or they may involve instances where people's rights are at stake. We would not permit rape even if it could be demonstrated that the rapist derived enormous happiness from his act, while the victim experienced only minor displeasure. We do not do cost-benefit analyses of freedom of speech or trial by jury. The Bill of Rights was not RARGed.[1] As the United Steelworkers noted in a comment on the Occupational Safety and Health Administration's economic analysis of its proposed rule to reduce worker exposure to carcinogenic coke-oven emissions, the Emancipation Proclamation was not subjected to an inflationary impact statement. The notion of human rights involves the idea that people may make certain claims to be allowed to act in certain ways or to be treated in certain ways, even if the sum of benefits achieved thereby does not outweigh the sum of costs. It is this view that underlies the statement that "workers have a right to a safe and healthy work place" and the expectation that OSHA's decisions will reflect that judgment.

In the most convincing versions of nonutilitarian ethics, various duties or rights are not absolute. But each has a *prima facie* moral validity so that, if duties or rights do not conflict, the morally right act is the act that reflects a duty or respects a right. If duties or rights do conflict, a moral judgment, based on conscious deliberation, must be made. Since one of the duties non-utilitarian philosophers enumerate is the duty of beneficence (the duty to maximize happiness), which in effect incorporates all of utilitarianism by reference, a non-utilitarian who is faced with conflicts between the results of cost-benefit analysis and non-utility-based considerations will need to undertake such deliberation. But in that deliberation, additional elements, which cannot be reduced to a question of whether benefits outweigh costs, have been introduced. Indeed, depending on the moral importance we attach to the right or duty involved, cost-benefit questions may, within wide ranges, become irrelevant to the outcome of the moral judgment.

In addition to questions involving duties and rights, there is a final sort of question where, in my view, the issue of whether benefits outweigh costs should not govern moral judgment. I noted earlier that, for the common run of questions facing individuals and societies, it is possible to begin and end our judgment simply by finding out if the benefits of the contemplated act outweigh the costs. This very fact means that one way to show the great importance, or value, attached to an area is to say that decisions involving the area should not be determined by cost-benefit calculations. This applies, I think, to the view many environmentalists have of decisions involving our natural environment. When officials are deciding what level of pollution will harm certain vulnerable people—such as asthmatics or the elderly—while not harming others, one issue involved may be the right of those people not to be sacrificed on the altar of somewhat higher living standards for the rest of us. But more broadly than this, many environmentalists fear that subjecting decisions about clean air or water to the cost-benefit tests that determine the general run of

decisions removes those matters from the realm of specially valued things.

II

In order for cost-benefit calculations to be performed the way they are supposed to be, all costs and benefits must be expressed in a common measure, typically dollars, including things not normally bought and sold on markets, and to which dollar prices are therefore not attached. The most dramatic example of such things is human life itself; but many of the other benefits achieved or preserved by environmental policy—such as peace and quiet, fresh-smelling air, swimmable rivers, spectacular vistas—are not traded on markets either.

Economists who do cost-benefit analysis regard the quest after dollar values for non-market things as a difficult challenge—but one to be met with relish. They have tried to develop methods for imputing a person's "willingness to pay" for such things, their approach generally involving a search for bundled goods that *are* traded on markets and that vary as to whether they include a feature that is, *by itself*, not marketed. Thus, fresh air is not marketed, but houses in different parts of Los Angeles that are similar except for the degree of smog are. Peace and quiet is not marketed, but similar houses inside and outside airport flight paths are. The risk of death is not marketed, but similar jobs that have different levels of risk are. Economists have produced many often ingenious efforts to impute dollar prices to non-marketed things by observing the premiums accorded homes in clean air areas over similar homes in dirty areas or the premiums paid for risky jobs over similar nonrisky jobs.

These ingenious efforts are subject to criticism on a number of technical grounds. It may be difficult to control for all the dimensions of quality other than the presence or absence of the non-marketed thing. More important, in a world where people have different preferences and are subject to different constraints as they make their choices, the dollar value imputed to the non-market things that most people would wish to avoid will be lower than otherwise, because people with unusually weak aversion to those things or unusually strong constraints on their choices will be willing to take the bundled good in question at less of a discount than the average person. Thus, to use the property value discount of homes near airports as a measure of people's willingness to pay for quiet means to accept as a proxy for the rest of us the behavior of those least sensitive to noise, of airport employees (who value the convenience of a near-airport location) or of others who are susceptible to an agent's assurances that "it's not so bad." To use the wage premiums accorded hazardous work as a measure of the value of life means to accept as proxies for the rest of us the choices of people who do not have many choices or who are exceptional risk-seekers.

A second problem is that the attempts of economists to measure people's willingness to pay for non-marketed things assume that there is no difference between the price a person would require for *giving up* something to which he has a preexisting right and the price he would pay to *gain* something to which he enjoys no right. Thus, the analysis assumes no difference between how much a homeowner would need to be paid in order to give up an unobstructed mountain view that he already enjoys and how much he would be willing to pay to get an obstruction moved once it is already in place. Available evidence suggests that most people would insist on being paid far more to assent to a worsening of their situation than they would be willing to pay to improve their situation. The difference arises from such factors as being accustomed to and psychologically attached to that which one believes one enjoys by right. But this creates a circularity problem for any attempt to use cost-benefit analysis to determine *whether* to assign to, say, the homeowner the right to an unobstructed mountain view. For willingness to pay will be different depending on whether the right is assigned initially or not. The value judgment about whether to assign the right must thus be made first. (In order to set an upper bound on the value of the benefit, one might hypothetically assign the right to the person and de-

termine how much he would need to be paid to give it up.)

Third, the efforts of economists to impute willingness to pay invariably involve bundled goods exchanged in *private* transactions. Those who use figures garnered from such analysis to provide guidance for *public* decisions assume no difference between how people value certain things in private individual transactions and how they would wish those same things to be valued in public collective decisions. In making such assumptions, economists insidiously slip into their analysis an important and controversial value judgment, growing naturally out of the highly individualistic microeconomic tradition—namely, the view that there should be no difference between private behavior and the behavior we display in public social life. An alternative view—one that enjoys, I would suggest, wide resonance among citizens— would be that public, social decisions provide an opportunity to give certain things a higher valuation than we choose, for one reason or another, to give them in our private activities.

Thus, opponents of stricter regulation of health risks often argue that we show by our daily risk-taking behavior that we do not value life infinitely, and therefore our public decisions should not reflect the high value of life that proponents of strict regulation propose. However, an alternative view is equally plausible. Precisely because we fail, for whatever reasons, to give life-saving the value in everyday personal decisions that we in some general terms believe we should give it, we may wish our social decisions to provide us the occasion to display the reverence for life that we espouse but do not always show. By this view, people do not have fixed unambiguous "preferences" to which they give expression through private activities and which therefore should be given expression in public decisions. Rather, they may have what they themselves regard as "higher" and "lower" preferences. The latter may come to the fore in private decisions, but people may want the former to come to the fore in public decisions. They may sometimes display racial prejudice, but support anti-discrimination laws. They may buy a certain product after seeing a seductive ad, but be skeptical enough of advertising to want the government to keep a close eye on it. In such cases, the use of private behavior to impute the values that should be entered for public decisions, as is done by using willingness to pay in private transactions, commits grievous offense against a view of the behavior of the citizen that is deeply engrained in our democratic tradition. It is a view that denudes politics of any independent role in society, reducing it to a mechanistic, mimicking recalculation based on private behavior.

Finally, one may oppose the effort to place prices on a non-market thing and hence in effect incorporate it into the market system out of a fear that the very act of doing so will reduce the thing's perceived value. To place a price on the benefit may, in other words, reduce the value of that benefit. Cost-benefit analysis thus may be like the thermometer that, when placed in a liquid to be measured, itself changes the liquid's temperature.

Examples of the perceived cheapening of a thing's value by the very act of buying and selling it abound in everyday life and language. The disgust that accompanies the idea of buying and selling human beings is based on the sense that this would dramatically diminish human worth. Epithets such as "he prostituted himself," applied as linguistic analogies to people who have sold something, reflect the view that certain things should not be sold because doing so diminishes their value. Praise that is bought is worth little, even to the person buying it. A true anecdote is told of an economist who retired to another university community and complained that he was having difficulty making friends. The laconic response of a critical colleague—"If you want a friend why don't you buy yourself one"—illustrates in a pithy way the intuition that, for some things, the very act of placing a price on them reduces their perceived value.

The first reason that pricing something decreases its perceived value is that, in many circumstances, non-market exchange is associated with the production of certain values not associated with market exchange. These may include spontaneity and various other feelings that come from personal relationships. If a good

becomes less associated with the production of positively valued feelings because of market exchange, the perceived value of the good declines to the extent that those feelings are valued. This can be seen clearly in instances where a thing may be transferred both by market and by non-market mechanisms. The willingness to pay for sex bought from a prostitute is less than the perceived value of the sex consummating love. (Imagine the reaction if a practitioner of cost-benefit analysis computed the benefits of sex based on the price of prostitute services.)

Furthermore, if one values in a general sense the existence of a non-market sector because of its connection with the production of certain valued feelings, then one ascribes added value to any non-marketed good simply as a repository of values represented by the non-market sector one wishes to preserve. This seems certainly to be the case for things in nature, such as pristine streams or undisturbed forests: for many people who value them, part of their value comes from their position as repositories of values the non-market sector represents.

The second way in which placing a market price on a thing decreases its perceived value is by removing the possibility of proclaiming that the thing is "not for sale," since things on the market by definition are for sale. The very statement that something is not for sale affirms, enhances, and protects a thing's value in a number of ways. To begin with, the statement is a way of showing that a thing is valued for its own sake, whereas selling a thing for money demonstrates that it was valued only instrumentally. Furthermore, to say that something cannot be transferred in that way places it in the exceptional category—which requires the person interested in obtaining that thing to be able to offer something else that is exceptional, rather than allowing him the easier alternative of obtaining the thing for money that could have been obtained in an infinity of ways. This enhances its value. If I am willing to say "You're a really kind person" to whoever pays me to do so, my praise loses the value that attaches to it from being exchangeable only for an act of kindness.

In addition, if we have already decided we

value something highly, one way of stamping it with a cachet affirming its high value is to announce that it is "not for sale." Such an announcement does more, however, than just reflect a preexisting high valuation. It signals a thing's distinctive value to others and helps us persuade them to value the thing more highly than they otherwise might. It also expresses our resolution to safeguard that distinctive value. To state that something is not for sale is thus also a source of value for that thing, since if a thing's value is easy to affirm or protect, it will be worth more than an otherwise similar thing without such attributes.

If we proclaim that something is not for sale, we make a once-and-for-all judgment of its special value. When something is priced, the issue of its perceived value is constantly coming up, as a standing invitation to reconsider that original judgment. Were people constantly faced with questions such as "how much money could get you to give up your freedom of speech?" or "how much would you sell your vote for if you could?", the perceived value of the freedom to speak or the right to vote would soon become devastated as, in moments of weakness, people started saying "maybe it's not worth *so much* after all." Better not to be faced with the constant questioning in the first place. Something similar did in fact occur when the slogan "better red than dead" was launched by some pacifists during the Cold War. Critics pointed out that the very posing of this stark choice—in effect, "would you *really* be willing to give up your life in exchange for not living under communism?"—reduced the value people attached to freedom and thus diminished resistance to attacks on freedom.

Finally, of some things valued very highly it is stated that they are "priceless" or that they have "infinite value." Such expressions are reserved for a subset of things not for sale, such as life or health. Economists tend to scoff at talk of pricelessness. For them, saying that something is priceless is to state a willingness to trade off an infinite quantity of all other goods for one unit of the priceless good, a situation that empirically appears highly unlikely. For most people, however, the word priceless is pregnant with meaning. Its value-affirming and value-protecting functions cannot be bestowed on

expressions that merely denote a determinate, albeit high, valuation. John Kennedy in his inaugural address proclaimed that the nation was ready to "pay any price [and] bear any burden . . . to assure the survival and the success of liberty." Had he said instead that we were willing to "pay a high price" or "bear a large burden" for liberty, the statement would have rung hollow.

III

An objection that advocates of cost-benefit analysis might well make to the preceding argument should be considered. I noted earlier that, in cases where various non-utility-based duties or rights conflict with the maximization of utility, it is necessary to make a deliberative judgment about what act is finally right. I also argued earlier that the search for commensurability might not always be a desirable one, that the attempt to go beyond expressing benefits in terms of (say) lives saved and costs in terms of dollars is not something devoutly to be wished.

In situations involving things that are not expressed in a common measure, advocates of cost-benefit analysis argue that people making judgments "in effect" perform cost-benefit calculations anyway. If government regulators promulgate a regulation that saves 100 lives at a cost of $1 billion, they are "in effect" valuing a life at (a minimum of) $10 million, whether or not they say that they are willing to place a dollar value on a human life. Since, in this view, cost-benefit analysis "in effect" is inevitable, it might as well be made specific.

This argument misconstrues the real difference in the reasoning processes involved. In cost-benefit analysis, equivalencies are established *in advance* as one of the raw materials for the calculation. One determines costs and benefits, one determines equivalencies (to be able to put various costs and benefits into a common measure), and then one sets to toting things up—waiting, as it were, with bated breath for the results of the calculation to come out. The outcome is determined by the arithmetic; if the outcome is a close call or if one is not good at long division, one does not know how it will turn out until the calculation is finished. In the kind of deliberative judgment that is performed without a common measure, no establishment of equivalencies occurs in advance. Equivalencies are not aids to the decision process. In fact, the decision-maker might not even be aware of what the "in effect" equivalencies were, at least before they are revealed to him afterwards by someone pointing out what he had "in effect" done. The decision-maker would see himself as simply having made a deliberative judgment; the "in effect" equivalency number did not play a causal role in the decision but at most merely reflects it. Given this, the argument against making the process explicit is the one discussed earlier in the discussion of problems with putting specific values on things that are not normally quantified—that the very act of doing so may serve to reduce the value of those things.

My own judgment is that modest efforts to assess levels of benefits and costs are justified, although I do not believe that government agencies ought to sponsor efforts to put dollar prices on non-market things. I also do not believe that the cry for more cost-benefit analysis in regulation is, on the whole, justified. If regulatory officials were so insensitive about regulatory costs that they did not provide acceptable raw material for deliberative judgments (even if not of a strictly cost-benefit nature), my conclusion might be different. But a good deal of research into costs and benefits already occurs—actually, far more in the U.S. regulatory process than in that of any other industrial society. The danger now would seem to come more from the other side.

Note

1. The Regulatory Analysis Review Group (RARG) was created by President Carter to improve the cost-benefit analysis of regulatory policy. It was subsequently disbanded by President Reagan. (editors' note)

Cost-Benefit Analysis Defended

Herman B. Leonard and Richard J. Zeckhauser

Cost-benefit analysis, particularly as applied to public decisions involving risks to life and health, has not been notably popular. A number of setbacks—Three Mile Island is perhaps the most memorable—have called into question the reliability of analytic approaches to risk issues. We believe that the current low reputation of cost-benefit analysis is unjustified, and that a close examination of the objections most frequently raised against the method will show that it deserves wider public support.

Source: The newsletter, *QQ: Report From the Center for Philosophy and Public Policy* at the University of Maryland at College Park, Maryland, Vol. 3, No. 3 (Summer 1983), pp. 6–9. Reprinted by permission.

Society does not and indeed could not require the explicit consent of every affected individual in order to implement public decisions that impose costs or risks. The transactions costs of assembling unanimous consent would be prohibitive, leading to paralysis in the status quo. Moreover, any system that required unanimous consent would create incentives for individuals to misrepresent their beliefs so as to secure compensation or to prevent the imposition of relatively small costs on them even if the benefits to others might be great.

If actual individual consent is an impractically strong standard to require of centralized decisions, how should such decisions be made? Our test for a proposed public decision is whether the net benefits of the action are positive. The same criterion is frequently phrased: Will those favored by the decision gain enough that they would have a net benefit even if they fully compensated those hurt by the decision? Applying this criterion to all possible actions, we discover that the chosen alternative should be the one for which benefits most exceed costs. We believe that the benefit-cost criterion is a useful way of defining "hypothetical consent" for centralized decisions affecting individuals with widely divergent interests: hypothetically, if compensation could be paid, all would agree to the decision offering the highest net benefits. We turn now to objections commonly raised against this approach.

Compensation and Hypothetical Consent

An immediate problem with the pure cost-benefit criterion is that it does not require the actual payment of compensation to those on whom a given decision imposes net costs. Our standard for public decision-making does not require that losers be compensated, but only that they *could* be if a perfect system of transfers existed. But unless those harmed by a decision are *actually* compensated, they will get little solace from the fact that someone is reaping a surplus in which they could have shared.

To this we make two replies. First, it is typically infeasible to design a compensation system that ensures that all individuals will be net winners. The transactions costs involved in such a system would often be so high as to make the project as a whole a net loss. But it may not even be desirable to construct full compensation systems, since losers will generally have an incentive under such systems to overstate their anticipated losses in order to secure greater compensation.

Second, the problem of compensation is probably smaller in practice than in principle. Society tends to compensate large losses where possible or to avoid imposing large losses when adequate compensation is not practical. Moreover, compensation is sometimes overpaid;

having made allowances *ex ante* for imposing risks, society still chooses sometimes to pay additional compensation *ex post* to those who actually suffer losses.

Libertarians raise one additional argument about the ethical basis of a system that does not require full compensation to losers. They argue that a public decision process that imposes uncompensated losses constitutes an illegal taking of property by the state and should not be tolerated. This objection, however strongly grounded ethically, would lead to an untenable position for society by unduly constraining public decisions to rest with the status quo.

Attention to Distribution

Two distinct types of distributional issue are relevant in cost-benefit analysis. First, we can be concerned about the losers in a particular decision, whoever they may be. Second, we can be concerned with the transfers between income classes (or other defined groups) engendered by a given project. If costs are imposed differentially on groups that are generally disadvantaged, should the decision criterion include special consideration of their interests? This question is closely intertwined with the issue of compensation, because it is often alleged that the uncompensated costs of projects evaluated by cost-benefit criteria frequently fall on those who are disadvantaged to start with.

These objections have little to do with cost-benefit analysis as a method. We see no reason why any widely agreed upon notion of equity, or weighting of different individuals' interests, cannot in principle be built into the cost-benefit decision framework. It is merely a matter of defining carefully what is meant by a benefit or a cost. If, in society's view, benefits (or costs) to some individuals are more valuable (costly) than those to others, this can be reflected in the construction of the decision criterion.

But although distribution concerns could be systematically included in cost-benefit analyses, it is not always—or even generally—a good idea to do so. Taxes and direct expenditures represent a far more efficient means of effecting redistribution than virtually any other public program; we would strongly prefer to rely on one consistent comprehensive tax and expenditure package for redistribution than on attempts to redistribute within every project.

First, if distributional issues are considered everywhere, they will probably not be adequately, carefully, and correctly treated anywhere. Many critics of cost-benefit analysis believe that project-based distributional analysis would create a net addition to society's total redistributive effort; we suggest that is likely, instead, to be only an inefficient substitution.

Second, treating distributional concerns within each project can only lead to transfers within the group affected by a project, often only a small subset of the community. For example, unisex rating of auto insurance redistributes only among drivers. Cross-subsidization of medical costs affects only those who need medical services. Why should not the larger society share the burden of redistribution?

Third, the view that distributional considerations should be treated project-by-project reflects a presumption that on average they do not balance out—that is, that some groups systematically lose more often than others. If it were found that some groups were severely and systematically disadvantaged by the application of cost-benefit analyses that ignore distributional concerns, we would favor redressing the balance. We do not believe this is generally the case.

will never fit in a cost-benefit framework and will have to be treated as "additional considerations" in coming to a final decision. Some, such as the inviolability of human life, may simply be binding constraints that cannot be traded off to obtain other gains. Nor can we carry out a cost-benefit analysis to decide which values should be included and which treated separately—this decision will always have to be made in some other manner.

These considerations do not invalidate cost-benefit analysis, but merely illustrate that more is at stake than just dollar measures of costs and benefits. We would, however, make two observations. First, we must be very careful that only genuinely important and relevant social values be permitted to outweigh the findings of an analysis. Second, social values that frequently stand in the way of important efficiency gains have a way of breaking down and being replaced over time, so that in the long run society manages to accommodate itself to some form of cost-benefit criterion. If nuclear power were 1000 times more dangerous for its employees but 10 times less expensive than it is, we might feel that ethical considerations were respected and the national interest well served if we had rotating cadres of nuclear power employees serving short terms in high-risk positions, much as members of the armed services do. In like fashion, we have fire-fighters risk their lives; universal sprinkler systems would be less dangerous, but more costly. Such policies reflect an accommodation to the costs as a recognition of the benefits.

Sensitive Social Values

Cost-benefit analysis, it is frequently alleged, does a disservice to society because it cannot treat important social values with appropriate sensitivity. We believe that this view does a disservice to society by unduly constraining the use of a reasonable and helpful method for organizing the debate about public decisions. We are not claiming that every important social value can be represented effectively within the confines of cost-benefit analysis. Some values

Measurability

Another objection frequently raised against cost-benefit analysis is that some costs and benefits tend to be ignored because they are much more difficult to measure than others. The long-term environmental impacts of large projects are frequently cited as an example. Cost-benefit analysis is charged with being systematically biased toward consideration of the quantifiable aspects of decisions.

This is unquestionably true: cost-benefit

analysis is *designed* as a method of quantification, so it surely is better able to deal with more quantifiable aspects of the issues it confronts. But this limitation is in itself ethically neutral unless it can be shown that the quantifiable considerations systematically push decisions in a particular direction. Its detractors must show that the errors of cost-benefit analysis are systematically unjust or inefficient—for example, that it frequently helps the rich at the expense of the poor, or despoils the environment to the benefit of industry, or vice versa. We have not seen any carefully researched evidence to support such assertions.

We take some comfort in the fact that cost-benefit analysis is sometimes accused of being biased toward development projects and sometimes of being biased against them. Cost-benefit analyses have foiled conservation efforts in national forests—perhaps they systematically weight the future too little. But they have also squelched clearly silly projects designed to bring "economic development" to Alaska—and the developers argued that the analysis gave insufficient weight to the "unquantifiable" value of future industrialization.

In our experience, cost-benefit analysis is often a tool of the "outs"—those not currently in control of the political process. Those who have the political power to back the projects they support often have little need of analyses. By contrast, analysis can be an effective tool for those who are otherwise not strongly empowered politically.

Analyzing Risks

Even those who accept the ethical propriety of cost-benefit analysis of decisions involving transfers of money or other tangible economic costs and benefits sometimes feel that the principles do not extend to analyzing decisions involving the imposition of risks. We believe that such applications constitute a *particularly* important area in which cost-benefit analysis can be of value. The very difficulties of reaching appropriate decisions where risks are involved make it all the more vital to employ the soundest methods available, both ethically and practically.

Historically, cost-benefit analysis has been applied widely to the imposition and regulation of risks, in particular to risks of health loss or bodily harm. The cost-benefit approach is particularly valuable here, for several reasons. Few health risks can be exchanged on a voluntary basis. Their magnitude is difficult to measure. Even if they could be accurately measured, individuals have difficulty interpreting probabilities or gauging how they would feel should the harm eventuate. Compounding these problems of valuation are difficulties in contract, since risks are rarely conveyed singly between one individual and another.

The problem of risks conveyed in the absence of contractual approval has been addressed for centuries through the law of torts, which is designed to provide compensation after a harm has been received. If only a low-probability risk is involved, it is often efficient to wait to see whether a harm occurs, for in the overwhelming majority of circumstances transactions costs will be avoided. This approach also limits debate over the magnitude of a potential harm that has not yet eventuated. The creator of the risk has the incentive to gauge accurately, for he is the one who must pay if harm does occur.

While in principle it provides efficient results, the torts approach encounters at least four difficulties when applied to many of the risks that are encountered in a modern technological society. The option of declaring bankruptcy allows the responsible party to avoid paying and so to impose risks that it should not impose. Causality is often difficult to assign for misfortunes that may have alternative or multiple (and synergistically related) causes. Did the individual contract lung cancer from air pollution or from his own smoking, or both? Furthermore, the traditional torts requirement that individuals be made whole cannot be met in many instances (death, loss of a limb). Finally, paying compensation after the fact may also produce inappropriate incentives, and hence be inefficient. Workers who can be more or less careful around danger-ous machinery, for example, are likely to be more careful if they will not be compensated for losing an appendage.

Our normal market and legal system tends to break down when substantial health risks are imposed on a relatively large population. These are, therefore, precisely the situations in which the cost-benefit approach is and should be called into play. Cost-benefit analysis is typi-cally used in just those situations where our normal risk decision processes run into dif-ficulty. We should therefore not expect it to lead to outcomes that are as satisfactory as those that evolve when ordinary market and private contractual trade are employed. But we should be able to expect better outcomes than we

would achieve by muddling through un-systematically.

We have defended cost-benefit analysis as the most practical of ethically defensible methods and the most ethical of practically us-able methods for conducting public decision-making. It cannot substitute for—nor can it adequately encompass, analyze, or consider—the sensitive application of social values. Thus it cannot be made the final arbiter of public de-cisions. But it does add a useful structure to public debate, and it does enable us to quantify some of the quantifiable aspects of public de-cisions. Our defense parallels Winston Chur-chill's argument for democracy: it is not per-fect, but it is better than the alternatives.

Ways Not to Think about Plastic Trees: New Foundations for Environmental Law

Laurence H. Tribe

Remember these things lost;
   and under the vaulting roof of the cathedral
      burn a candle to the memory.[1]

Baudelaire's *Rêve Parisien* paints what is quite literally a still life—a dreamscape of a metallic city where groves of colonnades stand in the place of trees and, in the place of water, pools of lead.[2] More prosaic but no less unnerving was the recent decision by Los Angeles County offi-cials to install more than 900 plastic trees and shrubs in concrete planters along the median strip of a major boulevard.[3] The construction of a new box culvert, it seemed, had left only 12 to 18 inches of dirt on the strip, insufficient to sustain natural trees.[4] County officials decided to experiment with artificial plants constructed of factory-made leaves and branches wired to

plumbing pipes, covered with plastic and "planted" in aggregate rock coated with epoxy.[5] Although a number of the trees were torn down by unknown vandals[6] and further plantings were halted,[7] the tale may not be over. For an article in *Science*[8] suggested recent-ly that, just as advertising can lead people to value wilderness and nature, so too it can "create plentiful substitutes."[9] The demand for rare environments is . . . learned," the *Science* article observes, and "conscious public choice can manipulate this learning so that the en-vironments which people learn to use and want reflect environments that are likely to be avail-able at low cost. . . . Much more can be done with plastic trees and the like to give most peo-ple the feeling that they are experiencing nature."[10]

While so explicit an acknowledgment of the acceptability of artificial environments may be unusual, the attitude it expresses toward the natural order is far from uncommon. In-creasingly, artificial objects and settings sup-plant those supplied by nature. Durable Astro-

Source: *Yale Law Journal*, Vol. 83, No. 7 (June 1974), pp. 1315–19, 1325–27, 1329–32, 1341–46. Reprinted by permission.

turf replaces grass in football stadiums and around swimming pools.[11] Guests at the Hyatt Regency hotel in San Francisco walk among more than 100 natural trees growing in the 20-story lobby but listen to recorded bird calls broadcast from speakers hidden in the tree branches.[12] And Walt Disney World offers a multitude of visitors what one *Newsweek* writer described as "a programmed paradise."[13]

I do not focus on Astroturf and the plastic trees of Los Angeles as harbingers of our most urgent environmental problems. Although the long-term prospects in this regard are probably more troublesome, I claim no imminent risk that we will too cleverly engineer ourselves into a synthetic hell. Quite apart from any such danger, I believe that such "nature surrogates" provide an illuminating metaphor through which to expose and criticize certain premises which underlie most current discussions of environmental thought, law, and policy.

While it might appear initially that nature surrogates would be antithetical to the ecological concern embodied in present environmental legislation and policy, a closer analysis leads to precisely the opposite conclusion. The perpetually green lawn and the plastic tree, far from representing the outcroppings of some inexplicable human perversion, are expressions of a view of nature fully consistent with the basic assumptions of present environmental policy. These assumptions, which are implicit in developing uses of policy analysis as well as in emerging institutional structures, make all environmental judgment turn on calculations of how well human wants, discounted over time, are satisfied.

This article will attempt to identify the roots and expose the inadequacies of this homocentric perspective and will tentatively outline the shape of an alternative foundation for environmental law.

I. The Limits of Analytic Sophistication: Nature and Reason in the Service of Man

Despite occasional probes in less familiar directions,[14] the emerging field of environmental law is being built on the basic platform of analytic sophistication in the service of human need. Statutes[15] and judicial decisions[16] typically mandate "systematic" and "interdisciplinary" attempts to "insure that presently unquantified environmental amenities and values may be given appropriate consideration in decisionmaking along with economic and technical considerations."[17] Public interest challenges to decisions alleged to be environmentally unsound are diverted by the pressures of doctrine and tradition from claims about the value of nature as such into claims about interference with human use,[18] even when the real point may be that a particular wilderness area, for example, should be "used" by no-one.[19]

A. Technical Capacities and Limitations

From the start, the aspect of environmental policy analysis that has most concerned students of the matter has been the supposed difficulty of ever incorporating certain *kinds of values* into systematic analyses of environmental problems, whether in the service of legislators, of planning agencies, of litigators, of private enterprises, or of courts. Variously described as fragile, intangible, or unquantifiable, these values have been widely thought to possess peculiar features making them intrinsically resistant to inclusion along with such allegedly "hard" concerns as technical feasibility and economic efficiency. In particular, those dimensions of a choice for which market prices do not exist have seemed to pose intractable obstacles to "objective measurement."

It does not take long to discover, however, that this emphasis on categorizing fragile values embodies a misleading formulation of the problem and an inadequate appreciation of the analytic capacities latent in the techniques under examination. To be sure, the aspirations of some policy analysts to an elusive "objectivity,"[20] the identity of their constituents,[21] and the advocacy role often expected of them by their clients,[22] induce certain practitioners to overlook or understress a variety of values that might, in context, be characterized as "fragile." More specifically, insofar as analysis is intended to help a decisionmaker persuade others of the justifiability and wisdom of his choice,[23] its usefulness in the absence of consensus as to goals is predictably reduced whenever it does not at least appear to point "objectively" and unambiguously toward a particular alternative. The users of policy-analytic techniques in advocacy situations are thus under constant pressure to reduce the many dimensions of each problem to some common measure in terms of which "objective" comparison seems possible—even when this means squeezing out "soft" but crucial information merely because it seems difficult to render commensurable with the "hard" data in the problem.[24] These tendencies are aggravated by the institutional and legal contexts in which analytic techniques are ordinarily used: Such techniques tend to be deployed as tools only by the individual combatants in policy conflicts; thus the only values consistently served are those strongly felt by persons motivated and able to seek a policy analyst's aid—a circumstance likely to exclude values too widely diffused over space, or too incrementally affected over time, to be strongly championed by any single client of a policy analyst; values associated primarily with persons not yet in being (future generations); and values not associated with persons at all (for example, the "rights" of plants or animals).

Having said all of this, however, one must concede that there is nothing in the structure of the techniques themselves, or in the logical premises on which they rest, which inherently precludes their intelligent use by a public decisionmaker in the service of these "intangible," or otherwise "fuzzy," concerns.[25] Despite what appears to be a widely held assumption to the contrary, all such concerns can in theory be incorporated in a rigorous analysis, either by using various market price or other numerical surrogates to value extramarket costs or benefits,[26] or by the technique of "shadow pricing"—that is, qualitatively describing as best one can the contents of a constraint as intangible as natural beauty or procedural fairness or respect for future generations, and then calculating the tangible benefits that would have to be forgone if one were to insist that one's policy conform to the constraint described.[27] . . .

Having considered the most serious technical obstacles to "good" environmental analysis and planning, one is therefore forced to conclude that none of these obstacles need prove insuperable: Each calls essentially for further research in preparation for more sensitive analyses and both greater creativity and closer vigilance in whatever environmental analyses are in fact conducted.

B. Ideological Boundaries

A final obstacle remains. Policy analysts typically operate within a social, political and intellectual tradition that regards the satisfaction of individual human wants as the only defensible measure of the good, a tradition that perceives the only legitimate task of reason to be that of consistently identifying and then serving individual appetite, preference, or desire. This tradition is echoed as well in environmental legislation which protects nature not for its own sake but in order to preserve its potential value for man.[28]

By treating individual human need and desire as the ultimate frame of reference, and by assuming that human goals and ends must be taken as externally "given" (whether physiologically or culturally or both) rather than generated by reason, environmental policy makes a value judgment of enormous significance. And, once that judgment has been made, any claim for the continued existence of threatened wilderness areas or endangered species must rest on the identification of human wants and needs which would be jeopardized by a disputed development. As our capacity increases to satisfy those needs and wants artificially, the claim becomes tenuous indeed.

Consider again the plastic trees planted along a freeway's median strip by Los Angeles county officials. If the most sophisticated application of the techniques of policy analysis could unearth no human need which would, after appropriate "education," be better served by natural trees, then the environmental inquiry would be at an end. The natural trees, more costly and vulnerable than those made of plastic, would offer no increment of satisfaction to justify the added effort of planting and maintaining them.

To insist on the superiority of natural trees in the teeth of a convincing demonstration that plastic ones would equally well serve human purposes may seem irrational. Yet the tendency to balk at the result of the analysis remains. There is a suspicion that some crucial perspective has been omitted from consideration, that the conclusion is as much a product of myopia as of logic.

II. Beyond Human Wants: A New Rationale for Environmental Policy

What has been omitted is, at base, an appreciation of an ancient and inescapable paradox: We can be truly free to pursue our ends only if we act out of obligation, the seeming antithesis of freedom. To be free is not simply to follow our ever-changing wants wherever they might lead. To be free is to choose what we shall want, what we shall value, and therefore what we shall be.[29] But to make such choices without losing the thread of continuity that integrates us over time and imparts a sense of our wholeness in history, we must be able to reason about what to choose—to choose in terms of commitments we have made to bodies of principle which we perceive as external to our choices and by which we feel bound, bodies of principle that can define a coherent and integrative system even as they evolve with our changing selves.[30]

To deny the existence of such bodies of principle is fashionable, but it is not inevitable. However obvious, it is worth recalling that most of the great philosophical systems of our own past—those of Plato and Aristotle, of Aquinas and the Scholastics, of Hegel and the Idealists—were grounded in the view that the highest purpose of human reason is to evolve a comprehensive understanding of mankind's place in the universe, not merely to serve as a detector of consistency and causality and thus as an instrument for morally blind desire. "The emphasis," as Horkheimer reminds us, "was on ends rather than on means." It is only recently that the concept of reason as calculation without content became central in the West—that reason began to liquidate itself "as an agency of ethical, moral, and religious insight." Unless we are to remain in the shadow of that intellectual eclipse, we cannot simply assume that we must stand mute when confronting the ultimate question of whether we want our children, and their children's children, to live in, and *enjoy,* a plastic world. . . .

Theoretically at least, policy analyses and legislative provisions can be so calibrated as to be sensitive to, and then to accommodate, whatever values individuals are capable of discerning. Yet it does not follow, simply because all values susceptible to human perception may thus be formally "included" in our designs, that an institutional system or an analytic technique which relentlessly treats all such values as manifestations of individual human preference will prove satisfactory. To reach such a conclusion would require another premise: that the act of characterizing all values as expressions of human preference does not affect their content or distort their perception. It is a premise that does not withstand scrutiny. Treating all values as based on personal preferences results in a major shift of focus: Attention is no longer directed to the ostensible content of the value but rather to the fact that it is a more or less abstracted indicium of self-interest. Even if one ultimately chooses the same actions under such a shift of focus, one may well end with the feeling that one has chosen them not out of obligation or for their own sake, but because their opportunity cost in terms of one's range of personal interests was low enough, thereby distorting the meaning of the choice and of the actions chosen.[31]

To offer a simple illustration, suppose a person feels an obligation to protect a wilderness area from strip mining. The initial perception of that obligation is likely to take the form of sympathy for the wildlife and vegetation which would be destroyed or displaced. Indeed, the perceived obligation may display at least the rudiments of an internal structure: Killing "higher" animal life may seem unjustifiable except for compelling reasons (to sustain, or to avert a direct threat to, human life, for instance); destroying plant life may seem improper if destruction can be avoided without "undue" cost. Certain categories of harm which might leave human civilization intact while threatening the global eco-system as a whole— severe radioactive contamination of the oceans, for instance—may seem wrong regardless of the strength of the countervailing human interest.

If the sense of obligation prompts the individual to undertake some concrete effort on behalf of the environment, such as making an adverse response to an environmental survey, initiating a suit to enjoin the strip mining, or advancing an argument in favor of preservation, a subtle transformation is likely to be occasioned by the philosophical premises of the system in which the effort is undertaken. The felt obligation will be translated into the terminology of human self-interest: It may be said that future generations will be deprived of contact with wildlife; that the aesthetic satisfaction of certain individuals will be diminished; that other recreational areas will become overcrowded. . . .

While the environmentalist may feel somewhat disingenuous in taking this approach, he is likely to regard it as justified by the demands of legal doctrine and the exigencies of political reality. What the environmentalist may not perceive is that, by couching his claim in terms of human self-interest—by articulating environmental goals wholly in terms of human needs and preferences—he may be helping to legitimate a system of discourse which so structures human thought and feeling as to erode, over the long run, the very sense of obligation which provided the initial impetus for his own protective efforts. . . .

To return to our example, once obligation has been transformed into a mere matter of personal preference, the tendency is inevitable to compare the value of wilderness with the value of strip mined coal in terms of self-interest. From there, it is but a short step to an even more blatantly reductionist approach: In order to insure that the comparison is "rational," the two values will almost certainly be translated into smoothly exchangeable units of satisfaction, such as dollars. While certain discontinuities may still be recognized—destruction of *all* wilderness areas may not be deemed worth even an infinite supply of coal—they will tend to be gradually eroded by the pressure toward analytic uniformity.

The translation of all values into homocen-

tric terms thus creates two distortions: First, an inchoate sense of obligation toward natural objects is flattened into an aspect of self-interest; second, value discontinuities tend to be foreshortened. It is important to emphasize again that these distortions do not follow as a necessary result from the theoretical premises of policy analysis. Although Aaron Wildavsky suggested in a 1966 critique that cost-benefit techniques structurally presuppose the individualistic premise that only personal preferences matter,[32] it is obviously possible to compute the costs of an activity in any terms one wishes or to impose whatever nonindividualistic constraint is deemed important. There is nothing in the logic of analytic techniques (or, for that matter, the logic of interest identification which precedes legislative enactment) that limits the use of such methods to the tradition of liberal individualism in any of its diverse forms.

The distortion occurs rather because the process of interest identification, as it is presently employed, interacts in a crucial way with the content of the interest being identified. The identification takes place in the context of a system of attitudes and assumptions which treat human want satisfaction as the only legitimate referent of policy analysis and choice. These assumptions, and the desire for analytic clarity which accompanies them, together exert an enormous reductionist pressure on all values which would otherwise seem incommensurable with a calculus of individual human wants. Thus the distortion results not from a logical flaw in the techniques of policy analysis but rather from what I have elsewhere described as the ideological bias of the system in which such analysis is imbedded, a system that has come to treat the human will and its wants as the center around which reason as calculation must revolve. . . .

III. The First Turns of the Spiral

. . . At a minimum, we must begin to extricate our nature-regarding impulses from the conceptually oppressive sphere of human want satisfaction, by encouraging the elaboration of perceived obligations to plant and animal life and to objects of beauty in terms that do not falsify such perceptions from the very beginning by insistent "reference to human interests." Thus environmental impact surveys and statements might make explicit reference to obligations felt toward nature. Resources might be devoted to improving our technical capacity to incorporate such felt obligations in policy analyses. And legislation might be enacted to permit the bringing of claims directly on behalf of natural objects without imposing the requirement that such claims be couched in terms of interference with human use.

A related proposal was recently advanced by Christopher Stone, who suggested the appointment of guardians or trustees for objects in the environment[33] as institutional embodiments of a perceived obligation to treat the world about us with respect, and as symbols of a recognition that persons are not the only entities in the world that can be thought to possess rights. Despite the protests of some that "man . . . can have no duty to any being other than man," and that, as a matter of "logic," only human beings can have "rights," the fact is that even our own legal system has long recognized entities other than individual human beings—churches, partnerships, corporations, unions, families, and occasionally even animals[34]—as rights-holders for a wide variety of purposes. Acceptance of the notion that some previously "rightless" entity enjoys legal protection is largely a matter of acculturation.[35]

Yet it remains true that treating a class of entities as rights-holders is consistent with regarding their protected status as a mere juristic convention. Thus, although American law has long accepted the independent juridical status of corporations, no one would suggest today that such entities are anything but legal constructs. No law prohibits the death or dismemberment of corporations on the basis of their intrinsic "right to life." No jurisprudence rationalizes the validity of corporate law in terms of "just" propitiation of the endogenous needs or wants of corporate entities.[36] It seems likely that contemporary observers would view the independent legal status of environmental objects in essentially the same way that they

view the concept of corporate existence. Affording legal rights to endangered species and threatened wilderness areas might thus be regarded as a convenient technique for concentrating congeries of otherwise diffuse aesthetic and ecological concerns ultimately reducible to human interest—in other words, as a useful but quite transparent legal fiction.

Even if this were the most one could hope for, the concept of rights for natural objects would probably represent a valuable doctrinal innovation. Whatever unnecessary threat the "standing" requirement continues to pose to effective environmental action would be avoided.[37] And procedural devices far less cumbersome than class actions would become available for challenging environmental abuses.[38]

But we might plausibly hope for more. At least so long as we remain within empathizing distance of the objects whose rights we seek to recognize, it seems reasonable to expect the acknowledgment of such rights to be regarded as more than fictitious. Thus, protecting cats and dogs from torture on the basis of their desire to be free from pain and hence their right not to be mistreated seems less jarring conceptually than protecting a forest from clear-cutting on the theory that the threatened trees have an inherent "right to life."

It is not surprising that one of the few pieces of existing federal law aimed unambiguously at protecting nonhuman interests—the Federal Laboratory Animal Welfare Act—limits its protection to mammals, whose perceptions of pain and discomfort we presume to be similar to our own. . . .

As the evolutionary distance between man and nonhuman rightsholders increases, the difficulty of analogizing to human experiences mounts. Torturing a dog evokes a strong sympathetic response; dismembering a frog produces a less acute but still unambiguous image of pain; even pulling the wings off a fly may cause a sympathetic twinge; but who would flinch at exterminating a colony of protozoa?

When legal protection is sought for plant life, the obstacles to convincing analogy are greater still. Yet even here the prospects are not altogether hopeless. Humans share certain fundamental needs with plants. Humans and plants both require water, oxygen and nutrition; both grow and reproduce; both die. A set of basic reference points for analogizing plant requirements to human needs thus exists. Some research even suggests that plants exhibit electrical and chemical reactions which are functionally analogous to pain.[39] And, once the bases for empathy are thus established, biologists and ecologists can obviously enrich our understanding of what "needs" exist for the other life forms with whom we have begun to feel new kinship.

What is crucial to recognize is that the human capacity for empathy and identification is not static; the very process of recognizing *rights* in those higher vertebrates with whom we can already empathize could well pave the way for still further extensions as we move upward along the spiral of moral evolution. It is not only the human liberation movements—involving first blacks, then women, and now children—that advance in waves of increased consciousness. The inner dynamic of every assault on domination is an ever broadening realization of reciprocity and identity. Viewed from a slightly different perspective, new possibilities for respect and new grounds for community elevate both master and slave simultaneously, reaffirming the truth that the oppressor is among the first to be liberated when he lifts the yoke, that freedom can be realized only in fidelity to obligation.

A passage in Faulkner's *Absalom, Absalom!* may hold the key: "Maybe happen is never once but like ripples maybe on water after the pebble sinks, the ripples moving on, spreading, the pool attached by a narrow umbilical water-cord to the next pool. . . ."[40] But there are some shores too remote for even these concentric circles to reach in the foreseeable future. When it is urged that legal protection be extended to nonliving entities like canyons and cathedrals, not for our sake but for theirs, it may be precisely such distant shores at which we are asked to gaze. Saint Francis of Assisi could embrace Brother Fire and Sister Water,[41] but Western societies in the last third of this century may be unable to entertain seriously the notion that a mountain or a seashore has intrinsic needs and can make independent moral claims upon our designs.

Still we can try. We can set aside resources and create public authorities for the specific purpose of preserving intact at least some major areas of real wilderness while we convert others into more Walt Disney Worlds and Coney Islands. The very process of treating some places with such respect may itself reveal and even create conceptual possibilities beyond our present capacities.[42] If, as I have argued elsewhere,[43] certain choices do not merely implement but radically alter the value systems within which they are made, then choosing to accord nature a fraternal rather than an exploited role—even when the resulting institutions resolve in particular cases not to forego certain human opportunities "for nature's sake"—might well make us different persons from the manipulators and subjugators we are in danger of becoming. . . .

Notes

1. Brower, in Time and the River Flowing 159 (F. Leydet ed. 1968) (writing of a great cavern, submerged during Lake Powell's creation in June, 1965, that had once been called the Cathedral in the Desert).

2. C. Baudelaire, *Rêve Parisien,* in Les Fleurs Du Mal 129, 347 (1955).

3. *See* L.A. Times, Feb. 8, 1972, § 2, at 6, col. 2. Plastic birds were subsequently added by unknown persons. *See* L.A. Times, Mar. 14, 1972.

4. *See* L.A. Times, Feb. 6, 1972. It may be that the decision to use plastic trees was also connected with the difficulty of sustaining natural plant life in the polluted atmosphere of Los Angeles County. *See* Chicago Tribune, Feb. 22, 1972, § 1, at 18, col. 2. ("Their admittedly logical argument is that little else will survive in that smogladen climate and that a plastic tree is more attractive than a dead and rotting one.")

5. *See* L.A. Times, Feb. 8, 1972.

6. *See* L.A. Times, Mar. 1, 1972.

7. *See* L.A. Times, Feb. 22, 1972.

8. Krieger, *What's Wrong with Plastic Trees?,* 179 Science 446 (1973).

9. *Id.* at 451.

10. *Id.* at 451, 453. Thus, when Roland Barthes saw in plastic "the stuff of alchemy" and in its

ubiquity the message that "the whole world can be plasticized," he foretold more than he could have known. R. Barthes, Mythologies 97–99 (A. Lavers transl. 1972).

11. The virtues of AstroTurf are amply extolled in Monsanto's advertising: At last, the work-free poolside! Simply install 'Round-the-Home Astro-Turf . . . it gives your poolside the look of lush grass, right up to the water's edge. Besides being bright, beautiful, durable and fade resistant, 'Round-the-Home AstroTurf is also easy to maintain—simply wash it with a hose. . . .
Monsanto Co. advertisement (on file with the *Yale Law Journal*).

12. Press release from Hyatt Regency San Francisco, May 8, 1973 ("Along the south side of the lobby runs a 130-foot long rock-lined 'babbling brook,' backed by a huge planter of shrubbery and live trees. Also located in this section of the lobby is a unique 'sound sculpture'. . . . Stereophonic speakers concealed in the foliage simulate the sound of songbirds flitting through the atrium.") (on file with the *Yale Law Journal*).

13. Morgenstern, *What Hath Disney Wrought!*, Newsweek, Oct. 18, 1971, at 38.

14. *See, e.g.,* Stone, *Should Trees Have Standing?— Toward Legal Rights For Natural Objects*, 45 S. Cal. L. Rev. 450 (1972).

15. *See, e.g.,* National Environmental Policy Act of 1969, 42 U.S.C. §§ 4321-47 (1970).

16. *See, e.g.,* Calvert Cliffs' Coordinating Comm., Inc. v. AEC, 449 F.2d 1109 (D.C. Cir. 1971).

17. National Environmental Policy Act of 1969 §§ 102(2)(A), 102(2)(B), 42 U.S.C. §§ 4332(2)(A), 4332(2)(B) (1970).

18. *See, e.g.,* United States v. SCRAP, 412 U.S. 669 (1973); Sierra Club v. Morton, 405 U.S. 727 (1972).

19. *See, e.g.,* 405 U.S. at 741 (Douglas, J., dissenting); *id.* at 755 (Blackmun, J., dissenting).

20. *See* Tribe, *Policy Science: Analysis or Ideology?*, 2 Phil. & Pub. Affairs 66, 84 (1972) ("[s]eeking to limit himself to matters about which he can be 'completely objective,' the policy analyst who must compare two alternative courses of action first focuses on the *consequences* of each alternative . . . and then on *objectively comparable features* of those consequences. . . .") [hereinafter cited as *Policy Science*], in Benefit-Cost and Policy Analysis 1972, An Aldine Annual on Forecasting, Decision-Making, and Evaluation 3–47 (W. Niskanen, A.

Harberger, R. Haveman, R. Turvey & R. Zeckhauser eds. 1972) [hereinafter cited as Aldine Annual].

21. *See Policy Science, supra* note 20, at 104 ("[q]uite obviously, the only values that can be served [by the analyst who accepts his client's ends as given] will be those strongly held by persons who seek a policy analyst's aid.").

22. *See* Tribe, *Technology Assessment and the Fourth Discontinuity: The Limits of Instrumental Rationality*, 46 S. Cal. L. Rev. 617, 627 (1973) ("[policy] analysis is often intended not only to aid the decisionmaker in choosing a course of action, but also to help him in *persuading others* of the justifiability and wisdom of his choice.") [hereinafter cited as *Technology Assessment*].

23. *See* Keeney & Raiffa, *A Critique of Formal Analysis in Public Decision Making*, in Analysis of Public Systems 64 (A. Drake, R. Keeney & P. Morse eds. 1972).

24. *Cf.* Tribe, *Trial by Mathematics: Precision and Ritual in the Legal Process*, 84 Harv. L. Rev. 1329, 1361–65, 1389–90 (1971) (discussion of the "dwarfing of soft variables").

25. *See Policy Science, supra* note 20, at 90–93, 106; *Technology Assessment, supra* note 22, at 630, 632–33.

26. *See, e.g.,* Knetsch, *Economics of Including Recreation as a Purpose of Eastern Water Projects*, 46 J. Farm Econ. 1148, 1150 (1964).

27. *See* McKean, *The Use of Shadow Prices*, in Problems in Public Expenditure Analysis 33, 47–48 (S. Chase ed. 1968).

28. In National Environmental Policy Act of 1969 (NEPA), § 101(b), 42 U.S.C. § 4331(b) (1970), Congress defined the goals of national environmental policy as follows:

In order to carry out the policy set forth in this chapter, it is the continuing responsibility of the Federal Government to use all practicable means, consistent with other essential considerations of national policy, to improve and coordinate Federal plans, functions, programs, and resources to the end that the Nation may—

(1) fulfill the responsibilities of each generation as trustee of the environment for succeeding generations;

(2) assure for all Americans safe, healthful, productive, and esthetically and culturally pleasing surroundings;

(3) attain the widest range of beneficial uses

of the environment without degradation, risk to health or safety, or other undesirable and unintended consequences;

(4) preserve important historic, cultural, and natural aspects of our national heritage, and maintain, wherever possible, an environment which supports diversity and variety of individual choice;

(5) achieve a balance between population and resource use which will permit high standards of living and a wide sharing of life's amenities; and

(6) enhance the quality of renewable resources and approach the maximum attainable recycling of depletable resources.

29. *Cf.* Frankfurt, *Freedom of the Will and the Concept of a Person*, 68 J. Phil. 5, 7–14 (1971).

30. *See Technology Assessment, supra* note 22, at 652–54. As I sought to show in *Technology Assessment*, such reasoned commitments can be shaped only in communities of persons whose shared experiences and understandings facilitate a common groping toward communal ends. *See also* R. Nisbet, The Quest for Community 229–32, 235–37, 241–47, 264–71, 276–79 (1953). This is so in part for contingent reasons—because it seems unlikely in this period of history that the search for ends can generate fruitful and convincing conclusions when pursued by isolated individuals—and in part as a matter of definition, because the wholeness that in fact seems threatened by freedom in the choice of ends is wholeness among persons (community) as well as wholeness over time (continuity). *See Technology Assessment* at 651 n.118.

31. *See* T. Nagel, The Possibility of Altruism (1970). The necessity to relate altruistic impulses to endogenous needs or wants of the object of altruism was recognized by Rawls. *See* J. Rawls [A Theory of Justice] at 189. ("There is . . . a peculiar feature of perfect altruism that deserves mention. A perfect altruist can fulfill his desire only if someone else has independent, or first-order, desires.")

32. See Aaron Wildavsky, The Political Economy of Efficiency, 26 Pub. Ad. Rev. 292 (1966).

33. *See* Stone, *supra* note 14.

34. A few courts have held that animals themselves enjoy rights under statutes prohibiting animal cruelty. *See, e.g.*, State v. Karstendiek, 49 La. 1621, 1624, 22 So. 845, 847 (1897). ("The statute [prohibiting cruelty to animals] is based on 'the theory, unknown to the common law, that animals have rights which, like those of human beings, are to be protected.'") Perhaps the most eloquent expression of this view is contained in an opinion written by a Mississippi judge in 1887:

Section 2918 of the Code, under which appellant was indicted, renders it a criminal offence for any person to cruelly beat, abuse, starve, torture or purposely injure certain animals, whether they belong to himself or another. This statute is for the benefit of animals, as creatures capable of feeling and suffering, and it was intended to protect them from cruelty, without reference to their being property, or to the damages which might thereby be occasioned to their owners. . . . [S]peaking for myself, I wish to say, that laws and the enforcement or observance of laws for the protection of dumb brutes from cruelty are, in my judgment, among the best evidences of the justice and benevolence of men. Such statutes were not intended to interfere, and do not interfere, with the necessary discipline and government of such animals, or place any unreasonable restriction on their use or the enjoyment to be derived from their possession. The common law recognized no right in such animals, and punished no cruelty to them, except in so far as it affected the right of individuals to such property. Such statutes remedy this defect, and exhibit the spirit of that Divine law, which is so mindful of dumb brutes as to teach and command not to muzzle the ox when he treadeth out the corn—not to plough with an ox and an ass together—not take the bird that sitteth on its young, or its eggs, and not to seethe a kid in its mother's milk. To disregard the rights and feelings of equals is unjust and ungenerous, but to wilfully or wantonly injure or oppress the weak and helpless is mean and cowardly. Human beings have at least some means of protecting themselves against the inhumanity of man— that inhumanity which "makes countless thousands mourn," but dumb brutes have none. Cruelty to them manifests a vicious and degraded nature, and it tends inevitably to cruelty to men. Animals whose lives are devoted to our use and pleasure, and which are capable, perhaps, of feeling as great physical pain or pleasure as ourselves, deserve for these considerations alone, kindly treatment. The dominion of man over them, if not a moral trust, has a better significance than the development of malignant passions and cruel instincts. Often their beauty, gentleness and fidelity suggest the reflection, that it may have been one of the purposes of their creation and subordination to enlarge the sympathies and expand the better feelings of our race. But, however this may be, human beings should be kind and just to dumb brutes, if for no other reason than to learn how to be kind and just to each other.

Stephens v. State, 65 Miss. 329, 330–32, 3 So. 458–59 (1887) (Arnold, J.).

35. See Stone, supra note 14, at 453–56. Arguing for "rights" on behalf of nonhuman entities should not be confused with suggesting that certain nonhuman interests should have absolute priority over conflicting human claims; recognizing rights in a previously rightless entity is entirely consistent with acknowledging circumstances in which such rights might be overridden, just as human rights may themselves come into conflict.

36. The legal protection afforded corporations is typically viewed as justifiable only insofar as it serves individual human needs. See, e.g., Rostow, To Whom and For What Ends Is Corporate Management Responsible, in The Corporation in Modern Society 63–71 (E. Mason ed. 1959). See generally J. Rawls [A Theory of Justice] 265–74.

37. Under current standing doctrine, a plaintiff cannot challenge an activity as injurious to the environment unless he has suffered or is likely to suffer personal harm as a result thereof. See United States v. SCRAP, 412 U.S. 669, 686–89 (1973).

38. For instance, administratively appointed guardians could bring actions to enforce the rights of environmental objects. See generally Stone, supra note 14, at 464–73.

39. See, e.g., Backster, Evidence of a Primary Perception in Plant Life, 10 Int'l J. Parapsychology 329 (1968); Lawrence, Plants Have Feelings, Too, Organic Gardening & Farming, Apr. 1971, at 64; Woodlief, Royster & Huang, Effect of Random Noise on Plant Growth, 46 J. Acoustical Soc'y Am. 481 (1969). See also Stone, supra note 14, at 479 n.93.

40. W. Faulkner. Absalom, Absalom! (New York: Random [Vintage], 1972), p. 261.

41. St. Francis of Assisi, The Canticle of The Sun, in Writings 153 (P. Robinson transl. 1906). ("Praised be my Lord for sister water,/The which is greatly helpful and humble and precious and pure./Praised be my Lord for brother fire,/By which Thou lightest up the dark./And fair is he and gay and mighty and strong.")

42. See, e.g., D. Rudhyar, Directives for New Life 21–23 (1971) (suggestion that the earth is a total "organism" in which mankind plays the role of articulating a planetary consciousness).

43. Technology Assessment, supra note 22, at 640.

Selected Bibliography

Note on using the bibliography: Many important articles are not listed below because they are found in the books listed. Further, the bibliography is intended to supplement earlier references in this volume. The bibliography also serves a start-up function; that is, it will lead the reader to other works that provide further bibliographical help—especially those classified under "General." Finally, we note the special usefulness of the one current philosophical journal devoted to concerns central to this volume: *Environmental Ethics* (published by Environmental Philosophy, Inc. at the University of Georgia, Athens).

General

Attfield, Robin. *The Ethics of Environmental Concern* (New York: Columbia University Press, 1983).

Barbour, Ian. *Technology, Environment, and Human Values* (New York: Praeger, 1980).

Blackstone, William, ed. *Philosophy and Environmental Crisis* (Athens: University of Georgia Press, 1974).

Elliot, Robert, and Gare, Arran, eds. *Environmental Philosophy* (University Park: The Pennsylvania State University Press, 1983).

Goodpaster, K. E., and Sayre, K. M., eds. *Ethics and Problems of the 21st Century* (Notre Dame: University of Notre Dame Press, 1979).

Mannison, Don, and McRobbie, Michael, and Routley, Richard, eds. *Environmental Philosophy* (Canberra: Research School of Social Sciences, Australian National University, 1980).

McCloskey, H. J. *Ecological Ethics and Politics* (Totowa, New Jersey: Rowman and Littlefield, 1983).

Merchant, Carolyn. *The Death of Nature: Women, Ecology and the Scientific Revolution* (New York: Harper and Row, 1980).

Partridge, Ernest. *What Good Is a Planet?* (Chicago: Nelson Hall, forthcoming).

Passmore, John. *Man's Responsibility for Nature* (New York: Scribner's, 1974).

Regan, Tom, ed. *Earthbound: New Introductory Essays in Environmental Ethics* (New York: Random House, 1984).

Scherer, Donald, and Attig, Thomas. *Ethics and the Environment* (Englewood Cliffs: Prentice-Hall, 1983).

Shrader-Frechette, K. S. *Environmental Ethics* (Pacific Grove, California: The Boxwood Press, 1981).

Part I

Clark, Stephen. *The Moral Status of Animals* (Oxford: Clarendon Press, 1977).

Feinberg, Joel. "The Rights of Animals and Unborn Generations" in *Philosophy and Environmental Crisis*, edited by William Blackstone (Athens: University of Georgia Press, 1974).

Fox, M. W. *Returning to Eden: Animal Rights and Human Responsibility* (New York: Viking Press, 1980).

Frey, R. G. *Interests and Rights: The Case Against Animals* (Oxford: Clarendon Press, 1980).

————. *Rights, Animals, and Suffering* (Oxford: Basil Blackwell Ltd., 1983).

Godlovitch, Stanley, and Godlovitch, Roslind, and Harris, John, eds. *Animals, Men, and Morals* (London: Gallancz, 1971).

Harrison, Ruth. *Animal Machines: The New Factory Farming Industry* (London: Stuart, 1964).

Inquiry Volume 22, Nos. 1–2 (Summer 1979). Includes a useful bibliography; the entire issue is about animals.

Johnson, Edward. *Species and Morality*, PhD dissertation in philosophy at Princeton University (1976); see University Microfilms International, 1977: Ann Arbor, Michigan.

Loftin, Robert W. "The Morality of Hunting," *Environmental Ethics* 6 (1984), pp. 241–50.

Magell, Charles. *A Bibliography on Animal Rights*

and Related Matters (Washington, D.C.: University Press of America, 1981).

Mason, Jim, and Singer, Peter. *Animal Factories* (New York: Crown, 1980).

Midgley, Mary. *Animals and Why They Matter* (Harmondsworth, England: Penguin Books Ltd., 1983).

————. *Beast and Man* (Ithaca: Cornell University Press, 1979).

Pierce, Christine. "Can Animals Be Liberated?" *Philosophical Studies* 36 (1979), pp. 69–75.

Regan, Tom. *All That Dwell Therein* (Berkeley: University of California Press, 1982).

————. *The Case for Animal Rights* (Berkeley: University of California Press, 1983).

Regan, Tom, and Singer, Peter, eds. *Animal Rights and Human Obligations* (Englewood Cliffs, New Jersey: Prentice-Hall, 1976).

Rollin, Bernard. *Animal Rights and Human Morality* (Buffalo: Prometheus Press, 1981).

Rosenfield, Leonora. *From Beast-Machine to Man-Machine* (New York: Columbia University Press, 1968).

Ryder, Richard. *Victims of Science: The Use of Animals in Research* (London: Davis-Poynter, 1975).

Singer, Peter. *Animal Liberation* (New York: A New York Review Book, distributed by Random House, 1975).

————. *The Expanding Circle* (New York: Farrar, Straus, and Giroux, 1981).

————. *Practical Ethics* (Cambridge: Cambridge University Press, 1979).

VanDeVeer, Donald. "Of Beasts, Persons, and the Original Position," *The Monist* 62 (1979), pp. 368–77.

Williams, William, and Miller, Harlan, eds. *Ethics and Animals* (Clifton, New Jersey: Humana Press, 1983). Williams also edits a useful newsletter by the same title; write the Department of Philosophy at Virginia Polytechnic Institute at Blacksburg, Virginia.

Part II

Abbey, Edward. *The Journey Home: Some Words in Defense of the American West* (New York: Dutton, 1977).

Barney, Daniel R. *The Last Stand,* Ralph Nader's Study Group Report on the National Forests (New York: Grossman Publishers, 1974).

Bugbee, Henry G. "Wilderness in America," *Journal of the American Academy of Religion* XLII (Dec. 1974), pp. 614–20.

Colinvaux, Paul. *Why Big Fierce Animals Are Rare* (Princeton: Princeton University Press, 1978).

Ehrlich, Paul, and Ehrlich, Anne. *Extinction* (New York: Random House, 1981).

Elliot, Robert. "The Value of Wild Nature," *Inquiry* 26 (Sept. 1983), pp. 359–61.

Engberg, Robert, and Wesling, Donald, eds. *John Muir: To Yosemite and Beyond:* Writings from the Years 1863 to 1875 (Madison: University of Wisconsin Press, 1980).

Frome, Michael. *Battle for the Wilderness* (New York: Praeger Publishers, 1974).

Glacken, Clarence. *Traces on the Rhodian Shore* (Berkeley: University of California Press, 1976).

Godfrey-Smith, William. "The Value of Wilderness," *Environmental Ethics* 1 (Winter 1979), pp. 309–319.

Hays, Samuel P. *Conservation and the Gospel of Efficiency:* The Progressive Conservation Movement, 1890–1920 (Cambridge: Harvard University Press, 1959).

Henberg, Marvin. "Wilderness as Playground," *Environmental Ethics* 6 (1984), pp. 251–63.

Katz, Eric. "Utilitarianism and Preservation," *Environmental Ethics* 1 (1979), pp. 357–64.

Lehman, Scott. "Do Wildernesses Have Rights?," *Environmental Ethics* 3 (Summer 1981), pp. 129–46.

Leopold, Aldo. "The Conservation Ethic," *Journal of Forestry* 31 (1933), pp. 634–43.

Lovelock, James. *Gaia: A New Look at Life on Earth* (New York: Oxford University Press, 1981).

Mannison, Don. "Nature May Be of No Value: A Reply to Elliot," *Inquiry* 26 (June 1983), pp. 233–35. (a reply to Elliot's "Faking Nature" in this volume)

Martin, John N. "The Concept of the Irreplaceable," *Environmental Ethics* 1 (1979), pp. 31–48.

Merton, Thomas. "The Wild Places," *The Center Magazine* (July 1968).

Myers, Norman. "The Whaling Controversy,"

American Scientist 63 (July–Aug. 1975), pp. 448–55.

Naess, Arne. "The Shallow and the Deep, Long-Range Ecological Movement," *Inquiry* 16 (1973), pp. 95–100.

Nash, Roderick, ed. *Wilderness and the American Mind* (New Haven: Yale University Press, 1973).

Norton, Bryan, ed. *The Preservation of The Species* (Princeton: Princeton University Press, 1985).

———. *The Spice of Life: Why Save Biological Variety?* (currently under review).

Pinchot, Gifford. *The Fight for Conservation* (Seattle: University of Washington Press, 1910).

Plumwood, Val, and Routley, Richard. "World Rainforest Destruction—The Social Factors," *The Ecologist* 12 (1982), pp. 4–22.

Regenstein, Lewis. *The Politics of Extinction* (New York: Macmillan and Company, 1975).

Rescher, Nicholas. "Why Save Endangered Species?" in N. Rescher, *Unpopular Essays on Technological Progress* (Pittsburgh: University of Pittsburgh Press, 1980).

Rodman, John (editor). "The Dolphin Papers," *The North American Review* (Spring 1974), pp. 13–26.

Rolston III, Holmes. "Values Gone Wild," *Inquiry* 26 (1983), pp. 181–207.

Routley, Richard, and Routley, Val. *The Fight for the Forests* (Canberra: Australian National University Press, 1974).

Sagoff, Mark. "On Preserving the Natural Environment," *The Yale Law Journal* 84 (Dec. 1974), pp. 205–67.

———. "On the Preservation of Species," *Columbia Journal of Environmental Law,* 7 (Fall 1980), pp. 33–67.

Sax, J. L. "Freedom: Voices from the Wilderness," *Environmental Law* 7 (Spring 1977), pp. 565–74.

Schwartz, William, ed. *Voices for the Wilderness* (New York: Ballantine Book, Inc., 1969).

Part III

Callicott, J. Baird. "Elements of an Environmental Ethic: Moral Considerability and the Biotic Community," *Environmental Ethics* 1 (1979), pp. 71–81.

———. "The Search for an Environmental Ethic," *Matters of Life and Death,* edited by Tom Regan, 2d ed. (New York: Random House, 1986).

Devall, William, and Sessions, George, eds. *Deep Ecology: Living As If Nature Mattered* (Salt Lake City, Utah: Peregrine Smith Books, 1985).

Ehrenfeld, David. *The Arrogance of Humanism* (New York: Oxford University Press, 1978).

Frankena, W. K. "Ethics and the Environment," *Ethics and Problems of the 21st Century,* edited by K. E. Goodpaster and K. M. Sayre (Notre Dame: University of Notre Dame Press, 1979), pp. 3–19.

Goodpaster, Kenneth. "On Being Morally Considerable," *Journal of Philosophy* 75 (1978), pp. 308–25.

Hill, Thomas, Jr. "Ideals of Human Excellence and Preserving Natural Environments," *Environmental Ethics* 5 (1983), pp. 211–24.

Johnson, Edward. "Animal Liberation Versus the Land Ethic," *Environmental Ethics* 3 (1981), pp. 265–273.

Marsh, George Perkins. *Man and Nature* (Cambridge: Harvard University Press, 1965).

Miller, Peter. "Value as Richness: Toward a Value Theory for an Expanded Naturalism in Environmental Ethics," *Environmental Ethics* 4 (Summer 1982), pp. 101–14.

Norton, Bryan. "Environmental Ethics and Weak Anthropocentrism," *Environmental Ethics* 6 (Summer 1984), pp. 131–48.

Pluhar, Evelyn B. "The Justification of an Environmental Ethic," *Environmental Ethics* 5 (Spring 1983), pp. 47–61.

Regan, Tom. "The Nature and Possibility of an Environmental Ethic," *Environmental Ethics* 3 (1981), pp. 19–34.

Rodman, John. "The Liberation of Nature?" *Inquiry* 20 (Spring 1977), pp. 83–145.

Rolston III, Holmes. "Is There an Ecological Ethic?," *Ethics* 85 (1975), pp. 93–109.

Routley, Richard. "Is There a Need for a New, An Environmental, Ethic?" *Proceedings of the Fifteenth World Congress of Philosophy* 1 (1973), pp. 205–10.

Routley, Val. "Critical Notice" (of John Passmore, *Man's Responsibility for Nature*), *Australasian Journal of Philosophy* 53 (Aug. 1975), pp. 171–85.

Schultz, Robert C., and Hughes, J. Donald, eds. *Ecological Consciousness: Essays from the Earthday X Colloquium*, University of Denver, April 21–24, 1980 (Washington, D.C.: University Press of America, 1981).

Shepard, Paul. *The Tender Carnivore and the Sacred Game* (New York: Scribner's Sons, 1973).

Taylor, Paul W. "Frankena on Environmental Ethics," *The Monist* 64 (July 1981), pp. 313–24.

White, Lynn, Jr. "The Historical Roots of Our Ecologic Crisis," *Science* 155 (March 10, 1967), pp. 1203–07.

Part IV

Ackerman, Bruce et al., *The Uncertain Search for Environmental Quality* (New York: Free Press, 1974).

Barkley, Paul, and Seckler, David, eds. *Economic Growth and Environmental Decay* (New York: Harcourt Brace Jovanovich, Inc., 1972).

Boulding, Kenneth. "Economics as a Moral Science," *American Economic Review* 59 (March 1969).

Broome, John. "Trying to Value a Life," *Journal of Public Economics* 9 (Feb. 1978), pp. 91–100.

Coleman, Jules. "Economics and the Law: A Critical Review of the Foundations of the Economic Approach to Law," *Ethics* 94 (July 1984), pp. 649–79.

Dales, J. H. *Pollution, Property, and Prices* (Toronto: Toronto University Press, 1968).

Daly, Herman E., ed. *Toward a Steady-State Economy* (San Francisco: W. H. Freeman and Company, 1973).

Dolan, Edwin G. *Tanstaafl: The Economic Strategy for Environmental Crisis* (New York: Holt, Rinehart, and Winston, Inc., 1969).

Dorfman, Robert, and Dorfman, Nancy, eds. *Economics of the Environment* (New York: W. W. Norton & Company, 1972).

Hardin, Garrett. "The Tragedy of the Commons," *Science* 162 (Dec. 13, 1968), pp. 1243–1248.

Held, Virginia, ed. *Property, Profits, and Economic Justice* (Belmont, California: Wadsworth Publishing Company, 1980).

Helfrich, Harold W., ed. *The Environmental Crises* (New Haven and London: Yale University Press, 1970).

Kelman, Stephen. *What Price Incentives?* (Boston: Auburn Publishing House, 1981).

Kneese, Allen V., and Schultze, Charles. *Pollution, Prices, and Public Policy* (Washington, D.C.: The Brookings Institution, 1975).

Krutilla, John. "Conservation Reconsidered," *The American Economic Review* 57 (Sept. 1967), pp. 777–786.

Kuperberg, Mark, and Beitz, Charles, eds. *Law, Economics, and Philosophy* (Totowa, New Jersey: Rowman and Allanheld, 1983).

Machan, Tibor. "Pollution and Political Theory" in *Earthbound*, edited by Tom Regan (New York: Random House, 1984).

Maclean, Douglas. "Valuing Human Life" in *Uncertain Power: The Struggle for a National Energy Policy*, edited by Dorothy Zinberg (New York: Pergamon Press, 1983).

Mishan, E. J. *Cost Benefit Analysis* (New York: Praeger, 1976).

Polinsky, A. Mitchell. *An Introduction to Law and Economics* (Boston: Little, Brown & Company, 1983).

Rhoads, Steven E., ed. *Valuing Life: Public Policy Dilemmas* (Boulder, Colorado: Westview Press, 1980). See this volume for a bibliography.

Sagoff, Mark. "Economic Theory and Environmental Law," *Michigan Law Review* 79 (June 1981), pp. 1393–1419.

Schelling, Thomas. "The Life You Save May Be Your Own" in *Problems of Public Expenditure Analysis*, edited by S. B. Chase (Washington: Brookings Institution, 1968), pp. 127–62.

Schwartz, William, ed. *Voices for the Wilderness* (New York: Ballantine Books, 1969).

Sen, Amartya K. "Rational Fools: A Critique of The Behavioral Foundations of Economic Theory," *Philosophy and Public Affairs* 6 (Summer 1977), pp. 317–44.

Sen, Amartya, and Williams, Bernard, eds. *Utilitarianism and Beyond* (Cambridge: Cambridge University Press, 1982).

Simon, Julian. *The Ultimate Resource* (Princeton: Princeton University Press, 1981).

Simon, Julian, and Kahn, Herman, eds. *The Resourceful Earth* (Oxford: Basil Blackwell, 1984).

Stokey, Edith, and Zeckhauser, Richard. *A Primer for Policy Analysis* (New York: Norton & Company, 1978).

Tribe, Laurence, "Policy Science: Analysis or Ideology?" *Philosophy and Public Affairs* 2, No. 1 (Fall 1972), pp. 66–110.

Westman, Walter E. "How Much Are Nature's Services Worth?" *Science* 197 (Sept. 2, 1977), pp. 961–64.

Organizations Concerned with the Environment and/or Animals

Environmental Defense Fund
1525—18th Street, N.W.
Washington, D.C. 20036

The Fund for Animals
Dept. P, 200 W. 57th St.
New York, NY 10019

Humane Society of the United States
Dept. P, 2100 L St., N.W.
Washington, D.C. 20037

International Society for Animal Rights, Inc.
International Headquarters
421 South State Street
Clarks Summit, PA 18411

The National Wildlife Federation
Department 107
1412 16th Street, NW
Washington, D.C. 20036

The Nature Conservancy
National Office
1800 North Kent Street
Arlington, VA 22209

People for Ethical Treatment of Animals
Dept. P, P.O. Box 42516
Washington, D.C. 20015

Sierra Club
530 Bush Street
San Francisco, CA 94108

United Action for Animals, Inc.
205 East 42nd Street
New York, NY 10017

The Wilderness Society
1400 Eye Street, N.W.
Washington, D.C. 20005

World Wildlife Fund—U.S.
1601 Connecticut Avenue, N.W.
Washington, D.C. 20009